R. L. S.

Stevenson's Letters to Charles Baxter

New Haven: YALE UNIVERSITY PRESS, 1956

LONDON: GEOFFREY CUMBERLEGE, OXFORD UNIVERSITY PRESS

R L S

STEVENSON'S LETTERS TO CHARLES BAXTER

Edited by D E L A N C E Y F E R G U S O N

and M A R S H A L L W A I N G R O W

Contents

Contents

INTRODUCTION

TO FANNY SITWELL, late in 1874, Stevenson wrote a list:

> Desiderata.
> 1. Good health.
> 2. 2 to 3 hundred a year.
> 3. O du lieber Gott, *friends!*

The first he never attained; the second he ultimately achieved many times over; the third was his in full measure, though marriage and death and division ended some of the relationships before his own demise.

Nearly a decade later he named over to W. E. Henley, in the order in which he had met them, the seven friends who had meant most to him. First of all was his cousin Bob (Robert Alan Mowbray Stevenson), whom he "had by nature"; the second was James Walter Ferrier. "Next I found Baxter—well do I remember telling Walter I had unearthed 'a W.S. that I thought would do.' " [1] The fourth and fifth were Sir Walter Simpson and Fleeming Jenkin; the sixth was Sidney Colvin; the seventh and last, Henley himself. Jenkin and Colvin were his seniors; the others his contemporaries. But of the seven friendships thus proudly enumerated, Stevenson carried only two to his grave.

Ferrier's death in 1883—the result of dissipation and tuberculosis—was what prompted the letter to Henley. Two years later death took Jenkin also. Simpson married a woman who disliked Stevenson, and drifted away. In time, too, the brilliant but unstable Bob also drifted away, though without open estrangement. The relationship with Henley ended in the famous quarrel detailed in these letters. Thus, of the seven, only Baxter and Colvin endured to the end, and of these it is Colvin, the later-comer, who has had most of the attention—in part because, as editor of Stevenson's letters, he gave himself the center of the stage.

But it should be noted that in his letters Stevenson always salutes his future editor as "My dear Colvin," whereas Henley is "Dear Boy" or "Dear Lad," and Baxter is usually "My dear

---

1. See below, p. xv.

vii

Charles." Britishers do not readily arrive at first-name terms; when they do, it means that all guards are down. Baxter, not Colvin, was Stevenson's crony in the tempestuous university and post-university days when the latter, in fairly regular conflict with his bewildered parents, was trying to find himself as man and writer. On Stevenson's exiguous allowance of ten shillings a week the two frequented pubs, and less decorous places, in the grimier streets of Edinburgh, acquiring a stock of memories which lasted them the rest of their lives. The prim Colvin shared no such adventures and memories; neither had he the command of broad Scots with which Stevenson and Baxter enlivened their relaxed moments. To the very end, Colvin still had to be assured that Scots idioms were not misprints.

The precise date at which the two youths met cannot be determined, but it must have been while Stevenson was still a student at the University. Baxter was the elder by almost two years: he was born 27 December 1848 and Stevenson 13 November 1850. They were fellow members of the Speculative Society and co-founders of the short-lived L.J.R. [2] Since their joint adventures in Edinburgh are a recurrent theme in these letters, it would be pointless to rehearse them here, but it must have been early in their association that they created the dramatic roles of Thamson (or Thomson) and Johnstone (or Johnson), whose disreputable Lowland characters pervade the correspondence. The usually accurate Baxter docketed as "Oct. or Nov. 1868" a note signed "Thamson" which was really written more than a decade later, and the error suggests that in his mind the dramatic personalities were almost coextensive with the friendship.[3]

Apparently their temperaments were as unlike as their physiques. Stevenson's frame was as nearly one-dimensional as human anatomy will permit; Baxter was stocky and tending to overweight. Stevenson was congenitally untidy in everything save his writing; Baxter's instinctive orderliness helped to make him first the secretary of the "Spec," later a successful lawyer. Stevenson was so mercurial that in his earlier years his gaiety sometimes reached the pitch of actual hysteria; Baxter was outwardly phlegmatic. But behind the lawyer's professional façade lurked an ir-

2. See below, p. 11.

3. The docket may be Colvin's; the handwriting is doubtful. In that case Baxter, it would seem, concurred in the attribution.

reverent imp. As cofounder of the L.J.R. he subscribed to its adolescent constitution, which is said to have opened with the words, "Disregard everything our parents have taught us." In his mature years he was one of the Edinburgh group who financed Henley's brilliant but unprofitable *Scots Observer*. But he was also the original of Michael Finsbury in *The Wrong Box,* whose imperturbable handling of the problem of disposing of an uninvited corpse supplies the broadest farce of that farcical tale. And in "Talk and Talkers" Stevenson averred that Baxter was "a person who attains, in his moments, to the insolence of a Restoration comedy, speaking, I declare, as Congreve wrote."

The two, in short, made a perfect team, with Baxter playing the straight man to Stevenson's imaginative soarings. Being straight man is an art in itself. That partner must be able to follow his companion's flights and to feed him the lines on which the success of the act depends. To this role of dead-pan collaborator Baxter brought genuine brilliance. When Stevenson gave him a lead, he played up to it.

Fortunately, no conjectural reconstructions of their youthful teamwork are necessary. The Baxter file includes a series of documents showing the pair reverting to their salad days. The year was 1886. Baxter and Stevenson were both in their later thirties—well established in their professions, married men, householders, outwardly pillars of Victorian society. On 18 June Stevenson, housebound at Bournemouth, answered at least four advertisements in the *Daily News*. One of his letters ended in Baxter's file; the nature of the others is easily reconstructed.

Two of the letters were to London house agents who had advertised property. The one which survives was addressed to Messrs. Wilde and Venables, 69 Moorgate Street, E.C.:

Antelope Hotel, Poole, 18 June 1886

Dear Sirs,

Observing in today's *Daily News* the advertisement of a house at Nunhead, and being myself on the move, I write to ask you to communicate with my lawyer, Mr. Charles Baxter, Writer to the Signet, 11 S. Charlotte Street, Edinburgh, and oblige

Yours truly,

Byron McGuinness

The unsuspecting agents accordingly forwarded a full description of the property. Baxter replied:

Dear Sirs,

Pray pay no attention to anything that comes from that man McGuinness. He is simply a monomaniac who knowing I have recently succeeded to some money pesters my life with what he considers eligible investments. I don't as it happens usually live in houses at £30.

May I ask if McG. has mooted any question of commission?

Yours truly,

Now thoroughly bewildered, Wilde and Venables forwarded the McGuinness letter. Baxter answered, though he failed to re-enclose the cause of it all:

Dear Sirs,

I return Mr. Byron McGuinness' letter. I did not know that it was in the capacity of his adviser that you had been requested to write to me.

Some years ago I did some business for him, but my bill has never been paid. What I would willingly submit to if I could only never hear his accursed name again!

Yours truly,

To another firm of agents, advertising a house in Portland Place, Baxter replied more conventionally. But he took the time to transcribe his answers for forwarding to Bournemouth. What is mainly notable in this first exchange is the lawyer's promptness in playing up to the leads given him. So far as the documents show, the correspondence descended on him without warning. Guessing its origin, he took his cue like an old trouper. But these bouts with the house agents were mere preliminaries.

Two other advertisements which Stevenson had answered were highly suspicious bids for persons with investment capital to become directors of newly formed stock companies. The first letter elicited from one A. Douglas Noll a detailed description of a cheap portable sewing machine. "A more bonafide business," Mr. Noll declared, "has never been put forward. I am satisfied that an enormous fortune will be realised through the invention, and had I the working capital, I would not have formed a company, but

advertised and carried on the concern myself." Baxter's acknowledgment was terse:

Dear Sir,

I am favoured with your letter of yesterday. May I ask (1) on
what grounds you wish Mr. McGuinness to become a director of
the proposed company and (2) why you write to me about it? Business is business: what good is it to be to me?

Yours truly,
Charles Baxter

Noll took the bait without a tremor. His response came by return of post:

Dear Sir,

Mr. McGuinness wrote me on the subject of becoming a director and desired me to send all particulars to you, as he stated
you were acting as his agent. Should our correspondence result in
business, I shall be most happy to place you on a proper footing
and will meet any reasonable suggestion you may make.

I am, yours faithfully,
A. Douglas Noll

Baxter underscored the operative words in Noll's final sentence,
wrote in the margin "I thought as much!" and forwarded the mis-
sive to Stevenson with a copy of his reply:

Confidential

Dear Sir,

When I wrote you, I had not heard from Mr. Byron McGuinness. I have since had a letter from him which explains matters.

Your undertaking seems a heavy one and your promises somewhat extravagant, but I shall see what can be done. Mr. McGuinness is a very shrewd man, and any arrangements as to my look-out
must be strictly confidential.

I can by no means undertake to make anything of Mr. McG.,
but will do the needful as far as possible. Who are the other directors? *This essential,* from circumstances of a delicate nature
occurring some years ago.

Yours truly,

P.S. I need not say that the circumstances were entirely unfounded.

Baxter was playing the old Thamson-Johnstone game to the hilt, cheerfully blackening his own character for the sake of the jest. Stevenson's acknowledgment was gleeful:

Dear C. B.

You would have "thought as much" many times over if you had seen McG.'s letter. He had "thought as much" himself on the terms of the advertisement, and wrote a low, boastful, and (constructively) dishonest letter; proving his ignorance of manners, business, and common decency, and giving as much as possible the idea of a vain theftuous dupe. And it drew! and yours drew! The Lord love us!

Yrs ever,
B. McG.

They have not *all* come off YET, my friend.

Indeed they hadn't. The fourth victim was George Thomson of Pendennis, Lee, Kent, who sent a twelve-page sales letter extolling an "Electric" Paint Remover. The prospective director of the company had to be prepared to invest £1,000, and Thomson closed with the statement that he already had fifteen applicants. This time Baxter played it differently:

Re Directorship

I am favoured with your letter of 21st inst. My client is a member of a very distinguished Irish family, and I could not advise him to incur the resentment of his relatives by entering the board of a company which, though doubtless strictly honest, is of a very *commercial* nature, and hardly such as an Irish Gentleman and landowner would care to put his hand to. My client's views are directed towards some of the leading Banks, Railways, or even Great Steamship Companies.

With many thanks for your communication, which shall of course be treated as strictly confidential, I am

Yours faithfully,

Mr. Thomson did not take this affront meekly. He retorted, on the letterhead of the City Carlton Club:

Re Directorship

Dear Sir:

Your letter to me is simply an insult to myself and my directors

—insinuating, as it does, that though we may be honest, our social position is not good enough for your client.

Let me inform you that our directors are men of very high social position in this *small City* of London and also men of considerable wealth—although not impoverished Irish landowners or men likely to be coerced by the petty whims of their relatives.

I myself can say that I should not have the privilege of being a member of this club—amongst whom, as its members, I mix with such men as the bankers of this City, Lord Geo. Hamilton, Duke of Portland, Earl Cadogan, Sir Robert Fowler (late Lord Mayor) etc., if my position was not equally good enough for your client. I should be very sorry to be rude in answer to your most insulting letter, but I cannot help saying that I should be sorry for the "Bank, Railway or Great Steamship Company" who elected a man whose agent was ass enough to imagine that such companies advertize as wanting a director with a qualification of £1,000.

My knowledge of such men is that they are found without advertizing, and that the qualification, though nominally 100 shares, is in reality much nearer £50,000. Perhaps the great banks you are connected with are satisfied with their directors having £1,000 in the business and an overdraft of several thousand. I am, Sir, Yours, etc.

G. Thomson

The bull had been sufficiently played. Baxter the matador closed in for the kill:

Dear Sir,

I am favoured with your letter of the 26th inst., upon the tone of which I shall make no comment except to say that it has apparently been written under some excitement. This is unfortunate for you, as it is distinctly libellous, and I have accordingly sent it to my London solicitors to proceed with, without delay.

Your assumption that my client is impoverished is warranted by his own folly in answering such an advertisement as yours; otherwise it is, like the remainder of your letter, grossly inaccurate.

If you are a man of business you ought to know that a parade of high sounding names such as you mention has no effect except to make one smile at the Cockney simplicity that imagines anyone will be influenced by them; but apparently the senile Tory belief in the virtues of the aristocracy is not yet extinct. It soon will be, however, thank God. I am, yours very truly,

Charles Baxter

If these letters represent Baxter's usual style when roused, it is easy to understand the twinge of envy which Stevenson confessed to in 1892: "I wish I had your gift—I have appeared rather freely lately as an insulting letter writer, but I do not consider I am fit to black your shoes."

Despite some undergraduate overtones, these pranks of 1886 merit attention for the retrospective light they shed on the earlier and less documented stages of the friendship. The two temperaments, outwardly so different, here and elsewhere fitted together like mortise and tenon. But though the friendship had begun in youthful escapades jointly accomplished, it was in no sense such a relationship as that of Robert Burns with Robert Ainslie, based on shared indecorum and withering as the erstwhile partners matured. As these two matured, they drew closer.

The recovery of some fifty letters from Baxter to Stevenson proves that neither lawyer nor author withheld anything in their exchanges. Though Baxter's side has survived haphazardly, with most of the letters belonging in the later years, they display a wide range of thought and feeling. Some phases of the lawyer's character come as a surprise. For instance, one would not, offhand, think of Baxter as a champion of the Established Kirk of Scotland; his delight in Scottish Rite Freemasonry, on the other hand, might have been expected in an alumnus of the L.J.R. Among Stevenson's other friends, Henley, but not Colvin, might have written such a bit of comradely invective as this:

Now then, for the third and last time: Where is that agreement with Longman about *Child's Garden?* Are you, or are you not, a man of biz? Do you, or do you not, reply to letters? Did you, or did you not, lie foully when you maintained at Monaco that your habits were more methodical than mine? And lastly, will you, or will you not, return that Agreement? [4]

But neither Henley nor Colvin seems likely to have experienced and confided such a mood as this:

4. CB to RLS, 26 January 1885 (Beinecke Collection).

I am going over all my letters just now. . . . I find the *whole* of your letters to me since I first knew you. First-rate reading they are. I intend making a careful arrangement of them. The number would surprise you. They may be useful to a biographer hereafter. I have been living for the last two days among the events of 1870–75. These old letters (all the female correspondence carefully preserved) come out with strange vividness. Sealed up as they were with the hot breath still on them, they seem to come out of their ten years' sleep living still. Last night my own house seemed strange and unfamiliar. I wondered what I was doing there with Gracie, and when I looked in the glass it seemed as if a curious kind of elderly stranger looked out at me. It was strange and eerie and not pleasant. . . .[5]

As for Stevenson's side of the correspondence, these are the frankest letters he ever wrote. Though it is rash to generalize when the letters to Colvin, Henley, and Bob Stevenson remain incompletely edited, it appears, for instance, that Baxter was the only friend save Henley to whom Stevenson confided the tremors of his relationship with Fanny Osbourne in 1878, as he was the sole friend to whom he wrote freely from the Pacific of his troubles with Joe Strong and his "Skimpolian family."

But the details of the friendship are here for the reading, including apposite parts of Baxter's share. It remains only to add a few factual items about the lawyer himself. For the non-Scottish, especially the American, reader, the professional title, Writer to the Signet, may need explanation. In Scots law a Writer to the Signet is what in England is called a solicitor—that is, a lawyer who deals in business management and civil law, as distinct from a barrister, who handles cases in court. Baxter was born, as above mentioned, 27 December 1848; he died 29 April 1919. On 24 July 1877 he married Grace Roberta Louisa Stewart, daughter of Major-General Robert Stewart, H.E.I.C.S.—the "Gracie" of these letters. They had three children: the daughter whose early death is mentioned below,[6] and two sons, who lived to maturity. Grace Baxter died 24 March 1893; two and a half years later the widower married Marie Louise Gaukroger of Longniddry.

To the reader of the ensuing pages Stevenson's personality will

5. *Ibid.*, 8 March 1886.
6. Page 107.

of course be the first to emerge. Stevenson was, above everything else, a skilled professional writer. Under his hand most of the people he alludes to acquire some touch of individuality. He was also a great conversationalist. The listener to one end of a telephone conversation ultimately forms a definite mental picture of the unheard speaker at the other. Hence we could deduce the essentials of Baxter's character, even without the help of his own letters. With that help, the interchange gains a three-dimensional quality not too often found in published letters.

With the coming of Fanny Osbourne the stereoscopic vision sharpens still further. Fanny was touchy, suspicious, on watch for slights or condescensions. She was also fiercely protective of her invalid husband, and thus in his behalf and her own became the disturbing element in more than one of his relationships—above all in his relationship with Henley. The latter, gifted and brilliant but also undisciplined and catty, had been jealous of Fanny long before he met her. Fanny in turn resented Henley's obtuseness to other people's comfort and convenience and dreaded the relapse which Louis was almost certain to suffer after a visit from Henley was over. Given two antithetical personalities, each with a proprietary interest in Stevenson, trouble was bound to come sooner or later. It is somewhat surprising that the explosion was delayed for eight years.

When it finally came, it tested Baxter's tact and intelligence to the utmost. He was fond of both men, and although convinced that the larger part of the blame was Henley's, he kept his temper, his integrity, and the affection of both. The young Stevenson had craved friendship above all things. Charles Baxter gave it.

The Letters and Their Publication

About 250 of Stevenson's communications to Baxter are known to survive, ranging in length from frugal British telegrams to twelve-page epistles. Of these, Sidney Colvin published part or all of thirty-nine in his 1899 edition of Stevenson's *Letters to his Family and Friends,* and added nine more in the enlarged edition of the *Letters* in 1911. Graham Balfour and J. C. Furnas, the only biographers who had access to the entire collection, have quoted from numerous others, but this is the first time that the complete correspondence has been printed.

Though Colvin thus used about one-fifth of the total, the ma-
jority of his texts are incomplete, frequently without marks of
omission. The reader who wishes to see in small compass the nature of the deletions need only compare Stevenson's anguished
letter about his parents' discovery of his "atheism" with Colvin's
dehydrated version. It would be a fair guess that almost 90 per
cent of the correspondence has not previously been collected.

The first and greatest debt of editor and reader alike is owed to
the admirable Baxter. He not only preserved the letters—in his
methodical lawyer's way he docketed most of them with either the
date of receipt or the postmark date, or both. Since Stevenson was
notoriously casual about dates, this habit of Baxter's clarifies many
points of chronology not otherwise easy of solution. Moreover,
when Baxter gave away autographs, he was usually careful to copy
in the margin whatever portions of the text were excised with the
signature. One's sole regret is that he failed to annotate the frequent allusions to minor persons whose identity is now hopelessly
obscure. But that is asking too much even of this "Prince of
Doers."

Nevertheless, Baxter did not preserve all his friend's early letters, and some of the later ones escaped his custody. As quoted by
Clement Shorter in connection with the publication of the letter
here printed on p. 6, Baxter recalled that in those youthful
Edinburgh days "R. L. S. had an engaging habit of calling promis-
cuously and—not finding me within—of leaving epistles, not always complimentary, lying open on my desk; often to the scandal
of my staid senior partner [Stevenson's 'Godkin' or 'Godlet'],
and sometimes even, to that of my more open-minded clerks."
Obviously these indiscretions were not filed.

Shorter was allowed to transcribe and publish this letter, but
Baxter retained the original. Three others, however, were given
to Shorter outright and by him were printed in a private edition
of twenty copies. One of the three was facsimiled; a second recently came on the market and has rejoined its fellows at Yale;
for the text of the third we are still dependent on Shorter's tran-
script. The Savile Club documents show that Baxter also gave
two letters to William Archibald and one to G. B. Burgin; these
are still lost, unless they are among the other strays which Mr.
Edwin J. Beinecke has acquired for the Yale collection. Three

brief notes, not elsewhere recorded, are now in the Henry E. Gerstley Collection at Princeton and are here included by permission of Mr. Alexander D. Wainwright, the University Librarian. Other unrecorded manuscripts may still be hidden in private hands, but the essential integrity of the collection is demonstrated by the fact that more than half a century after he handled them only three of the letters have here to be given from Sidney Colvin's text.

The main part of the collection is known as the Savile Gift. In May 1906 Baxter wrote to Sir Herbert Stephen of the Savile, asking if the Club would accept the confidential custody of the documents.

I *cannot* [he said] like worthy Dr. Andrew Lang, burn them, still less sell . . . I propose to make over these letters as the absolutely free property of the Savile: knowing that Stevenson would rather have them there than anywhere. (I am not superstitious, I hope. But not long ago being in want of money I was tempted with a big price. Listen, now: in a dream, I heard his voice, which said: *don't sell my letters, Charles,* and then I wondered what to do. I saw you one night in the Savile, and then I saw) . . . As to future publication of any interest, this is in the discretion of those to whom they belong. I accept the condition always of "no sale." . . . I ought to add that the distressing letters about Henley are not there, but I will send a sealed letter stating in whose custody they are—*in case of need,* as they say. In the meantime, believe me I never quarrelled with either one or tother, in testimony of which I send (for return) Henley's last two letters. The fault *was all* of W.E.H. and this I know and say on my word of honour.

The "quarrel letters" were deposited in the Advocates' Library (now the National Library of Scotland), Edinburgh, where they remain and where all restrictions on their use have expired. The Savile Gift remained with the Club until after the Second World War, when, through the good offices of Mr. Beinecke, it was conveyed to the Sterling Library of Yale University. The letters are now printed with the permission of Mr. Beinecke, the Yale authorities, and Messrs. Alan and Lou Osbourne. It will be noted that Baxter imposed no restraint upon ultimate publication; neither did Stevenson himself.[7]

One letter from Stevenson to Sir Walter Simpson and several to Henley found their way to the Baxter file, which also contains a mass of other documents, among them many letters from Fanny Stevenson, Margaret I. Stevenson, and Lloyd Osbourne. All the Stevenson letters are here printed, and also such of those by his mother, wife, and stepson as add appreciably to the biographical record. But a whole sheaf of Lloyd's letters to Baxter relates solely to the business details of transferring the family possessions to Samoa and to ordering supplies for Vailima. Inasmuch as some readers may think that Stevenson's own letters dwell too heavily upon business, none of this material is included.

Even at its best, Stevenson's handwriting is not always easy to read, and many of these letters were written during illness, or in haste. It is too much to hope that there are no misreadings. For the previously published letters, I made my own transcriptions from the manuscripts; on comparing these with the printed texts I found that Colvin had misread words at least as often as I had. (Where indecorous words are indicated by dashes or other symbols, the reticences are Stevenson's own.) But "there are bits of R. L. S. manuscript one may have doubts about to the end of time," as Mr. Park of the National Library consolingly remarked after he had deciphered for me some passages which I found illegible in microfilm. This is particularly the case with foreign words and names. Moreover, Henley's and Fanny Stevenson's hands are frequently just as baffling.

Such being the facts, I am personally indebted to the American Philosophical Society, Philadelphia, for much more than a convenience. They gave me a grant-in-aid which enabled me to have the entire Savile Gift photostated, and in dealing with such handwritings it is an inestimable privilege to have photographic copies at hand for study and restudy. The documents relating to the Henley quarrel are transcribed from microfilm supplied by courtesy of the National Library, Edinburgh, and the Princeton and Clement Shorter texts from photostats. Messrs. Charles Scribner's Sons have kindly granted permission to reprint those portions of

7. See below, pp. 321–2.

the text which appear in Sidney Colvin's *The Letters of Robert Louis Stevenson,* 1911, 1940.

The editors have divided the labor. I originated the project, and made the basic transcripts of all the documents except the letters from Baxter to Stevenson. Mr. Waingrow collated my transcripts with the originals, catching numerous misreadings, and, by establishing accurate dates, reordered the sequence of portions of the correspondence. The Stevenson Calendar is his. The notes and the index are our joint production.

DeL. F.

Falls Village, Conn.
March 1956

Our thanks go out to a long list of librarians and others who have contributed in one way or another to the making of this volume: Derek Colville, Howard B. Garey, Gordon S. Haight, and Richard L. Purdy, all of the Yale faculty; James T. Babb, Marjorie G. Wynne, and Helen Chillman, of the Yale Library; David H. Horne, of the Yale University Press; W. David Patton, of New Haven; W. Park, M. R. Dobie, William Beatty, David M. Lloyd, and James Ritchie, all of the National Library, Edinburgh; J. R. Johnstone, former honorable secretary of the Speculative Society, Edinburgh University; Ruth Erlandson and Nory Edwards, of Brooklyn College; A. P. DeWeese, of the New York Public Library; Edwin J. Beinecke, of New York City; George L. McKay, compiler of the catalogue of the Beinecke Collection; Charles Neider, of New York City; Mrs. H. H. Bretnor, of the Bancroft Library, University of California; Charles R. Sanderson, of the Public Library, Toronto; Alexander D. Wainwright, of Princeton; and finally, J. C. Furnas, whose *Voyage to Windward* has superseded all other biographies of Stevenson, and whose courtesy and helpfulness equal his erudition.

DeL. F.
M. W.

Editorial Note

In presenting the texts of these letters, the editors have sought to mediate between the interest and convenience of the reader on the one hand and the style and spirit of the writer on the other. The following procedures are the result:

The letters have been made to conform to modern rules and practices respecting punctuation, capitalization, the use of quotation marks and italics, and paragraph division, except where the original form was thought to be meaningful in its irregularity. The principal exception to this general process of normalization is the retention of personal spellings (in foreign languages as well as in English). Abbreviations (a form of spelling) have also been kept, though special signs, such as the ampersand, have been expanded. Obvious inadvertences in spelling have been silently corrected; superscripts have been lowered; flourishes have been ignored.

Since the datelines of the letters may serve as a convenient means of reference, we have been particularly concerned to adjust their chronic irregularities of position, style, and content to standard form, except (again in accordance with our general rule covering exceptions) when the original wording is of special interest. As it has worked out, the dateline is in many cases largely or entirely the composition of the editors. Despite Baxter's helpfulness in frequently supplying the date of postmark and/or receipt, the dating and placing of the letters remained a major editorial problem. Regarding Baxter as an editorial collaborator, we have not distinguished between his dates and ours (square brackets being the sign of both), though the distinction in most cases should be apparent. A "received" date is of course his. An exact date (day, month, and year) is also his—taken from the postmark—unless the evidence of the text or notes clearly points to another authority. An incomplete or approximate date is likely to be ours, and the evidence for it will be found either in the letter itself, its position with respect to letters before and after, or in the notes. Dates and places supplied from the postmarks of the few surviving envelopes are so indicated. Again, we have not distinguished between handwritten and engraved or printed addresses, but in most cases letterheads will be apparent from their form or content. It might be noted here that most of Baxter's surviving letters are written on his official stationery, the letterhead of which ("Chambers, 11 So. Charlotte Street, Edinburgh") we have reduced to "Edinburgh."

The main purpose of the headnotes is to give the present location of the manuscript and its principal printed version, if any; reprintings and the casual printing of small extracts have generally been ignored. If no printed version is mentioned, it is to be assumed that the letter is here being published substantially for the first time. In the few instances where the manuscript could not be found, the text was taken from the printed version.

In the footnotes we have not, except when quoting directly, given the sources of our information when these sources are the standard works of reference or the standard biographies and editions of Stevenson; out-of-the-way authorities have been cited.

M. W.

New Haven, Conn.
March 1956

The following short titles are used:

Balfour.	Graham Balfour, *The Life of Robert Louis Stevenson,* 2 vols. New York, 1901.
Colvin or *Letters.*	*The Letters of Robert Louis Stevenson,* ed. Sidney Colvin, 4 vols. New York, 1911.
Connell.	John Connell [John Henry Robertson], *W. E. Henley,* London, 1949.
Diary.	"Notes about Robert Louis Stevenson from His Mother's Diary," in Vol. 26 of the Vailima edition of his works, 1923.
Furnas.	J. C. Furnas, *Voyage to Windward: the Life of Robert Louis Stevenson,* New York, 1951.
Poems.	*Robert Louis Stevenson: Collected Poems,* ed. Janet Adam Smith, London, 1950.

CALENDAR

A CALENDAR of Stevenson's movements is largely a record of his poor health and his attempts to relieve it, though the impulse to adventure, matrimonial and otherwise, is to be found behind some of his more dramatic excursions. The details which explain the movements are set forth in the correspondence itself. Many of the dates here reduced to month and year are more precisely fixed in the letters and the notes. Many of the lesser jaunts are ignored. A selection of Stevenson's publications (in book form) has been inserted as a reminder of productivity maintained in spite of sickness and stability wrested from a lifetime on the move.

1850   13 November.   Born, 8 Howard Place, Edinburgh.
1867   November.   Enters Edinburgh University.
1869   2 March.   Elected to Speculative Society.
1871   April.   Gives up engineering for law.
1872   Spring.   Bridge of Allan and Dunblane.
        July.   Visits Germany with Sir Walter Simpson.
        9 November.   Passes preliminary examinations for the Scottish bar.
        December–
1873   –January.   Bridge of Allan and Malvern.
        July.   Meets Sidney Colvin at home of Cousins Babington, Cockfield Rectory.
        November–
1874   –April.   Menton.
        May–June.   Edinburgh and Swanston. London and Hampstead, with Colvin. Elected to Savile Club, 3 June.
        July–August.   Cruises the Inner Hebrides with Simpson.
        November.   Resumes law classes.
        December.   London and Cambridge, with Colvin.
1875   February.   Meets W. E. Henley in Edinburgh Infirmary.
        March–April.   Visits art colonies of France with Bob Stevenson.
        July.   Admitted to Scottish bar. Returns to France. Meets Mrs. Fanny Van de Grift Osbourne.
        September.   Returns to Edinburgh.

1876   January.   Walking tour in Ayrshire and Galloway.
      April–May.   London.
      August–October.   Canoe trip with Simpson.
      Autumn.   Grez and Barbizon.

1877   January–February.   London.
      June–July, August–November.   France.
      December–

1878   –March.   Paris.
      April–May.   Edinburgh and Swanston. *An Inland Voyage*
      (May).
      June.   Paris, as secretary to Fleeming Jenkin at the Exposi-
      tion.
      August.   London and Paris. Fanny Osbourne returns to
      America.
      September–October.   Walking trip through the Cévennes.
      October–December.   London. Returns to Edinburgh, 21
      December. *Picturesque Notes on Edinburgh* (December).

1879   January.   Swanston, with Henley, writing *Deacon Brodie*.
      February and May.   London.
      June.   France (Cernay-la-Ville). *Travels with a Donkey*.
      July.   Edinburgh and London.
      August.   Embarks for America.
      September–December.   Monterey, California, with Fanny
      Osbourne and family.
      December–

1880   –May.   San Francisco (Fanny living in Oakland). Married
      19 May, San Francisco.
      June–July.   Honeymoon at Silverado, Napa County.
      August.   Returns to England with wife and stepson Lloyd.
      August–September.   Strathpeffer and Edinburgh.
      November–

1881   –April.   Davos, Switzerland. Meets John Addington Sy-
      monds. *Virginibus Puerisque* (April).
      May.   Sojourns in France, on return to Scotland.
      June–July.   Pitlochry.
      August–September.   Braemar.
      October–

1882   –April.   Davos. *Familiar Studies of Men and Books*
      (March).

April–June. London and Edinburgh.

June–July. Stobo Manse, near Peebles.

July–August. Kingussie. *New Arabian Nights* (August).

September. Explores south of France for residence, with Bob Stevenson; rejoined by Fanny at Marseilles.

October. Campagne Defli, St. Marcel, near Marseilles.

December. Marseilles and Nice.

1883 March. Chalet "La Solitude," Hyères.

July–August. Royat.

December. *The Silverado Squatters* and *Treasure Island.*

1884 January. Visited by Baxter and Henley at Hyères. Excursion to Nice, where RLS is taken ill.

February. Returns to Hyères.

June–July. Royat. Outbreak of cholera at Hyères; returns to London, end of July.

Late summer. Bournemouth.

1885 Spring. Settled at "Skerryvore," Bournemouth. *A Child's Garden of Verses* (March). *More New Arabian Nights,* with Fanny (May).

November. *Prince Otto.*

1886 January. *Dr. Jekyll and Mr. Hyde.*

July. *Kidnapped.*

November. London, with Colvin.

1887 May. Edinburgh. Death of Thomas Stevenson. Return to Skerryvore.

August. *Underwoods.* Sails for America with Fanny, Lloyd, and Mrs. Thomas Stevenson, 22 August; arrive New York City, 7

September. Newport, R.I. Settle at Saranac, end of September.

December. *Memories and Portraits.*

1888 March. Fanny leaves for California to visit relatives. Letter from Henley, 9 March, touching off quarrel.

April. New York City.

May. Manasquan, N.J.

June. San Francisco. Sets out on first South Seas voyage, aboard the *Casco,* 28 June.

July–August. The Marquesas.

September. The Paumotus.

October.   The Society Islands.

December.   The Sandwich Islands. December–

1889   –June.   Honolulu. *The Wrong Box,* with Lloyd Osbourne
        (June). Sets out on second cruise, aboard the *Equator,* to
        the Gilbert Islands.

        September.   *The Master of Ballantrae.*

        December.   Samoa. Purchases estate ("Vailima") in Upolu.

1890   February.   Sydney.

        March.   *Father Damien.*

        April–August.   Third cruise, aboard the *Janet Nicoll,* to
        Gilberts, Marshalls, and other islands. Week's stay, Au-
        gust, at Noumea, New Caledonia, while Fanny and Lloyd
        continue cruise.

        August–September.   Sydney.

        October.   Settles in Samoa.

1891   January.   Excursion to Sydney, to meet mother returning
        from Scotland. *Ballads.*

        March.   Excursion to Tutuila, with the American Consul,
        Harold B. Sewall.

1892   April.   *Across the Plains.*

        August.   *A Footnote to History.*

1893   February.   Sydney.

        April.   *Island Nights' Entertainments.*

        August.   Outbreak of war in Samoa; defeat and banish-
        ment of Mataafa.

        September–October.   Honolulu. *David Balfour* (Septem-
        ber).

        November–

1894   –December.   Vailima. *The Ebb-Tide,* with Lloyd Os-
        bourne (September). Dies, 3 December.

THE LETTERS

MS, Yale.

17 Heriot Row [1] [Edinburgh] 31 October [1871]

My dear Baxter,

Thursday the 16th is the important day, 6:30 the eventful hour.[2]
Be early, be early!

Yours very sincerely,
LOUIS STEVENSON

MS, Yale.

[Edinburgh, 1871–72?]

My dear Baxter,

If you cannot bring down my copy tonight *in propria,* I shall
call for it tomorrow a little after one.

Yours sincerely,
LOUIS STEVENSON

MS, Yale.

[Edinburgh, 1872?]

Accept the enclosed, and thank you.

Tomorrow about five-ten I shall come for you with the carriage
to Charlotte Street.[3]

Ever yours,
ROBERT LOUIS STEVENSON

1. Address and date in the hand of RLS's mother.
2. "On the 16th October we hear that Louis is to get a £3 prize for his improvement on lights ["A New Form of Intermittent Light for Lighthouses"] and he
says: 'No one can say that I give up engineering because I can't succeed in it, as I
leave the profession with flying colours.' . . . He gets his prize on his 21st birthday
[13 November] in the evening, so it is celebrated on the 16th [of the same month] by
a young dinner party of nineteen . . ." (*Diary,* p. 322).
3. CB's office, 11 South Charlotte St.

MS, Yale.

[Edinburgh, 1872?]

Dear Charles,

Couldn't you look down this afternoon, or at ½ past eight this evening and play one game of chess? I'll stand Sam.[4]

Yrs,

R. L. S.

I'm confined to the house.

MS, Yale.

[Edinburgh] Thursday, 3 March (or April) [5] 1872

My dear Baxter,

Like one full of new wine—and so indeed I was, for I had a cab at my disposal this lovely evening—I went and called on you. I learned you were out at dinner, and then indeed, O person well known unto R. L. Stevenson, then indeed did I remember the tale known unto men, how that on this night of all nights you should tread to the Thessalian measure, being girt with the skins of leopards and your temples girt with ivy leaves and shining as to your face with ruddy Bacchus. Then indeed, then indeed did I recollect that you should deftly move forth your patent-leather footsteps, swaying as to your auburn head in the measure of them that touched the reed and your left arm curved about the slender waist of one fair among the virgins.

It is necessary to explain, O Argive youth, that I have been reading the translations of Bohn,[6] cunningly written with a reed upon the well-prepared tablets.

"But wherefore, O son of Stephen,[7] dost thou stay my footsteps, already bent, as it were unwillingly, unto the court of writers?" [8]

4. I.e. treat.

5. The 3d of March 1872 was a Sunday, 3d April a Wednesday; originally RLS wrote "Monday." Cf. the dating of the next letter.

6. RLS "was ignorant of Greek, and preferred the baldest of Bohn's translations to more literary versions that might come between him and the originals" (Balfour, 2, 122).

7. The remainder of the letter is cast in the form of a dialogue between RLS and CB.

8. I.e. Writers to the Signet (see Introduction, p. xv). RLS was himself preparing

"He that is hasty with his questioning lips is not judged wise among the prudent."

"Yea, but the man of many verbal words—he that explaineth nought with his much-sounding lips—what is he?"

"Thy words are sharp."

"Thy words indeed, as it seemeth to me, are many; but the purport lingereth."

"Hear then, O much writer, unto the plain sense that abideth ever behind my spoken words. Her that brought me forth, nowise unjustly judging herself indebted unto thee, bids me, touching the ground as to my forehead and as it were with the folded hands of him that hath an obligation, offer unto thee her grattitude,[9] thus tardily, thus tardily coming toward thee, O thou crafty employer of scribes."

"Now indeed, O son of Stephen, thou speakest well. But has the pious woman, her that intromits with furthest India, concealed with due regard my complicity in her diminutive game?"

"Truly thou art one of little reverence."

"As why, O sick man?"

"Dost thou take us, perhaps, for those that have the colour in our eyes of dewy lawns, not trodden save by the flocks, whom the careful shepherds drive to and fro at morning and even?"

"Thou speakest doubtfully with thy lips."

"Not so, O writer; but the doubtful hearer ever heareth things equivocal. Thy name, indeed, is hidden. And it seemeth, forsooth, a great thing, this name of thine; having once drawn forth the exchangable money, what import, thinkest thou?, has the name of the son of him that checketh the doings of the writers. Go to! thou art one of a swelling vanity, whom shall the gods chasten in due time. Neither is it for nothing that thou art held as a pointing of fingers, in that thou wearest the long robe called after him of Fame, the great chieftain, fiery as to his head, even him that, being great, is small. For thou also, though thou art great, art small, O employer of scribes."

R. L. STEVENSON BOHN

---

for the Scottish bar and was for some months during 1872 and 1873 engaged as a scribe in the office of Messrs. Skene, Edwards, and Bilton, Writers to the Signet. His mother noted: "he likes it very much because he has no trouble only to copy and then he gets paid so much a page!" (*Diary*, p. 323).

9. The nature of Mrs. Stevenson's indebtedness to CB is not known.

Epilogue
O thou, wearied with much Bohning, I am asked, I am asked that
I should further open unto thee this riddle.
(*My mother has been ill*)
O thou etc. . . . .
I could Bohn till doomsday.
(*and so could not write*)
O Bohn! Bohn! O Argive maidens!
(*herself.*)

MS, Yale. Letters, *1, 38.*

Dunblane,[10] Friday, 5 [11] March 1872

My dear Baxter,
    By the date you may perhaps understand the purport of my letter
without any words wasted about the matter. I cannot walk with you
tomorrow and you must not expect me. I came yesterday afternoon
to Bridge of Allan [1] and have been very happy ever since, as every
place is sanctified by the eighth sense, Memory. I walked up here
this morning (three miles, tudieu! a good stretch for me) and passed
one of my favourite places in the world, and one that I very much
affect in spirit, when the body is tied down and brought immovably
to anchor in a sick-bed. It is a meadow and bank at a corner on the
river, and is connected in my mind inseparably with Virgil's
Eclogues. "Hic corulis mistas inter consedimus ulmos," or something like that the passage begins [2] (only I know my short-winded
latinity must have come to grief over even thus much of quotation);
and here, to a wish, is just such a cavern as Menalcas might shelter
himself withal from the bright noon, and, with his lips curled back-

    10. "Lou's classes finish in March [1872]. He has got through the winter pretty well
and has been able to fulfil most of his engagements . . . He rather breaks down when
his work is over and goes to Bridge of Allan and Dunblane for a change, coming back
every few days for Prof. Jenkin's theatricals at which he is to act this year" (*Diary,*
pp. 322–323).
    11. The 5th of March was a Tuesday.
    1. A popular health resort near Stirling, to which RLS was taken several times in
childhood and youth. "I shall never forget some of the days at Bridge of Allan; they
were one golden dream" (RLS to his cousin, Henrietta Traquair Milne: *Letters, 2,*
185).
    2. "hic corylis mixtas inter consedimus ulmos?" (*Eclogues* 5.3): "why not seat us
among these elms, with hazels interspersed?"

ward, pipe himself blue in the face, while Messieurs les Arcadiens ("Arcades ambo") would roll out these cloying hexameters, that sing themselves in one's mouth to such a curious lilting chaunt.

In such weather, one has the bird's need to whistle; and I, who am specially incompetent in this art, must content myself by chattering away to you on this bit of paper. All the way along I was thanking God that he had made me and the birds and everything just as they are and not otherwise; for although there was no sun, the air was so thrilled with robins and blackbirds that it made the heart tremble with joy, and the leaves are far enough forward on the underwood to give a fine promise for the future. Even myself, as I say, I would not have had changed in one *iota* this forenoon, in spite of all my idleness and Guthrie's lost paper,[3] which is ever present with me—a horrible phantom; except perhaps in that one direction in which I have so sorely over-ridden and disenchanted my poor mind and body.

No one can be alone at home or in a quite new place. Memory and you must go hand in hand with (at least) decent weather, if you wish to cook up a proper dish of Solitude. It is in these little flights of mine that I get more pleasure than in anything else; and yet I am not really happy. Happiness is a matter of bottled stout and roast beef—by the way, how memory loves to dwell over that rare joy, a really good roast of beef. Now, at present, I am supremely uneasy and restless—almost to the extent of pain; but O! how I enjoy it and how I *shall* enjoy it afterwards (please God) if I get years enough allotted to me for the thing to ripen in. When I am a very old and very respectable citizen, with white hair and bland manners and a gold watch and an unquestioned *entrée* to the Sacrament, I shall hear these crows cawing in my heart, as I heard them this morning. I vote for old age and eighty years of retrospect. Yet, after all, I daresay a short shrift and a nice green grave are about as desirable.

Poor devil! how I am wearying you! Cheer up: two pages more and my letter reaches its term, for I have no more paper. What delightful things inns and waiters and bagmen are! If we didn't travel now and then, we should forget what the feeling of life is.

---

3. Charles John Guthrie, fellow member of the Speculative Society (see below, p. 10); later Lord Guthrie, senator of the Scottish Courts of Justice. The paper, read at the "Spec" 20 February, was entitled "American Peculiarities and English Prejudices."

The very cushion of a railway carriage—"The things restorative to the touch." [4] I can't write, confound it. That's because I'm so tired with my walk. I wish I could think of something else to say, for when this letter is done, I shall be handed over to my own restlessness for several hours; and then not all my weariness will be able to keep me still, and walking is the devil and all for my health. Such a nice little girl went past the window just now, in black and as *mignonne* as your warmest mood could fancy, that I felt inclined to run out and kiss her for her mother. I know exactly the sort of warm, brown, melting hand the little darling would and *must* have; but the gloomy waiter "held me with his [5] eye." He seemed to have all the beadle-staves and constable-batons of united respectability under his arm, instead of one poor napkin.

Believe me, ever your affct friend,

R. L. STEVENSON

MS, Yale. Printed by Clement K.
  Shorter, Sphere (*London*), 65 *(1916),*
  96; reprinted, Bookman (*N.Y.*),
  43 (1916), 369.

[Dunblane, spring of 1872] [6]

Mon cher Baxter,

After several years of feeble and innefectual endeavour with regard to my third initial (a thing I loathe), I have been led to put myself out of the reach of such accidents in the future by taking my two first names in full.[7] It is perhaps as well from another point of

4. "The thing's restorative,/I' the touch and sight" (Browning, *The Ring and the Book,* I, 89).

5. MS, "glassy" deleted. Cf. Coleridge, *The Rime of the Ancient Mariner,* line 13.

6. Writing to Shorter on 16 February 1898 (see Introduction, p. xvii). CB gave the opinion that this letter belonged "to the early part of 1872." In a MS note to the letter Colvin comments: *"about* that year *certainly."* CB's dating is corroborated by *Diary,* p. 322: "In the spring of 1872 Louis was in a very depressed state . . . He wrote one terribly morbid letter to me from Dunblane all about death and Churchyards—it vexed me so much that I put it in the fire at once."

7. RLS was christened Robert Lewis Balfour, the third name being for his mother, Margaret Isabella Balfour. A desire to distinguish himself from his cousin Bob (Robert Alan Mowbray Stevenson), who always signed his three initials, may have influenced the decision. Though he adopted the French spelling of his second name, he always gave it the English pronunciation.

view, as I am going to land fame wholesale under the same designation; and as such will probably be the superscription on my *tooomb* in W[estm]inster Ab[be]y, as well as on the marble tablet to be let into the front of the house of my birth, No. 8 Howard Place.[8]

I have seen nothing else to change except a numeral which you had omitted to change yourself, while working off the rest.[9]

Your caution about being funny and clever on the proof, D[ea]r C., was unnecessary. I call various celestial persons to witness that I would gladly be as funny as old Harry just now, if I could, and simply can't. If you want epitaphs, apply to sincerely-yours; but this is not the booth for humour. Life, my dear Charles, is real, life is earnest. Death is a sort of roaring lion that produces itself between three and four in the morning and at divers other disrespectable hours. I may also observe, in the same connection, that the worm dieth-not quite free. No one is so good at not-dying as the worm. Even the devil requires a dyke-side to do not-do it at for any considerable lapse of time.[1]

Yours gloomilly and intellectually-feebly,
R. L. S.

Flourish.[2]

MS, Yale.

[Dunblane] 28 March 1872

My dear Baxter,

Damn you for a cold-hearted knave. Quoy?[3] est ce qu'on escrit de telles espitres aux amys qui sont malades et ont besoigne de consola-

8. Now the Robert Louis Stevenson Museum.

9. Perhaps with reference to an essay for the Spec, though "proof" (next sentence) suggests a publication, and the addresses before the Spec were not regularly printed.

1. "Long e'er the De'el lye dead by the dike side": Scottish proverb spoken in anticipation of the death of a wicked person.

2. Alluding to a scrawl around the initials.

3. RLS is here imitating Balzac's imitation of Rabelaisian French, though he frequently lapses into shaky modern French. "How is this? does one write such letters to friends who are sick and in need of consolation and not, by Heaven, of such damned beastly blasts of east wind. Here I am before a pleasant fire; I was smoking joyously and reading the *Droll Stories* of the late Master Balzac, who was by Jove a good man and one who could bring laughter, if one wanted that; and here they hand me a letter from my very dear and very respected friend Mr. Baxter, which I had thought would contain many pretty turns of phrase and many kind remarks; and here I am terror-struck at the discovery of nothing but dirty and filthy things that could never be to

tions, de par dieu!, et non pas de telles inhumaines bouffees de vent mauldict de l'est. Ores, me vecy avant ung bien joli feu et qui fusmait a faire joye et lisait les "contes drolatique" de nostre feu Maistre de Balzac, qui etait ma foi homme de bien et scavoit a faire rire, si on le veult; et vecy qu'on m'apporte ung lettre de mon tres cher et tres respectez amy, le sieur de Baxter, que je jugeais de contenir moult jolis facons de parler et moult gentils proupos; et me vecy espouvantez d'y trouver rien que de choses sales et ordureurses et qui ne plaisent poinct aulx gens de bien et ceulx qui ont les haults gouts de la vie et sachent a vivre et a laisser vivre. Mais suis gen de bien moi mesme, et sache pardonner, estant tres jolyment enseignez par la Soulffrance, en bon maistre d'escholle, qui est, pour vraye dire, restez chez moi et pas mesme mis pied hors la

---

the liking of good men or men with a gusto for life and the talent for living and letting live. But I am a good man myself, and know how to forgive, having been very nicely instructed by Suffering, who has been a good schoolmaster to me, and who, truth to tell, has been with me without once setting foot outside my door these past five or six days. Now be something of a good fellow and pay me a visit; and throw out the window all that secretary's frigidity and pomposity which has wounded me so much, so that you may come to see me as a good friend and nothing else. Furthermore, I would like to tell you something quite profitable to know: that the *Droll Stories* I mentioned are as good as could possibly be and that you should read them to become a good Pantagruelist, which many men here, otherwise "droll" enough and with high relish for life, can never be, for want of knowing this queen of languages, the Gallic—which arouses great pity in the hearts of good men. In all truth, my friend, I cut a pretty roguish figure here in writing this language, but I'm doing my best always, and am learning fairly well how to spell badly—which, if you will believe me, is as difficult a task as the contrary. I will also tell you, for a moment, how I have been all this time I haven't seen you. I was bedfast till Tuesday evening; a little more comfortable afterwards, but still sad "like the dove alone in her nest bereft of her mate," and most inactive, as you may well believe, since I could not move my head for the great pain, and in fine more dead than alive.—By the way, read "The High Constable's Wife," a fine tale, with some of the elements of real tragedy. The mere reading sets one aflame. If only we here weren't so valiant and of such prepossessing appearance, like the late Pharisees, I would imagine its being a great drama; but it comes to no close, as it should—otherwise it's a fine subject. And now, how cast down and otherwise destroyed are all our beautiful dreams of Springtime! They have passed on, one after the other, and have left no successors! And now, fine sir, you who are such a great man and such a redoubtable secretary, you must stoop just a little to visit the sick and console them and let them know about all that's new and diverting in the great city. To all those wonderful sights and sounds I am but a poor blind and deaf man, being here as if in prison; indeed I am literally a prisoner here, as I shall explain to you.—And I shall hope, fine sir, to see you again soon; as I shall hope you will succeed in deciphering this letter, which I greatly doubt, and that you will be able to admire my laboured ingenuousness, which I personally cherish; and I shall remain always, believe me, your servitor in the arts and sciences, Louis Stevenson."

porte pour ces darreniers cinq ou six jours. Et maintenant faites ung peu le bonhomme et venez me visiter; et jectez par fenetres tout cettuy dignitez et froide pompe de secretaire qui m'a tant blesse, á ce que vous pouvez venir me veoir en bon amy et poinct aultre chose. Aulsi, vouldrai vous dire ung chose qui est bien prou-fictable a scavoir: que les dictes contes drolatiques sont on ne peult plus mieux, et que debvrez les lire pour desvenir bon Pantagrueliste, ce que beucoulp de gens icy, qui sont aultrement assez drosles et bons viveurs, ne peuvent jamais, faulte de scavoir cette reine de langues, la langue galloise—qui faict grant pitiez ez coeurs de gens de biens. Vrayement, mon amy, suis jolyment villain, moy, a escrire cettuy langue, mais fais toutsjour de mon mieulx et apprends tant bien de mal espeller—ce qui est ung mestier aulsi difficile a apprendre que son opposé, si vouldrez bien me croire. Aulsi vous dirai çy, ung petit moment, comment je me suis portez, pendant que je ne vous ai pas veu. Et premier, dans mon lict jus-qu'au mardi soir; aspres suis ung peu mieulx a mon aise, mais touts-jours suis triste "comme est la palumbe seule en son nid par mort du compaignon," et bien resveurs, comme vous poulvez croire, ne pouvant moulvoir mon teste a cause de si grants douleurs, et estant, pour en finir, plus mort que je ne fus vif.

A proupos, lisez "La Connestable," belle conte, qui ne manque d'elements vrayements tragiques. Ça brusle a lire seulement. Si seulement nous n'estions pas icy tant preudes et de bonne mine, comme feu Messieurs Les Pharasiens, j'en resverais ung beau drame; mais ca n'ha poinct de fin, comme ça debvrez—aultrement c'est ung beau subject. Et maintenant, comment sont dejectez et aultre-ment detruicts touts nos beaux resves du Printemps! Sont depassez, ung apres l'aultre, et m'ont poinct laissez de successeurs! Et main-tenant, beaux sire, qui est si grant homme et si redoubtable secre-taire, debvrez vous humilier ung petit peu pour visiter les malades et les reconforter, eulx, et leurs donner touts ces jolys nolveutez qui sont en train dans la grante Ville. Moy, suys ung paulvre sourd a tous ces beaulx rumeurs, et ne voys poinct ces belles visions; estant icy comme en prison; et suys vrayement en prison sans detours, comme je vous l'expliquerai.

Et esperai, beaulx sire, de vous reveoir bientost; aulsi que vous estes parvenuz a dechiffrer cettuy espitre, comme moultement me redoubte, et que sachez assez pour admirer tous mes laborieulx naivetez, qui me sont trez amables, a moy; et restrerai toutsjours, si croyez, vostre escuyer ez arts et sciences,

LOUIS STEVENSON

MS, Yale. Letters, 1, *40.*

Dunblane, Tuesday, 9 April 1872

My dear Baxter,

I don't know what you mean. I know nothing about the Standing Committee of the Spec,[4] did not know that such a body existed and even if it doth exist, must sadly repudiate all association with such "goodly fellowship." I am a "Rural Voluptooary" at present. *That* is what is the matter with me. The Spec may go whistle, may go be ——. As for "C. Baxter Secy"—who is he? I know one Charles Baxter (or Bagster), Jinkster, Jokester, —ster, —ster; but I know nought of this *"Secy."* "One Baxter, or Bagster, a secretary," I say to mine acquaintance, "is at present disquieting my liesure with certain illegal, uncharitable, unchristian, and unconstitutional documents called *business letters: the affair is in the hands of the POLICE."* Do you hear *that,* you evil-doer? Sending business letters is surely a far more hateful and slimy degree of wickedness than sending threatening letters; the man who throws grenades and torpedoes is less malicious. The Devil in red-hot hell rubs his hands with glee as he reckons up the number that go forth spreading pain and anxiety with each delivery of the Post.

I have been walking today by a colonnade of beeches along the brawling Allan. My character for sanity is quite gone, seeing that I cheered my lonely way with the following, in a triumphant chaunt: "Thank God for the grass, and the fir-trees, and the crows, and the sheep, and the sunshine, and the shadows of the fir-trees." I hold that he is a poor mean devil who can walk alone in such a place and in such weather and doesn't set up his lungs and cry back to the birds and the river. Follow, follow, follow me. Come hither, come hither, come hither—here shall you see—No enemy—except

4. The Speculative Society is Edinburgh University's oldest (unofficially connected) student organization. A literary and debating club whose members are elected "from among undergraduates of presumed intellectual promise," it was founded in 1764 and numbered Sir Walter Scott among its early secretaries. The "Standing Committee" meets once a year, between March and October, i.e. during the "close season."

a very slight remnant of winter and its rough weather. My bedroom, when I awoke this morning, was full of bird-songs—which is the greatest pleasure in life. Come hither, come hither, come hither; and when you come, bring the 3rd Part of *The Earthly Paradise;* [5] you can get it for me in Elliot's [6] for two and tenpence (2s/10d) (*business habits*). Also bring an ounce of Honey Dew from Wilson's.[7]

The whole of the latter part of this letter was written to a chaunt, and may be read in a similar style by the judicious reader, if he be as light-hearted.

Do come. I think you will find me nice, but know not, as I speak very little.

I send here competition sonnet to the L.J.R.; [8] you will soon get one from Bob, and will please consider yourself as judge and law-giver over us in this matter.

To the Members of the L.J.R.

As Daniel, bird-alone in that far land,
Kneeling in fervid prayer, with heart-sick eyes,
Turned thro' the casement toward the westering skies;
Or as untamed Elijah, that red brand
Among the starry prophets; or that band
And company of faithful sanctities
Who, in all times, when persecutions rise
Cherish forgotten creeds with fostering hand;
Such do ye seem to me, light-hearted crew,
O turned to friendly arts with all your skill,[9]
That keep a little chapel sacred still,
One rood of Holy-ground in this bleak earth
Sequestered still (an homage surely due!)
To the twin gods of mirthful wine and mirth.

R. L. Stevenson

5. The third and final volume of William Morris' poem had appeared in 1870.

6. Andrew Elliot, bookseller, 17 Princes St. He had published anonymously in 1866 RLS's first printed work, *The Pentland Rising*.

7. H. Wilson, tobacconist, 9 Leith St.

8. The L.J.R., which met at a pub in Advocate's Close, 357 High St., was a discussion club organized by RLS, his cousin Bob Stevenson, CB, J. W. Ferrier (see below, p. 15), and others. Its constitution is said to have begun: "Disregard everything our parents taught us." The initials stood for Liberty, Justice, Reverence.

9. MS, "That follow joy with all your store of skill" deleted.

MS, Yale.

17 Heriot Row, Edinburgh, 28 April 1872

My dear Baxter,

Not being *in propria* able to appear before you and charm away
your evil spirit, I must see what I can do by proxy; especially as
I am myself somewhat gloomy, owing to having had no sleep whatever last night with toothache. I had a pretty bad time of it. Could
niether lie in bed nor stay out of it, and passed a fairish slice of the
night in dressing and undressing. About two I came downstairs
and had a pipe and a couple of glasses of wine, which did me good
for the time being; but I heard every hour until eight, which I
missed dozing in the arm chair waiting for breakfast. I kept pretty
cheery until about five, when I began to throw pillows about and
swear (in the words of Billy Taylor) [1] "most horribel." I thought
to myself that I should look pretty blue if this were some persistent
malady and I were to be told next morning that I should spend
all my remaining years without intermission of pain. However, I
kept up my spirits by imagining worse cases: as, for example, the
same degree of toothache in a draughty common stair—*Pouah!
enfin, c'est assez, n'est-ce-pas?*

I don't know that I am very fit to write, and I have a hideous
tendency to relapse into bad French, which I mean to resist and to
keep on the Queen's Highway and Queen's English if I can.

In fact I can't write.

Yours very sincerely,
Your most obedt. servt.,
Yours faithfully,
L. S.

(2nd attempt)

I *will* write. Do you know what a hard thing it is to resist sleep
and what a terrible thing it is to strive with wakefulness? I tried last
night to play the one off against the other and to pretend to my
own heart that I wished to keep awake in order to hear the next
hour strike, in hopes that I should cheat the devil and get to sleep;
but it wouldn't do—he has not been going to and fro upon the
earth all these thousand years for nothing, and he saw thro' my

1. Not identified.

honest deceit as tho' I had been glass. I could hear him sniggering in the corner.

This morning the *pain-wrinkle* that I have over one eye was deeper than I have ever seen it. I shall pretty soon have a permanent brand there. It is principally an autograph of Tick [2] (tic, tik, tique, comme vous voulez).

I can't help being egotistical, as you know already, but I feel that this letter does require an apology. Pain concentrates one's feelings so inordinately that it takes one a while to get them spread again. One walk in the sun, and a lungfull or two of spring air, will send all the morbid de[vils . . .] they [. . .].[3] I shall gradually recollect that there are other people in the world besides myself and to like those other people (sometimes a great deal too much) and to insist on speaking to them and hearing them speak. I have written another page I see, but I am no nearer writing you a letter than I was at the beginning; therefore,

Ade,

MS untraced (see Introduction, p. xviii).
  Letters, 1, 53.

Boulogne Sur Mer,
Wednesday, 3 or 4 September 1872 [4]

Blame me not that this epistle
  Is the first you have from me.
      Idleness has held me fettered,
      But at last the times are bettered
And once more I wet my whistle
  Here, in France beside the sea.

All the green and idle weather
  I have had in sun and shower
      Such an easy warm subsistence,
      Such an indolent existence

2. Perhaps a pun on Ludwig Tieck (1773–1853), German writer and critic.
  3. Gaps made by CB's cutting out the signature overleaf. About eight words are missing.
  4. Wednesday was the 4th. "On July 20th Lou starts for Germany with Sir Walter Simpson [see below, p. 16]. We follow in August and join him at Baden Baden on August 23rd. While we are there Louis goes for a short walking trip in the Black Forest; we return home by Strasburg, Paris, and Boulogne" (*Diary*, p. 323).

I should find it hard to sever
   Day from day and hour from hour.

Many a tract-provided ranter
   May upbraid me, dark and sour,
     Many a bland Utilitarian
     Or excited Millenarian,
—*"Pereunt et imputantur* [5]
   You must speak to every hour."

But (the very term's deceptive)
   You at least, my friend, will see,
     That in sunny grassy meadows
     Trailed across by moving shadows
To be actively receptive
   Is as much as man can be.

He that all the winter grapples
   Difficulties, thrust and ward—
     Needs to cheer him thro' his duty
     Memories of sun and beauty
Orchards with the russet apples
   Lying scattered on the sward.

Many such I keep in prison,
   Keep them here at heart unseen,
     Till my muse again rehearses
     Long years hence, and in my verses
You shall meet them rearisen
   Ever comely, ever green.

You know how they never perish,
   How, in time of later art,
     Memories consecrate and sweeten
     These defaced and tempest-beaten
Flowers of former years we cherish,
   Half a life, against our heart.

Most, those love-fruits withered greenly,
   Those frail, sickly amourettes,

5. "Bonosque/Soles effugere atque abire sentit,/Qui nobis pereunt et imputantur" (Martial, *Epigrams* 5.20): "And he feels the good days are flitting and passing away, our days that perish and are scored to our account."

How they brighten with the distance
Take new strength and new existence
Till we see them sitting queenly
Crowned and courted by regrets!

All that loveliest and best is,
Aureole-fashion round their head,
They that looked in life but plainly,
How they stir our spirits vainly
When they come to us Alcestis-
like returning from the dead!

Not the old love but another,
Bright she comes at Memory's call
Our forgotten vows reviving
To a newer, livelier living,
As the dead child to the mother
Seems the fairest child of all.

Thus our Goethe, sacred master,
Travelling backward thro' his youth,
Surely wandered wrong in trying
To renew the old, undying
Loves that cling in memory faster
Than they ever lived in truth.

So; *en voilà assez de mauvais vers.* Let us finish with a word or two
in honest prose, tho' indeed I shall so soon be back again and, if
you be in town as I hope, so soon get linked again down the Lothian
Road by a cigar or two and a liquor, that it is perhaps scarce worth
the postage to send my letter on before me. I have just been long
enough away to be satisfied and even anxious to get home again
and talk the matter over with my friends. I shall have plenty to tell
you, and principally plenty that I do not care to write; and I daresay you too will have a lot of gossip. What about Ferrier? [6] Is the

6. James Walter Ferrier (d. 1883), son of James Frederick Ferrier (1808–64), meta-
physician and professor of moral philosophy and political economy at St. Andrews
University. RLS remembered his friend as "gifted with very considerable abilities; he
was by nature the most complete and gentle gentleman (I must risk the pleonasm) I
have known.—I never knew any man so superior to himself. The best of him only
came as a vision, like Corsica from the Corniche. He never gave his measure either
morally or intellectually. The curse was on him. Even his friends did not know him
but by fits. I have passed hours with him when he was so wise, good, and sweet, that

L. J. R. think you to go naked and unashamed this winter? He with
his charming idiosyncrasy was in my eyes the vine-leaf that preserved our self-respect. All the rest of us are such shadows, compared to his full-flavoured personality; but I must not spoil my own
début. I am trenching upon one of the essayettes which I propose
to introduce, as a novelty, this year before that august assembly. For
we must not let it die. It is a sickly baby, but what with nursing and
pap and the like, I do not see why it should not have a stout manhood after all, and perhaps a green old age. Eh! when we are old
(if we ever should be) that too will be one of those cherished memories I have been so rhapsodizing over. We must consecrate our
room. We must make it a museum of bright recollections, so that
we may go back there white-headed and say *Vixi*. After all, new
countries, sun, music, and all the rest can never take down our
gusty, rainy, smoky, grim old city out of the first place that it has
been making for itself in the bottom of my soul, by all pleasant and
hard things that have befallen me for these past twenty years or
so. My heart is buried there—say, in Advocate's Close!

Simpson [7] and I got on very well together, and made a very
suitable pair. I like him much better than I did when I started,
which was almost more than I hoped for.

If you should chance to see Bob, give him my news, or if you
have the letter about you, let him see it.

> Ever you affct. friend,
> R. L. Stevenson

I never knew the like of it in any other" (Balfour, *1*, 106). He died of tuberculosis and
dissipation, his promise unfulfilled. RLS's finished portrait of him appears in the
essay "Old Mortality" in *Memories and Portraits*.

7. Sir Walter Grindlay Simpson (*d.* 1898). See above, n. 4; he was later RLS's companion on the "inland voyage." In 1870 he had succeeded to the baronetcy of his
father, Sir James Young Simpson (1811–90), pioneer gynecologist and obstetrician.
"I think his special character was a profound shyness, a shyness which was not so
much exhibited in society as it ruled in his own dealings with himself. He was shy
of his own virtues and talents, and above all of the former. He was even ashamed
of his own sincere desire to do the right. More than half the man, as you first knew
him, was a humbug; and that was utterly the worser part. But this very foible served
to keep clean and wholesome the unusual intimacy which united him, Baxter, and
myself; for he would permit no protestations and scarce any civility between us.
It is odd that this had to be dropped in time; for, as we went on in life and became
more seriously involved, we found it then more necessary to be kind. Then, indeed,
Simpson could show himself not only kind but full of exceptional delicacies" (Balfour, *1*, 107). He appears frequently in this correspondence—as "Grindlay," "Simp,"
"the Bart," and other titles not sanctioned by Debrett. In "Talk and Talkers" he
appears as Athelred.

MS untraced (see Introduction, p. xviii).
Sold at Sotheby's, 17 February 1932.
Letters, 1, 57.

17 Heriot Row, Edinburgh, October 1872

My dear Baxter,

I am gum-boiled and face-swollen to an unprecedented degree. It is very depressing to suffer from gibber that cannot be brought to a head.[8] I cannot speak it, because my face is so swollen and stiff that enunciation must be deliberate—a thing your true gibberer cannot hold up his head under; and writ gibber is somehow not gibber at all—it does not come forth, does not *flow,* with that fine irrational freedom that it loves in speech—it does not afford relief to the packed bosom.

Hence I am suffering from *suppressed gibber*—an uneasy complaint, and like all cases of suppressed humours, this hath a nasty tendency to the brain. Therefore (the more confused I get, the more I lean on Thus's and Hences and Therefores) you must not be down upon me, most noble Festus,[9] altho' this letter should smack of some infirmity of judgment. I speak the words of soberness and truth; and would you were not almost but altogether as I am, except this swelling. Lord, Lord, if we could change personalities how we should hate it. How I should rebel at the office, repugn under the Ulster coat, and repudiate your monkish humours thus unjustly and suddenly thrust upon poor infidel me! And as for you—why, my dear Charles, "a mouse that hath its lodging in a cat's ear"[10] would not be so uneasy as you in your new conditions. I do not see how your temperament would come thro' the feverish longings to do things that cannot then (or perhaps ever) be accomplished, the feverish unrests and damnable indecisions that it takes all my easy-going spirits to come through. A vane can live out anything in the shape of a wind; and that is how I can be, and am, a more serious person than you. Just as the light French seemed very serious to Sterne,[1] light L. Stevenson can afford to bob about over the top of

8. RLS was studying for his preliminary examinations in law.
9. Acts 26:25 ff.
10. Webster, *The Duchess of Malfi,* IV.2.134.
1. "But the French, Mons. le Count, added I . . . have so many excellencies . . . they are a loyal, a gallant, a generous, an ingenious, and good-temper'd people as is under heaven; if they have a fault, they are too *serious.*"—"*Mon Dieu!* cried the Count, rising out of his chair" (*A Sentimental Journey,* "Character: Versailles").

any deep sea of prospect or retrospect, where ironclad C. Baxter would incontinently go down with all hands. A fool is generally the wisest person out. The wise man must shut his eyes to all the perils and horrors that lie round him, but the cap and bells can go bobbing along the most slippery ledges and the bauble will not stir up sleeping lions. Hurray for motley, for a good sound *insouciance,* for a healthy philosophic carelessness!

My dear Baxter, a word in your ear: "DON'T YOU WISH YOU WERE A FOOL?" How easy the world would go on with you— literally on castors. The only reason a wise man can assign for getting drunk is that he wishes to enjoy for a while the blessed immunities and sunshiny weather of the land of fooldom. But a fool, who dwells ever there, has no excuse at all. *That* is a happy land, if you like—and not so far away either. Take a fool's advice and let us strive without ceasing to get into it. Hark in your ear again: "THEY ALLOW PEOPLE TO REASON IN THAT LAND." I wish I could take you by the hand and lead you away into its pleasant boundaries. There is no custom-house on the frontier, and you may take in what books you will. There are no manners and customs, but men and women grow up like trees in a still, well-walled garden, "at their own sweet will." [2] There is no prescribed or customary folly, no motley, cap, or bauble; out of the well of each one's own innate absurdity he is allowed and encouraged freely to draw and to communicate. And it is a strange thing how this natural fooling comes so nigh to one's better thoughts of wisdom, and stranger still that all this discord of people speaking in their own natural moods and keys masses itself into a far more perfect harmony than all the dismal, official unison in which they sing in other countries. Part-singing seems best all the world over.

I who live in England must wear the hackneyed symbols of the profession, to show that I have (at least) consular immunities, coming as I do out of another land, where they are not so wise as they are here, but fancy that God likes what he makes and is not best pleased with us when we deface and dissemble all that he has given us and put about us to one common standard of—Highty-Tighty!—when was a jester obliged to finish his sentence? I cut so strong a pirouette that all my bells jingle, and come down in an attitude, with one hand upon my hip. The evening's entertainment is over—"and if our kyind friends"—

2. Wordsworth, "Composed Upon Westminster Bridge."

Hurrah! I feel relieved. I have put out my gibber, and if you have read thus far, you will have taken it in. I wonder if you will ever come this length. I shall try a trap for you and insult you here, on this last page. "O Baxter, what a damned humbug you are!" There —shall this insult bloom and die unseen, or will you come toward me, when next we meet, with a face deformed with anger, and demand speedy and bloody satisfaction? *Nous verrons,* which is French.

R. L. STEVENSON

MS, Yale.

Private

17 Heriot Row, Edinburgh, 31 October 1872

My dear Baxter,

I have been quite depressed all day about this rotten, carious job of yours with that poor, honest, childish weakling, John Forman.[3] I can always say more in pen and ink than I can *viva voce;* and so I may say now (what I had on my tongue a dozen times this afternoon) that whereas this would have been a funny story to me in ordinary circumstances, it becomes a matter of great concern to me from the moment that my friend is involved in it. I do think, my dear Charles, that from beginning to end you have played niether a wise nor a kindly part in the affair. (I know I am speaking like a parson, but I'm damned if I can help it.) You might, I think, have felt yourself above taking revenge on such a shorn lamb as J.F., instead of answering his inefficacious pebbles with such a boulder as you sent upon his poor, frail head; and certainly, after you had done so—after you had played a part so far off magnanimity, you might have taken a lower key and done your best to heal your own bruises by healing his.

I do wish you would think better of this matter and give Forman something in the way of reparation. Apology is from the strong to the weak. A big man is never so big as when he apologises to a little whelk of a creature such as our poor, *invalide* Forman. If you cannot see your way to writing something, for the love of God, old man, let me call and I'll eat all the necessary onion—yea, and relish

3. Perhaps John Forman, W.S., who lived at 8 Heriot Row. The circumstances of the quarrel remain obscure.

it. I shall say that you were hasty and told a foolish story, without any wish to hurt his (J.F.'s) feelings, that you were riled at the way he took to shew his displeasure, that—*enfin,* old man, that you are plucky enough and *man* enough to apologise because you find your-self involved in a duel with a child. For God's sake, don't deny me this favour. I shall count it a real proof of friendship. I shall take it more gladly than I would a ten-pound note, and you know what that means for an impecunious, extravagant, hand-to-mouth, poor devil such as I. I know well enough that you are not so mean as to desire a fight with so feeble an adversary. I know that you must feel the *hate* of such a man a slur upon your tact and magnanimity, and I want—I really do wish and hope, in spite of all this cursed pulpit phraseology, that you will either write or let me go on your part and do the immediate leek-eating.

Don't let me have a friend who isn't bold enough to say *"I was wrong"* to such a ——— as J.F.

For God's sake don't take this amiss. However much you dislike it or think it strained and foolish, it is the best proof of friendship you have ever got, or are ever likely to get, from

Your afft. friend,

R. L. STEVENSON

MS, Yale.

[Malvern?] [4] December 1872

Secretairy,

Quite contrairy,
How did the voting go?
Did the president's rule
Make you look like a fool?
Or were you at the head of the row?

As for me, I am a harmless, necessary —ster. "If you want to see — A —— come to me." Seriously, old man, I'm limed, and my lookout for life is a pretty bad one. I gave myself a good cross-examination this morning, and ever since I have been—I don't say

---

4. "Louis was not very strong in Dec. and after trying a change to Bridge of Allan without result he and I are ordered to Malvern where we stay for three weeks and he comes home much better" (*Diary*, p. 324).

indifferent, for I should like to live—but *easy* as to the result. I don't take so unkindly to death, especially as I see a course about which anon and in your private ear. I don't think much of my own chance, for I think I have a regular skinful, and I fancy the doctor thinks so too. I feel somehow as if I were in the roads already, and casting anchor, but eh good God! they may be a long way off, and there may be a nasty surf on the bar when I come to cross. We shall hope, however, 1st for a good recovery, and 2nd for an easy passage, if No. 1 be denied.

Enough of the mortuary. I have started an essay for Simpson's night, "Law versus Legislation." [5] It is *terribly* broad, and will bring anyone who may happen to listen on my head.

I wish to God I had five years more, for if I went on as I have been doing, I think I shd not have been so useless—should not feel myself a cancelled cipher when I came to the end.

Ever your sincere friend,
R. L. S.

MS, Yale.

Imperial Hotel, Great Malvern, 16 January 1873

My dear Baxter,

Without, it rains—within, muddle o' the brains. The damp weather has played old billy with such gray matter or convolutions (or whatever it is) as I possess, and the result is incapacity to do more. I have been stewing up spiritualism and just began an article on it [6] yesterday: fresh, gay, breeze blowing, streamers flowing. And now O pitiable sight!—we have missed the tide and I and my new embarcation lie stranded together on the broad, wet flats of idiocy. No gibbering here—all things are too despondent and wet; it requires an effort but I shall throw off mine inactivity, drop down by the fore-chains, and take a reach over the swampy sands—who knows but I may stumble on an oyster or two?

The fact is, I have a hidden grief and am letting concealment, like a worm i' the bud, prey on my damask cheek.[7] But—chut!—

5. On 11 February 1873 at the Spec, with Simpson in the chair, RLS read an essay entitled "Law and Free Will," with what may be a subtitle, "Notes on the Duke of Argyll."

6. Not recovered.

7. Cf. *Twelfth Night,* II.4.112–113.

not even in the privacy of this epistle can I be *bass* enough to breath—I really ought to be very glad and shall be by tomorrow or perhaps earlier; but in the meantime this blessing wears about as offensive a disguise as he could well have laid his hands upon—I should say, figuratively speaking, that he wore a white hat—and the double knocker of not being able to work coming on the back of it has played the devil with me altogether.

Charles Baxter, I am demoralised. There is no use attempting to deny it. I am unstrung, undone, mind and body. O Writer to the Signet, that thou wert here and this black hour consoling!

I shall go shortly and play billiards with the waiter, which is my one, forlorn, and dissipated amusement in this place. Said waiter is intelligent, but he has such good manners and talks so *point-de-vice,* that I have to be on my *p*s and *q*s with him. He is too good society for me—is that waiter! It is such a strain to be always a gentleman and never to be allowed to say——.

I had a card from Hodgson,[8] in which he said that he hungered and thirsted (Mrs. H. *de meme*) after my company on some specified evening in the "Halls of the Society of Art" [9]—I *think* that was the expression, but as I had lost the ticket before I answered, I didn't of course enter these details. If you go, you must tell me all about it.

I must say that I am damned tired of this place. My mother and I talk little except at meal times, and I write or read straight on, except when I betake me to my waiter.

But today, O spes naufracta, O scribendum opus, O blokus pokendum! (Please construe and pause.) Nigri diaboli sunt in corde mea et illic saltant et ludunt veterem Henricum generaliter; quod est lugendum. "Ne sit ancillae tibi amor pu—." Non plus, non plus—silentium est vestrum ludum, R. L. Stevenson, in meano tempore.[10]

8. William Ballantyne Hodgson (1815–80), professor of commercial and political economy at Edinburgh University. RLS had just taken his course in political economy, in which "he gained a certificate of merit for essays; he enjoyed this class very much" (*Diary*, p. 324).

9. It was at the Royal Scottish Society of Arts that RLS read his paper on "Intermittent Light for Lighthouses" (above, p. 1 n. 2).

10. "O shipwrecked hope, O work to be written, O bloke to be prodded! Black devils are in my heart, and there dance and play Old Harry generally; which must be deplored. 'You need not be ashamed [*pudori*] of your love for a servant lass' [Horace, *Odes* 2.4.1]. No more, no more—silence is your game, R. L. Stevenson, in the meantime."

My brain is just like a wet sponge: soft, pulpy, and lying spread out, flat and flaccid, over my eyes.

If I could call up the devil just now, wouldn't I do it pretty quick niether! The devil! why I'd be glad of John the Baptist. The fact is, that waiter is a strain on me. I am not framed for such damned good society. And it rains. And I can't walk—drink—work —play—; but I *can* smoke, and I'm going to.

I feel as if I could write poetry today; probably shall, before night.[1]

O Lord, old man, I'm getting tired of this whole life business. If I could find any other investment, I should take out my capital. When I think of how much country lies behind me since November, country that I had never thought to travel in at all; when I think of how deep a quagmire I have been puddling in this whole winter through—well you don't suppose the retrospect *égayant,* do you? O fie, fie upon the whole foolish, violent, and wearisome game, say I. Let me get into a corner with a brandy bottle; or down on the hearthrug, full of laudanum grog; or as easilly as may be, into the nice, wormy grave. I give up my chair to whoever wants it: here gentlemen is the refuse of what was never a very good hand and the one or two counters still left to me—share them and Adieu!

R. L. S.

Please see that I am not done brown at the Speculative.

R. L. S.

MS, Yale. Letters, 1, *61.*

17 Heriot Row, Edinburgh,
Sunday, 2 February 1873

My dear Baxter,

The thunderbolt has fallen with a vengeance now. You know the aspect of a house in which somebody is still waiting burial: the quiet step, the hushed voices and rare conversation, the religious litterature that holds a temporary monopoly, the grim, wretched faces; all is here reproduced in this family circle in honour of my (what is it?) atheism or blasphemy. On Friday night after leaving you, in the course of conversation my father put me one or two questions as to beliefs, which I candidly answered. I really hate

1. Cf. RLS's verses, "Ne sit ancillae, etc." (*Poems,* p. 332).

all lying so much now—a new-found honesty that has somehow come out of my late illness—that I could not so much as hesitate at the time, but if I had foreseen the real Hell of everything since, I think I should have lied as I have done so often before. I so far thought of my father, but I had forgotten my mother. And now! they are both ill, both silent, both as down in the mouth as if—I can find no simile. You may fancy how happy it is for me. If it were not too late, I think I could almost find it in my heart to retract, but it is too late; and again, am I to live my whole life as one falsehood? Of course, it is rougher than Hell upon my father, but can I help it? They don't see either that my game is not the light-hearted scoffer, that I am not (as they call me) a careless infidel. I believe as much as they do, only generally in the inverse ratio; I am, I think, as honest as they can be in what I hold. I have not come hastilly to my views. I reserve (as I told them) many points until I acquire fuller information. I do not think I am thus justly to be called a "horrible atheist"; and I confess I cannot exactly swallow my father's purpose of praying down continuous afflictions on my head.

Now, what is to take place? What a damned curse I am to my parents! As my father said, "You have rendered my whole life a failure." As my mother said, "This is the heaviest affliction that has ever befallen me." And, O Lord, what a pleasant thing it is to have just *damned* the happiness of (probably) the only two people who care a damn about you in the world. You see when I get incoherent, I always relapse a little into the Porter in *Macbeth*.

I should like to——blast!

I think if Cambridge could be managed, it would be the best thing. A little absence is the only chance.

Imagine, Charles, my father sitting in the arm chair, gravely reading up Butler's *Analogy* [2] in order to bring the wanderer back. Don't suppose I mean this jocularly—damn you. I think it's about the most pathetic thing I ever heard of—except one, and *that* I could not tell, but I can write it. My mother (dear heart) immediately asked me to join Nicholson's [3] young men's class: O what a

2. Joseph Butler (1692–1752), Bishop of Durham. For more than a century his *Analogy of Religion* (1736) was widely regarded among Protestants as second in authority only to the Bible.

3. Probably the Rev. Maxwell Nicholson (1818–74), minister of St. Stephen's Church, Edinburgh. On 30 December 1874 CB wrote to RLS: "Be as careful as you can how your father hears of Dr. Nicolson's death (this morning at 3 o'c). It might be

remedy for me! I don't know whether I feel more inclined to laugh or cry over these naivetés, but I know how sick at heart they make me.

What is my life to be, at this rate? What, you rascal? Answer—I have a pistol at your throat. If all that I hold true and most desire to spread is to be such death, and worse than death, in the eyes of my father and mother, what the *devil* am I to do? Here is a good heavy cross with a vengeance, and all rough with rusty nails that tear your fingers; only it is not I that have to carry it alone: I hold the light end, but the heavy burthen falls on these two.

Charles Baxter, if you think it likely that you will ever beget a child, follow Origen's specific; [4] it is painful, but there are worse pains in this world.

If PEOPLE ONLY WOULD admit in practice (what they are so ready to assert in theory) that a man has a right to judge for himself, and is culpable if he do not excercise that right, why, it would have been better for a number of people—better for Wycliffe and Servetus and even Whitefield,[5] nay and even me. Better, on the other hand, for many a doubting Torquemada, and for my father and mother at the present date.

Don't——I don't know what I was going to say. I am an abject idiot—which all things considered is not remarkable.

Ever your affectionate and horrible Atheist,

R. L. STEVENSON, C.I., H.A., S.B.,[6] etc.

MS, Yale.

Private

17 Heriot Row, Edinburgh [October? 1873]

My dear Baxter,

I wished to say a little word to you last night, and much of it I managed to say, yet left that unsaid that was made all the more important as I went forward. I wish you to understand that what I said to you is not to be judged exactly as other matters that go betwixt

---

a dangerous shock; at least I know I have made my mother very ill by coming out with it too plainly. What a merry Xmas for us both!"

4. I.e. castration.

5. All of them heretics against the established religions of their day.

6. Careless Infidel, Horrible Atheist, Son of Belial(?).

me and my friends, and to ask you, as a very particular act of friendship, two things: (1st) that you will not mention anything of what
you have heard from me to *anyone* else, and (2nd) that you will
not recur to the matter unnecessarily with me.

Please, old man, do not misunderstand this note. You will know
how serious I am when I tell you that I had little sleep last night
because I had omitted to add these two requests, which I know you
will very kindly grant. Indeed it is perhaps better that they should
be made to you in writing. You need not answer this note, either
by word or in writing.

Believe me, ever your friend (as I hope you to stand mine),

ROBERT LOUIS STEVENSON

You know there are some things, old man, on which chaff is not
quite on the spot. Let this little note of considerable pain on my
part be forever among the number of such things, and pardon me
for having written it.[7]

R. L. S.

MS, Yale.

15 Chepstow Place, Bayswater, London
[after 24 October 1873] [8]

My dear Charles,

Your kindness put me in rather an odd little difficulty on Saturday morning. Please send the letters to this address—the first word
is "Chepstow," in case you can't read it—in a large envelope. My
paper will appear in the *Portfolio* for December,[9] where you may
look for it.

I am really very far from well, and so you must pardon me for

7. No clue to these confidences survives.

8. When RLS left Edinburgh for London (*Diary*, p. 325).

9. "Roads," a description of the roads in Suffolk; it appeared in November
(*Portfolio, 4*, 1873, 185). "I have finished *Roads* today [12 September], and send it
off to you to see. The Lord knows whether it is worth anything!—some of it
pleases me a good deal, but I fear it is quite unfit for any possible magazine. However, I wish you to see it, as you know the humour in which it was conceived,
walking alone and very happily about the Suffolk highways and bye-ways on several
splendid sunny afternoons. . . . *Monday*.—I have looked over *Roads* again, and I
am aghast at its feebleness. It is the trial of a very ' 'prentice hand' indeed. Shall
I ever learn to do anything *well?*" (RLS to Mrs. Sitwell, *Letters, 1*, 73).

writing very briefly. My head swims so devilishly I can hardly see to write. I have been to see a swell London doctor,[10] who thinks I shall pull round, on a diet etc. etc.

The Lord help you in that dammed town, whose name even makes me shudder!

Years hence I think I shall be able to tell you something that will make you [1] respect me, although that sentiment sounds somewhat burlesque in connexion with

Ever your friend,
R. Louis Stevenson

This is the skeleton of what I would write to you if my head were stronger.

MS, Yale.

Private—a few! [2]

[London] Satingty [3] [1 November 1873]

My dear Charles,

The doctor has just told me that I have succeeded in playing the devil with myself to a singular degree. That walk down from Queen Street has made a fine sore of my burning, and here I am. There is not much gibber about me, alas! Like bad soda water, the cork has come out and my spirit does not pour forth in foolery, as I had wished. It is difficult to gibber with a sore and after having written two and twenty pages for Hodgson. Still I must do something light and festive.

Talking of soda water, I have a vapid, dead taste in my mouth as if I had been drinking some and it was *very* bad. I see the colourless pools on the table with the bubbles in them, and the green bottle and the wire and the spittoons—*Fi! fermons les yeux!* We are in a public house, and somebody was drunk last night. This is a most intolerable vision, isn't it? I have had it about me all morning, and you never saw such a sour, saw-dusty, cold, matutinal

---

10. Dr. (later Sir) Andrew Clark (1826–93). He ordered RLS to the Riviera, without his parents (*Diary*, p. 325).

1. MS, "me."

2. I.e. and how!

3. MS obscure; apparently a facetious spelling of "Saturday."

public-house in your life, as is this one that I inhabit in spirit. I cannot get rid of this.

The general chorus of all my thoughts just now is

"Over the hills and far away," [4]

as it must be of any well-regulated person in this double-damned place at the beginning of winter. It is a terrible long dark vault, this winter, for a man to enter into; not so long, however, but what I can see—far away, at the other end—the sun shining in next spring. Aren't you made hungry, or thirsty, or something, by the mere word? Spring, that dear delusion, that jolly old impostor, that I know will be cold and rainy and unutterably filthy after all!

I feel very sentimental. The sun is shining just now, by the bye, right into the room, and that has dispersed my visionary public and terrible depressing potash water—a new form of nightmare and very horrid.

I don't like the slowness with which this drivel comes away. Is the cask running dry? Is the issue of my foolishness ceased? God forbid.

You can't tell how much I want to stand on my head—just because I've got a sore, altho' you know I couldn't stand on my head even if I hadn't a sore.

Who the devil's that knocking in the lower flat? Knocking stopped. Do you remember the knocking in *Macbeth?* That is some pumkins. There is not much knocking about the world that can come up to that. The Porter is a man I have a great respect for. He had a great command of language. All that he says, curiously enough, my mother left out when she read *Macbeth* to me—I suppose it was too affecting. By jingo! I remember the day my mother read *Macbeth* to me. A terrible, black, stormy day, when niether of us could go out of the house, and so we both sat over the fire and she read and I had snakes and newts and others to crawl up and down my spine.

There is blasted little to think about in this world. This letter is quite a chronicle of all my thoughts, except that whenever a cart passes, I should like to go and look at it to see what is in it, and then don't so, and then am sorry for not having done so.

I have left out some of my thoughts here. The spirit of the Porter entered into me for a space. If I were a medium, I should call up

4. Cf. RLS's "A Song of the Road."

the spirit of that Porter and just sit and listen to him by the hour. I don't think anything could soothe me so.

Words can't express how empty my head is. I have entirely exhausted it over Pol. Econ. By the bye, wouldn't it be fun to borrow a motto for Hodgson from the Porter's speech?

I feel as if I had taken hands with certain personnified execrations and was dancing with them in a sort of Bacchanalian jinga-ring, all about the vacant but sensitive floor of my mind. *Damn* is a short, burly fellow; he is not much at dancing; he is sort of solid and serious and dances away with gravity. —— is lean and feathers his toes like anything. But the life and soul of the party is my little immortal soul, who skips and leaps and cancanises and drags the whole ring hither and thither, and faster! faster!—step out, damn! —Evoë!—round and round and round goes my immortal soul and all the personnified oaths.

The real truth is, I was able to eat nothing at breakfast, and I am quite giddy and light-headed with work and tea and want of food. My head rolls about on my shoulders like a great big peony on the end of a blade of spear-grass. And O! I am in a hell of a state— venus, mind, and body.

Distractedly yours,

R. L. STEVENSON

I shouldn't wonder if there are some oaths in this letter. I now believe that story about Swinburne and the bell-pull.[5]

I really am not drunk, altho' I feel quite drunk, for I have tasted *nothing* but tea today.

MS, Yale.

[London, 4 November 1873]

My dear Baxter,

Please redeem my *Democratic Vistas* by W. Whitman from Wilson, Tobacconist, in Lieth Street. Miss Mason has charge of it— not old W. himself; so please explain to her my movements and how my health it is all ruinèd and I'm a-goin' south.

In a little while I think you will receive my *Leaves of Grass* also,

5. Possibly a variant of "Oh God, if there is a God, which there isn't, where are those damned boots?"

when you will be decent and cheery enough to do them both up discreetly into a parcel and forward them [6] to the address that I shall have sent you before then.

Let Simpson etc. know of my movements. I think my last blow was that Sunday night. I never got properly well again. My parents utterly puzzle me: I have sometimes a notion that the atheist son is almost in the way. My head is about done for, so goodby, old man. Post Restante, Mentone, is my next address.

                                                          R. L. S.

MS, Yale.

                                        [London, 4 November 1873] [7]

My dear Charles,

Le grand moment est arrivé. Ce soir, avant que je me couche, je saurai ce que j'ai encore d'espoir. Je me sens au bord du gouffre. Un indicible vertige m'engourdisse toutes les facultés. Une heure—et je serai je ne sais où. It is my final cast, old man, for happiness in this unhappy world.

And yet I have strength enough to say that I have received your notice and to bid you, O perfidious man, tremble upon your tottering throne.

5.45—Spec Rooms. And I dine at six!

O what a low and detestable proceeding.

Goodbye.

                              Yours, on the red-hot tenterhooks,
                                                    R. L. S.

MS, Yale.

Private

                    Hotel du Pavillon, Menton [15 November 1873]

My dear Charles,

I feel that I ought to write to you, though after all you never write to me, and yet I [am] not in good enough spirits to be tonight a very pleasant correspondant. I am only gradually finding out how

6. For an essay he was writing on Whitman (see *Letters, 1,* 106).

7. A Tuesday, on which day the Spec regularly met. RLS left London for France the next day.

nearly done for I have been. I am awfully weary and nervous, I cannot read or write almost at all, and I am not able to walk much; all which put together leaves me a good deal of time in which I have no great pleasure or satisfaction. However, you must not suppose me discontented. I am away in my own beautiful Riviera, and I am free now from the horrible worry and misery that was playing the devil with me at home. A friend in London,[8] I must tell you, had a conversation with my father (this is in the strictest confidence— I am not supposed to know of it myself) and explained to him a little that I was not the extremely cheerful destroyer of home-quiet that he had pictured to himself, and that I really was bothered about this wretched business; and I hope some good out of that if I can only pull my health round. I hope you will write to me and write something amusing. I shall write shortly to J.W.F. and Simpson, and you will oblige if you will announce this my intention (should you have an opportunity) in order that I may enjoy some grattitude *avant le coup,* if either of them has any grattitude in him.

If you have any cheerfulness in you, write cheerfully, for all my correspondents, I am sorry to say, are in a somewhat chill-blained humour. Bob [9] writes sadly from Antwerp, where he feels lonely as yet, and there are other troubles besides my own that make the pack a little heavy just at present; I wish I could get it off my aching shoulders for half an hour. If I were pious, I should pray for a night's sleep, for I slept badly yesterday, and that plays one out when one is seedy.

I do not know how I am to apologise to you for this Jeremiad, which is not like the usual run of my correspondance with you at all; but the truth is, I am out of heart at this knock-down blow just when I was beginning to get a possibility of good work and a livelihood. It is beastly to have a bad head like this, and to have to pay for half an hour's thinking with a bad night or an hour or two of miserable nervousness. However, we keep our weather eye open, and still hope greatly. I cannot be a heretic to my own favourite gospel of cheerfulness altogether, and I have my jolly hours too, I can promise you, when the sun shines and the lemon gardens perfume everything about them more sweetly than the most delicate 'air oil.

8. Probably Mrs. Sitwell, the chief confidante of RLS's youth; later Lady Colvin. See Furnas, p. 84.
9. Bob Stevenson, who was studying art in Belgium.

Next night

I am placidly ignorant of the day of the week, but I think it is the sixteenth of the month. I had a good night, without specially committing myself to the Powers that be, and woke in time to see a magnificent dawn. I am in somewhat cheerier humour than before. Bob gave me the messages about the *Portfolio*. You will like it, I think; Simpson had better go without his number as he will contemn and loathe the article.[10] It is to be signed L. S. Stoneven, which makes not a bad name. O! what about the Spec! Do for the Lord's sake clear me of responsibility, and write and tell me how you get on this session. I do think that the Spec is about the only good thing in Edinburgh.[1] I should like to be present at a meeting tonight—O awfully. I would open a debate about the game-laws, or defend the Xian religion, or make the coffee outside with Clers,[2] or support the secretary in his tyranny, or do anything mean, sordid, and disreputable for that inestimable favour. Shouldn't I have a nice pipe in the lobby—no, up at the far end of the library, sitting on the steps. Tell me how many of you are drunk at Barclay's[3] dinner.

I have just put another billet on the fire, and it is most cheerful and companionable, and gossips and chirps away to me like an old friend. The sea is quieter tonight, but it always wails among the shingle uneasily. It is a quiet, dark night outside, with stars. I wonder strangely what everyone is about tonight—friends in London, Antwerp, Edinburgh; and me alone here up at the top of the house, with my two little windows shining, two little lighted beacons over the peaceful Meditteranean.

Talking of which, old man, take care of yourself like a good chap, won't you? And believe me

Ever your afft friend,

R. L. STEVENSON

10. "Roads."

1. On the evening of 25 March of this year RLS was to have read to the Spec, in the office of president, the valedictory address which concluded each session, but because he had been taken ill, CB read it in his place. It was entitled "The Best Thing in Edinburgh" (see edition by Katharine D. Osbourne, wife of RLS's stepson Lloyd, San Francisco, 1923). Though RLS had become an inactive member on 11 February, he continued to read essays and even to hold office during the years following (*History of the Speculative Society 1764–1904*, Edinburgh, 1905, pp. 41, 42).

2. Apparently so spelled. Not identified.

3. Thomas Barclay (1851–1940), president of the Spec, 1873–75; barrister at the Inner Temple, London, 1876.

When you get *Leaves of Grass,* you'll send the 2 books off, won't you?

MS, Yale.

CB TO RLS

[Edinburgh] Sunday, 16 November 1873

My dear Louis,

I duly received your letters announcing your unexpected orders for the South. I needn't say to you how sorry I was for the cause of them, but I've no doubt being away from this land of civil and religious liberty will do a good deal to restore *tone* to your nervous system, which I imagine is about all that is wanted. You are lucky enough, too, old fellow, to be sent away at this time, for now chill Novr. has settled down upon us with his usual cheerfulness, and we wander about with red noses stillicidal as to their extremities, say our prayers, and try to think we are thankful to God for being Christians and having the inestimable blessing of residing in His modern paradise hight Scotland. But it *don't* do; honesty will out and we grumble as heartily now and then as if we were poor heathens.

How strangely our côterie has broken up! With scarcely a word of warning, almost imperceptibly, the L.J.R. is scattered far and wide over the face of the earth; its times seem almost a part of antiquity, dim and fading away in the shadows of the past. Only now by times two or three old antiques, such as Simpson and myself or maybe [   ] [4] coming together over our cups, feebly chirp with small weak twitterings of the brave times so long gone by. Brave days they were; step not too close, Mr. Connoisseur, you ought to know that the blurs and blotches are not the picture—but back a little, let the time-distance soften and mellow, and see the delicate genial *genre* picture, coarse tho' the subject be—(how shall we call it?)—"Boors carousing in a tavern."

Here wipe we dry the sentimental tear and turn we now to things more practical. I called as desired at Wilson's and got the *Vistas.* I am keeping them till the fulfilment of the mysterious prediction of the arrival of the *Leaves.* Why these hidden things and dark allu-

4. Name illegible.

sions? I gave in for you a resignation of your Presidentship at the
Speculative. Thomas Barclay, a gentle youth albeit of no high degree, now reigns in your stead. The room has secured, and indeed
I think merits, universal approbation, and our meetings have been
remarkably pleasant. Not that there have been no personal on-
slaughts, for there have been more than there used to be; but somehow there is a better tone, no one is intoxicated, and members stay
in the room during the evening. Graham Murray's [5] opening address was very successful, being not much of a discourse such as we
have usually had, but rather a smart satirical attack upon the leading members of the Society, among whom were specially distinguished yourself and your humble servant. I shall try to send you a
copy of it, as I think it would amuse you. Simpson reads on Tuesday a "View of the Doctrine of the Trinity in the first Three
Centuries," at which he has been working pretty hard and which I
imagine will touch up our orthodox brethren.

Are you still suffering from the paroxysm of virtue which charac-
terised your last days here? Write me thereof, and of Mentone: is
the sky blue? and does the sun shine? is the song of the labourer
heard in the morning, and do you hate existence no more? Is it
better to be a Mentonian (I'm blessed if I know where the place is)
than a Scotchman? are his wives prettier? his daughters more vir-
tuous? his life purer, and his end happier? or is it that—the surface
cleared away—the doctrine of averages prevails, and Mentonians
are just Scotchmen after all, with a darker hue, another tongue, and
less *canniness?* To these and other suggested queries I will that you
write me faithful answer. Remember, if I seem to neglect you, that
I have much to do, that my leisure is for the most part only the
putting off of weariness, and that of all things, the thing I like least
is writing letters. Such considerations will I hope convince you that
tho' out of sight you are never out of the mind of your friend and
brother in mischief, and

Yours affectionately,

C.

5. Andrew Graham Murray (*b.* 1849), member of parliament for Bute, 1891, and in
1905, as Lord Dunedin of Stenton, Lord Justice General and Lord President of the
Court of Session.

MS, Yale. Letters, 1, *106.*

[Menton] 4 December [1873]

My dear Baxter,

At last, I must write. I began a letter to you before, but it broke miserably down, and when I looked it over it seemed so contemptible a fragment that I have put it in the fire. I must say straight out that I am not recovering as I could wish. I am no stronger than I was when I came here, and I pay for every walk beyond say a quarter of a mile in length by one, or two, or even three days of more or less prostration. Therefore let nobody be down upon me for not writing. I was very thankful to you for answering my letter; and for the princely action of Simpson in writing to me—I mean before I had written to him—I was ditto to an almost higher degree. I hope one or other of you will write again soon, and remember, I still live in hope of a reading of Grahame Murray's address. I do so much want somebody to be rude to me! The *Leaves of Grass* has not, I suppose, turned up. Damn. Not that it matters really, as I could do no work to it even if it were here. Of course, you must keep my cheerful auguries about my health to yourself, or any of trustworthy ear who may be interested therein, but I do somewhat portend that I may not recover at all, or at best that I shall be long about it. My system does seem extraordinarilly played out.

Yes, I am as moral as ever; more moral. A man with a smashed-up constitution and "on a diet" can be moral at the lowest possible figure, and then I always was a bit of a Joseph, as you know. My whole game is morality now, and I am very serious about it. Indeed I am very serious about everything, and go to the boghouse [5a] with as much solemnity as another man would go to church with. I can't laugh at a mosquito, and I have not made a joke, upon my living soul, since I left London. O! except one, a very small one, that I had made before, and that I timidly repeated in a half-exhilirated state towards the close of dinner, like one of those dead-alive flies that we see pretending to be quite light and full of the frivolity of youth in the first sunshiny days. It was about Mothers' meetings, and it was damned small, and it was my ewe lamb—the Lord knows I couldn't have made another to save my life; and a clergyman

5a. Privy.

quarrelled with me, and there was as nearly an explosion as could be. This has not fostered my leaning towards pleasantry. I felt that it was a very cold, hard world that night.

My dear Charles, is the sky blue at Mentone? Was that your question? Well, it depends upon what you call blue; it's a question of taste, I suppose: it's only about as blue as Hell, that's all, or bluer. Is the sky blue? You poor critter, you never saw blue sky worth being called blue in the same day with it. And I should rather fancy that the sun did shine, I should. And the moon doesn't shine niether. O no! (This last is sarcastic.)

Mentone is one of the most beautiful places in the world, and has always had a very warm corner in my heart since first I knew it eleven years ago.[6] I went back certainly not [7]

11 December

Let us, dearly beloved brethern, start fresh. I got a most charming letter from Simpson today at dinner, which has braced up my nerves considerable, and I shall try now to finish mine epistle.

I know here the comicalest of cusses: one in appearance somewhat like an educated goat, with a negro's wig on, called Argyll-Bates,[8] or (in the orthography of the *Courrier de Menton*) Arpel-Batts. Argyll-Bates and I became acquainted while he stayed at this hotel,[9] and both Dowson [10] and I knew he would turn out excentric. He asked me to go a drive with him to Bordighera, and I expected all sorts of strange manoeuvres. I thought he would bring out a long flute or fife in joints, out of different places of concealment about his person (having previously turned up his cuffs so as to convince me that there was no deception, spring, or false bottom) and that having put them together, he would pass his fingers through his hair, knock his hat in, hastilly black his face and hands with a burnt cork, and, standing up in the open carriage, begin to play wild music; or I thought he would play the banjo; or that he would bring out globes of water with gold fish in 'em. But he didn't.

6. RLS's first visit to Menton, January–March 1863, was the result of his mother's poor health, not his (*Diary*, p. 300).

7. The sentence breaks off.

8. Not identified.

9. Hôtel du Pavillon.

10. Alfred C. Dowson, father of the poet Ernest Dowson. He was the translator (from the French) of *Bordighera and the Western Riviera* (1883), by Frederick Fitzroy Hamilton.

He only brought out a black bottle and drank Marsala from the neck. He herded much with gipsies when he was young, and he sang me gipsy songs. The other evening I went along to his rooms, and he read aloud to me a burlesque of his own composition. (O Lord! how our sins do find us out, how of our pleasant vices are fashioned the scourges wherewithal our buttocks tingle! [1] But I never read anybody *a burlesque*.) He plays very well on the piano, and that is about the best of him.

So you read an essay to the Spec? [2] And they didn't know very much more about J.P. after it than they had known before? And that was damned little, you bet? Well, well, there have been other great works coldly looked upon; and verilly, I say unto you, you ——, you have your reward. I think I see J.P. rubbing his shadowy palms together in Hell and thanking God that he has been understood at last. When I say I think I see him, I don't mean anything very definite, for I shouldn't know him from Job if I were to see him. He didn't wear a collar, if I remember rightly? That was his best holt, wasn't it? It was very good—ha, ha! He didn't wear a collar! O Lord, that's rich! What a humourist! And the exquisite sense of fitness, too, that kept him from overdoing the pleasantry and not wearing trousers either! I wish he hadn't worn trousers, though. I could then have capped the jest so well by kicking his bottom. I hope I don't hurt your feelings. That chef-d'oeuvre about not wearing a collar is all I know about J.P., but, as I said before, I think that capital.

This is the 26th consecutive day without rain or cloud. (That's not English, but that don't matter much.) You see the Mentonese is rather on the spot about weather, isn't he? His wife, about whom you asked with a spasm of ill-concealed Satyriasis, is pretty for a short time, and then goes in for tempus edax what'shisname [3] without farther scruple. I don't know whether she is faithful to him or not, but I should fancy she had few temptations after a certain age.

I live in the same Hotel with Lord Salisbury. [4] Ahem. He has black whiskers and looks not unlike Crum Brown, [5] only rather

1. Cf. *King Lear*, V.3.170–171.
2. On Jean Paul Richter (1763–1825). It was read on 2 December.
3. Rerum: Ovid, *Metamorphoses* 15:234.
4. Robert Arthur Talbot Gascoyne-Cecil (1830–1903), 3d Marquis of Salisbury; later thrice prime minister.
5. Alexander Crum Brown, M.D., professor of chemistry, 1869, at Edinburgh University.

more of Crum B. than there is in the Edinburgh edition. He has been successful (or his wife has) in making some kids; rather a melancholy success: they are weedy looking kids, in highland clo'. They have a tutor with them who respires Piety and that kind of humble your-lordship's-most-obedient sort of gentlemanliness that noblemen's tutors have generally. They all get livings, these men, and silvery hair, and a gold watch from their attached pupil; and they sit in the porch and make the watch repeat for their little grandchildren, and tell them long storys beginning "when I was private tutor in the family of etc.," and the grandchildren cock snooks [6] at them behind their backs, and go away whenever they can, to get the groom to teach them bad words. My friends, let us all kneel down and thank God that he has never made us tutors in a nobleman's family; there are some fates too pitiable for tears. I would sooner be a Macer. (Talking of whom, is there anything new about Johnny Adams? [7] Dear man! how my heart would melt within me and the tears of patriotism spring to my eyes if I could but see him reel towards me in his dress clo' like a moon at midday and smiling his vulgar, Scotch grin from ear to ear!) Can I do anything for you with Lord Salisbury? Ahem.

Foot-note in small print: Is he a dook, marquis, earl, or paper Lord? [8]

I see with pain that you are still as dissipated as the devil. Upon my word, Charles, I do not think you ought to leave the parent nest. I speak very seriously. I doubt if you would not be much the worse for it. Remember what is the invariable result of their absence, and perpend, my man, perpend. Seriously, if it can be managed, stay where you are. It seems a rude thing to say, but I do think the terrors of the law are not unnecessary for you.

I question if anybody ever had such cold hands as I have just now; however, wonderful to state, I have no blood to the head, and so can go on writing.

I am reading Michelet's *French Revolution,* having somewhat surfeited myself on George Sand. [9] Even the most wholesome food

6. I.e. thumb noses.

7. Actually "Adam," a bibulous clerk of court in Edinburgh. See RLS's Burnsian verses "To Charles Baxter, on the Death of Their Common Friend, Mr. John Adam, Clerk of the Court."

8. I.e. a judge of one of the high courts, whose title was not hereditary.

9. On Sunday, 30 November, RLS had written to Mrs. Sitwell: "I have found here a new friend, to whom I grow daily more devoted—George Sand. I go on from one

palleth after many days banquetting, and History's little dishfull of herbs seemed at last preferable to the stalled ox of pampered fiction.

Sidney Colvin [1] will arrive here on Saturday or Sunday, so I shall have someone to jaw with. And seriously this is a great want. I have not been all these weeks in idleness, as you may fancy, without much thinking as to my future; and I have a great deal in view that may or may not be possible (that I do not yet know) but that is at least an object and a hope before me. I cannot help recurring to seriousness a moment, before I stop, for I must say that living here a good deal alone and having had ample time to look back upon my past, I have become very serious all over—not in religion, as you may fancy, but morally. If I can only get back my health, by God! I shall not be as useless as I have been. By God, or by Satan, or by the Unknowable, or by the Universum, or by Myself (because there is none greater alas!) or however we shall have to swear nowadays, when we have laid aside your religion, my gentle communicant,

Ever yours, mon vieux,
ROBERT LOUIS STEVENSON

(Soon to Simpson.) Health really on *the improve.*

MS, Yale.

Monaco, 20 December 1873

My dear Baxter,

There is a large wooden chest (plain deal) in my sitting room; in that box many papers, and among these papers two stories: one (which you read a long while ago) called *The Curate of Anstruther's Bottle;* the other called *The Devil on Crammond Sands.*[2] Both are written on single leaves of white, ruled foolscap, and I should think they would be close together. They cover each about

---

novel to another and think the last I have read the most sympathetic and friendly in tone, until I have read another. It is a life in dreamland" (*Letters, 1,* 103).

1. RLS had first met his future editor, then Slade Professor of Art at Cambridge, in the late summer of this year at the home of his cousin, Maud Balfour Babington, at Cockfield, Suffolk. His mother noted: "and they were fast friends ever after. Prof. Colvin encouraged him in his literary aspirations and I always called him his literary godfather" (*Diary,* p. 325).

2. Neither of these stories was ever published. The outline of "The Curate" is preserved in RLS's essay, "Random Memories: the Coast of Fife."

30 leaves written on one side only—O! the last leaves of the second story are on another sort of paper, not-ruled I think, which you might be apt to forget. If they are not in the chest (but I am almost sure they are) they are in one of the long drawers of the kist of drawers in the same room.

Now, if you will dedicate ten minutes of your time to this brief search, and send the papers to me by Book Post, you will be a very good and acceptable person, and I will forgive you your unaccountable inaction about W.W.[3] and a certain breach of confidence of which I say nothing now.

Do work this off for me, without delay, as it is of a little importance to yrs truly, or may be. Please shew the accompanying certificate to my people, as it may amuse them.

Ever your friend,
R. L. STEVENSON

Admit ——————————
—— Charles Baxter, Esqr hunter to her
Majesty's Signet, —————
—— to view the Shrine
R. L. Stevenson
On Secret Service

To one Steward (a Stewardess)
of [my] Heart Row.

MS, Yale.

[Hôtel Mirabeau, Menton, January 1874]

My dear Charles,

I am here in a funny little Society: an American called Johnson,[4] one of the best story-tellers in the world, a man who can make a

3. Walt Whitman (see above, p. 29).

4. Or Johnstone. The family is mentioned in other letters from Menton (*Letters, 1*, 114 ff.) but is not further identified.

whole table d'hote listen to him for ten minutes while he tells how he lost his dog and found him again; Mme Johnson, his wife, a good woman, pious, stupid, who removes herself from the con- tamination of our games on the Sunday night (we play games in the Salon); his daughter May, a little girl of eight, very pretty and wild; M. Robinet, a French painter,[5] a very good fellow; Mme Zasetsky, a Russian Princess, and Mme Garschin, her sister,[6] two very nice women; Mme Garschin's little daughter and Mme Zaset- sky's, my adorable little Nelitchka, two and a half years old, talking the wonderfullest jargon of German, English, Italian, Russian, and Polish. I shall be better able to tell you of all this when I see you, as there are certain things that I do not care to write about. Don't open your eyes—the length they would occupy stands for the better part of my discretion. I hope you will be able to read this scrawly hand. Everybody is very jolly and we live just like a family; d——d like a family in fact: family secrets are produced right and left and I could tales unfold etc. You have no idea of how things are man- aged in such a Society. The Stool of Repentance, for example, at which we play often, is really a serious censorship: nobody dreams of giving any opinion that they do not mean, and one is told the cheerfullest home truths to one's face, seated on a chair in face of laughing audience. You have no idea what fun it is, especially on the sort of tentative terms on which we all are, to hear what people are thinking about you in the clearest terms—I was going to say English, but it's French. I have scarcely spoken a word of English today, so you may conceive what debauched French I serve myself with.

You are a good fellow to send me all these things, a beastly good fellow. The Lord bless you. Have you been revivalled yet?[7] They sent me magazines about it: the obscenest rubbish I was ever ac- quainted with. Simpson tells me MacGil[8] has stopped liquoring;

5. Gustave Paul Robinet (1845–1932), "sometimes in his days known as *le Raphael des cailloux,* from the minuteness of detail which he put into his Provençal coast landscapes, was a chivalrous and affectionate soul in whom R.L.S. delighted in spite of his fervent clerical and royalist opinions" (*Letters, 1,* 117, headnote).

6. Furnas (pp. 88–91) gives a lively sketch of these ladies and of RLS's relationship with them. See also *Letters, 1,* 117 ff. and RLS's verses "To Mesdames Zassetsky and Garschine" (*Poems,* p. 102).

7. The American evangelist team of Dwight L. Moody and Ira D. Sankey were conducting their first joint revival tour of the British Isles, and held services in Edinburgh from the end of November 1873 to late January 1874.

8. Not identified.

he will take to buggery likely. I bless God I am an infidel when I
read of such nervous fiddle-de-dee; and these people are down upon
the spiritualists! Why, I saw that bald-headed bummer J. Balfour [9]
had been describing a meeting he was at. He said, "They then enjoyed very precious and manifest tokens of the Lord's Presence."
If I had been there and had sworn upon all the obscene and
blasphemous phrases in my large repertory that God had *not* been
there, they would have told me it was because my heart was hard;
and yet when the poor humble spiritualist tries to cock up his little
tail on the same pretext, they say it's a manifest imposture and bend
their brows on him as if he were a thief. *O sapristi!* if I had hold
of James B. by the testicles, I would knock his bald cranium against
the wall until I was sick.

Eh bien, et comment ça va-t-il, mon Ecrivain au Signet? Est-ce
que vous vous portez bien, ou avez vous une——?

Imagine my position: when we were playing at a game in which
one has to finish a word, I had both *bou* and *fou* given to me; the
first time I saved myself with bou*quet,* but the second I could think
of nothing but what thou wottest of, and so was silent and paid my
forfeit. I shall now shut up. *Baisez mon cul.*

Ever yours,

ROBERT LOUIS STEVENSON

MS (postcard), Yale.

[London, 25 June 1874] [1]

Très affairé, je ne trouve pas le temps de vous écrire. Pardonnez
moi, donc. Tout va bien. Je suis l'intime des rédacteurs; [2] j'ai même
l'espoir de visiter Carlyle,[3] mais je ne sais pas encore trop comment.

---

9. James Balfour, 13 Eton Terrace. See *Narrative of Messrs. Moody and Sankey's
Labors in Great Britain and Ireland,* etc., New York, 1875, p. 20.

1. Postmark.

2. On 3 June RLS was elected a member of the Savile Club, having been proposed
by Colvin and supported by Andrew Lang, among others. The editors included
C. E. Appleton of the *Academy,* Walter Pollock of the *Saturday Review,* John Morley
of the *Fortnightly Review,* and William Minto of the *Examiner,* the latter of whom
was elected at the same time as RLS. Another editor, Leslie Stephen, had left the
club in 1870 (*The Savile Club 1868 to 1923,* 1923, passim).

3. "His great and natural desire to see Carlyle was frustrated, for Mr. Stephen,
on whose kind offices he depended, found the sage in one of his darker moods and at
a moment of irritation; and when Stevenson was mentioned as a young Scot who was

J'ai reçu cinq livres pour les *Fables,* ce qui était plus que je n'ex-
spectais.[4]

R. L. S.

MS, Yale.

[Edinburgh, fall of 1874]

Dear Charles,

Cold—in house—pity sorrows—not able to dine tomorrow—
visit acceptable—also, if attainable without trouble, volume of
Vasari from Spec containing the Life of M. Agnolo Buonarotti
Esqr., an Italian artist of some reputation, now deceased.[5] Don't
bother about this, you know; it was said only in case you might be
in the nieghborhood.

Ever thine,
ROBERT LOUIS STEVENSON

MS, Yale.

Savile Club, 15 Savile Row W.
[London, 28 July 1875]

My dear Charles,

Damned nice of you to write. Grindley and I were awful ill with
headache on the voyage,[6] and Grindlay spewed; so we also have had

---

most anxious to meet him, and who had taken to the study of Knox, the senior would
only say that he did not see why anybody should want either to see his 'wretched
old carcase' or to say anything more about Knox, and that the young man had better
apply when he had put his studies into an articulate shape. So Stevenson never met
his fellow-countryman . . ." (Balfour, *1,* 149–150).

4. RLS had reviewed Lord Lytton's *Fables in Song* for the *Fortnightly Review,*
new ser. *15* (1874), 817 ff. To Mrs. Sitwell he wrote: "I have been very cynical over
myself today, partly, perhaps, because I have just finished some of the deedest rubbish
about Lord Lytton's *Fables* that an intelligent editor ever shot into his wastepaper
basket. If Morley prints it I shall be glad, but my respect for him will be shaken"
(*Letters, 1,* 154).

5. A complete English translation of Vasari's *Lives of the Most Eminent Painters,
Sculptors, and Architects of Italy* (1550), by Mrs. Jonathan Foster, was published this
year. RLS may have wanted the life of Michelangelo for source material for a tale
he was writing called *When the Devil Was Well* (see Furnas, p. 120, and *Letters, 1,*
201).

6. ". . . on the 24th he sailed for London with Sir Walter [Grindlay] Simpson
en route for France" (*Diary,* p. 328).

our perils of the deep. It was in consequence of the most high-
handed overfeeding Grindlay spewed most gay and free. Since we
have been here, you should see him trying to get wound up of an
evening with (what they call) Brandy and Seltzer: Seltzer and some
colouring matter unknown is the right name for it. He just gets
bagged and bagged and better bagged and ever more baggeder, and
has to go to bed in the end, sick and sober, with a haggard light in
one eye.

Who should we meet but Glasgow Browne? [7] All right seemingly.
Coins, weeds, clo': all as before; telling great tales of bonnes for-
tunes among ladies of title, whereat I and Grindlay shake the head
of incredoolity. There are hitches: for instance—no I'm too tired.
God bless Parnes.[8] Write again. O, when we woke in London docks,
the first steamer I saw go past was the "Charles," and the next the
"Cygnet." I was afraid to look any more, I felt so eerie; but of course
I *know* the third was the "Baxter." We leave tonight: address Chez
Siron, Barbison, Seine et Marne, France.

                                             Ever yours,
                                             R. L. S.

MS untraced. Sotheby, 9 May 1949, 60.
   Letters, 1, 235; corrected text from
   Poems, p. 104.

                                    [Edinburgh, October 1875]

        Noo lyart leaves blaw ower the green,
        Reid are the bonny woods o' Dean,
        An' here we're back in Embro, frien',
            To pass the winter.

   7. Robert Glasgow Brown (*d.* 1879), associate of RLS on the short-lived *Edinburgh
University Magazine*, editor of *Vanity Fair* 1875–76, founder and first editor of *London*
(see below, p. 51). "I best remember him . . . tall, slender, with a not ungraceful
stoop; looking quite like a refined gentleman, and quite like an urbane adventurer;
smiling with an engaging ambiguity; cocking at you one peaked eyebrow with a great
appearance of finesse; speaking low and sweet and thick, with a touch of burr; telling
strange tales with singular deliberation and, to a patient listener, excellent effect.
After all [his] ups and downs, he seemed still, like the rich student that he was of yore,
to breathe of money; seemed still perfectly sure of himself and certain of his end.
Yet he was then upon the brink of his last overthrow" ("A College Magazine," in
Memories and Portraits). He died of tuberculosis.
   8. Not identified.

Whilk noo, wi' frosts afore, draws in,
　　An' snaws ahint her.

I've seen's hae days to fricht us a',
The Pentlands poothered weel wi' snaw,
The ways half smoored wi' liquid thaw,
　　An' half congealin',
The snell an' scowtherin' norther blaw
　　Frae blae Brunteelan'.

I've seen's been unco sweir to sally,
And at the door-cheeks daff an' dally—
Seen's daidle thus an' shilly-shally
　　For near a minute—
Sae cauld the wind blew up the valley,
　　The deil was in it!—

Syne spread the silk an' tak the gate,
In blast an' blaudin' rain, deil hae't!
The hale toon glintin', stane an' slate,
　　Wi' cauld an' weet,
An' to the Court,[9] gin we'se be late,
　　Bicker oor feet.

And at the Court, tae, aft I saw
Whaur Advocates by twa an' twa
Gang gesterin' end to end the ha'
　　In weeg an' goon,
To crack o' what he wull but Law
　　The hale forenoon.

That muckle ha', maist like a kirk,
I've kent at braid mid-day sae mirk
Ye'd seen white weegs an' faces lurk
　　Like ghaists frae Hell,
But whether Christian ghaists or Turk
　　Deil ane could tell.

9. Parliament House, Edinburgh. "For a few months Louis went every day to the Parliament House and it was hoped that he might carry on his writing in the library but he soon found that it was impossible; the Parliament House was too pleasant a place to be idle in and he told his father that he would fall between two stools if he went on, so the pretence was given up and he stayed at home and worked busily and happily at his literary work. He got four briefs in all" (*Diary,* pp. 328-9).

The three fires lunted in the gloom,
The wind blew like the blast o' doom,
The rain upo' the roof abune
     Played Peter Dick—
Ye wad nae'd licht enough i' the room
     Your teeth to pick!

But, freend, ye ken how me an' you,
The ling-lang lanely winter through,
Keep'd a guid speerit up, an' true
     To lore Horatian,
We aye the ither bottle drew—
     To inclination.

Sae let us in the comin' days
Stand sicker on oor auncient ways—
The strauchtest road in a' the maze
     Since Eve ate apples;
An' let the winter weet oor cla'es—
     We'll weet oor thrapples.

MS, Yale. Written on CB's official sta-
   tionery; see above, Introduction,
   p. xvii.

Chambers, 11 So. Charlotte Street,
Edinburgh [fall of] 187[5]

My dear Charles,

I want you to see my answers to condescendances (and d——d condescending condescendances they were) before they go. Now I have hung about in the rain for 40 minutes, and will no longer hang about in the rain. Can you make it convenient to call up at the Spec after five? Je vous attendrai, jusqu'à cinq heures et demi.

I have been as nice as treacle and as good as gold with Master Ingram,[1] and done as you proposed.

Tout à vous,
R. L. S.[2]

1. John H. Ingram, whose edition of Edgar Allan Poe RLS had reviewed in the *Academy*, 2 January of this year.
2. Followed by four attempts at a monogram.

I say that's the most practicable looking thing I ever made for myself. *Practical* was the word I employed, sir. Not *pretty*. You must have misapprehended me grossly, sir. Look here.[3]

MS, Yale.

> 17 Heriot Row, Edinburgh
> [29 February 1876]

My dear Charles,

My mother will be obliged if you will dine here on Wednesday at seven.

Let me add that I will be pleased also, and all the more if I have assured news of the decease of a certain colonel with whom I walked once of an afternoon. I like Charles Baxter very much, but I am quite unable to bear company to the Colonel. For the love of God, appear again in your own colours, or—go to the devil, for I am weary of "Colonelling." Colonel me no colonels; but remember, although somehow or other I seem to have deeply offended you, that I *have* been very intimate, and niether can nor will go back to such sickening games as this of chronic colonelship.

I write in the forms of jest, but, believe me, quite in earnest, *quant au fond.*

It is to meet Mrs. McKenzie,[4] Auchenbeglish, my mother asks you. Mrs. M. has testified a desire to meet you, strange as it may seem. Therefore, come without fear.

> Yours,
> ROBERT LOUIS STEVENSON

MS, Yale.

> Albemarle Club, 25 Albemarle Street W.
> [London, 1876]

My dear Charles,

Herewith sheets of the prints ($£1500$'s worth) stolen from Colvin on Saturday morning. C. is answerable for value. Will you

3. Monogram.
4. Not identified.

kindly hand one in at Hill's and other print gents, as we fear the thieves may try Edinr. Full details when I arrive. The Police are humbug.

Yours ever,
ROBERT LOUIS STEVENSON

*MS untraced. Printed, with facsim-
ile, in Clement Shorter, Letters to
Charles Baxter by Robert Louis
Stevenson, London, 1914?.*

[Fontainebleau? early July 1877]

My dear Chawles,

I shall make my arrangements. The convoy shall be followed; and sincerely, it will give me a very hearty pleasure to be chief mourner.[5] I do not know whether I am quite following out your jest in a jesting spirit, or with a modicum of whimper. But the fact is that I have felt a great pleasure in your request; and damn it all, I am not eloquent. I'll hold the bottles. And I wish you a rare good time, and plenty of children. If you have as good a time in the future as you had in the past, you will do well. For making all allowance for little rubs and hitches, the past looks very delightful to me: the past when you were not going to be married, and I was not trying to write a novel; the past when you went through to B[ridge] of Allan to contemplate Mrs. Chawles in the house of God, and I went home trembling every day lest Heaven should open and the thunderbolt of parental anger light upon my head; the past where we have been drunk and sober, and sat outside of grocers' shops on fine dark nights, and wrangled in the Speculative, and heard mysterious whistling in Waterloo Place, and met missionaries from Aberdeen; generally, the past. But the future is a fine thing also, in its way; and what's more, it's all we have to come and go upon. So, let us strike up the Wedding March, and bedeck ourselves with the loose and graceful folds of the frockcoat, and crown ourselves with Sunday hats as with laurel, and go, leaping, and singing, and praising God, and under the influence of champagne and all the finer feelings of humanity, towards that sacred edifice, or secular

5. CB was married on 24 July to Grace Roberta Louisa Stewart.

drawing room, from whence you, issuing forth, shall startle mankind with the first splendours of the wedded Chawles. Proudest moment of my life, C.B.

Ever your old friend,
LOUIS STEVENSON

Commend me to the Object, as Lang [6] used to call his one.

I'll likely come home for it; awful expense, you'll say, but I really should like to do the part, for auld lang syne.

MS, Yale.

Savile Club, 15 Savile Row W.
[London, 23 December 1877] [7]

My dear Charles,

The Blow has fallen. I am swept from my native Heaths. Those who may once have shared with me the Innocent Levities of Youth will now be so very kind as to cash the enclosed and forward by return of post a ten-pound note in a registered letter addressed: R. Stevenson, 5 Rue Ravignan, Paris.[8] "R." only, mark you, Charles, for that's a piece of the business. I am dead beat. I could not sleep last night, and the degree to wh. my bones ache can be represented by no figure in my repertory. As to the rest of the coins, I shall write again.

Will you please manage this? If my indorsation is insufficient, please send the coins anyway.

Yours,
WILKINS MICAWBER
alias
ROBERT LOUIS STEVENSON

6. Andrew Lang (1844–1912), critic and minor poet. RLS's friendship with him had begun at Menton.

7. "On the 22nd Dec. Lou starts suddenly for London by night train much to our disappointment; he returns to Paris.—About this time Louis became rather impatient of the restraints of civilisation . . ." (*Diary*, p. 331).

8. The address of Mrs. Fanny Van de Grift Osbourne, estranged from her husband and studying art in Europe. RLS had met her first at an artists' colony at Grez, where she was known as "la belle Américaine."

MS, Yale.

[Paris, 29 December 1877]

My dear Baxter,

Thanks, it's received: £10 received from Messirs. Mitchel [9] and Baxter. God has come to the front and I'm all right. Public news: I am going to stay a day or two on the coast of France before returning to London, when my business will be ripe; I am overworked. Private news: ditto. Publish this abroad with sound of tetrumpet. As soon as I find my new address, I shall telegraph, and then please forward the rest of my coin thither at once. Say, in two letters: addressed Robert Louis this time.

Ever yours,
R. L. STEVENSON

MS, Yale.

[Paris? early 1878]

My dear Charles,

I am ashamed of my silence. But what the devil! we all know what a nasty thing letter-writing is. This may reach you while you are lying a bleeding corse under the southern palms, or you may be engaged in performing that feat at present. Well, God help us, such is life. My *Obus* is in an irritable condition, but has not yet exploded. The man with the linstock is expected in May; [10] it makes me sick to write it. But I'm quite insane; and when the mountain does not come to Mahomet, Mahomet will to the mountain. The Simp is also close hauled with all manner of troubles and trials; [1] love (the course of true) never did run smooth. The little bow-boy plays such almighty Hell in these nieghbourhoods, and everybody has been thumped under the left pap to such an egregious degree, that nothing, by your leave, will satisfy any of us but marriage. Dear

9. William Mitchell, CB's senior partner.

10. RLS had apparently been living with Fanny Osbourne—a potentially explosive situation; hence "obus," a bombshell. The "obusière" below is Fanny; the man with the linstock, presumably her husband, Samuel C. Osbourne.

1. Sir Walter Simpson had married, 13 January 1874, Anne Fitzgerald Mackay. This is the first of a series of obscure references to family disturbances caused by the marriage.

God, where are the old days—but where are the snows of yester year?

Give my love to your Americans and French; as also, to the Dey of Algiers; and tell the latter that my heart is in the Highlands where-ever I go. Also, my mother bids me bind my hair in the old manner, but I have promised to my *obusière* to wear it after a patent of hers. Also, whene'er I take my walks abroad, how many poor I see,[2] but I am reluctantly obliged to pass them by with averted countenance as I am engaged in economising for another and, I trust, speedy course of *obusery*.

You will observe that my once powerful genius is in a state of pitiable decline. It is true. *London* is rapidly hustling me into the abhorrèd tomb; I do write such damned rubbish in it,[3] that's a fac', and I hate doing it so inconceivably. I declare I would ten times rather break stones, or—or in short do anything that didn't involve an office. As for offices, the abhorrèd tomb aforesaid seems to me welcome in comparison. At least you have only to go *once* to that office. And then, you know, according to some writers of re-pute, its business exterior is no more than a trap for the Ingenuous Public; and after being past through a few benches and ledgers and Ghaelic clerks in the front appartment, you escape into a large back garden, covered with daisies and umbrageous trees, where there are swings and croquet sets for giddy youth, while austere age is supplied with rocking chairs, tobacco, summer beverages of an eminently intoxicating character, and the light and vicious litera-ture of France. Hence, Charles, we should never presume to pass a judgment on the arrangements of providence. His little games are so dark and wily that, for anything we know, they may be intended for the best; and the Mind that created Johnny Adam [4] and Eben Scott,[5] and placed them in the same town is surely far beyond the reach of our feeble comprehension.

I suppose you are going to turn upon me like a wild beast and say you wanted news. Well, it's a pity. All our news is so damned compromising that I prefer not writing it. And at any rate, I hate

2. Cf. Isaac Watts, "Praise for Mercies" (*Divine Songs for Children*).
3. "A Plea for Gas Lamps," 27 April; "Pan's Pipes," 4 May; "El Dorado," 11 May; "New Arabian Nights," 8 June–26 October; "Providence and the Guitar," 2–23 November. The magazine was now being edited by W. E. Henley.
4. See above, p. 38.
5. Not identified.

news. Love to the Dey. To Hell with the Pope. A man's a man for
a' that. And three merry men are we: I on the Land (that's to say
high and dry—no coin)—Thou on the Sand (Afric's golden sand,
down which the sunny fountains pour)—And Simp on the Gallows
Tree! (or at least he ought to be—so should you for that matter—
but you and I have chosen the better part, and each sits merrily on a
little *obus* of his own, awaiting the moment when—paff!—no more
obus and no more man of good fortunes!).

> Yours ever,
>
> Tommy make room for your uncle.

> R. L. Stevenson, *Duc et pair*

Tell me Shepherds have you seen my Flo-ora pass this way
Tol de rol de rol de rol de rol. Singing Rule Brittannia, Brittannia
rules the waves.

MS, Yale.

> Hotel Mirabeau, Paris [June 1878] [6]

My dear Charles,

You see you were right. I only write to ask a service. £100 quid
must be had. You choose any interest. But send me necessary papers
to sign at once to above address. God bless you. This is the last 20
days of my passion.[7] 'T will then be over for good. They are steep.

> Ever yours in the worst case, as his handwriting attesteth,
>
> Robert Louis Stevenson

MS, Yale.

> Hotel Mirabeau, Paris, 26 June 1878

My dear Charles,

I thank you a thousand times for your kind promptitude. Hell
is already beginning to decrease in temperature. It was none of my

6. ". . . on June 7th he leaves for Paris with Prof. Fleeming Jenkin who is to be a
juror at the International Exhibition and Louis is to be his secretary" (*Diary*, p. 332).
CB dated the letter 5 June.

7. Fanny Osbourne was preparing to return to California in August, after a stay
in London.

making this particular manifestation of the underworld, but I had to bear the scorching.

Two remarks first: 1°. I shall most likely require nearly the whole 400 [8] before I am done, and all this within a month. You shall judge for me what ought to be done. 2°. As to payment, I am and have been of more than your opinion, although I feared to speak of it. Proper charges shall be made out of the 400, which will leave a large débris. And if ever I get plugged up, wh. is not likely (see last *Academy*),[9] I shall come and spunge on you without a thought, if you should be able for the passive in that form of relation at the time.

Again: 1°. Can a man, a British subject of age, marry an American girl (of age, *if necessary*) [1] in Scotland? If so, with what delay and under what conditions? 2°. Would this be easier managed in England by special license?

These would be a good thing to have answered soon.

The Debenture tomorrow.

Ever yours,

R. L. S.

MS, Yale.

Paris [August 1878]

My dear Baxter,

Poste Restante, Montargis,[2] till further notice. Thanks for your letter. You must have Deb. by this time; if not, I still preserve receipt of registration. Have you seen my people of late? Tell me about them; also tell me how I should address you. God bless you. I feel pretty ill and pretty sad, as you can fancy.

Ever yours,

R. L. S.

8. This draft, with the later one for Katharine de Mattos (below, p. 59), accounts for 90% of the £1,000 advanced by Thomas Stevenson to RLS in 1875, when the latter was admitted to the Scottish bar.

9. In which *An Inland Voyage* was reviewed by P. G. Hamerton. "I wonder how many people there are in England who know that Robert Louis Stevenson is, in his own way (and he is wise enough to write simply in his own way), one of the most perfect writers living, one of the very few who may yet do something that will become classical?" (*Academy*, *13*, 1878, 547).

1. I.e. if it is necessary to mention her age.

2. He was preparing for his "travels with a donkey."

Had to work 9 hours yesterday, and am cocked hat in conse-
kwents.

MS, Yale.

[Le Puy, Haute-Loire, 28 August 1878] [2]

My dear Baxter,
This is the new address: Poste Restante, Le Puy, Haute-Loire.
If any other letter went to Montargis except the first, please tell me.
I am so ill and tired that I can scarce finish these words.

Yours,

R. L. S.

*MS, Princeton (Henry E. Gerstley Col-
lection).*

Chez Morel, au Monastier, Haute-Loire
[6 September 1878] [4]

My dear Charles,
I send a word to say that I have received yours, and that I am with
you in spirit. By this time you will know the best and worst, and it
seems impossible to say much, in case it should fall out of tune with
your circumstances when this arrives. I am not much given to the
praying, except in burlesque, but I do heartily supplicate God for
you and your wife and your child. May all go better with you, old
man, than it has gone with me. I find it damned hard work to keep
up a good countenance in this world now-a-days, harder than anyone knows, and I hope you may never have cause to feel one half
as sad as I feel. Good luck to you all, with all my heart.

ROBERT LOUIS STEVENSON

3. Postmark.
4. Postmark.

MS, *Princeton (Henry E. Gerstley Collection).*

Chez Morel, Monastier, Haute-Loire
[9 September 1878] [5]

My dear Charles,

How is your wife? And have you received no letter for me? One
was to have come to your care, and I think should be there now.

I am here alone in a hill village, with the ponts et chaussées person, a first commis de la régie, a receveur d'enregistrements, and a
percepteur d'impot. Gloomy rather, full of quarrels, bitter, voluble,
quarrelsome, cowardly; not a pleasant lot; but the engineer is very
decent.

I meant a letter and stick.

R. L. S.

MS, *Yale.*

Chez Morel, au Monastier, Haute-Loire
[11 September 1878] [6]

My dear Charles,

I shall never have a more permanent address than this, where I
have been a fortnight and shall stay another week or ten days. I
burn to hear from you. I am glad the trial is so early; supporting so
big a family, and all in different quarters, leads to expenses, I promise you.

I inclose two indorsed cheques and a signed receipt for Smith,
Elder and Co.,[7] 15 Waterloo Place (15),[8] London, which please forward when you have fingered the marrow and fatness in question.

Ever yours,
R. L. S.

5. Postmark (year illegible).
6. Postmark.
7. Publishers of the *Cornhill Magazine,* to which RLS had contributed several essays
this year, including "Aes Triplex."
8. Inserted because RLS thought the first "15" not legible.

MS, Yale.

[Monastier, 16 September 1878] [1]

Dear Charles,

I beg your pardon for the telegram. Five wise heads, including that of a judge, were of my way of thinking; but now the other is received. Thanks. I leave, I hope, on Saturday morning.

Yours ever,

R. L. S.

*MS untraced. Printed in Shorter, Let-
ters to Charles Baxter by Robert
Louis Stevenson.*

Chez Morel,[2] Le Monastier, Haute-Loire,
17 September 1878

My dear Charles,

I shall soon go off on a voyage, for which I think I shall buy a donkey, and out of which, if I do not make a book, may my right hand forget its cunning. I am busy all day long: writing, sketching, shooting with a revolver, dining with excisemen and ponts et chaussées people. For the first time for near a year I feel something like peace; it is like gold—yea, much fine ditto; it is like the dew of Hermon, or the pomade on Aaron's whiskers.[3]

In view of the journey I think forty quid would be a good thing; you might send it in a cheque on the Compagnie Générale at Le Puy. With that I shall not fear to go on my travels.

Ever yours,

ROBERT LOUIS STEVENSON

Do write a word some of these days, and let me hear the news.

1. Postmark. Note by CB: "Starting on travels with a donkey 1878."
2. Shorter: "Marcel."
3. Psalms 133.

MS, Yale. Letters, 1, *264.*

Morel's, God knows what date, *vide* postmark
[19 September 1878]

My dear Charles,

Yours (with inclosures) of the 16th to hand. All work done. I go to
Le Puy tomorrow to dispatch baggage, get cash, stand lunch to engineer who has been very jolly and useful to me; and hope by five
o'clock on Saturday morning to be driving Modestine towards the
Gévaudan. Modestine is my *anesse:* a darling; mouse colour; about
the size of a newfoundland dog (bigger, between you and me); the
colour of a mouse; costing 65 francs and a glass of brandy. Glad you
sent on all the coin; I never know when I may have to send off
coins to other gents, you know, and was half afraid I might come to
a stick in the mountains, donkey and all, which would have been
the devil.

Have finished *Arabian Nights* [4] and Edinburgh book,[5] and am
a free man. Next address: Poste Restante, Alais, Gard. Give my
servilities to the family. Health bad; spirits, I think, looking up.

Ever yours,

R. L. S.

MS, Yale.

Address me at Poste Restante, Lyon.
Date of this Oct. 5th [1878]
Alais, Gard. Business habits, if you please.

My dear Charles,

Le tour est fait. I received the 3 letters, for which I was glad and
heartbroken. I return the two cheques endorsed, and have directed
Seeley [6] to pay you my little bill on them (the Seeley's, I mean). I
had a pleasant journey and sold my ass for thirty francs at the end. I
hope you will hear details in a book before very long. But the
Lord knows what is in store for us. I have given up forecasting.

Ever yours, dear Charles,

R. L. S.

4. See above, p. 51 n. 3. The tales did not appear in book form until 1882.

5. *Picturesque Notes on Edinburgh,* published in December. It appeared serially in
the *Portfolio* from June to December.

6. Richmond Seeley, publisher of the *Portfolio* and *Picturesque Notes on Edinburgh.*

MS, Princeton (Henry E. Gerstley Collection).

[France, October? 1878]

Dear Baxter,

Cursèd luck; I thought you had had all the 50 from my father. Try and squeeze out another drop; sell the thing, or anything, and then pay yourself and send me anything.[7] If it's only 10/- it would be a desirable feature in the scene.

I am still in France, please. Please remember that.

More again.

Ever yours,

R. L. S.

MS, Yale. Note by Colvin: "These [this and the next two letters] relate to ultra-private matters concerning a cousin (Mrs. de Mattos) and her separation from her husband, and shd certainly be withheld or destroyed."

New address:[8] 4 Earl's Terrace,
Devonport Rd., Uxbridge Rd.W.
[London] 28 October 1878

My dear Charles,

What is to be done to make it clear to you? I don't know what is going to become of me, I don't know what I ought to do, and I have not a notion what I want to do.

One thing is certain: sell the Debenture and chuck the money into the bank on deposit. Bank rate should be good with all these smashes, and I hope to leave it there a long while. I have now got upwards of eighty pounds together by payment for work and one thing and another; so that's all plain for the present. What I require is to know I have money at hand, and the loss I suppose is not

7. At the top of the letter two very dim words are penciled in RLS's hand. They appear to be "Chez Henley" and probably mean that RLS wanted the money sent there against his return to London.

8. W. E. Henley's.

so great if I reflect how long I should probably have to pay the 7 per cent.

I am only in great suspense from almost the most threatening news possible, and I wish to be ready in an emergency. The Lewis's deny all knowledge of all the bad features of the case you know of; lay all blame on Gibson, Craig, Dalziel and B.[1] and say it was bad conduct. Nice fellows you lawyers. The visit of the clerk to K.d.M.[2] they say is a malicious invention; such a thing, they say, could never happen in business. Nice fellows again.

As I see this is confusing, I must tell you the news is purely American. America is a great country.

The birds referred to, in the Bart's epistle, were scattered, along with much else, by the action of Law. They were the apple of my eye, for a while, but now they are the apple of somebody else's. Well, sich is life.

Yours ever,
R. L. S.

Note business letter enclosed; it's [3] in it.

MS, Yale.

Savile Club, 15 Savile Row W.
[London, November 1878]

My dear Charles,

Recd 100 quid, for which God bless you. Enclosed Debenture endorsed as per invoice.

I have found out what was the matter with Katharine: it was her kid, about which honestly I had forgot. The kid, if you report favourably of our position, shall be forwarded afterwards.

I propose the husband to say: (1) That he had met Katharine in

1. Gibson-Craig, Dalziel, and Brodies, 5 Thistle St., Edinburgh. The Lewises are not identified.

2. Katharine de Mattos, Bob Stevenson's sister. Her family had opposed her marriage to W. Sydney de Mattos because he was reputed to be an atheist, but that may not have been why the marriage failed. After her separation she supported herself and her daughter by journalistic endeavor. Later she figures prominently in RLS's quarrel with Henley. It may be worth noting that this is the third occasion on which RLS's knight-errantry involved him with unhappily married women; the other two were Fanny Sitwell and Fanny Osbourne.

3. Presumably Simpson's letter; both are missing.

town and thought her looking ill and packed her to the country.
(2) After a few days, that he believed she couldn't stand this excitement and had packed her abroad. Then, as it seems to me, he could
send the child after, and, sticking to the same story, refuse her
address.

This system I shall develope to the husband tonight; should you
not think it good or safe, or should your studies convince you we
are dealing with a more ticklish state of affairs, please advise him
to that effect. W. Sydney de Mattos, 17 St. Leonard's Terrace,
Chelsea. I doubt if I shall finally slip my cables before Wednesday.

Yours ever,

R. L. S.

MS, Yale.

Private

Savile Club, 15 Savile Row W.

[London] Friday [29] November 1878

My dear Charles,

You did perfectly right to send the money. Indeed, under the
circumstances, I do not see that you could have done anything else;
and I thank you for having done so. I had already sent money to
France, but in the matter of money, the more the merrier.

For my own part, I am more or less displeased. If people, out of a
singularly futile delicacy, delay writing for money till they are
cleaned out, and if I, through no possible fault of mine, do not
receive the letter for two days, I question the right of anyone to
telegraph in the terms communicated by you.[4] It may be thought
that I should spend my life waiting for letters in a given back
parlour, but this is a view of human liability to which I demur.
Nor do I demur any less distinctly to the view of politeness which
prompted the telegram in question. Our man makes about as much
as I do, has more to do with this complication, and has had no
heavier load upon his shoulders. If it would do anything else but

4. Telegram, dated 23 November 1878, from W. S. de Mattos, 10 Holden Terrace,
London, to Charles Baxter: "Lewis grossly careless Send ten pounds to Katharine
D M to poste restante Paris to avoid subpoena Will write you" (MS, Yale).

bring trouble on his wife, I should write myself and advertise him of my views. As it is, if you have a *natural* means of commenting on his conduct in a business way, I should not mind your hinting that his action was a little more than cool, and his language a thought less than—well, let us say—considerate.

At any rate, honour no more telegrams from him, or we shall be having one from Saxon, in the interests of his system.[5] On the other hand, should Katharine (separately) ask an advance, do not hesitate to honour it.

Please let me know if the money was sent to the man; for if so, I shall see myself that it gets to its proper destination.

I enclose a little cloud of checques: 3, 3, 3, and 15 quid: total £24.

How are you getting along? I am in the midst of much work and much idleness: in a mixed, amphibious walk of life. The great drammy of *Deacon Brodie, or the Two Lives* nears an end. Shall we find anyone to play it? Echo is fondly hoped to echo Irvine.[6] We are as modest as that.

But it's all in the hands of the Right Honourable Member for Heaven.

God speed the plough.

Look out for *The Pavillion on the Links* in London.[7] It is a tale, sir, which would harrow up etc.

I have been absolutely bust in health and spirits: a kind of dead body with a capacity for disintegrating emotion; but I am better a good deal. My cure began with winning a bottle of champagne from a Prof. of Physiology on a bet. I drank it, and began to revive.

Yours ever,

ROBERT LOUIS STEVENSON

Ought I to send a receipt for the £10? If so, send me one to sign.

5. Not identified.

6. The play, by RLS and Henley, was based on the life of William Brodie (hanged 1788), an Edinburgh cabinetmaker by day and burglar by night. Henry Irving refused it, but it was acted in 1883 and later in the United States by a touring company led by Henley's brother Edward.

7. Not published until September–October 1880, in the *Cornhill Magazine*.

MS, Yale.

Chambers, 11 So. Charlotte Street,
Edinburgh [after 21 December] 187[8] [8]

Dear Charles,

Dear camerado, I engage you with an engagement for Saturday.
If the weather favours, I may depart on the Sunday morning. Come
and dine with le Ferrier and me at 17 Her. Row on that day at your
own hour, with the boathouse key, and thence to Granton.[1]

You are now engaged with an engagement.

W. WHITMAN [2]

MS, Yale.

17 Heriot Row, Edinburgh [early 1879]

My dear Charles,

I hope you have got your books—I saw your letter to Henley, and
I confess a hit. I am not so young as once I was; there is a relish of
time in me: I find myself heavy and a little sad-hearted in comparison with the past, and above all, laughter, the old incontroll-
able, hyperbolical laughter that took you by the midriff and kept
you crowing until the tears came into your eyes, laughter is all
extinct. We laugh in echo now-a-days. But I don't think the play is
at an end, and

Though nothing can bring back the hour
Of splendour in the grass, of glory in the flower,[3]

I pretend to be a pretty sound and merry liver, after all. I like my
work as I never did before; I like my solitary walks in the country;
I like a good talk, a pipe of tobacco, a glass of liquor. O damn it,
no, the pipe is not yet smoked; and I purpose to be a better old man
than ever I was a young. Cheerily, old man, cheerily. A dull humour
is worse than most complaints. And as long as people have their

8. "*At last* on the 21st [of December] after being more than six months away
Louis came home" (*Diary*, p. 332).

1. On the Firth of Forth.

2. RLS's essay, "The Gospel according to Walt Whitman," had appeared in the
New Quarterly Magazine for October.

3. Wordsworth, "Ode: Intimations of Immortality from Recollections of Early
Childhood."

wits, and a good heart, and a good digestion, and a tolerably clean conscience, I am for sweeping all these maudlin, piping sentimentalities into the common sewer. We are a little too old for greensickness and Wertherism. If we haven't cleared our spirits of that unripe rubbish by this time, I wonder how we expect to die.

This has been lying a long while. I must send it off in proof I didn't quite forget you. I saw yours to the Baronick, and was surprised at one piece of intelligence therein contained. Mine are always married before I begin, which simplifies things. At least, there's always one fewer misfortune to apprehend. It's a poor consolation. Damn.

I hear you are going to return soon. The weather is not gay, rather the reverse in fact; I should half recommend you to delay yet a bit, but I suppose it's dull. I saw the Godkin [4] at his desk past six the other night, and blessed him unawares. The great waters rather went over Henley's head the other day,[5] but I cannot bring myself to relate how. You will hear from himself. He and I have a little surprise for you, which will probably embitter your return. I am damnably in love, a good deal in debt, and yours ever,

ROBERT LOUIS STEVENSON

MS, Yale.

Savile Club, 15 Savile Row W.
[London, May 1879] [6]

Dear Charles,

Please excuse long silence—though it's you that owes me a letter, and an apology too—and send off in the most compendious form—cheque I should think on a San. Fran. bank—£20 (twenty pounds) to Jacob Van de Grift,[7] Riverside, California.

Yours ever,

ROBERT LOUIS STEVENSON

4. Mitchell, CB's senior partner.

5. In a letter to RLS, undated but probably written about this time, Henley reports that his wife had suffered a stillbirth (MS, Yale).

6. "In the beginning of May he has a bad attack of neuralgia and leaves for London and Paris on the 9th" (*Diary*, p. 333).

7. Jacob Vandegrift, Fanny Osbourne's only brother, had recently gone to California for his health. The £20 may have been for him, or for Fanny.

MS, Yale.

Arts Club, Hanover Square W.

[London, 19 May 1879]

My dear Charles,

I explain nothing. Wild work, very wild, but it is a wild world. We [8] are now chez the Arts undergoing reparations. It is a wild world. My mind is affected.

Yours,

R. L. S. [1]

MS (telegram), Yale.

London, 9 June 1879

Address chez Leopold Cernay la Ville Seine et Oise and please tell Ferrier

MS, Yale.

Chez Léopold, Cernay-la-Ville,

Seine et Oise

[14 June 1879] [2]

My dear Charles,

I shall call at Printing House Square [3] on my way back about 1st July. I am much tempted to close with them; at least I'll talk it over.

I send you a sola bill of exchange, on the back of which my fervid pen has traced a little original literature; if it is not enough, send it back and I'll put on more. Pay yourself and clap rest into bank for me. Bless you.

R. L. S.

8. I.e. the Savile Club.
1. The remainder of the page has been torn off just below the signature.
2. Postmark.
3. Address of the London *Times,* where RLS apparently had some hope of employment (see next letter). But nothing came of it.

MS, Yale.

[France, 25 June 1879]

Address Savile Club. Am on way home. Shall see *Times* on the way. What to say know not. Puzzling for gent so vague as sincerely y. Shall probably be éconduit without trouble on my part. Leave the Show-the-door part of it to Able Bodied Editor. Shall serrer your mang avang peu. Love to all the world.

Je me suis foutu une dyspepsie. Ça embete, ce machin là.

R. L. S.

MS, Yale.

Savile Club, 15 Savile Row W.
[London, 4 August 1879]

Dear Charles,

All well. Please send my last batch of letters (should there be any) to Mr. Robert Stephenson, Passenger per *Devonia*,[4] c/o Henderson Brothers, 49 Union Street, Glasgow, where I shall be able to get them both on Wednesday and Thursday morning.

Yours with diarrhea,

R. L. S.

MS, Yale.

[Glasgow, 6 August 1879]

My dear Charles,

Here I am in the Glasgow, my traps aboard and the deep C, or natural B—,[5] in front of me. Colvin is to send you the books; two vols. are for Douglas and Foulis,[6] after which it is probable that the J.W.F. will come a-hawking. I have been ill, and took a blue pill. It's but little of my native land I'll carry off with me, it seems: some of the blue pill and my clothing I take it. I am in fair spirits, but a little off my nut and quite off my feed. I read Aimard's

4. Which was sailing for the United States on the 7th.
5. Apparently a musical joke.
6. Booksellers and publishers, 9 Castle St., Edinburgh.

novels [7] to teach me independance and philosophy and learn something of the ways of New York; so, you see, prudence rules. I write
this in a subterranean smoking room, with a bar maid not far off,
also writing. I don't like it. You will address me to Post Office,
N.Y., will you not, mon brave? and generally will not forget

Yours,

JOHNSON

Remember me in the kindest way to the Ferrier and to yourself,
old man. Je te serre la main. Portes toi bien.

MS, Yale. Furnas, p. 158 (extracts).

RLS TO W. E. HENLEY

[New York City, 17 August 1879]

Dear lad,

I have passed the salt sea with comparative impunity, having only
lost a stone and got the itch. I could not eat, and I could not sh—
hush!—the whole way; but I worked,[8] I worked, and am now des-
patching a story as long as my arm to the vile Paul,[9] all written in
a slantindicular cabin with the table playing bob-cherry with the
ink bottle. The voyage was otherwise great fun: passengers singing
and spewing lustily, and the stormy winds did blow.

My news is bad and I am wet to the skin. F. has inflammation of
the brain, and I am across the continent tonight.

Address under cover to Joseph D. Strong,[10] Monterey, Cal.

I am ever your sincere and wet and scented American, lodging
in a shilling Irish boarding house with a flee in my lug; and the
itch—or at least an unparallelled skin irritation [11]—sometimes
stings like a whiplash; and sleep is impossible to me. Last night I
did not close an eye, but sat on the floor in my trousers and
scratched myself from ten P.M. to seven, when I arose much the

7. Gustave Aimard (1818–83), French romancer who wrote numerous stories with
American settings.

8. Two or three words deleted.

9. *The Story of a Lie,* published in the October number of the *New Quarterly
Magazine,* edited by C. Kegan Paul, who also published RLS's *Inland Voyage* (1878)
and *Travels with a Donkey* (1879).

10. The young San Francisco artist who was soon to marry Fanny's daughter, Isobel.

11. "very similar to syphilys . . ." deleted.

better for the exercise. A little Irish girl just bursting into figure but dirty is now reading my book [1] aloud to her sister at my elbow; they chuckle, and I feel flattered.

Yours,
R. L. S.

P.S. Now they yawn, and I am indifferent: such a wisely conceived thing is vanity!

MS, Yale.

CB TO RLS

Edinburgh, 19 August 1879

My dear Louis,

Call for letters addressed Mr. Robert Stephenson. I hope to hear from you soon. I suppose you should have landed on Sunday or yday.

Ever yours,
C. BAXTER

MS, Yale.

Union Pacific Transfer, Council Bluffs, Iowa,[2]
U.S., Friday [22 August 1879]

Dear boy,

Have been on cars since Monday and have still a week before me. Tired, but not so much as one would have feared. Am now quite the accomplished emigrant. Still suffer greatly from my complaint, which it seems, so says an apothecary, doth from the liver rise. "The ills that from the liver rise, Do ask a drug divine," [3] and this the 'pothecary failed to supply. I make an oath six or seven times a day that I will scratch no more. If I could keep it, I should be an ancient hero. Man cannot work in the cars; I write, however, much poetry, very illegibly in a halfpenny note book. The muse is niether kind

1. *Travels with a Donkey.*
2. Where RLS changed to an immigrant train for the rest of the journey westward. See *The Amateur Emigrant.*
3. Cf. "Drink to Me Only with Thine Eyes."

nor copious. And my transcontinental poems will rather stop a gap in the present than go down singing to posterity. I keep in truly wonderful spirits, all things considered, and beyond a capsize in New York, have kept right side up and smiling all the time. When you write you must give me news of my parents. The enclosed please forward to my governor. Remember, Charles, you give my address to *no one,* not even the Queen; it is no part of my programme to bestrew America with my brains. On the same principle address to me *under cover* to Jos. Strong (Monterey, Monterey Co., Cal.) or again you will sell me up. Believe me

Ever your friend,

R. L. S.

MS, Yale.

[Monterey, California, 9 September 1879]

My dear Charles,

Address me c/o Jos. D. Strong, Monterey, Monterey Co., Cal. This is not a letter, for I am too perturbed. You may use my own name on the letter, and say where I am, giving my father 2 or 3 days to tell it the first. (I went over here for literary purposes in order to write up emigracy.) I am still thirty pound to the good. You had better send me fifty of that hundred in circular letters or something on San Francisco. My news is nil. I know nothing, I go out camping, that is all I know. Today I leave, and shall likely be three weeks in camp. I shall send you a letter from there with more guts than this, and now say good bye to you, having had the itch and a broken heart.

R. L. S.

MS, Yale.

c/o Jos. D. Strong, Monterey,
Monterey Co., Cal.
[24 September 1879]

My dear Charles,

I write you from an Angora goat ranche where I live with some frontiersmen, being fallen sick out camping. I am not yet recov-

9 Sep 79

My dear Charles

Address me c/o Jas. D. Strong.
Monterey, Monterey Co., Cal. This is not a
letter, for I am too perturbed. You may use
my own name on the letter and say where I
am & giving my father 2 or 3 days to tell it
the first (I went over here for literary
purposes in order to write-up emigracy) I am
still thirty pound to the good. You had better
send me fifty g[illegible]hundred in circular letters
on something on San Francisco. My news is
nil. I know nothing, I go out camping, that
is all I know; today I leave, and shall
likely be three weeks in camp; I shall send
you a letter from there with more guts than this
and am very good hype to you, having had the
itch and a broken heart.

R.L.S.

69

ered up to the point of being good for much; indeed I am pretty well dished in the meantime; but my fever has gone, and though I cannot yet walk about at all, I both eat and sleep, and if you come to that, work. Talking of that, for anything I understand of times and seasons, which are now quite beyond me, perhaps you will receive £50 to my account before you have to send me the 50 I asked in my last, which would save lifting the £100, and I believe I have told them to send it you. I am in no need, but helpless if anything happened; and that I must not remain. Whether anything will recur is another matter. Things are damned complicated, and I have had the art to complicate 'em more since my arrival. However I hope for the best.

Why don't I hear from you, split me? 'Tis too mean by God, when I give you my news so free. I am lying in an upper chamber nearly naked, with flies crawling all over me and a clinking of goat bells in my ears, which proves to me the goats are come home and it will soon be time to eat. The old bear hunter is doubtless now infusing tea, and Tom the Indian will come in with his gun in a few minutes. How's that for Beadle's American Library? [4] Yet all true. How about J.W.F.? and how for God's sake about my father? Tell me, please, Charles. Since I have gone away I have found out for the first time how much I love that man: he is dearer to me than all except F. How is your mother? and your wife?

Ever yours,

R. L. S.

MS, Yale.

CB TO RLS

Edinburgh, 30 September 1879

My dear Louis,

I was glad to get your letter of the 9th, as your long silence was becoming rather oppressive. I should be glad also to have another, a little more intelligible, as with the exception of the fact that you are alive I can't say that I have obtained *much* more information. But as you promise one with some more guts in it, I shall be patient and hope for the best.

4. A monthly series of novels, published by the English branch of Beadle and Co., which flourished during RLS's youth.

My wife is a good deal perturbed today as a second little B. is on its way and giving both her and itself a good deal of pain and worry. Let us wish them well through with it.

I send as requested £50 in circular notes, and in another envelope the circular which you should sign and keep constantly separate from the notes. The one can't be got without the other. Acknowledge receipt.

Ever yours,
C. BAXTER

MS, Yale.

Private and Confidential

R. L. Stevenson, Monterey,
Monterey Co., Cal.,
15 October [1879]

My dear Charles,

A thousand thanks for your letter, the third altogether I have received from Europe since I left. I have written to N.Y. about the remittance, but I fear it will come to nothing. I was deeply vexed to hear of your mother's death; if I were not under a cloud I should have liked to send a message to your father, but I believe I am better employed in trying to find messages to my own. Indeed I wish they would cheer up. In coming here I did the right thing; I have not only got Fanny patched up again in health, but the effect of my arrival has straightened out everything. As now arranged there is to be a private divorce in January, after the girls are married; [5] and yrs truly will himself be a married man as soon thereafter as the law and decency permit. The only question is whether I shall be alive for the ceremony. You know that all last year I was sorely worried. This journey, the dreadful anxiety I was in for a month after my arrival, and the continual necessity to work when I am scarce able for it, are all leaving their marks upon me. First, I ran for a fever; then I was supposed to have started a decline; now my face is elegantly covered with burning raw spots. I can just do some work and lie on a bed after it, and though I have some appetite, I cannot digest. Still, so far as it has gone, it has been

5. Nellie Vandegrift, Fanny's sister, married Adolfo Sanchez of Monterey; Isobel Osbourne, her daughter, married Joseph Strong.

an upward grade, and with care, I believe I shall pull through. I need not say, my dear Charles, that every word of this is for your private ear.

I asked you for £50 and you say no word of it; I suppose it must have been in another letter and that I may soon look for it. To tell the truth I was a good deal muddled in the early days of my stay.

You will see by enclosed cutting that I am not your only old friend in California.[6] I thought to send you a former notice, but it was unkind in spirit, and I did not like to send a sneer so far.

Ever yours,
ROBERT LOUIS STEVENSON

Do write to me, Charles.

MS, Yale.

[Monterey, 29 November 1879]

My dear Charles,

If no money has been sent by my people in answer to that telegram, please send me £50 as before. I am sick both at heart and in body today and you must excuse this note. I have done towers of work since I have been here, and am not afraid for the next twelve months at least. By the beginning of January, if my health holds out, I should have made about the worth of £300 since I started on this journey; it is true I shall have spent £140 or thereby (not so much), but then the journey is made.

Yours ever,
R. L. S.

MS, Yale.

608 Bush Street, San Francisco, Cal.
[9 January 1880]

My dear Baxter,

I received the state of account and the cheque, which I herewith return endorsed. You will oblige me by returning the amount less charges as soon as possible. I am let in for heavy expenses for per-

---

6. The actress Adeline Stanhope, mentioned below, p. 78.

haps another couple of months; it is very unpleasant, but once that is over, life will go cheaper. I have three people to support and perhaps four, instead of one or two.[7] I can only send you a note, for my last mail has taken away from me any desire for correspondence.[8] I did not like to write business to my father, but I wish my books sold.[9] My papers had better be put together, and perhaps someone can, and will, give them house room; if not, I shall be obliged if you will store them for me. I daresay they might just as well be burned, but one never knows. Among my books there is one, Aikman's *History of the Persecution* or *History of the Covenanters* [10] in the shelves immediately behind one as one sits at the business table, on which I think you will find my name written by my father; if this is so, please keep it; if not, and I am not asking too much, look out some other book that is, and keep that. I wish I could keep them all, but just now a pound or two is very near. O—and pray keep the *Procès de Jeanne d'Arc* in 5 vols., the *Reign of Charles VII* by Vallet de Viriville, the *Nouveaux Aperçus sur Jeanne d'Arc*,[11] and the *Monstrelet*, edition Panthéon Literaire.[12] When I can afford, I will have these sent to me.

I hate to ask you to do so much for me, my dear Baxter, but I shall try and not trouble you so much in future. I remain,

Very sincerely your friend,
ROBERT LOUIS STEVENSON

P.S. I regret that you should have communicated my news to my father and mother as it seemed to me more respectful they should hear from me direct, and I believe I marked the letter *private*. However, all that is of very small moment, and need not cost anyone two thoughts. What has to be, has to be; and whether in one way or another, is none the less painful.

R. L. S.

7. Sam Osbourne had lost his job, leaving Fanny, their young son Lloyd, and perhaps also their daughter Isobel and Nellie Vandegrift dependent upon RLS.

8. He was receiving uncomprehending and hortatory letters from his friends at home, particularly Colvin and Henley.

9. This sale of his library was not carried out, as his parents rallied to his support.

10. James Aikman, *Annals of the Persecution in Scotland from the Restoration to the Revolution* (1842); *A Historical Account of Covenanting in Scotland* . . . (1848).

11. Auguste Vallet de Viriville, *Procès de condamnation de Jeanne Darc* . . . (1867); *Histoire de Charles VII, Roi de France, et de son epoque* . . . (1862–65); *Nouvelles recherches sur la famille et sur le nom de Jeanne Darc* . . . (1854).

12. *Chroniques de Monstrelet* . . . (1861).

MS, Yale.

608 Bush Street, San Francisco
[20 January 1880]

My dear Charles,

I see I have been unjust to you. You must not blame. I have truly
been so damnably pulled about that it need not surprise you if I
have forgot the terms of my own letters, and I hope it need not irri-
tate you against me.

Thank you for drinking my health. It is better a great way,
though I still suffer a little, and have now a rheumatic stitch in the
muscle of my chest which incommodes me to write and is pretty
sharp.

I own I was surprised at the vivacity of my father's feelings, for
I went so completely out of my way, and his, to prepare him, that
I did not imagine he could be taken unawares.

Osbourne is behaving better and seems to be going to keep his
bargain after all. Whenever he shows symptoms of behaving well,
I relapse into my wonderment. His whole conduct is an undecipher-
able riddle. But I suppose the truth of it is that he changes his mind
and sometimes wants only money and sometimes both money and
respect. I hope he will cherish this last inclination steadily as it tells
upon my pocket when he varies, and indeed might plunge me under
water altogether. He has made several attempts to find out how
much I am worth, and for what reason I cannot fathom, keeps
himself informed of my address.

Mrs. Louis Stevenson is probably still far into the future; even
the divorce has not yet been told to her family from considerations,
the serious illness of a sister being the chief. It may be six months
before we can come to the scratch, and we shall be in no hurry, I
promise you. This is not the time for it.

I lead a pretty happy life, though you might not think it. I have
great fun trying to be economical, which I find as good a game of
play as any other. I have no want of occupation, and though I rarely
see anyone to speak to, have little time to weary. I keep thoughts at
a distance, except when I go out to walk, for then one can bear
disagreeable matters with less concern.

The unbound 3 vol. (not the bound 2 vol.) Molière might also
be kept back from sale, and de Musset's *Comédies,* and Hazlitt's
Table Talk and *Plain Dealer,* and my Boswel's *Johnson* in one vol.

I owe a guinea to William Mackintosh,[13] which I wish you would pay him.

Your afft friend,

ROBERT LOUIS STEVENSON

MS, Yale. Letters, 1, 320.

608 Bush Street, San Francisco, Cal.,

26 January [1880]

My dear Charles,

I am truly glad you paid back the £50. I was almost afraid it might have hurt their feelings, but in their letter to me, they seemed to think I had sent for my father to Paris [1] (I did not *send* for him, at all, to begin with) to get money out of him, and I do not desire such a supposition to go forward.

I am reminded of this by another telegram I found the other day lying waiting for me at the hotel. It was so kind, I did not know what to do, but answering their telegrams is steadily running away with coin. The Osbourne continues to promise money, but as none comes, I suppose it is a mere flourish, and in the meantime, we have to go on as best we can. I have to drop from a 50 cent to a 25 cent dinner; today begins my fall. That brings down my outlay in food and drink to 45 cents, or 1/10½ per day. How are the mighty fallen! Luckily, this is such a cheap place for food; I used to pay as much as that for my first breakfast in the Savile in the grand old palmy days of yore. I regret nothing and do not even dislike these straits, though the flesh will rebel on an occasion. It is today bitter cold, after weeks of lovely warm weather, and I am all in a chitter. I am about to issue [forth] for my little shilling and half-penny meal, taken in the middle of the day, the poor man's hour, and I shall eat and drink to your prosperity.

Ever yours,

R. L. S.

The large French atlas in my room belongs to Wheatley of Williams and Norgates; [2] return it to him with my best thanks, if not

13. RLS's numerous cousins included a family of Mackintoshes; this is probably one of them.

1. In February 1878.

2. Williams and Norgate, London publishers.

sold; if it is, it must be bought back *at any price* for him. Remember me to him most kindly; he is a nice fellow.

MS, Yale.

608 Bush St., S.F., Cal., 22 February [1880]

My dear Charles,

I have received yours of Jan. 29; also one containing a letter of credit; and a notice of a registered letter which I can't get till Monday, but which I presume is from you and contains the dibs. I take you, I think: a wife,[3] a sister-in-law,[4] five cats, two dogs, three horses (it's true we're trying to sell them) and occasional descents of a son-in-law [5] from a boarding school. And then, mind you, I have to support a two-and-three-penny bachelor [6] out of the house; 'tis him that I curse, for that is all thrown away; if I could live at home, it would cost no more in housekeeping.

I see how the mistake occurred, but you see I had been quite ready to believe the mistake was my own (as it was for producing ambiguous literature).

I am no longer a ⅔, but a two-dollar bachelor, having been sharply ill again, but now convalescent. I have just been waiting this money to go into the country with for my health. I had an acute pleurisy, upon the pain and misery of which I look back with some horror. I do not want a repetition. We were nearly married right away, in consequence, but my father's letter came in time.

I was a little morbid a month or two ago, being far from well, and in the receipt of a correspondence that would have taken the starch out of Mark Tapley. People rolled letters onto me like boulders, and then ran away and pelted me with notes like road metal. I feared to open an envelope: there was sure to be some damned torpedo or, at the least, some Waterloo Cracker that would singe my whiskers.

I inclose the London correspondents of my people here, Falkner, Bell and Co.; please in future just pay into them for me and

3. I.e. wife-to-be.
4. Nellie Vandegrift.
5. I.e. stepson: Lloyd Osbourne.
6. RLS was trying to live on sixty cents a day, with a twenty-five cent table d'hôte as his chief meal.

let us have no more letters and agonies. I have been telegraphed to and written to about some £100, which I now believe never to have existed out of Colvin's head, but I assure you, I went round from bank to bank here, and wrote and telegraphed and so on, till all California rang with it. I am now ashamed to be seen upon the streets. I am the man that lost a hundred pounds, and in that capacity, as I now believe, a lying swindler.

Ever yours,

R. L. S.

How are my people? and your father? and your wife? and—I've been afraid to ask, but I must get it over now—and Ferrier? [7]

MS, Yale.

[East Oakland, April–May 1880]

My dear Charles,

I am guilty indeed. But I have been engaged in preparing to go to another world so long that I have partly learned to neglect the affairs of this one. I have not yet found your receipt but I am going to have another look, which I hope may be more successful. I have been engaged in being sick-nursed and jockied, and I do think I am going to recover and be as well as ever, but I am still very weak and sensitive to the weather. It was a considerable shock to my pride to break down, but there—it's done, and cannot be helped. I have had a pretty rough time, and God bless my people for coming round when they did, or instead of being able to rest just now, I should have been trying to work and succeeding in—dying, I fancy.

Do you remember Corkleroy, Mr. Johnson? I beg your pardon, that's a kind of an anglified expression, sich as I abominate. But do ye mind of Corkleroy? [8] an' Bathgate? an' Miss Stewart? [1] an'

7. Ferrier's health was breaking.

8. Also spelled Cocklerye. A hill about two miles SSW of Linlithgow and not much farther from Bathgate. Cf. RLS's poem, "The Scotsman's Return from Abroad (In a Letter from Mr. Thomson to Mr. Johnstone)," which begins:

> In mony a foreign pairt I've been,
> An' mony an unco ferlie seen,
> Since, Mr. Johnstone, you and I
> Last walkit upon Cocklerye. (*Poems*, p. 167)

1. ". . . the scene, the Royal Hotel, Bathgate; I went there with a humorous friend

the Arthur? [2] Eh! man!!!!! These would have been my last adventures in patria mea—may be still, for all I know—but I believe I shall have another innings now. Corkleroy! I repeat it with my best accent, and the room smells of Ferintosh [3] and sporrans.

Do write and tell me your news. I am waiting till I get in my new teeth, the old ones having been gently removed with a pair of plyers; then I go to Sacramento to marry, and thence to Shasta county in the mountains to seek a place for my household gods. Address P.O. San Francisco, Cala. My father has promised me, of his own motion, 250 quid per annum. Fifty he has sent me, and if you would be so good as ask, perhaps he might take up your credit of a hundred; and so anything that may come from my work would remain in your hands clear—for a while. It will not be much—had my health held out another month, I should have made a year's income, but breaking down when I did, I am surrounded by unfinished works. They taunt me with my present uselessness, and do naught to feed my family and hapless babes; it is a good thing my father was on the spot, or, as I say, I should have had to work and die. I had a wierd letter from the Simp, which some day I shall answer. It was plainly begun when the writer was sober—unmistakeably finished when he was drunk. Eh losh! what ongoin's! The last time I was drunk was in the emigrant train with a Pennsylvania Dutchman, ex-naval apothecary and ex-farmer's boy. I shall never, I fear, be drunk again; I grow more respectable daily and am more than half ashamed of it. A. Stanhope [4] again in San Francisco, I see by the papers, playing hell with "her sympathetic voice."

Ever yours, my dear Charles,
THE GAY JAPANEE [5]

---

to lunch. The maid soon showed herself a lass of character. She was looking out of window. On being asked what she was after, 'I'm lookin' for my lad,' says she. 'Is that him?' 'Weel, I've been lookin' for him a' my life, and I've never seen him yet,' was the response. I wrote her some verses in the vernacular; she read them. 'They're no bad for a beginner,' said she. The landlord's daughter, Miss Stewart, was present in oil colour; so I wrote her a declaration in verse, and sent it by the handmaid. She (Miss S.) was present on the stair to witness our departure, in a warm, suffused condition" (RLS to Edmund Gosse, 29 July 1879; *Letters, 1,* 275).

2. Apparently an inn or pub.

3. Whisky. Cf. Burns' "Scotch Drink."

4. Adeline Stanhope, later Mrs. Nelson Wheatcroft (1853–1935). During April of this year she was playing the part of Lillian Vavasour in Tom Taylor's *New Men and Old Acres* at Baldwin's Theatre, San Francisco.

5. A low hostelry frequented by RLS and his companions in their youth.

> Alas how changed from then!
> No more he tastes the barley bree
> With Simpkins and the bold C.B.,
> All in the farmer's den.

MS, Yale.

Ben Wyvis Hotel, Strathpeffer
[August–September 1880] [6]

My dear Cherls,

Enclosed is a receipt with which I know not what to do—do you? I am well, but have a little overtired myself, which is disgusting. This is a beastlyish place, near delightful places, but inhabited alas! by a wholly bestial crowd. Fanny will write for an affidavy and, what will be better, a certificate of baptism (Christian). I now send you a copy of a poem.

On Some Ghastly Companions at a Spa

> That was an evil day when I
> To Strathpeffer drew anigh,
> For there I found no human soul,
> But Ogres occupied the whole.

> They had at first a human air
> In coats and flannel underwear.
> They rose and walked upon their feet,
> And filled their bellies full of meat.
> They wiped their lips when they had done—
> But they were ogres every one:

> Each issuing from his secret bower,
> I marked them in the morning hour.
> By limp and totter, list and droop,
> I singled each one from the group.

6. RLS and Fanny Osbourne were married on 19 May and, with Lloyd, came to Scotland for a visit with RLS's parents in August. Late in August or early in September they all went to Strathpeffer "that Louis might have more mountain air" (*Diary*, 334–5). Another letter to CB—in the form of the verses, "The Scotsman's Return from Abroad"—was written about this time (see *Diary*, p. 336; *Poems*, p. 490).

I knew them all as they went by—
I knew them by their blasted eye!

Detected ogres, from my sight
Depart to your congenial night.
From these fair vales, from this fair day,
· Fleet, spectres, on your downward way,
Like changing figures in a dream,
To Muttonhole or Pittenweem!
Or, as by harmony divine
The devils quartered in the swine,
If any baser place exist
In God's great registration list—
Some den with wallow and a trough—
Find it, ye ogres—and be off!

Yrs,
R. L. S.

*MS (telegram), Yale. Addressed: To
Charles Baxter, 3 West Bay, North
Berwick.*

17 Heriot Row, Edinburgh, 8 September [7] 1880

I am not allowed to come Can I not see you even for twenty minutes ere you go I write

MS, Yale.

Chambers, 11 So. Charlotte St., Edinburgh
[late September-early October?] 188[0?] [8]

Share Moshew,

Jay essayay de voo vwar, may ne puvee pa ploo longtong demurray eesee; ains, m'en vais. Peutetre, viendras tu me voir? J'aurais des choses à vous demander à propos de votre organisation, et, comme je suis fatigué au point de ne plus pouvoir rien faire, je ne pourrai

7. According to *Diary* (p. 336) the Stevensons did not return to Edinburgh until the middle of the month; yet the date on the telegram is reasonably clear.

8. The letter is written on the back of CB's official stationery.

promettre de revenier moi-même. Tachez donc de me faire visite et bientôt.

THAMSON

MS, Yale.

Troyes [28 October 1880]

Dear Charles,

Herewith a cheque and the old divorce. I have been pretty seedy and am just creeping towards Davos in the midst of wind, rain, coughing, and night sweats. This is a stuning place; it consists pretty considerably of churches, but not (strange to say for a French place) of soldiers. I eat main well; wherefore, I believe I shall continue to inhabit the spacious firmament yet a while. I have a picture for Simp's study, tell him, but it's astray just now, and he must wait. You had better add that it was made by me, or he may think I have bought him a *vioo maistre, ce qui n'est pas.* The dog [9] has bogged more upon this hostile soil, with a preference for hostile carpets, than could be believed of a creature so inconsiderable in propor-tions. The cat [1] bogged so free (not having a tail, niether, to conceal consequences) that she was left in England. I regret the dog was not left also, grudging so much manure to a foreign land. Yet we all adore that dog.

Yours ever,

R. L. S.

I told my people to repay you the £40; no word of Colvin.[2] Ad-dress Hotel Belvedere, Davos-am-Platz, Grisons, Switz.

MS, Yale.

[Davos Platz, Switzerland, November 1880]

My dear Baxter,

I have had the money paid and send herewith the receipt and extract of divorce, the latter to put in my little drawer in your place

9. Later known as Woggs, or Bogue; sketched in detail in "The Character of Dogs" (*Memories and Portraits*). He was given to RLS and Fanny by Simpson.

1. A manx cat, given by Simpson's sister Eva.

2. See next letter.

of business. I have been very miserable and pretty sick, but feel better now. The Grosvenor Hotel killed me. Also I had the dry rot, and did not know what to do, nor how to do it.

The money advanced is not truly from Colvin; my people are to pay it back; it is only supposed to have been advanced from Colvin to me in London.[3] As soon as I can write home properly, all —as the melodramas say—will be clear.

Yours ever,
R. L. S.

MS, Yale.

Hotel Belvedere, Davos Platz, Switzerland
[November 1880]

My dear Charles,

Herewith a cheque and F.'s certificate—what a piece of machinery! The South wind blows, which unfits me for anything but ill temper and a pain in the back of my neck. F. is not well either, and is on a diet of food; I on a diet as to tobacco [4]—blame' noosance. The snow will not fall, owing to my presence in my well known impersonation of the Prophet Jonah. More Rigs with the Keganic Paulus, who wants to buy my books up (both of them) [5] for £20 quid: kind, but not good enough.

Adoo,
R. L. S.

MS, Yale.

[Davos Platz, received 11 December 1880]

My dear Charles,

Of course I have something to ask; else I would not write: that is plain to the meanest capacity. However, to my news first. I found out on coming here that there was more the matter than I thought;

3. RLS had spent £46 during an extravagant week's stopover in London and was rescued by Colvin, who arranged through CB to have £40 awaiting RLS and Fanny in Paris. Colvin had regarded this sum as part payment of a debt he owed RLS, but the latter knew that Colvin could ill spare the sum and therefore asked his father to repay CB.

4. Under the care of Dr. Karl Ruedi, tuberculosis specialist.

5. I.e. the copyright of *An Inland Voyage* and *Travels with a Donkey*. See next letter.

the cold hearted leech [6] says I may be 2 years anyhow ere I recover, and indeed, after a full month's rest, I believe he may be right. I do not exactly pick up hand over hand. Paul is going to bring out a 3/6d edition of my 2 books, but I do not know how near he is going to cut me. I must give way of course, for the advertisement is very valuable; yet I hate to be shorn as he wishes to shear me: 2d a copy, and in the *I.V.* not till 500 are sold. His first proposal, which I loathingly repudiated, was to buy both outright for—£20. *Assez calme.*

How goes on the Bart's infatuation? Seems d——d odd, d——d odd; where'n hell's he going to bring up? An old roué. The more you study Charles the Second, the more you will find him to be precisely Simp. I suppose you must be Charles the 1st, or Charles the XIIth, at that rate; or rather Charles the Nonpareil—thank God!

How's the missis, and the paw-paw? An' eh! Johnson, here's a bit jobbie for ye, man. Do ye ken America? an' Indianny? an' Hendricks Co? an' a place there they ca' Clayton? God a'michty, they are unco steigh words for an honest Scotsman. Weel, there's a Mrs. Betty Patterson [7] dwalls there; an' ma mannie, if ye would be sae guid's send her twa pund sterlin', niether mair nor less, by a Post Offish order, I wad be real blyth an' tak' it real kind o' ye, an' maybe we micht arrange thon auld sair bit about the Session funds—*an' the Han' in the Plate,*[8] eh, Johnson? I'll no promise, but we'll see. £2, 0, 0 to Mrs. Betty Patterson, Clayton, Hendricks Co., Indiana, U.S.A. This is to defray expenses about that d——d certificate of birth.

Yours ever,

ROBERT LOUIS STEVENSON

MS, Yale.

[Davos Platz, February 1881]

My dear Charles,

First: business. (1) Enclosed cheque. (2) Herewith second note to Simp. (3) Send the bill to Saml. Osbourne, Nevada Block, Pine

6. Dr. Ruedi.

7. Elizabeth Vandegrift Patterson, the third of the five Vandegrift daughters, of whom Fanny was the eldest.

8. Cf. below, p. 85.

and Montgomery, San Francisco, Cala., U.S.A., filled up for 200 dollars; and to oblige a friend, in the note with it say that I have been ill (which is true), which explains the lateness of this arrival (which is false—it was *in curia*). Do nothing to make it obliged to be paid; say that your client merely wishes to hand it over to him till his convenience. I am determined I shall get no money, and can only get harm from hostility.

Second: shpart. The public of Edinburgh may be damned for me. They have behaved most beastly to the Simp, they and their lying forces.[9] I feel awfully hot against poor Eva.[1] Of course she did not and does not know, as I know, how he (the Simp) lay to for her sake, but it does seem a low and a rough return for even his ordinary and patent kindness.

It's a' true; it was me and the Perfesser.[2] We had a rummer thegither ae nicht, an' says I, "Man," I says, "ye ken verra weel," says I. "Nane better," says the Perfesser. "Sir," says I, "ye're in the verra bit—nane better." "Aye," says the Perfesser, steerin' at the toddy. "Aye," says he, "and what's mair, as a Christian man"—"The verra word," says I, "ye've said the verra word—A Christian man. O!" says I, cuistin' up my een, "it's a bony word,—think o' that, man," says I. "And," says I, "think o' the clavers."[3] "Ye micht be an elder," says the Perfesser. "Ye micht be a beylie," says I. "Dam'd," says he, "dam'd, but ye hae me there," he says, "I wouldnae gien a fahrt to be an elder," says he, "but, dam'd, man, I would like fine to be a beylie." An' that's the hale truth, as God sall answer to me in the great day o' jidgement. *Explicit fabula.*

My dear Charles, the changes were indeed kaleidescopic—in swiftness at least. Write me again soon like a good soul, as a flesh and blood C.B. and not as a mythical partner in a W-S-ery. I'm to stay another year here, but don't give me up. I shall return, shining as to my physiognomy. I'm still worth writing to. I believe, upon my soul, I am not bound for the grey ferry, and shall drink with C.B. before I haggle with Charon. When I do the last, I shall leave a word with him, and pay your *obolus,* if he looks honest; for I don't fancy, even in Shakespeare's bosom, I should quite outgrow an un-

9. MS, possibly "farces."
1. Cf. below, pp. 155, 299, 302.
2. Sidney Colvin, who was Slade Professor of Art at Cambridge.
3. Idle talk.

regenerate hankering after the Green Elephant. Odd now, that of
all these hostelries yours only should remain. The Twinkling Eye,
the Gay Japanee, alike with shutters closed; but as I pray God, to
reopen them again for some immortal years and hear, to a modified
degree, the chimes again at midnight. Midnight, I mean, in my
most rosy forecasts, shall not be greatly later than the wholesome,
almost chick-like, couching hour of 1 P.M.

I must catch this old post—honest and true, or would have writ
longer.

R. L. S.

MS (telegram), Yale.

Davos Platz, 27 February 1881

Stop bill Frisco by telegram Letter

MS, Yale.

[Davos Platz, received 4 March 1881]

My dear Charles,

This is only a line to say why I telegraphed to stop the bill. I must
have mis-expressed myself like ein beast of the field. I meant the bill
to be sent back to him [4] as a free gift, to do what he thought fit
with, and had written to tell him so. Now there is one thing I won't
do and that is to let myself be let into explanatory or apologetic
letters to that putrid wind-bag; hence my anxiety to stop your measures. His—the wind-bag's—last was to wish to send his daughter to
a whore's lying-in hospital,[5] where the women go by numbers, no
men are admitted, and kids are given for adoption. This he actually proposed to the girl's husband; which, from a man who makes,
I find, 2,400 a year, is steep.

Man, yon was awfu' aboot the plate. I aye tell't ye, ye werenae fit
to be an elder. I could see your elbow yeukin [6] ower a fat collection;
your moo wad be hingin' doon an' your e'e fair dazed. "Dod," says
I, "yon's no a man to be sae near the plate." But ye ken the auld

4. Sam Osbourne, Fanny's ex-husband.
5. For the birth (18 April 1881) of her son, Austin Strong, later famous as a
dramatist.
6. Twitching.

sayin', "the nearer the kirk." Ae thing onyway: I dinnae ken
muckle o' ony comi*tee*, and I ken naething o' yours by ordinar, but
my fegs, they arenae gentlemen. A gentleman, to my thinkin' o't,
's a guid, plain, straucht, fine, canty, honest body, aye ready for
a dram an' to be jōlly wi' a freen; but the Lard safe us frae your
Edinburry gentry wi' their gesterin ways an' markit sixpences. I've
kennt mony a leery [7]—aye and ne'er saw'm sober forbye—'at wad
hae scunnered [8] at the thocht. But man, Tamson, that's life. I'll
drink your bonny guid health, sir, an' wishin ye weel ower a' this
bit clavers—it'll shune blaw by: I've had the like mysel—I'll jist
awa to ma bed.

R. L. S.

MS, Yale.

[Davos Platz, *ca.* 2–3 March 1881]

My dear Charles,

It was I, as you now know, who telegraphed *in propria*. Many
thanks for the remittance. Receipt enclosed. I have no time to add
a word, however short.

Yours ever,
R. L. S.

MS, Yale.

[Davos Platz, 4 March 1881]

My dear Charles,

What a solemn thing is regret, what a consequential matter is
neglect. In your attractive letter I had passed over one detail; of
that I have been reminded and hasten to respond to the reminis-
cence. It is à propos of the p.o. order to my sister-in-law; this, LET
ME TELL YOU, SIR, SHOULD BE ADDRESSED AS FOLLOWS: the order
taken out as payable in Indianapolis, and forwarded to Mrs. Betty
Patterson, at Clayton, Hendricks Co., Ind. Do you twig, my lovely
friend? if not, you may retire up your own fundament as soon as
look at it.

Yrs ever,
R. L. S.

7. Rascal.
8. Sickened with disgust.

P.S. Twig. Take out game for Indianapolis and send it to other shop. Yours ever. P.S. This ink is too annoying: with good ink, I could write the Bible IN A SLEEVE LINK. In spite of this folly, please understand that there is sense in these Brief Lines: to take out the P.O.O. for Indianapolis, and *send* it to t'other shop, which is within reach.

MS, Yale.

[Davos Platz, 12 March 1881]

Dear Charles,

Enclosed two cheques. I fear I must ask you to send me four pounds of the total here; which, as I am going to spring a damned bookseller's bill on you, will vastly baffle me in my present object to get clear of debt in your direction. Still, as this makes not much under thirty quid I shall have sent you this while, I must have made a little progress. And there will be more to come. I must not be blamed if I do little work, nor even if I write few letters: I am really not the thing yet; mighty easy to get out of health, by no means easy to get in again. I heard from Barty t'other day, but have not yet got up the pluck to answer. Really feel very incapable, but this, as the resident nurse says, is the bad time of the year: 4 have dropped off of late in the two hotels in which I am intimate, and one if not 2 more daily looked to follow. A party with a wolverine on his back does well if he carries it through this pass. Afterwards, we mean, sir, to begin to convalesce in earnest.

Yours ever,
R. L. STEVENSON

MS, Yale.

[Davos Platz, received 28 March 1881]

Dear Charles,

Dam proud it's so little. Harriet[?] [9] and Lady propose to meet us: Italian Lakes. Not been well; then been better; then double summersault, landing twice on crown of head: speed calculated 45

9. MS obscure. It is tempting to read "Baronet."

miles an hour; consequent stiff neck and blasted depressing hem-
orage this morning. Otherwise cheery; wish I were a bird; seductive
Rutherford's; [10] 15 minutes talk, return, wish I were bird. Breath-
less style; unwillingness to write; wish were bird; sincerely yours,
R.L.S.

It had better be explained that I am niether drunk nor mad, but
only hideously lazy.

MS, Yale.

Hotel Saint Romain, 5 et 7 Rue Saint-Roch,
Paris [26 April 1881]

My dear Charles,
I have received the £10, for which I enclose the receipt. I was
rather down on my luck generally, not only in health but credit.
Last night, under a nightmare dread of a hoemorrhage—a night I
shall not forget in a hurry—I conceived a design which I have not
the slightest intention of carrying out, but it amuses my somewhat
perturbèd spirit; so if you come across old Robb,[11] please find out
how much it would take to print in the worse possible manner, "on
grey paper in blunt type," [12] 200, 300, or 400 verses; if it could be
done for next to nothing—well, anyway, it would amuse me to
know and I could live a while longer in my day dream. We all
know we can't get to Kingdom Come, but we all like to go through
the early stages. I half hope you may see me yet in Edinburgh.

Yours ever,

R. L. S.

Please pay my debt and offer my resignation to the Canoe Club.

R. L. S.

10. An Edinburgh pub, called "The Pump," which RLS frequented in his youth.
11. George Robb, printer, 3 Thistle St., Edinburgh. The verses to be printed were
the burlesque sonnet sequence, "Brashiana."
12. Browning, "Soliloquy of the Spanish Cloister."

MS, Yale.

Fisher's Hotel, Pitlochrie, Perthshire
[*ca.* 3–5 June 1881]

My dear Charles,

The will seems to me to be a sweet thing. Two remarks only occur to me: Sam's name is "Samuel Lloyd Osbourne"; Fanny was baptised Frances Matilda, but has always been called and signed herself "Fanny." So you can judge and tell us what to do. The will, returned herewith.

I suppose our address will be Post Office, Pitlochrie; we shall soon be in lodgings.

We shall not trouble about that clary wine this shoot. Nice up here, tho' somewhat chilly. I had quite a friendly letter from Simkin, and answered in part. I hope all is right on my side. But if they do come up to see us—the baith o' them [1]—I shall wish that veesit weel ower.

Yours ever,
R. L. S.

1. Simpson and his wife.

MS, Yale.

Mrs. Thomas Stevenson to CB

Kinnaird Cottage, Pitlochry, 8 June [1881]

My dear Mr. Baxter,

I began this note on Saturday but was so tired that I got no farther, and since then we have been busy house hunting and moving. Now I am glad to tell you that we are comfortably settled in a nice little Highland cottage with a pleasant talkative mother to cook for us and a cheery daughter to do the waiting. Not much of this last is possible as you will understand when I tell you that when we are seated at table it is impossible to get round it. Both Louis and I enjoy getting above the pomps and vanities for a little. We are two miles from Pitlochry—high above it. I was afraid it might be rather bleak for Louis, so we have just taken it by the week; but the air is delightful and we are all eating splendidly and sleeping like tops, so I hope it may do. We have a nice little spare room with a beautiful view of Ben-a-Vrackie, which is heartily at your service if you can run up for a day or two. But you must be content to live on milk, cream, eggs, butter, and meat, without either soup or fish.

I have never got to the brandy yet: it arrived in safety and was much approved of—very many thanks for it. I think Louis has stood the sudden change in the weather wonderfully well, which is a good account of him.

I hope you have good news of your wife. With kindest regards to her and you and the babies, I am ever,

Yours most truly,
M. I. Stevenson

MS, Yale.

Kinnaird Cottage, Pitlochry, Perthshire,
[8? July 1881]

My dear Charles,

I have been writing off my fingers about this chair of Mackay's,[2] or I would sooner have thanked you for your welcome tellygram.

2. RLS was trying to get the appointment to the professorship of history and constitutional law at Edinburgh University, which Aeneas James George Mackay (1839–1911) had just resigned. See *Letters*, 2, 37 ff.

Exit (then) that Monstrous Fraud, the R.—not the O.R.; [3] may shame lie light upon his putrid spirit, may he wallow in the underclothing of shopgirls and quench his thirst with the cooling whiskey straight, and after a few happy years rejoin his fond creator, naked and unashamed! I wish him no worse than to shake off this mortal coil before he can say Jack Robinson.

The good news had better, by word of mouth, be broken to my mother; we cannot write, as it would blow the gaff to dear papa, and be, even in retrospect, the death of him.

Droll about the chair, isn't it? They all say I'm too late, but it will do me good to go on: all means Mackintosh,[4] Crichton [5] and David Douglas [6] and Jenkin.[1]

Ever your friend,
R. L. S.

If you weren't such a humbug, you'd come and see me.

MS (telegram), Yale.

Pitlochry, 22 July 1881

Weather bad and I still have cold Better not come

MS, Yale.

[Kinnaird Cottage, Pitlochry, 29 July 1881]

My dear Charles,

I suppose you have heard that I have been ill: beastly out of sorts, and not even yet much to brag of. We go, if I am able, to

3. Possibly "old Robb" (see above, p. 88).

4. John Mackintosh (1833–1907), Scottish historian; author of *History of Civilization in Scotland* (1878–88).

5. David M. Lloyd of the National Library of Scotland writes: "There were two Crichtons (David and James Arthur) among the Curators of Patronage of the University, but RLS did not come up before them for election to the Chair." The Vice-Dean of the University was also named Crichton, but he was the nominator of the successful candidate, John Kirkpatrick.

6. David Lloyd: "I have not been able to trace him. It would appear that any support he gave RLS must have been unofficial, as there is no mention of it in the Faculty minutes. Could he have been the Edinburgh publisher who died 4 April 1916?"

1. Henry Charles Fleeming Jenkin (1833–85), engineer and electrician; professor of engineering at the University (see above, p. 52 n. 6); cf. RLS's *Memoir of Fleeming Jenkin* (1888).

Braemar on Monday. I wish to God I had not come to Edinburgh. I
have payed smartly for it. I send you herewith a cheque for £16, 16.
Soon, in a few days, I will send you another for £8, 8. And please at
once send £20 to Falkner, Bell and Co., San Francisco for Joseph
Dwight Strong. I hate sending it cruelly, but needs must. This is an
admirable specimen of my correspondence: ask a service and hush
up. But truly I am not very fit just now.

How do you and the Bart get on? I was glad, for one reason, I
went to Edinburgh, as I found out one misconception in his mind.
Kind friends (let us never say who) had told him you showed your
letters with peals of laughter, and he concluded you were, from
first to last, enjoying yourself in that sub-impish fashion of which
we have known examples. This explains his explosions, and I was
glad to be able to assure him you were really and seriously moved.

Yours ever,

R. L. Stevenson

MS, Yale.

[Braemar, early August 1881]

My dear Charles,

Herewith a cheque which I have been trundling for days in my
pocket for lack of energy. What's new with ye? I am better, but of
course I have not yet got rid of the effects of my cold, nor shall for
a while yet, I suppose. I had a real mean day following the one I
saw you, lying on a sofa and spitting blood like winking: a most
depressing employment. This is a fine place: H.B.M.[2] and several
other mountains in the vicinity; a Free church with a clock; an
R.C. ditto with a bell; an Established do. with nothing that I know
of; 2 large hotels, several Williams, a lawn tennis ground, many
well-dressed girls, rivers and geographical and -detical incidents
going to projuce a real effect of scenery seldom offered to the dis-
criminating public.

Here's to you—in fancy: no drink brandy, the liver slightly inactive, tongue clogged; but the human heart, sir, still in the right
place.

2. Queen Victoria's summer home was Balmoral Castle, near Braemar.

I have just looked at the cheque; what do they mean by not negociable: that I can't get the dibs, eh? Dam farceurs, va!

Ever yours,

R. L. S.

MS (telegram), Yale. Addressed: Chas. Baxter, 4 Rubislaw Terrace, Aberdeen.

Braemar, 8 September 1881

No telegram received Perceive with glee that you come tomorrow [3] Please wire by what train you leave Aberdeen Answer paid

MS, Yale.

[Davos Platz,[4] 19 October 1881]

Dear Charles,

Many thanks for your promptitude and kindness. I have not lost a moment in replying. Only arrived last night. Feel very well though tired. If the capitalist is still with you—meaning the nouveau riche, or Henley [5]—tell him he shall hear as swiftly as I can manage; tomorrow I will try to get something done.

I cannot say how much obliged I am to you for this kindness about K. d. M. A firm hand is needed to keep her to it, but I believe a good solicitor would do the trick. Shall write again. Enclose wierd shot at business letter.

Yrs ever,

R. L. S.

3. "Mr. Gosse, Mr. and Mrs. C. Baxter, Prof. Sidney Colvin, and Dr. and Mrs. Balfour all pay us pleasant visits" (*Diary*, p. 338).

4. "Dr. B[alfour] orders Louis away from Braemar. The cold has really been as great as winter. . . . Louis and Fanny return to Davos for the winter—this time they have a chalet to themselves which they greatly prefer to hotel life; it is in connection with the Hotel Buol" (*Diary*, pp. 338–9).

5. Henley had just been appointed editor of the *Magazine of Art*.

[Enclosure] [6]

Davos Platz, Wednesday, 19 October 1881

Charles Baxter, Esq., W.S.

My dear Sir,

Will you be so kind as to inspect on my behalf the Marriage Contract of Mr. and Mrs. Sydney de Mattos and the securities of the investments. Mr. Robertson, S.S.C.,[7] Queen Street, my co-trustee and the agent of the trust, will I am sure be delighted to afford you every facility; my continued absence and ill-health make it desirable, and I suppose this letter will be as I intend it to a sufficient authorization. Believe me, my dear Sir,

Yours sincerely,

ROBERT LOUIS STEVENSON

MS, Yale.

[Davos Platz, 14 November 1881]

My dear Charles,

I have long been meditating a letter to you, when here came this abominable business one.

I am disgusted my balance should be so far to leeward, but I must just ask you to let it go farther and dub up the 99 dollars, for this accursed house must be kept up. Pray lose no time in letting Young [8] know. My object in having him is just that we may not have to pay delinquent fines every blessed shot.

I must have some money soon; indeed I have written to demand some already—I don't know how much it will be—from that classical periodical *Young Folks.*[9] I hope you observed that the readers thereof spew me, as an author, out of their mouth. That is surely the nadir of reputation.

I suppose you know I have been ill—we have been ill: Fanny and I both in bed together, with a hired sick nurse; Wogg wailing with an abscess in his ear; and Sam [1] with his right hand in a splint. We are all better, but none to boast of. I only sleep with a pretty

6. Copy by CB.
7. Solicitor Supreme Court.
8. E. B. Young, the agent in charge of Fanny's property in Oakland.
9. In which *Treasure Island* was being serialized.
1. I.e. Lloyd Osbourne.

little flask of chloral and haschisch at my side, my cough is so violent at night. Otherwise, I am swiftly picking up, and today feel really well. Weather lovely.

I enclose a cheque to cash: it is for Sam, but I'll pay him. Meanwhile let it vanish into my deficit. It will always reduce it that much. I am about spun or I would write further. Indeed I'll try to give you a proper letter soon.

The blamed "abstract of the property," if I did not give it to you, is lost. Pray lose no time about this: these taxes do so mount.

We both beg you to hold us in esteem and to remember us with all good wishes to your wife. Indeed we have had a wretched time. I had a fine hoemorrhage the other day. I was pleased the chair was over; I could not have taken it, if I had got it. Gibson'll [2] be *graaaaaand*. We are a great nation.

Yours ever,
R. L. S.

I return Young's letter.

MS, Yale.

Hôtel and Pension Buol, Davos Platz
[November 1881]

My dear Charles,

This is intolerable, but we have been very unhappy—dog ill, wife ill, and the rest, and you must try to excuse me. Anyway, here is the receipt at last with best thanks. Fanny is, I think, going to be able to hold out here yet awhile, so the money was not as necessary as I feared it would be; but I'll keep it, for God knows it will be wanted ere we leave.

I am getting a steady, slow, sluggish stream of ink over paper, and shall do better this year than last.

Your remarks about your business forcibly recalled the early days of your connection, and the twopence that we once mustered between us in the ever radiant Lothian Road.

O sweet Lothian Road . . .
O dear Lothian Road . . .

Ever yours,
R. L. S.

2. Alexander Gibson was proposed for the professorship by the Lord Advocate, but the election actually went to John Kirkpatrick.

Ode by Ben Johnson, Edgar Allan Poe, and a bungler.

Long, long ago,
(It was in the Lothian Road)
I saw two fellows wander long ago.
So merrily they strode
So high their spirits glowed,
With twopence in their pockets long ago.

Brash,[3] Brash is dead
That immortal Brash is gone
And the crowds go streaming on,
They go streaming, streaming forward, seeking Brash!
But he
I can see
On the great Olympus dwells, dispensing trash,
Gin, gin he sells,
Then as now;
And with infuriate brow
Light-minded drinkers forth he drives, who bow
Not duly unto Brash.

Brash, Brash, Brash,
How musical they clash
Words of pleasant savour, words endeared of yore!
But Brash has gone before,
Godlike Brash is gone.
From earth's phantasmal shore
In a flash
Immortal Brash
Burst, like Elijah, upward and was gone!

Yet fear not we shall follow; for wherever
Great Brash his way made plain, the common herd
May follow that extraordinary turd
And that with no unusual endeavour:
Brash was not wise, nor amiable nor clever;
Brash was a beast as I have always heard;
Fate could not act more palpably absurd
Than the dead Brash from other fools to sever.

3. Thomas Brash, the ill-tempered publican of "Brashiana."

Let us be fools, my friend, let us be drunken,
    Let us be angry and extremely silly;
      Then though divines and commentators clash,
We, when once dead and dry, dusty and shrunken,
    Buried and bundled hence, shall, willy-nilly,
      Share the eternal destiny of Brash.

MS, Yale.

Davos Printing Office
Managed by Samuel Lloyd Osbourne and Co.,
The Chalet [November 1881]

My dear Charles,

I enclose a cheque for thirty pound and never was anybody gladder to do so; does that help up the balance much? I've lost your letter, and don't know. I only know that other 7 dollars ought to go to Young, the S.F. party, and that a cheque for £16, 0, 0, in favour of Dr. Carl Ruedi, Davos, sent in a cover to me, would be as good as a holiday. I have written something like 35,000 words since I have been here, which shows at least I have been industrious. My wife is still very seedy, has just been four days in bed, and is not now, I think, fit to be up. I am much better, though today I got a chill; but I believe I have stodged it—I don't want to boast—let us say I hope I have.

Weather lovely: absolumong. Only too hot; yet parties are skating—have been for a week.

Yours ever,
R. L. S.

MS, Yale. Letters, 2, 73 (misdated 5 December).

Davos, 15 December 1881

My dear Charles,

That cheque to Ruedi has been lost; for God's sake stop it and supply another. I lost it. I ought to have written about this before, but we have been in miserable case here: my wife worse and worse, and now sent away, with Sam for sick nurse, I not being allowed to go down.[4] I do not know what is to become of us, and you may imagine how rotten I have been feeling, and feel now, alone with my weasel-dog and my German maid, on the top of a hill here, heavy mist and thin snow all about me, and the devil to pay in general. I don't care so much for solitude as I used to: results, I suppose, of marriage.

Pray write to me something cheery. A little Edinburgh gossip, in heaven's name. Ah! what would I not give to steal this evening with you through the big, echoing college archway, and away south under the street lamps, and to dear Brash's, now defunct! But the old time is dead also, never, never to revive. It was a sad time too, but so gay and so hopeful, and we had such sport with all our low spirits and all our distresses, that it looks like a lamplit, vicious fairy land behind me. O for ten Edinburgh minutes, sixpence between us, and the ever glorious Lothian Road, or dear mysterious Lieth Walk! But here, a sheer hulk, lies poor Tom Bowling [5]—here in this strange place, whose very strangeness would have been heaven to him then—and aspires—yes, C.B., with tears —after the past.

See what comes of being left alone. Do you remember Brash? the L.J.R.? [6] the sheet of glass that we followed along George Street? Granton? the night at Barrymuirhead? the compass near the sign of the Twinkling Eye? the night I lay on the pavement in misery?

> I swear it by the eternal sky
> Johnson—nor Thomson—ne'er shall die!

Yet I fancy they are dead too; dead like Brash.

R. L. S.

MS, Yale.

[Davos Platz, January 1882]

Dear Charles,

No sooner yours came than down I sat and penned the enclosed.[7]

---

4. "Fanny gets ill and is ordered away to Berne—Louis has to go after her to take her home and on Christmas day they travelled seven hours in an open sleigh in the midst of fearful cold—and wonderful to relate they were none the worse" (*Diary*, p. 339).

5. Hero of a once-popular song by Charles Dibdin (1745–1814).

6. See above, p. 11.

7. Part of the Brashiana series of burlesque sonnets.

I could go on a while longer, but these shall go. I think number 4 very fine; I dote on the last line of No. 2; I like the simile at the beginning of No. 1; and the sestett of No. 3 is just. If you like 'em, I'll do more.

I have gone mad wood-engraving; we have published a volume,[8] of which I inclose an advertisement. I cannot afford to buy any more, and I send a specimen of my last—no bad, eh? Man, I'm grand of it.

I don't actually remember if T.B.'s counter was zinc; I now believe it was wood, but the license, at least, is fair.

I wish you God-speed through your troubles, old man; I can, at this distance, do no more than send you Brasheana; and yet no— I'll go another ninepence—here's a copy of *Moral Emblems* inclosed. If these combined do not cheer you, the devil's in it. I wish I were in Edinburgh, to give you a philip.

Ever yours,
R. L. S.

MS, Yale.

Private and Confidential

Hôtel and Pension Buol, Davos Platz,
2 February 1882

My dear Charles,

I had written a letter to you some time back, but it was, by opinion of counsel, put in the fire. It bore on a subject which is going to trouble both you and me, and far worse I fear, a dear friend of ours. Look out for squalls: there will be quarrels flying, if you don't take care.[9]

I now enclose Robertson's account,[10] and a correspondence I have been having with him which has put me in a state of blue suspicion, probably unworthy. In my answer to the first letter, I put both questions on the same basis, asking more light on both, and meantime withholding my consent to both. Behold his eager retort. My

8. One of the series of *Moral Emblems*—verses and woodcuts by RLS—printed by Lloyd Osbourne on his toy press. The whole series was published with an introduction by Osbourne, New York, 1921.

9. See below, pp. 100 f.

10. See above, p. 94.

answer I inclose in this. What means this haste? Possibly dead
stupidity, perhaps Robertsonism; but I don't like it. It has put the
hair up all along my back, and I won't consent till I choose, and I
don't feel much like choosing. Does it seem wise to you? We *can*
keep the policies up; then why not? It don't seem natural to me.
We, as trustees, have the children to look to, g-d d--n me. Tell us
how it strikes a stranger.

Yours ever affectionately,
R. L. S.

MS, Yale.

Hôtel and Pension Buol, Davos Platz
[6 February 1882]

My dear Charles,

Will you mind raising me what you can on that hundred quid
that I'm to get from Chatto,[1] and letting me have it by return if
possible. I have given up this place—I can stand it no longer; all
seems beginning over again—I mean my wife's illness, and I want
to get off, clean and clear, without getting more direct from my
people than I can help. I shall just *pine* for this. With that and what
I've sent for, we can escape I hope with flying colours. I am very
wretched as you may imagine.

Yours ever affectionately,
R. L. S.

MS, Yale.

Hôtel and Pension Buol, Davos Platz
[received 14 February 1882]

My dear Charles,

I told you I had written a more explicit letter; I will and I can
write no more. I am very sorry I did it, but I meant friendly, and I
thought it would so naturally join on to talks that we had held that
you would at once understand. Indeed it was a trouble to me, and I
even felt that a hint might seem disloyal; and then again I thought
that a word might prevent some chance *nothing* which, in an apparent state of tension, would set all afire. I hardly understand my-

1. Chatto and Windus were the publishers of *Familiar Studies of Men and Books*
(March) and *New Arabian Nights* (August).

self, for I was horrid pained by your letter. I had meant so creamy by everybody that I am knocked up to find I have made you miserable.

I now see that my ambiguity may have made a hell of an unpleasant effect, and to clear the field, I will, in absolute confidence, add a general reflection: A lady of title [2] will not rest (and at present she is not resting by any means) till she has cleared every manjack of her husband's friends out of the boutique.

But now, when all's over, was so much anger necessary? I meant well; I was an ass to write so; but it is not likely it would comfort me to know I had made you miserable.

I surely need not protest my sincere affection for you. I only meant to warn you to be circumspect just now. Put yourself in my shoes: nothing was written against you; if there had been, it would not have been fair to speak of it; yet I saw that somebody was blowing my correspondent that way, I remembered how we had both agreed that we would not be made to quarrel, I thought a word might put you on your guard, and with some misgivings, as you see by the destruction of my first letter, I sent that word. Too doubtfully as I now see. But indeed I had no thought but my affection for both concerned; and I hope you will forgive

Your sincere, obscure friend,

R. L. S.

All is well about the policies; again, it was only the man's singular idiocy that fills one continually with suspicions. He seems to have had no object, and the policies are to go on.

MS, Yale.

Hôtel and Pension Buol, Davos Platz

[14 February 1882]

My dear Charles,

For God's sake give me an answer in peace. I am quite sewn up; your letter haunts me o' nights. I will truckle or eat dust. Give me an answer in peace. What was well meant, however idiotic, scarce deserves this burthen. My conscience is quite overlain.

Yours,

PENITENT THIEF

2. Lady Simpson.

MS, Yale. Letters, 2, 77.

Hôtel and Pension Buol, Davos Platz
[22 February 1882]

My dear Charles,

Your most welcome letter has raised clouds of sulphur from my horizon. I was able to unbosom my agonies to my wife, and finally, which is much better, to dismiss them from my mind. I cannot tell you how uncomfortable I felt.

I see that we feel exactly the same about the S. connection: I echo your sentiments exactly, and I share your fears for the future of the one most interested. I could sometimes blame myself for the part I have played in that marriage, but I should not: that was the best thing to be done then; the error was made before. And yet will not S. have to pay dearly for his good act—for it was a good act? Perhaps, after all, not so dear as we fancy. She was his choice; God knows, he had time to judge. And God bless him anyhow.

I am glad you have gone back to your music. Life is a poor thing, I am more and more convinced, without an art. That always waits for us, and is always new. Art and marriage are two very good stand-bys.

In an article, which will appear sometime in the *Cornhill,* "Talk and Talkers," and where I have full-lengthed the conversation of Bob, Henley, Jenk, Simp, Symonds, Colvin, and Gosse, I have, at the end, one single word about yourself.[3] It may amuse you to see it.

We are coming to Scotland after all, so we shall meet, which pleases me, and I do believe I am strong enough to stand it this time. My knee is still quite lame.

My wife is better again; so if you have not yet raised the money, do not. I think we can stay on here after all a while longer. But we take it by turns: it is the dog that is ill now!

Ever yours,

R. L. S.

3. In that essay, which appeared in two parts (April and August), Bob Stevenson is Spring-Heel'd Jack, Henley is Burly, Fleeming Jenkin is Cockshot, Simpson is Athelred, John Addington Symonds is Opalstein, and Edmund Gosse is Purcel. Colvin does not appear in the published text. The characterization of CB is quoted in the Introduction to the present volume, p. ix.

MS, Yale.

Hôtel and Pension Buol, Davos Platz
[received 11 March 1882]

My dear Charles,

I meant a long while ago to write to you on two subjects: your wife and mine, and here comes a cheque, not uncomfortable either in itself, which puts me on the task.

First as to your wife. God bless her for teaching us that patience. We play it literally all DAY LONG—and niether of us can get beyond ten in counting: instead of eleven, twelve—we go knave, queen, and one. 'Tis a most fascinating folly.

Second as to mine, I think you ought to know that she is very grateful to you, and when I heard it I became equally grateful, for some kind words you said last year at Braemar the malarious. She was about beside herself, and your sympathy did her all the good in the world. I think it is pleasant to have your bread come to you thus, after many days, so I mention the fact.

Altogether the Baxter stocks are high.

Yours ever,
NINE POUNDS

Hello—after this was in the envelope, came the firm's, so now I sign myself

AHUNDREDANDNINEPOUNDS

I was told in your firm's letter to sign and return a receipt—for what I know not—why who shall say?—where was it? God knows. Business people are sometimes maculate themselves.

MS, Yale.

Stobo Manse [4] [near Peebles] 1 July 1882

Dear Baxter,

I inclose an account—no, it is needless. Please send £1, 17 from me to Donald Noble, Photographer, Oban. I can no more.

Yours ever,
R. L. STEVENSON

4. "On the 26th June we go to Stobo Manse which we have taken, without seeing it, for summer quarters" (*Diary*, p. 339).

MS, Yale.

Chambers, 11 So. Charlotte Street,
Edinburgh [July] 188[2]

Received Donald Noble's Voucher for payment of £1,17,3.[5]
Not known and not admitted.

R. L. STEVENSON

MS, Yale.

Hotel, Kingussie,[6] 28 July 1882

Dear Charles,
Please receive and act as a good father of a family (*tanquam bonus paterfamilias*) to the inclosed Commercial Instrument. I remain, Dear Charles,

Thine,

ROBERT LOUIS STEVENSON

Charles Baxter, Esq., W.S.

P.S. Pray pay the enclosed bill for me, and bless you.

MS, Yale.

Terminus Hotel, Marseilles,
Tuesday [10] October 1882 [7]

My dear C. B.,
I suppose you have heard that I have had a beas'ly time. It is so. I had a very dull, grimy time. After being used to marriage, it is damnable to be alone—and ill. I hope you will be spared the second; and I do sincerely pray God your child may soon be better; I was real vexed to hear of its illness, and of your wife's absence. Long absences are not good for husbands.

5. In CB's hand.
6. ". . . Louis gets ill and is ordered off. He goes to London and sees Dr. Clark who advises him to try Speyside. So he goes off to Kingussie to look for a house" (*Diary*, p. 339). Colvin notes that RLS spent three weeks with him at Kingussie (*Letters*, 2, 95, headnote).
7. In late August RLS left Kingussie and, accompanied by his cousin Bob (the ailing Fanny remaining behind), set out to explore the south of France for a suitable residence. At Montpellier he suffered a hemorrhage (*Diary*, pp. 339–340; Furnas, p. 209).

I am much better since I came to Marseilles; though today it blows a sirocco and I feel damp and nervous and remorseful, as people do under that infliction. I think the phrases are good: damp and nervous and remorseful.

Have you ever got back your "Brasheanna"? If you have and still incline to print them, I will cut an emblematic wood cut for the lot. Poetry and Painting at the Tomb of Brash, or something of that sort, with a romantic landscape behind.

Please send a cheque for £10 to Dr. Carl Ruedi, DavosPlatz, Grisons: I have announced it to him.

Yours afftly,
R. L. S.

MS, Yale.

Terminus Hotel, Marseille, 17 October 1882

Dear Charles,

As usual nae receipt, but I'll alloo 'at I hae gotten a cheque; I hope it'll be honoured. We have gotten a braw bit hoosie: [8] nine

8. ". . . Fanny joins him [at Marseilles], travelling alone from Edinburgh. We are anxious about her but 'through idiocy and being an American she made it out.' On the 16th October we hear that they have taken a house five miles from Marseilles called 'Campagne Defli' and they are both charmed with it" (*Diary*, p. 340).

rooms, twa dressin' rooms, and I dinnae ken hoo money presses. Forbye, we hae gotten a big hash o' a weedy [9] for a servant lass; she says she can cook grand. Ma wife (Mrs. Johnson) tells me to tell ye that it'll be a grand ploy for ye some o' thae days to get into the train and be huusled doon here to Marseilles and tak a bit keek at Campagne Defli, St. Marcel, Banlieue de Marseille. We'll likely gang in there on the Sunday, but I'll tell ye when ance we're fair settled.

THAMSON

Doubts of the Poet Thamson

Campagne De—fli:
  O me!
Campagne De—bug:
  There comes the tug!
Campagne De—mosquito:
  It's eneuch to gar me greet,[10] O!
Campagne De—louse:
  O God damn the house!

MS, Yale.

Campagne Defli, St. Marcel,
Banlieue de Marseille,
1 December 1882

Dear Charles,

This, which my wife had lost, comes to you late; pray attend to it. It will be covered by the cheque I sent your firm some time ago, and which has not yet been acknowledged.

Your Mr. Baxter has imitated your firmal reserve, and never written to, nor acknowledged the communications of,

A

POOR

INVALID

Je la trouve mauvaise. Write like a good lad, and give us news of your baby.

Yours ever,

R. L. S.

9. Lump of a widow.
10. Make me cry.

MS, Yale.

[Campagne Defli, St. Marcel, December 1882]

My dear Charlie,

I cannot say how much shocked we were to hear of your loss; there is nothing, in such cases, to be said but that the child has not lost, and is done with suffering and dying. God doeth all things well; it is somehow best the way it is—that I know, but it is not a thing to be proved. Had I died long ago when I was a child, I should have lost a great deal of pleasure I know, but how much misery would have been spared both to myself and those I love. And when you remember how a sick child suffers, it seems good that your daughter should have gone so quickly and be at rest.

Please remember me to Mrs. Baxter.

I write, as people always think they must, in the vein of consolation; but though I am no father, when I remember that it might have been Sam, I hold my peace.

Ever, my dear Charles, your affectionate friend,

ROBERT LOUIS STEVENSON

My dear Friends,

I have lost a child myself,[1] and I have no word of consolation to offer. I know too well that there is nothing to be said. I thought once that I could not lose my child and live: such sorrow seemed impossible to bear. But I had to bear it, and I lived. I think there is no time day or night when I am awake that the remembrance of it is not with me. I can only offer my sympathy to you in your bitter affliction. I know that is nothing: I feel the poorness of words as I write. It seems but a mockery to say anything.

Truly yours,

FANNY VdeG. STEVENSON

MS, Yale.

Campagne Defli, St. Marcel,
Banlieue de Marseille
[December 1882]

Dear Charles,

Herewith these—how shall I call them?—proofs de luxe.[2] I

1. Fanny's youngest child, Hervey Osbourne, had died in Paris in 1876.
2. Of "Brashiana." A set of proofs was pulled, but the work was not published.

should have sent them back smarter, but I have had another go of illness, and some beastly nuisances of business that I had not the strength to attend to. Le pauvre Thomson,[3] il a été bien bas, savez-vous; il ne valait pas un pétu, lui; coquin de dieu, ce qu'il a dé-gueulé de sang, ce qu'il a sué—pis qu'un fromage de Suisse, ce qu'il a pâti, nom de Dieu—mai, là, c'était assomant, je ne vous dis que ça. Avec ça, l'appoplexie; seulement ce n'était pas le vrai, vraie appoplexie—c'était de l'indigestion, quoi! Mais il se croyait foutû pour de vrai, tout d'même, allez. Mais c'est un gaillard, je n' vous dis qu' ça; il a mangé—ce qu'il a mangé, tout d'même!—et puis dormi—et pissé, par d'ssus l'marché—pour n' pas dire autre chose, rapport aux dames. Car on est chevalier francais ou on n' l'est pas, coquin de Dieu! Moi, je suis comme ça, gros comme le bras, sâle comme une peigne, bête comme le Bon Dieu, je n'vous dis qu'ça —mais galant, savez vous, galant à ne pas plus pouvoir lacher un pet que d'faire ça. Voile comme je suis, moi, et solide!

Farceur, va!

MS, Yale.

[Campagne Defli, St. Marcel, December 1882]

My dear Charles,

I send a damned dominie's [4] account. I know I have no money, but what then? The poor rogue must be imbursed, I fancy. It is more regular they should be paid; and as the friend of regularity and no enemy (as I misread thee) to a liberal and judicious education, I do now call upon thee, by all thou holdst most binding—let the man be paid.

3. The French of this letter is in imitation of the language of the Parisian man-in-the-street—salty, racy, with shrugs of resignation and the curled lip of scorn, but on a firm foundation of courage and a sense of proportion: "Poor Thomson, he was pretty low, y' know; he wasn't worth a straw, him; God, the way he threw up blood, the way he sweated—worse 'n a Swiss cheese the way he suffered, my God!—but then, it was crushing, I tell you. On top of that the apoplexy! only it wasn't the real one, real apoplexy, it was indigestion, that's all! But he thought he was really done for anyway. But he's a plucky one, I tell you; he ate, O how he ate, all the same!— and then slept—and pissed, into the bargain—not to mention something else, having to do with the ladies. For either you're a French gallant or you're not, by God. Me, that's how I am, big around as your arm, filthy as a comb, foolish as the Lord, I tell you—but lusty, you know, so lusty as to be no more able to let a fart than to do *that*. That's how *I* am—tough.—Go on, you joker!"

4. The Rev. Henry John Storrs, vicar of Eastham, Bournemouth, 1871–80, "a tutor

In order to somewhat soften the blow, I have sent off some MS to Longman, and unless some strange revolution should intervene, I should be able to send you the money inside ten days. Of course, strictly speaking, I *could* send it you now, but it would be beastly inconvenient, and if your firm will advance the amount for the time mentioned, I shall be obliged. (Je tire la langue.) If your firm won't, I shall have to gently but firmly change my legal advisers: which I believe involves your fall. Seriously, if you won't advance it, telegraph, as I don't want Storrs to wait longer than can be helped.

I am in pretty poor health, yet better and better pleased with myself. I long for more proofs. I hope you are going in for a great preface. "Make it a great book, Sir. Make it a folio," as the great Johnson said.[5] How many copies are you going to print? I declare I would get a person to do a picture of Brash's shop for a frontispiece. Copies can be sold ultimately to members of the aristocracy and book collectors for prices variing from £10 up to £45. Pray let me hear you have *sat down* to your preface. It should contain a life of Brash, which your knowledge and imagination admirably qualify you to supply: 1. His name. 2. His probable ancestry and birth. 3. Speculations concerning his education (if any). 4. Choice of a profession. 5. His homes and haunts. 6. Celebrity bursts upon our hero. 7. His mysterious death. 8. Funeral—the last coronach in Scotland. 9. Speculations as to his place of sepulture. 10. Critical view of his philosophy and ethos by a divine of the United Presbyterian Church. 11. A note on his sense of humour by John Wardrop Tawse.[6]

Yours ever,
ROBERT LOUIS STEVENSON

MS, Yale.

Grand Hôtel, Nice,[7] 7 January 1883

My dear Charles,

Enclosed is the cheque of which I spoke to you as in a parable in my last. The publisher was prompter to shell out than you to re-

---

who had half a dozen resident pupils," Lloyd Osbourne among them (Osbourne, *Moral Emblems*, New York, 1921, p. xvi).

5. Boswell's *Life of Johnson*, 19 October 1769.

6. John Wardrobe Tawse (1813–87), of Stobshiel, W.S.

7. "We always feared that there must be something wrong as it [Campagne Defli]

ässure my mind. I have been pretty dam bad, but took a cut along
here and have much bettered myself, though still lean and twittery.

A few days longer in St. Marcel

And I'd have had to pack my parcel.

St. M. does not work me off. Many good wishes from me and mine
to you and yours for this coming year. In the few hidebound
scratches I have had from you, you have never said how it was with
your son. Pray repair this, and believe me, Dear Charles,

Affectionately yours,

ROBERT LOUIS STEVENSON

MS, Yale.

[Gare de Nice, Alpes Maritimes,
12 January 1883] [8]

Dear Charles,

Thanks for your good letter. It is true, man, God's trüth, what ye
say about the body Stevison. The deil himsel, it's my belief, could
nae get the soul harled oot o' the creature's wame, or he had seen
the hinder end o' they proofs. Ye crack o' Maecenas; he's naebody
by you! He gied the lad Horace a rax forrit [9] by all accounts, but
damn! he never gied him proofs like you. Horace may hae been a
better hand at the clink than Stevison—mind, I'm no sayin' 't—but
onyway he was never sae weel prentit. Damned, but it's bony! Hoo
mony pages will there be, think ye? Stevison maun hae sent ye the
feck [10] o' twenty sangs—fifteen I'se warrant. Weel, that'll can make
thretty pages, gin ye were to prent on ae side only, whilk wad be
perhaps what a man o' your *great* idees would be ettlin' at, man
Johnson. Then there wad be the Pre-face, an' prose ye ken prents
oot langer than po'try at the hinder end, for ye hae to say things
in't. An' then there'll be a title page and a dedication and a index
wi' the first lines like, and the deil an' a'. Man, it'll be grand. Nae
copies to be given to the liberys!

---

was too cheap for a place that sounded so delightful. Sure enough Louis never was
well there and before Christmas a bad attack of fever broke out and Louis had to
take flight to Nice. The change at once did him good" (*Diary*, p. 340).

8. Postmark. Envelope marked "Private."

9. Helpful shove.

10. Bulk.

I am alane mysel, in Nice, they ca't, but damned, I think they micht as weel ca't Nesty. The Pile-on,[11] 's they ca't, 's aboot as big as the river Tay at Perth; and it's rainin' maist like Greenock. Dod, I've seen's had mair o' what they ca' the I-talian at Muttonhole. I-talian! I havenae seen the sun for eicht and forty hours. Thomson's better, I believe. But the body's fair attenyated. He's doon to seeven stane eleeven, an' he sooks awa at cod liver ile til it's a fair disgrace. Ye see he tak's it on a drap brandy, and it's my belief it's just an excuse for a dram. But the creature was aye drucken, that's weel ken't, an' sma' shame to'm. He an' Stevison gang aboot their lane, maistly; they're company to ither, like, an' whiles they'll speak o' Johnson. But *he's* far awa, losh me! Stevison's last book's [12] in a third edeetion, an' it's bein' translated (like the psalums o' David, nae less) into French; and a damned eediot they ca' Asher [1] —a kind of a rival of Tauchnitz [2]—is bringin' him oot in a paper book for the Frenchies an' the German folk in twa volumes. Sae he's in luck, ye see.

Yrs,
THOMSON

MS, Yale.

Marseilles [received 25 January 1883]

Dear Charles,

To explain my movements were impossible.[3] I have telegraphed hence tonight for twenty pounds. I shd have telegraphed for more but for the enclosed,[4] which pray attend to, and for God's sake believe this damned kick-ba' they ca' Thamson ever, dear Johnson, yours,

L.

11. The River Paillon.
12. *New Arabian Nights.*
1. Asher and Co., Berlin.
2. Christian Bernhard von Tauchnitz (1816–95), who had founded his famous publishing house in Leipzig in 1841. He specialized in reprinting English books for circulation on the Continent. See below, p. 149.
3. In a letter to John Addington Symonds (*Letters*, 2, 112) Fanny tells of an anxious week following RLS's departure for Nice, during which communications between them had broken down.
4. See next letter.

MS, Yale.

Hotel des Iles d'Or, Hyères, Var,
Sunday 11 [March 1883]

My dear Charles,

My people are away from home, and I have already written to them for money and fear it will come too late. Pray telegraph £20 to me. It won't be for long, for I have a book [5] being debated now between Henley and a brutal and licentious publisher. And this money should arrive, I reckon, if you telegraph it, on Wednesday; and on Thursday I shall be entering on possession of Chalet la Solitude, Hyères-les-Palmiers, Var, France, and in great need of money. Pray manage this: your own terms of course for interest; and as I say, it should not be for long. TELEGRAPH.

My health is much better, but my wife is no great shakes. It has been snowing, freezing, and blowing great guns for three mortal days. The cold is ultra-Swiss, ultra-Polar, in these pasteboard houses. You never answered my last (business) letter,[6] probably undated, inclosing one from Young of San Francisco. I pray God it came to hand.

Much hurried and chilled and savage,
R. L. S.

MS, Yale.

Chalet la Solitude, Hyères, Var, 21 April 1883

Dear Sir,

Your undated favour of the twenty-second caused me repeatedly to vomit. Nails are steady 1/5@ 6. O.P.[7]

Yours commercially,
MASON, DUDLEY, AND CUTLER

Dear Sir,

Enclosed please find a cheque for £45 and a note and bill from H. J. Storrs.[8] Putting this and that together, you will see what is to

5. *Treasure Island.* See below, p. 114.
6. The preceding.
7. Official Prices?
8. See above, p. 108 n. 4.

be done. The ballance, if balance it may be called—balllance me that—please retain in your commercial custody.

I am sir,

Yours with sublime precision,

R. L. S.

Dear Charles,

> How's that for clear and calculated?
> Can skill be overestimated?
> Or can the business virtues fail
> To keep a man in beef and ale?
> "It cannot"—with commercial pride,
> The actuarial umpire cried—
> "All who go in for dates and dockets
> Glory in well-filled guts and pockets;
> But they who do not date their letters
> Perish at last in straw and fetters!"

The Inspired Bard

Dear Sir,

In reply to your insulting and undated favour (postmark, Hanwell) [1] I have the pleasure to inform you that I despise your bestial rancour, and that your crude, unclean, and cruel imputations fall powerless from the shield of my commercial honour.

The kitchen maid, to whom you refer, was already in the family way when she entered the service of my family. The page was dismissed by myself and not, as you dare to insinuate, by an outraged spouse. I resigned from the Kirk Session because of the pressure of my commercial affairs, and although it may be true that I have, in earlier and more thoughtless years, been unjustly condemned for forgery, arson, stilicide, public butlery, and rape followed by murder on the person of twelve infant and flaxen-headed children of different sexes, I cannot see what connection the most infernal malignity can trace between these early errata and misfortunes, and my present honourable and, I may add, envied status.

I am, dear sir, with every sentiment of loathing and repudiation for your vomitable and degraded nature,

Respectfully yours,

WILLIAM FIGG

1. Famous lunatic asylum in West London.

MS, Yale.

[Hyères, received 23 April 1883]

My dear Charles,

I am not a man of business. There! Get back your twenty pounds for God's sake, and never mention them again. They are at Toulon [2] and I cannot get them any way, and have done without them. Colvin gave me his interest, which is thus discharged.

O those twenty pounds—Grrrr! I am,

Yours,

TWENTY POUNDS

Twenty Pounds

£20

How much will this fiasco have cost me? Well, let me not hear of it: when the bill comes, we shall pay. Hell! I am not a man of business.

Twenty Pounds

P.T.O.

[*overleaf*] Twenty Pounds

MS, Yale.

Chalet la Solitude, Hyères-les-Palmiers,
Var, France, 8 May 1883

My dear Charles,

Did you not receive a cheque for £6,15? If not, stop it at once through Cassell's, who drew it in my favour.

Also pray send me what money I have: I guess about £20? I hope so. I am very tired; I am working like a tiger: sometimes seven or eight *Cornhill* pp. a day, if you can imagine what that means. A novel is the rig: *Prince Otto.* I am to get £100 from Cassell's for *Treasure Island,* which puts me fairly on my feet, and if health only holds good, there I should remain. À-propos, Henley will probably ask you to communicate my bargain about *Treasure Island* with James Henderson,[3] as the Cassells must see it; this, then, pray do.

2. Where RLS stopped on his way to Nice.
3. Editor of *Young Folks,* in which *Treasure Island* had been serialized.

Who would have thought *T. Id.* would have so splendidly panned
out? Honour to Piracy, up with the flag!

Ever yours,

R. L. S.

My wife is not well. I have written to Henley a note to show to [4]
the Savile Committee.[5]

MS, Yale.

[Hyères, 20 May 1883]

—— Johnson Esq.

Dear Sir,

Enclossed please find a recipe for that twenty pound ye sent me.
I'll sune have a hunner o' my ain; it'll no last very long, but the
Lord'll can Provide.

> O dinnae mind the drams ye drink
> Nor whatten things betide.
> There's naething maitters noo or syne:
> The Lord'll can provide!
>
> Tho' weans, frae different mithers, thrang,
> O dinnae cease to ride!
> It's only haulf-a-croon a week:
> The Lord'll can provide!
>
> Tho' muckle-bellied creditars
> Spring gleg [6] on ilka side,
> O borrow, borrow, borrow the mair:
> The Lord'll can provide!
>
> Tho' jolterin hands the toddy spill
> An' Tremens claim his bride,
> O never ye fash,[7] for health or cash:
> The Lord'll can provide!

4. MS, "to at."
5. Henley was elected to the Savile Club this year; CB, in 1885.
6. Quickly.
7. Bother.

Of a' the wauf and shiftless lairds
  Frae Coppersmith to Clyde,
What maitters if the warst's yersell:
  The Lord'll can provide!

What though your wee bit shoppie's steeked? [8]
  An' what though alms' denied?
An elder still you'll hae your will:
  The Lord'll can provide.

THOMSON
Toddy Hill
by Sculduddery
Glen Tosh

MS, Yale.

The Solitude, Hi-ears the Pawm Trees, Var
[May–June 1883]

Dear Cherls,

Here's a bit checky, chuckie. It micht hae been mair; and it's His Mercy it's nae less. Hoots. Write to a buddy. Sair, sair hadden doon by the Bubblyjock,[1] and that's wark. I wark frae fower to five hours a day, clerk-clerkin' awa'. It's my idey that mebbe I'll can shupport mysel—that's if I've nae mair damd illnesses. But that's a' to be seen.

Ye'll hae to acknowledge my checky, do ye ken that?

Eh, man, ye're grand of it: there's naebody like you, by your way o't. Eh, Thomson.

When I was young and drouthy
  I kent a public hoose
Whaur a' was cosh an' couthy; [2]
  It's there that I was crouse! [3]
It's there that me an' Thamson
  In days I weep to mind,

8. Shut.
1. Held down by the turkey cock, i.e. by work.
2. Snug and comfortable.
3. Cheerful.

Drank wullywauchts [4] like Samson
    An' sang like Jenny Lind.
We cracked o' serious maitters,
    We quarrelt and we grat; [5]
Like kindly disputators
    Our whustles weel we wat.

A grieve frae by Langniddry,
    Wha drank hissel to death,
Was great upon sculdiddry
    And curious points o' faith.
The grieve was in the centre,
    Wi' Thamson close anigh,
An' Doctor Brown's [6] prezentor (pron: prezentor)
    Was often there forby.
Wi' mair I neednae mention
    Tho' a' were decent folk—
That public hoose convention
    Is now forever broke!

                    Air: Jerusalem the Golden.
For some are died an' buried
    An' dootless gane to grace;
And ither some are married,
    Or had to leave the place.
And some hae been convertit
    An' weirs the ribbon blue;
And few, as it's assertit,
    Are gude for muckle noo!

MS, Yale.

              La Solitude, Hyères-les-Palmiers, Var,
              21 June 1883

Dear Charles,

    I enclose two bargains, which I beg you to add to my archives in the halls of the Baxterium.

4. Hearty draughts.
5. Wept.
6. Dr. John Brown (1810–82), author of *Rab and His Friends,* to whom RLS addressed a set of Scots verses (*Poems,* p. 174).

I have no good news: Sam, Fanny, and the dog have all been ill, and my life is become so merely a question of aperients and from five to seven hours a day of clerking that I have nothing to relate. Hitherto, the ship swims. How long it may continue to *vogue*, I cannot fancy. Grim spirit of Finance, how you displume romance! O, lies there not some *anse* Along the shores of France Where breakers never prance And Sal and Tom and Nance May wanton in the dance And with enamoured glance Defying time and chance In that delightful stance Far from both kirk and manse Melt time into a trance! There sure should I enhance My meagre corpul*ance*. O, that would be my Fanc— Y for a Perman*ance*. Et settery.

Adoo.
R. L. S.

MS, Yale.

FANNY STEVENSON TO CB

La Solitude, Hyères-les-Palmiers, Var
[June 1883]

My dear Mr. Baxter,

Many thanks for settling the question of my identity so far as it can be settled. The new element of uncertainty concerning that dynamite explosion sometimes called Jaickson [7] was too much for my shattered frame. My frame is greatly shattered, but we all hope for repairs at Royat.[8] We start tomorrow. My mind is so dulled that the Tauchnitz affair [1] will not understand itself. The Bogue has the mange. He is very like Jaickson. He is so thoroughly convinced of his deserts and our affection that he bites and worries us just as he likes. We think of having them both vaccinated by Pasteur against the "rage." We tell Jaickson that we want him to come and write plays, but that is only a ruse to get him into the hands of the unscrupulous Frenchman. Louis seems to be daily gaining strength,

7. Henley. The effort to bring him into the Scots fellowship, as co-partner of "Thomson" and "Johnstone," seems not to have been very successful.

8. "His father was far from being well this summer and was recommended to take baths, so we arranged to go to Royat where Louis and Fanny could join us" (*Diary*, p. 341).

1. See below, p. 149.

but he needs the change, as do we all, extremely. The poor Coggie [2] is quite knocked up by the summer weather and complains of softening of the brain. It is odd how many people suffer from softening of the brain, and how few from softening of the heart. I don't mean Coggie: she has the best heart in the world. I tremble to think what we should have done without her. I never in my life met a creature of such crystalline honesty and frankness. There is Louis' bell—I suppose for me. Much love to you and yours, and believe me always,

Truly yours,
F. VDEG. STEVENSON

MS, Yale.

Clermont-Ferrand, Hotel de la poste.
Soon to go to Royat. [5 July 1883]

My dear Charles,

Henley says, and I obey, that I am to instruct you to request Paul to inform us what has become of *Trs with a Dy* and *An Id Vge;* and that I am at the same time to request you to inform him (Henley) what he (Paul) shall say to you (Baxter) about my (Stevenson's) works: with a ri dum, ro dum, Henley Paul and Me! The point is about the conflagration and the great exasperation of the authors' congregation with Pauline swindleation: [3] with a ri dum, ro dum, Henley Paul and Me!

Your letter came to hand. I count the *Deacon* [4] dead as mud. Managers, I suppose, are like publishers. But the truth is, the sanguine Henley, that dog-like optimist, hopes against despair. If it failed in Glesga, as I gather it did, it's a dead rat. Glad it produced as much as it did.

You will hear my address from my people. Sam is better; Fanny

2. Elizabeth Anne Ferrier; sister of James Walter Ferrier, who died in September of this year.

3. A fire in Kegan Paul's warehouse had destroyed some of the unsold copies of the books named. The publisher did not share the insurance money with the authors whose books were lost.

4. See above, p. 61.

ditto; George North [5] do. 'Tis plain, the latter is just killing *Young Folks.*

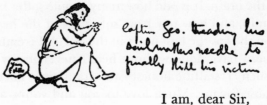

I am, dear Sir,
Yours ever,
GEORGE NORTH

MS, Yale.

Royat, 20 July 1883

Dear Charles,

Pray find inclosed cheque for £10, and bill to Arnaud et Pélissier, 38 Rue St. Férreol, Marseille, B[ouches] du Rhone, which pray pay. I can no more, being begrimed with ink and sweat, and the pale devotee of constipation.

Ever yours,
R. L. STEVENSON

MS, Yale.

[Royat, 7 August 1883] [6]

Dear C. Baxter,

Blame fool! don't reduce weight like that. Excessively dangerous. Monstrously dangerous. Quit it. Weight should be attacked most tenderly and gravely and gently.

Yours,
T. BRASH
Wine and Spirit Merchant,
Edinr, N.B.

5. *Treasure Island* was serialized under the pen-name of Captain George North.
6. Postmark.

MS, Yale.

[Hyères, September 1883] [1]

Dear Baxter,

Please give the bearer, one S. L. Osbourne, not (I believe) un-known to you, the magnificent sum of five pounds sterling (£5, o, o), for which I shall gladly regard myself as, dear Baxter,

Your indebted,
ROBERT LOUIS STEVENSON

Charles Baxter Esq.
 P.S. You shall hear soon.

MS, Yale. Envelope marked "Private."

3 Encl.[2]

Chambers,[2] La Solitude,
Hyères-les-Palmiers, Var,
3 October 1883

My dear Charlie-over-the-whisky-and-water,

Your despatch of the 1st duly to hand—Encl., ahem! Encl. We shall say nothing of any serious topic, for they are all the devil. Coggie is a capital person. I wish I could get among you all. Encl. Selah.

"Encl.," says he, "Selah," says she.
We're both as happy as happy can be.

I think I'll keep your cheque, though I do not immediately need it, being at length floated by the incompetent Cassells. Cassells in the air. That firm is doomed. To a man who is not a model of business habits, their neglect, delay, and abject and general con-fusion strikes amaze. Encl. I wrote and—Encl.—told them so.

I hesitate between viewing "Encl." as the equivalent of "ahem" or as a sort of drear solemnity like "Selah" in the psalmns. What is Encl? ANYWAY?

Did you hear of the *"Strages Bankerorum"*—when I smote a whole banking house hip and thigh—arranged their papers for

1. Lloyd went to Scotland in September 1883 for a stay with RLS's parents.
2. In imitation of CB's official stationery.

them—and was conducted to the streets by louting managers and sec.s? It took place at Clermont-Ferrand, and I had a medal struck —Encl.

> I am,
> Yours enclitically,
> R. L. S.

The B—k better; stocks rising; nails firm; alcohol plentiful; hardware tender.

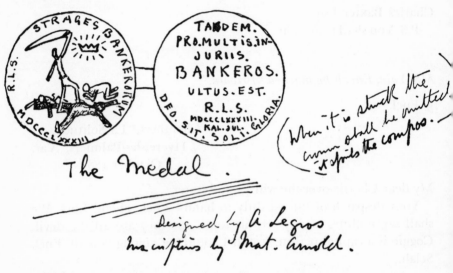

The Medal.

(When it is struck the crown shall be omitted. It spoils the compos.)

Designed by A. Legros
Inscriptions by Mat. Arnold.

[Alphonse Legros (1837–1911), painter and etcher, Slade Professor of Fine Art, University College, London, 1876–93.]

"Encl" breathed the rustic maid,
"Encl" the sighing shepherd said,
 Till all the meadows rang.
The birds among the thorn,
Through all the rosy morn,
Still nothing else but "Encle, encle" sang.
The sun that through the upper blue
His fainting, flaming furrow drew,
 In tune with others sang;
The forest and the field
Were with that music healed;
And from the rocks the holy accents rang.
O shepherd! and O! rustic maid,

What was the song, the song you played,
  And what the words you sang?
That mute, mysterious word
Shall still on earth be heard,
And mankind hearken to that music's clang.
For though Dodona's vocal oaks
Now nod before the woodman's strokes,
  And now precarious hang;
Still as they nod to fall,
They shall confirm you all,
And echo "Encle" in their dying bang!

MS, Yale.

> La Solitude, Hyères-les-Palmiers, Var
> Eicht October Auchty three

Dear Charlie-over-the-whiskey-and-water,

I enclose a chequie; it's aye drib-dribblin, like an auld man's water—fegs! or mines! [3]

I hear you're aiblins [4] for Highairs aboot the New Year.

MAN, COME!

The wife's greetin' fain to see the baith o' ye; and for mysell, I haenae been what ye would richtly ca' sober sin' the news cam' in.

EH, MAN, COME!

For society, there isnae sae muckle; but there's myself—the auld Jonstone, ye ken—he's the real Mackay,[5] whatever; and there's the wife, puir wean; an' there's Powel the druggist,[6] a fine canty body; and, man, there's a grog shop, whaur every afternoon twa auld men sit crackin, that taydious that the diel wad die o't, an' it's grand sport for ance in the week.

> Yours te-tŏtally,
> DRUCKEN AN'RA

Thomson Esq., Toddy Vale, Talisker, Glen-Tremens, Argyll.

3. My own.
4. Perhaps.
5. This occurrence of the allusion shows that all of the reference works are wrong about its origin, including the usually admirable Eric Partridge.
6. Lot 840 in the Spoor sale at the Parke-Bernet Galleries, New York City, 3–5 May 1939, was a copy of the trial-proof edition of *The Silverado Squatters*, inscribed by RLS to "Walter A. Powell the celebrated Scoto-Welshman of Hyères," with the date 17 October 1883.

MS, Yale.

Encl. a cheque.

La Solitude, Hyères-les-Palmiers, Var [19 October 1883]

Cherlie-over-the-whiskey-and-water,

> Here is a checkie, ye see;
> Please pit it doun to me;
> And I will be
> Yours as he oughter
> Robert Louee.[7]

That's Louis, in their French way: Louee, to rime wi' free. Eh me! do ye see? I've been spittin some mair blood, but I dinnae wish my faither tauld o't. I'm that üsed wi' it mysel that I dinnae mind it a damn. But I'm feared to annoy the auld man; he's no sae cheery onyway as I wad hae likit to see. Louee. Eh me! whuskey's better nor tea. That rhyme's ower muckle for me; I cannae resist it—he—he! Toots, gang to the D.

> Yours,
> LOOEE

Yon's a lie aboot the Bankeri; I mean a lee aboot the Bankeree; and there I'm again in the deep sea; nae help for me, but to rime till I dee.

> Looee
> peepee
> hee-hee

1. If your sister merried an' had a wean, what wad that wean ca' ye? Encl. Cherlie!

2. When ye dinnae ken a thing, whar do ye gang? To the Encl.-paedia.

3. What is the commonest plant in lawyers' chalmers? The Encl.osier.

> O!
> Down by the streams o' writin' ink
> The Encl.osier blows.
> Shakespeare (Wully)
> Awa, and tak a dram
> Scots champagny.

7. Robert Louis, a Frenchman, was Lloyd Osbourne's tutor at Hyères.

MS, Yale.

Encl. £5, 5

La Solitude, Hyères-les-Palmiers, Var
[October 1883]

Verily, verily, I say unto thee, it is not those that say unto me, Encl, Encl, but those who acknowledge cheques, who enter into the kingdom of the cygnet.

2. And the Scribe was sore abashed, for he was a damnable correspondent, and he had not acknowledged a draught of twenty five shekels of silver,

3. And he lifted up his voice and wept.

4. And behold it came to pass that the sound of his lamentations came to the ears of Johnson,

5. And Johnson lifted up his eyes and saw him afar off beside a public urinal.

6. And he hasted and went and came to him, even as a man running.

7. And when he was near at hand, the Scribe lifted up his voice, and put shit upon his hair, and refused to be comforted,

8. Continually crying, "I have sinned in thy sight, O Johnson, and am no more worthy to be called thy Thomson."

9. And the evening and the morning were the fourth day; but the morning and the evening were the fifth.

10. This is a hard saying and worthy of Bedlam.

Here endeth the Second Lesson.

But the third, I warrant, shall be somewhat sharper.

MS, Yale.

[Hyères, after 27 October 1883] [8]

Here, Thomson, is a checkie.
I am yours, Johnson.
Here, Johnstone, is a checkie.
I am yours, Thomson.

8. Written on the back of an advertisement bearing this date.

MS, Yale. Furnas, p. 497. Envelope
marked "Private."

Toddy Vale, by Kilrummer
[Hyères, 7 December 1883] [9]

Thomson,

It's done. I'm a dissenter. I kenned fine frae the beginning hoo it would a' end; I saw there was nae justice for auld Johnstone. The last I tauld ye, they had begun a clash aboot the drink. O sic a disgrace! when, if onything, I rayther drink less nor mair since yon damned scandal aboot the blue ribbon. I took the scunner as faur back as that, Thomson; and O man, I wuss that I had just left the estayblishment that very day! But no, I was aye loyal like them that went afore me.

Weel, the ither day, up comes yon red-heedit, pishion-faced creeter—him a minister! "Mr. Johnstone," says he, "I think it my duty to tell 'ee that there's a most unpleisand fama aboot you." "Sir," says I, "they take a pleesure to persecute me. What is't noo?"

What was't? Man, Thomson, I think shame to write it: *No Bony-Feed wi' the plate.* Is'n that peetiful? The auld, auld story! The same weary, auld, havering [10] claver 'at they tauld aboot Sandie Sporran—him that was subsekently hanged, ye'll mind. And wi' me —hoo improabable! But it a' comes o' that silly hash aboot my brither Sandy's trust: a thankless office, the trustees!

Whatever, I saw that I was by wi't. Says I, "I leave the Kirk." "Weel," says he, "I think youre parfitly richt" and a wheen mair maist unjudeecial and unjudeecious observations. Noo, I'm a Morisonian,[11] an I like it fine. We're a sma' body, but unco tosh.[12] The prezentar's auld, tae; an' if ye'll meet in wi' our opeenions— some o' them damned hetrodox by my way o't, but a body cannae have a'thing—I mak nae mainner o' doobt but what ye micht sucred him. I'm a great light in the body; much sympathy was felt for me generally among the mair leeberal o' a' persuasions: a man at my time o' life and kent sae lang!

Aw. Johnstone

9. Postmark.

10. Chattering.

11. Two James Morisons founded minority religious sects in Scotland. The first, of Perth (1762–1809), founded a new sect after seceding from the Glassites; the second (1816–93) founded the Evangelical Union in 1843.

12. Fancy.

P.S. I'll hae to pay for the wean. In a so-ca'd Christian country! Mercy me!

MS, Yale. Envelope marked "Private."

La Solitude, Hyères-les-Palmiers, Var
[14 December 1883] [13]

My dear Charles,

What is this I hear from Henley, that you are hesitating? [14] Here am I working double tides to have liesure and money for a holiday, and my wife and I proposing to go, all four of us, to Nice and Monte Carlo—if you don't come, I don't believe we can either of us forgive you. Don't dash away this cup after having offered it. It's not decent. I insist upon your coming. My wife insists upon it.

Thomson, if you stay at hame, damnd, I'll be done wi' ye. You a prezentar! Damd! A common, low wawf eediot.

Come.
Come. Come.
R. L. S.

MS, Yale.

FANNY STEVENSON TO CB

La Solitude, Hyères-les-Palmiers, Var
[15 December 1883] [15]

My dear Mr. Baxter,

I hope to receive by return mail the date of your departure from Edinburgh en route for Hyères. Strange reports of intended dishonourable conduct on your part have reached our unwilling ears, but the noble natures of your friend and your friend's wife refuse to entertain suspicions so derogatory to your character as a Christian gentleman. I hardly suppose you know that it was the expectation of your visit that made Louis decide finally to throw over the Island scheme,[1] which would have brought him in four hundred and

13. Postmark.
14. CB and Henley were planning to spend Christmas in Nice.
15. Postmark.

1. RLS had toyed with the idea of a trip to the Greek islands, to gather material for another book of travels.

fifty pounds, a book in the future, and given him a chance to see places that have been the dream of his life. And of course it is not possible that you could know that not so much as a shoestring has been bought for me this autumn and winter, because we have been saving our money to spend when you come. Your rooms, too, are engaged, but that is a small matter. Of course I know you are not so heartless as to offer the cup to the lips of a poor invalid like Louis, whose life is so dull (his only companions month in and month out a cross dog and an overbearing wife) only to dash it to the earth after he has refused everything else that could either cheer or inebriate. The thought is too inhuman. You see friends every day and do not realize what the disappointment would be to Louis. The truth is I cannot have Louis disappointed. You *must* come. You made the offer so long ago that we had time to throw over all our own plans and begin upon the new basis of your proposed visit. Ask Mrs. Baxter; I know she will send you at once, as I should send Louis to you were you the consumptive exile begging for a sight of your friends. Please let me know when you will start, and about when you will arrive. Give my love to Mrs. Baxter, pray, and tell her I should send other messages but that my mind is so engrossed in the matter in hand: my determination (*determination!*) that my dear Louis is not to be disappointed in what he so very much desires. According to your intentions, believe me to be more or less sincerely yours,

F. VdeG. STEVENSON

MS, Yale.

[Hyères, December? 1883]

Dear C. B.,

I inclose a further bulletin of the great crash of Johnstone.

Pray send me any money I may have. I have much need, but plenty coming in.

Also, that I may square my accounts, oblige me with a note of what the *Deacon* produced. I have made upwards of £350 this year; next I shall do better. If I could only live at a little less than £50,000 a year, I might yet do well.[2]

2. Not signed.

MS, Yale.

[Hyères, December 1883]

Dear Charles,

I inclose a receipt with thanks. Henley of that ilk bids me explain to you Cook's tickets, and how they allow you to travel in first class carriages at second class fare. But this they do not necessarily do. They only allow you to mount in first class *trains. Du reste,* consult *Cook*—he hath an office everywhere; consult him, fall on his buzzim.

R. L. S.

turn over

My dear Mr. Baxter,

A word. Leave your blue ribbon at home, and at whatever cost to health or morals, *drink no water* on the journey. A woman is just dead here from drinking water in Paris. No siphon—abjure the siphon, if that is the way to spell it. St. Galmier is the *only* safe beverage. Siphon is made possibly of poison water. We are in fluttering expectation of your visit.

My regards, please, to your wife, and this time

Most sincerely yours,

F. VdeG. STEVENSON

MS (postcard), Yale.

CB TO MRS. BAXTER

Hotel des Iles d'Or [Hyères] 8 January 1884

My dearest Gracie,

Louis has been most dangerously ill, but the bleeding has now stopped. He is not allowed to speak, but he is up and has been immensely cheered by our [3] arrival. Mrs. L. was at her wits' end all alone, and she too feels all right now that she has people to be with her. H. and I have just had lunch with them, and I have come back to the Hotel to write to you. The pen is horrible. Just fancy: it is as hot and bright as summer. Palm trees and olives and oranges all

3. CB and Henley.

about. The sky clear and the sea blue. Truly a wonderful difference.
I wish you were here with the children to enjoy it. It would be life
to Eddie.[4]

Ever with love yours,
C. B.

MS (postcard), Yale.

CB TO MRS. BAXTER

Monte Carlo, 13 January [1884]

My dearest Gracie,

We came on to Monaco last night, and as it is only ten minutes
walk from there, I came up here this morning. It is certainly a most
lovely place, a sort of heaven made by deils. They are all at it playing away for dear life, Sabbath the day notwithstanding. I think we
shall stay a day or two and then begin our road back. Henley has
business to do on Saturday in Paris, so I hope to be back on Monday
morning at the latest. I think I have sent you more missives than
you have sent me this time, but Henley even—the perfect—has
only written once to his wife. In this country there is absolutely
no accommodation for writing and the pens are like needles. It is
like a summer day. Just now, 1:30, I suppose you will be at the
Square.[5] Louis is improving daily.

Ever yr affte husband,
C. B.

MS, Yale.

RLS AND FANNY STEVENSON TO CB AND HENLEY

[Pension Rose, Nice, 20 January 1884]

Our dear Couple,

When, upon your departure, you left the pair of us bitterly snivel-
ling, a sight to the toothless waiter, the principal object of interest
in the garden house, little did we fancy that we could so soon be

4. Edmund, CB's son.
5. Probably Rutland Square, the address of CB's parents.

employed in the language of pleasantry in connexion with this bereavement. I, the dictator, felt that the world had come to an end, and I, the dictatee, came to dreadful grief, presenting all the appearance of the dreaded coppery oyster poison. I, the dictator, finding the toothless one looking at me with great curiosity, turned for comfort towards the dictatee, and found her on the brink of the friendly hysteric. I, the dictatee, am ordered to fill in with a sentence —"I'll do nae mair," says Johnson, "if you don't." I, the dictator,— the gross dictator—declare that Charles Baxter and William Ernest Henley have deserved nobly of their native land—that no array of terms can depict the debt of gratitude below which they have buried me. I, the dictatee, need no command from Mr. Thompson to subscribe to those true words. I, the dictator, being, by the rules of this game totally ignorant of what has just been interpolated by the enslaved and blighted dictatee, and being therefore in a false position and immediately threatened with the literary doom of repetition, do nevertheless openly, signed sealed and delivered, declare, publish, and decree that *this must be repeated.* I, the dictatee again, agree with Mr. Thompson, not that this nonsensical letter is to be repeated, but the visit. I, the dictator, am quite the pertater; she, the dictatee, is hardly a praty; I, the dictator, grow greater and greater, and siezing the pen conclude the letter by stating that I am still a pallid *prisonnier* in the Pension Rose, and that no array of terms can explain my feelings.

And I, now that I am able to break free from Louis' trammels of nonsense, will tell you that Louis is better in some ways, but naturally much weakened, having started night sweats. They began with Dr. West's [6] medicine, though I suppose they would have followed later on without it. We find the *pension* most delightful and the table very good; the only trouble is that it is so cheap that we feel like swindlers when we ask for anything. I have learned more of Dr. West since I came here, and I do not care to have anything more to do with him. I have been, ever since you left, crushed with fatigue. I fall asleep while I sit in my chair. I knew you would be anxiously looking for word from Louis, and though there is nothing new, I felt I must send a line, however dull. I do not hear from Sam, which troubles me, as the last letter said he was not well. If you know how he is, pray tell me. I send my love to you both, my

6. Dr. Charles West, Nice; M.D. Berlin, 1837.

dear kind true friends. There is also an inarticulate message from
Bogue. Please give our loves to your wives if they are with you, and
believe me,

Sincerely,
F. VDEG. STEVENSON

Money [7] come this morning (Monday). Self better, wife naturally
worse. We still shall stick a day or two at the Pension Rose.

MS, Yale.

FANNY STEVENSON TO CB

[Pension Rose, Nice, 22 January 1884]

Louis is much worse, the doctor says in great danger, almost no
hope. Congestion of the lungs and kidneys, consultation this afternoon. Sent for Sir Walter and after consultation suppose for the
family. The doctors fear the family, a moment's agitation could be
fatal, if there is absolutely no hope will send, somebody had better
say something to the mother. I know Louis better than doctors and
I do not give him up yet. At the Pension Rose.

F. VDEG.

MS (telegram), Yale. Addressed: To
Sir Walter Simpson, Randolph
Cliffe, Edinburgh.

FANNY STEVENSON TO SIR WALTER SIMPSON

Nice, 22 January 1884

Consultation more satisfactory Better [1]

MS (telegram), Yale.

FANNY STEVENSON TO CB

Nice, 23 January 1884

Wonderfully better

7. Postscript in RLS's hand.
1. MS, "Beater."

MS (telegram), Yale.

FANNY STEVENSON TO CB

[Nice] 24 January 1884

Critical but better

MS, Yale.

FANNY STEVENSON TO CB

[Nice, received 27 January 1884]

My dear Mr. Baxter,

Louis thinks I have not written to you, so I am to write a letter this afternoon. After this, letters that are written in the sick room will have two marks—thus—under my name, so do not place too much reliance. I have not heard yet from Sir Walter, but I do hope he is on his way. I *cannot* get on without the help of a man. This morning Louis very nearly passed away. He fainted, and it was just a chance that he came through it. At the same time, in many ways he is much better. I think I might have saved even the fainting fit this morning had Sir Walter been here. Another time it might mean saving his life. I long and hope that Sir Walter is on his way. I write to you and not to Henley because I do not know where Henley is, and know that you will tell him. A letter came from you last night which made Louis very happy; nothing can give me happiness in this black hour, but your sympathy and friendship is something to which I hold fast. Give my love to Mr. Henley, and to your wife. Letters do Louis great good; at least they give him pleasure. If you see reviews, would you kindly send them, paper and all?

Sincerely yours,

F. VdeG. STEVENSON

MS (postcard), Yale.

FANNY STEVENSON TO CB

[Nice, 26 January 1884] [2]

My dear Mr. Baxter,

I cannot understand whether S. is coming or not. Hope deferred maketh the heart sick. Louis is worse again today, and my faith is at a low ebb. The fever is frightful, and the cough excruciating. He is very weak. If S. is not coming, I must have Bob. I still hope S. may be on today's train. If you know that S. is not coming, please ask privately Louis' mother and to telegraph Bob money and let him come *quickly*. It is very serious. Think of the state of mind I was in when I was asked to assist in writing that letter, the first.[3] I saw what was coming then. Is Henley with you still? Please all write letters to Lo., showing that you know that he is seriously ill, and yet cheerful. He is hurt, now that the whole world does not know it. Let everybody write.

F.

MS (telegram), Yale.

FANNY STEVENSON TO CB

[Nice] 26 January 1884

Has Simpson started If not send money to Bob quickly Answer

MS, Yale.

FANNY STEVENSON TO CB

[Nice, end of January 1884]

My dear Mr. Baxter,

Louis has passed a much better night: but little pain and no wandering in his mind. The night before was horrible: an agony of pain, and struggling with delirious fancies all night. He was already better when the consulting doctor arrived, an old friend of

2. Postmark.
3. Of 20 January.

Dr. George Balfour,[4] and of the Simpsons. He spoke with great affection of "Watty" and said, "Ask Watty if he remembers Dr. Drummond." [5] He was most kind and sympathetic, and I think if you would like to know more clearly what he thinks of Louis, you might write to him and I am sure he would give you a detailed answer. I should be very glad if you did, for I do not think he told me the whole truth. He says that the momentary danger is over, though it might return, but that the case is a grave one. He told Louis that the fever he has had is malarial, but to me he said it was simply hectic fever, which he would probably never be free from. At the same time he says that he has known men as far gone as Louis pull themselves together and make a new start that carries them on for years. The fact that he is alive now says much in his favour. The whole thing was so sudden and violent. I never before had much to do with a frightened doctor, but the first one was frightened out of his life almost. I have got a very nice little English nurse [6] to help me, and this morning Louis is well enough to watch her with great amusement, though her first appearance was an awful shock to him. She at once offered to take his shirt off, which [was] drenched with cold sweat; but this morning he is regarding her as a very nice bit of machinery. I don't know whether I am sorry that I sent for Sir Walter or not; when the doctor told me to send for him, he said, "Your husband will be dead before anybody can arrive, so you had better send for a man"; wasn't that awful? And then I had to go up smiling to Louis. As they want to get him away from Nice as soon as possible, I should be so glad to have someone to help me get him home: it will not be an easy thing to manage. I have such faith in Louis' friends that I feel no hesitation in asking any service of them for him. I shouldn't think of doing it for myself, but for him I do not think twice—nor need I, I am convinced, and he deserves all their affection and kindness.

I find I must stop now: the nurse needs me. Much love to your family.

Sincerely yours,

F. VdeG. Stevenson

4. "That wise youth, my uncle": Dr. George Balfour (1823–1903), physician to the Royal Infirmary, 1867–82, and author of numerous medical works.

5. Dr. James Drummond, Promenade des Anglais, Nice; M.D. St. Andrews, 1852.

6. Mrs. Burgess, for whose son RLS later tried to get a nomination to Christ's Hospital. See *Letters*, 2, 250 ff.

MS, Yale.

Fanny Stevenson to CB

[Nice, received 4 February 1884]

My dear Friend,

I send the enclosed. I believe it should be sent to the firm, but I do not understand business matters, so just for once it will go to you privately.

Louis was much better yesterday morning when Bob arrived, and also this morning, but within the last two hours something seems to be a little wrong. He sleeps stupidly, and then sweats heavily, and complains of griping pains. He is very pale with it. Take it altogether he is better, I think. I must send this off without another word, as all the rest of the time I have I must take for him. Bob and your letter arrived together. Much love to you all.

F. VdeG. Stevenson

Will write more tomorrow. Have had good counsel from another doctor, but it is to be kept a secret on account of physicians' etiquette.

MS (telegram), Yale.

Fanny Stevenson to CB

Nice, 2 February 1884

Parents not necessary Much better

MS, Yale.

Fanny Stevenson to CB

[Nice, 4 February 1884]

My dear Mr. Baxter,

Why is all this sudden excitement going on with Louis' parents? When Louis was so very bad, they just wrote as though they thought it was nothing but nerves that ailed Louis, though they had had letters and telegrams from both me and the doctors on the subject. Now that they have been assured in every way possible that Louis is doing as well as could be expected or hoped, come these letters and telegrams on all sides. It is *impossible* to say or do more than we have done: Bob sent a telegram, I sent a telegram, Dr. Wakefield [7] sent a telegram, and we all wrote letters all of the same purport. There is no other step to take. I believe that finally Dr. Drummond sent a telegram, though it is nearly a fortnight since he saw Louis, and he says he knows nothing whatever about him now. Dr. Drummond refused to answer telegrams that should have been addressed to Dr. Wakefield, and it is only in sheer despair that he sent one last night at Wakefield's request. I do wish they wouldn't do it: they put us in such a horrid position. If Louis were not really better, I should be in a fearful state, as any moment they might throw the case over, and there is no other doctor here—not even old West, who has gone to England. As to Dr. Williams, there is no such person in Nice; [8] there is a *dentist* Dr. Williams, but not a doctor. It seems to have been a mistake, Wakefield being the man meant most probably. Please show this to Mrs. Stevenson; you had better, because it is so *very* important not to offend the only doctors there are past bearing. If Louis got worse and they refused to have anything to do with us, what would become of us? Dr. Drummond is so angry and indignant that I dare not go back to him. He has been of the greatest help to me, but secretly and quite in private. Now he suspects me, very justly, of having let everything out and told that he was acting in an unprofessional manner. Do beg them not to do wild things. They have been told *everything*, except that I would not send for them in the beginning. I was convinced that if Louis died it would kill his father, so why not give his father the chance of the doubt—while there is life there *is* hope. Anyhow they seem to think I should not have sent for anyone, to come so far. I said to show this letter, but you had better read what is necessary; leave out all about Dr. Drummond's giving me advice privately. He is to pretend utter ignorance of my and Louis' movements and affairs, but, *this in strict privacy,* he is sending me to Cannes to see a great swell there named Frank,[9] a brother-in-law to

7. Dr. William Wakefield, M.D. Glasgow, 1864. The *British Medical Directory* gives his address as Paris.

8. There was a Dr. David William Williams, M.D. St. Andrews, 1858. The *Directory*, however, lists his addresses as Menton and Geneva, and he may have been in the latter place at this time.

9. Dr. Philip Frank, M.D. Berlin, 1837; Fellow of the Royal College of Physicians, London, 1871.

a duke. I daren't tell this to Louis' people: they are too wild, and will do something that may make more trouble. I am writing the things to you that I wish to say to them because writing and telegraphing to them has no effect whatever, and your last telegram says to answer to you—or if it doesn't say so I inferred so. I answered your telegram, and also sent another one to Heriot Row, though they had already had one that same morning, and one the night before. Dr. Wakefield has written another letter to them, but after that he will not do anything more, and Dr. Drummond will have nothing to [do] with anything. I am very sorry, for I am afraid to go back to Dr. Drummond for final instructions. I suppose he would put me to the door as an informer. I shall however do as he told me and go to Cannes. I have been an informer insofar as telling you is concerned, but I have told no one else, though it must look like it to Dr. Drummond. I have written to Henley lately, and I suppose he has sent you the letter. I believe Bob also has written to him. Your letters, the letters of both of you, have been a great delight to Louis. I want, before I forget it, to say one thing. The doctors both said that Louis had been preparing for an illness for some months, and that he was bound to have it sooner or later. I hope and trust that you never thought that your visit did him any harm. I don't think that Louis ever was more delighted in his life than by your visit, and I believe that the pleasure and excitement did him good rather than harm. We shall never forget it, either of us, though it now all seems, as I said it would, like a dream.

Bob went over to Monaco yesterday, but they would not let him into the gambling rooms. What is it that is stamped upon the Stevenson brow that makes them seem unfit to enter even the lowest gambling house? Louis looks innocent as a babe. Perhaps that is it. He may look too innocent.

I have things to do now, so I will stop. Louis is still improving, and I hope we will very soon get him to Cannes. The great trouble will be getting him from Toulon to Hyères. I might get some sort of waggon thing and have a bed laid on it and drive straight through, as it will be more tiring to make all the changes at the trains. It will be long before he will be strong enough to sit up so far.

Please make my excuses to your wife for not speaking of her, nor sending any messages to her. I do not think she will misunderstand me. If you were in Louis' place, she would most probably do just as I do and forget everything that was not at the moment more or less intimately connected with her husband. I hope you found your child better. I have often thought of it, though I always forgot to ask you when I wrote. Louis has read this letter and says, "What an angry woman": I *am* annoyed, I confess, by being placed in such a false position with Dr. Drummond. I went to him personally with Sir Walter Simpson's letter, which he said he would answer immediately, though he could not say anything at that time, but he thought that then he had done enough. He asked most earnestly after all the Simpsons, and seemed to remember them with great affection. It seemed quite impossible for him to realize that Sir Walter could be old enough to have a boy. He looked up at me over the letter and said, "A boy! Watty Simpson's got a boy! I must be growing old!"

I enclose an account for books which Louis asks you to pay. There are other papers, with the Chatto and Windus thing that I keep for a stronger envelope. Our best regards to your family and yourself, and believe me,

Most sincerely yours,
F. VdeG. STEVENSON

MS, Yale.

FANNY STEVENSON TO CB

[Nice, February 1884]

My dear Mr. Baxter,

Louis says please negociate this bill. He also says to write hereafter to Hyères, which I think is a little premature; still a letter sent there is sure to follow us. I am thankful to tell you that Louis is going on very well indeed, though he has had a shock that will probably last a long time. Mrs. Stevenson has the full report of Louis' case which the doctor sent her in the beginning of this illness, and I think he has written one since he has been better. I am very sorry no answer has come to his letter, for he has been most kind, and has, I fully believe, saved Louis' life. All other doctors are now cut off from us, owing to the wild folly of the parents, and we can only now go back to Hyères to Dr. Vidal.[1] Why this man

1. Dr. L.-Emp. Vidal, of Hyères; M.D. 1863.

has not turned from us I don't know. He has explained that he has been shamefully treated, but that he doesn't care. He does care, though. He is to spend next summer at Royat, which is a comfort as he now knows so much of Louis' constitution, and last year there was no doctor there that we cared for.

While I am writing I am giving Louis his breakfast, which makes a very jolty sort of letter. I cannot tell you how very kind the Gorellis [2] have been all through this dismal time. I am more thankful than words can express that you brought us here. I am horribly ashamed that I forgot to send your book until yesterday. I shouldn't have remembered then had Louis not reminded me. You have never said how you found your child. I do trust it is better. The weather here is superb, and makes us quite homesick for La Solitude, which must be lovely now. I wish I could send you a bit of garden and sunshine for nursery use, and so, I am sure, does your wife. Pray give her my love, and believe me sincerely yours,

F. VdeG. Stevenson

MS, Yale.

Fanny Stevenson to CB

La Solitude, Hyères-les-Palmiers, Var
[25 February 1884] [3]

My dear Mr. Baxter,

Louis wishes me to ask you to send to Bob twenty pounds immediately. I am sorry to say that Louis is not so well as he was. He had a sharp hemorrhage yesterday, but we managed to stop it, though it was very alarming in the beginning. I find it quite impossible to make anyone understand how very ill Louis has been, and how weak he is now. He can do absolutely *nothing*. We suppose that the hemorrhage was caused by Bob and my having read a manuscript work aloud the evening before. Bob leaves us tomorrow to my infinite regret. Had he not come I should never have got Louis home again. We had the most *awful* time with the doctors before we left. They both consider that they have been bitterly insulted by Louis' people. I am not going to say anything about this

2. Proprietors of the Pension Rose.
3. Postmark.

hemorrhage to them. It is so difficult to know what to tell and what to keep. I have so much to do with my dear invalid that I have not much time to write letters. Dr. Vidal gives exactly the same report of him that Wakefield did to Mrs. Stevenson, though he never heard of Wakefield.

I suppose you know Bob's address? No. 9 Alpha Place, Regent Park, London N.W. Give our love to your wife, please. Thanks for your last letter, which Louis enjoyed very much.

Truly yours,
F. VdeG. Stevenson

You won't forget the Exam papers for Sam, will you?

MS, Yale.

Fanny Stevenson to CB

La Solitude, Hyères-les-Palmiers, Var
[3 March 1884] [4]

My dear Mr. Baxter,

Will you please send forty pounds to Louis? I am so tired with not sleeping for several nights and general anxiety that I find I cannot write a letter. Louis has not been so well the last few days. In fact since Bob left. I am writing to Henley to get advice from Mennell,[5] so have to keep my head clear for that. I have had such a wild letter from the dear madman that I feel almost as wild myself. I think Louis is a little better today. The weather has changed, which is a good thing. Louis or else I have a thousand or more letters to write, so pray excuse this scrawl and believe me,

Truly yours,
F. VdeG. Stevenson

Send us for God's sake £60, or more if we have it. The £40 is our rent due in a few days.

4. Postmark.

5. Dr. Zebulon Mennell, Oxford House, 31 Shepherd's Bush Rd. W. "I found that C. Baxter and Mr. Henley when they heard of the attack had sent Dr. Mennell out from London to see Louis. . . . Mennell's report was that no artery had given way but the bleeding had proceeded from a gorged part of the lung . . . and with perfect rest and great care he may recover perfectly" (*Diary*, p. 342).

What has become of "Brashiana"? At any rate send me copies; I
do so want to see them.

Yours,

Jōhnston

MS, Yale.

[Hyères, 7 March 1884] [6]

Dear Cherrels,

       Here is a chaquey.

Yours, Drucken Jackey

*MS, Yale. Note by CB: "£50 remit-
ted."*

La Solitude, Hyères-les-Palmiers, Var
[14 March 1884] [7]

Dear Thomson,

    I'm glad it's as muckle; it micht be waur. Do ye ken, man Thom-
son, yon debatchery o' yours at the Coantinental's fair disgraced
me wi' a'body here. I was kind o' respeckit, as it were, or you and
Jaickson cam. An' noo! losh, the very weans strone upon the door-
step. They say, Mr. Johnstone, ye may be a very decent-like kind of
a man yersel but ye keep damd low company whatever—folk says.
An' what can I dae? Naething. Yon freend o' yours, folk says, he'll
be a kind of a drouthy customer, I'm thinkin'. What can I say? It's
üseless to deny ye were the waur o't. I never sae muckle's smelt it
off him, of me. Ay, they say, it's a kind of a cōmmon accident up
your way.

II to Thomson in Gaol [8]

Thomson, what did I tell ye? What did I hammer in the lugs of
ye? Choky; that was what a said—and there ye are. Of coorse, it's
a sair affliction to see a man that I hae been ower muckle mixed up

6. Postmark.
7. Postmark.
8. CB's note.

wi'—no to say, indentifeed—come to sic hōrrible example; but still
and on, it's a consolation to ken that, whatever, I dinnae ken the
disgrace o' a gaol, airns, an' cōmmon malefactors. Be damd, you're
in it noo! A bony exhibeetion. O Thomson, and me that has aye
befreendit ye! But what did I say? No faurrer back nor Mononday,
I said to a fine canty man, Thomson's in the wrang gait, I said,
Thomson's fair lost. The warst 'at onybody could say o' me was jist
maybe that I had been singl'erly oonfortinate in ma law cases, and
had less nor justice frae *weeg'd puggies* like Deas,[9] so ca'd Lard—a
paper Lard! His language was actionable; and him on the bench—
a man that should be an example. But even he said that he regretted
he had nae poo'er to commit me. Aye the same impotent malice:
Deas and Ingles [1] and a man they ca'd Hope [2]—Despair wad hae
been a better name for him; aye the same story: lōngin' to persecute
me and no able, gnashin' their auld stumps on Jōhnson, an' Johnson still defeein' them.

But you're on the justeeshiary side, my buckie. That's beyond a
jest. They'll hang you—*I* tell ye—*you*'ll see. You're by wi' it. And as
for that meeserable attemp' to get up releegion— Tht, think shame.
Ye've been, since ever 'at I kent ye, a drunkard, a whoremonger, a
blasphemer, and mair that I wouldnae like to name, you bein'
whaur ye are and your letters likely opened. But ye need fear nae
evidence frae me. The deil himsel couldnae harle me into a witness
boax. I've been there ower often, and never heard a ceevil word but
frae my ain advocate; and the judges themsel, that should set the
example, fair hōrrifyin' me wi' their low, wauf expressions: "essentially fraudulent," "ashamed of himsel," "disgraceful exhibeetion,"
"never had heard sic an exhibeetion," "the defender's evident bad
faith," "the carreer o' seemin'ly random falsehood" (maist offensive), "the cruel, heartless, and unnatural behaviour of the defendant" (the defendant was aye me: catch me goin' to law if I could
win oot of it). "The defendant's statement (this was Deas) may be
dismissed, as not containing one word of truth." "The defendant
may congrattilate himsel that he escapes a criminal persecution."
"The defendant disn't appear for the first time (whae's fau't was

9. Sir George Deas (1804–87), Lord Ordinary of Session and Lord Commissioner of
Justiciary. He lived at 32 Heriot Row. *Weeg'd puggies:* bewigged judges.
1. John Inglis, Lord Glencorse (1810–91), Lord Justice General of Scotland.
2. No one named Hope is listed among the Lords of Session at this date.

that?) before this court; I would ca'tion him no' to appear again; he may not always be so fortinate." Me that never gained a case. Onyway that' a bad language and nae mair. I despise scurreelity— let-a-be frae the Bench.

Yours,

T. JOHNSON

MS, Yale. Addressed: "Mr. Thomson
c/o Charles Baxter" etc. Note by
CB: "III to Thomson after his trial
and Glorious Acquittal."

La Solitude, Hyères-les-Palmiers, Var
[15 March 1884] [3]

Jist what I said frae the first o't. Leave him alane, I said; nae fear o' Thamson; he'll worm through. Folk here werenae for believin't. I ken ye aye said sae, Mr. John'son, says they; we ken ye were aye thriepin't [4] ower upon us; but wha (says they) wad hae believed it? Yon man Thomson! (they says). A man in physognomy fair brandit wi' drink an' gallows! Hooever, they says, we'll hae to allow that ye were right, Mr. John'son, and telled us exac'ly hoo it wad lie.

Eh, man, what a triump! An ovawtion! An' yon Lard Bung [5] (what a bonny name he his!)—a ceevil, daycent Lard! Whaur d's he sit? Damd, I'll bring an action! Yon's the man for me! But, man, whatten a clan ye got thegither! Jaickson, by all! An' yon plumber! Gude guide us, what's the courts comin' tae. Onyway, ye confüsed them wi' evidence. But Lard Bung was by ord'nar. Ye may thank your sakes it wasnae Deas or Ingles: they wad hae had Jaickson heels ower cran, ayther one o' them, afore he'd weel begude. [6] I fand a cuttin o' the möckery o' justice that I had and send it ye. Ye can see what like it was wi' Deas: diffrent from Lard Bung—a true Lard him—a real honest Scotsman—the Lard bless him.

THOMAS JOHNSTONE

3. Postmark.
4. Asserting it.
5. No one whose name could be parodied into "Bung" is listed among the Scottish judges, unless it is George, Lord Young, Lord Commissioner of Justiciary.
6. Begun.

Droll Scene in Court: Pettigrew *v.* Johnstone

This case came up for proof today, and much mirth was occasioned by the cross examination of the defendant—a solemn, dissipated looking man.

Cross examined by the Solicitor General: You were till recently an office bearer in the church?

—Whatten church? I am now an office bearer in the Morrisonian body.[7]

Q. In the Church of Scotland?

—I had a difference.

Q. You were advised to retire?

—That's a calu'ny. I wasnae pleased with the minister: I didn't think he was spiritual enough.

Q. Or Spirituous. (Laughter in Court) Come now, Mr. Johnstone, we will not be hard upon you. You have been a bankrupt?

—Five times. (Laughter in Court)

Q. You have been in trouble?

—Nothing was ever proved upon me.

Q. No, there have been no convictions, but you must allow you have been rather unfortunate in the number of accusations under which you have laboured. Neighbours somewhat calumnious?

The witness (with emphasis): Jealous. (Laughter in Court)

The Sol. Gen.: You have been fined for shebeening? [8]

The witness: That was a mistak'. (Laughter in Court)

Q. You have been accused of reset of theft? [9]

—It was not proved.

Q. You had an unpleasant case, I think, with the trustees of your brother's children?

—I had.

The Court: I mind that case. It was a very bad one. I remember regretting at the time, and I expressed my regret, that I was unable to prosecute the present defender. I had forgot him. I am very much obliged to you, Mr. Macdonald,[10] for putting it in my head. (To the witness:) I spoke very sharply to you, Sir.

---

7. See above, p. 126.
8. Selling liquor at illegal hours.
9. Receiving stolen goods.
10. Perhaps John Hay Athole Macdonald (1836–1919), Dean of the Faculty of Advocates, 1882–85; Lord Advocate, 1885; Lord Justice Clerk, 1888. He was knighted in 1900.

—*Witness:* There was a great prejudice against me.

Lord Deas (continuing): I gave you a warning, I believe?

—Yes, my lord.

Q. What have you been doing since I saw you?

—I have been a grocer, and kept a public house, and I have had misfortunes, my Lord, and now I'm retired upon my means.

Q. Do you mean that you have no ostensible means of livelihood?

—No, my Lord.

Q. What do you mean?

—Thank you, my Lord. (Laughter in Court)

Lord Deas: Silence. This is most unseemly. What is your trade, man?

—I am a tout, my Lord.

Q. What for?

—For a number of gentlemen. (Laughter in Court)

(His Lordship threatened to clear the court at once on any repetition of the disturbance.)

Q. In what trade are these gentlemen?

—Publicans, my Lord, and hotel-keepers.

Q. Do you mean that you are paid to bring people in to drink?

(The witness was silent.)

The Sol. Gen.: My Lord, the man is a pimp.

Lord Deas: Now, Thomson, how does this come about? When first I saw you, you were a man in a very humble way, and a poor creature, but had a kind of decency about you; and then I warned you. Then you were a baker and a precentar, if I remember; and how does it come about that you should have sunk to this most degraded position that you now occupy? Here you are, as I foretold, fallen from the very poor position that you then occupied to be a perfect byword in a court of justice. I have had my eye on you for long. You had better be very careful, sir.

The Sol. Gen.: Thank you, my Lord. (To witness:) You may go down.

Scotsman [11]

A prevarication of justice!

T. J.

11. I.e. the newspaper, the letter being a parody of one of its legal reports.

(Summing up.) *Lord Deas:* This is a case of evidence and the value of witnesses. The pursuer seems to be a very decent man. As for the defender, his own account of himself is a very poor one—I never had a poorer in my experience. It is for the Jury to consider what confidence they are inclined to put in the statements of this man, Johnstone. They have heard and seen him, and heard something, although far from all, of his antecedents. His statement is not in itself impossible, but it is certainly one of the most improbable that ever I heard. There is nothing against nature in this man's allegations; but they are of that description that the Jury must lay a great stress upon the honesty and worth of his entirely unsupported testimony—a great deal more than perhaps any man's evidence would bear or justify—if they were to pay the slightest attention to any single word that had fallen from his lips. The man's scandalous bad character and obvious prevarication must be carefully weighed and must be allowed to influence the conclusions of the Jury. A man of reasonably decent character was of course to be preferred to a man who had made a mere exhibition of himself in court, and who was besides not even able to deny the charge of following a most infamous trade.

MS, Yale.

FANNY STEVENSON TO CB

[Hyères, 29 March 1884] [1]

My dear Mr. Baxter,

It is a shameful time since I have written to you. This is my excuse: Louis strained his eyes and started some mischief in one, and has been for some time condemned to darkness, double green goggles, and a shade. Of course he could do no work, so I have been writing to his dictation until my own eyes have given out. In consequence my letter must be short. Louis is otherwise much better daily. Encl. a cheque. Much love to your wife. Love from Louis to you both. How are the babes?

Sincerely yours,

F. VdeG. STEVENSON

1. Postmark.

MS, Yale.

FANNY STEVENSON TO CB

La Solitude, Hyères-les-Palmiers, Var
[received 16 April 1884]

My dear Mr. Baxter,

Louis is stronger and the weather good, so we leave, nothing happening to the contrary, tomorrow. I find this letter among some things Louis gave me to burn and thought I had better send it to you. Would you please send those examination papers of which I spoke, for the preliminary medical, to Sam, whose address is Eastham, Bournemouth? In *awful* haste. My love to your wife; am glad to hear the child is better.

F. VdeG. STEVENSON

MS, Yale.

Encl.

La Solitude, Hyères-les-Palmiers, Var
[28 April 1884] [2]

Dear Cherls,

Encl. please find a cheque for £40—Storrs' [3] bill of £39 odds—and Storrs' letter, directing how he wishes to be paid. Apply business talents and serve hot.

I have been faur frae weel this whylie, but I keep pushin forrit. I have sent Sam a draught on your firm. I am generally all there, what there is o' me, includin a skyatica. It's grand, the skyatica. It's a kind of an alto pain, a kind of a piccoly pain, like thon orchestry whustle ye üsed to toot upon yoursel, Mr. Thomson—an' a grand feggure you were, sir, though no sae muckle soond as was expeckit frae your feesognomony. Prood was I to hear ye.

Yours ever,
R. L. S.

Whan first upon the alto flute
Great Mr. Thomson tried to toot;
Tho' *Piccolo* was what its name was,

2. Postmark.
3. See above, p. 108 n. 4.

Sae great that eident [4] player's fame was,
An' he could blaw sae sma' and skilly,
They changed the name to *Piccalilly*.

MS, Yale.

[Hyères, May? 1884]

Dear Charles,

Herewith the cheque. I am muckle obleeged to you for a' 't's come and gane. I'm a wheen be'er. The deevil an' me's no dune yet. It's lang ar the deil. I am, dear Cherls,

Yours entirely,
THOMSON

My first name is Dauvit. Do ye mind when I was a baker at Kirkintilloch? Yon were braw days! And when I keepit a wee, bit, tosh, laigh, canny dram shop at Camlang? Eh, it was grand! Noo, I'm a mere wauf, randy beggarman.

I never was what ca'd an honest man, and I was aye keen fur the siller. But man, can ye no get Jaickson to ca' cannier? I dinnae mind muckle, but yon puir Tauchnitz (if that be his name) comes between me and my vivers.[5] It's a dam shame, by what I can see—a fair disgrace—and him a common German. Tauch! says you. Nitz! says I, and gives ye them!

D. THOMSON

4. Diligent.
5. "Tauchnitz junior" had written to Henley from Leipzig, 30 April 1884: "Dear Sir,—Some time ago, my friend Mr. James Payn suggested to me that I should include in my cheap Continental Series Mr. Louis Stevenson's *Treasure Island* and at the same time he told me that I had to refer to you with respect to that work.— I have not had the pleasure till now to publish any of Mr. Louis Stevenson's books, but I should be quite willing to try the publication of the above mentioned work. As it is rather a small book, filling only *one* of my cheap volumes, I suppose I might have it at a moderate price, say Fifteen or Twenty Pounds? Perhaps you kindly send me a line upon the subject and, if my proposal is convenient to you and Mr. Stevenson, I shall not fail to settle the matter at once. . . ." (MS, Yale). The book was published as vol. 2255 of Collected British Authors (Leipzig, 1884).

MS, Yale.

RLS TO SIR WALTER SIMPSON

[Hyères, May? 1884]

My dear Simpson,

The Bag has not yet turned up; but the letter did and greatly pleased us. It was the most Simpsonian thing ever penned—the essence of Stravon.[6] The Bag will be acknowledged in due season.

I must tell you a joke. A month or two ago, there was an alarm: it looked like family.[7] Prostration: I saw myself financially ruined, I saw the child born sickly, etc. Then, said I, I must look this thing on the good side; proceeded to do so studiously, and with such a result that when the alarm passed off—I was inconsolable!

You like accounts; observe this partial budget:

Earnings		
£365	rent	£80
215	Sam's school	£135
		£215

£150 to live, laugh, love, and pay the taxes with. I pushed the budget no farther. Next year I shall make £500: that is if I keep well. I have been spitting blood for a week,[8] but now it has stopped. When I spit blood I write verses: same principle as the ancient phlebotomy.

I have written a novel; curious to hear your views of it. It will probably not appear for a year yet.[9] My own belief is that I have made a spoon; [10] anyway it is a step. I have worked round to be able to tell a story in my way. It's a queer way, but I think it has merit.[11]

6. Strathavon, Sir Walter's home. Most of RLS's letters to Simpson are said to have been destroyed. This one escaped by somehow getting into CB's file.

7. Cf. RLS's verses, "God Gave to Me a Child in Part" (*Complete Poems*, New York, 1923, p. 434).

8. ". . . on the 14th of May I received a most alarming letter from Fanny telling me that Louis had had a dreadful attack of hemorrhage" (*Diary*, p. 341).

9. *Prince Otto.* It was serialized in *Longman's Magazine*, April–October, and published in book form, November 1885.

10. I.e. succeeded: "To make a spoon or spoil a horn."

11. Not signed.

MS, Yale.

RLS to Henley

Highcliff Hotel, Bournemouth [1]
[August–September 1884]

Dear William Ernest Hart,[2]

What is the reason of things? The piratic and obscure Mennel [3]
came, interviewed my uncle,[4] and then, without a word, fled, leaving me unadvised; since when I have not seen him. My uncle
praised the pirate, said he agreed with him, said I was quite well,
said my hemorrhage was all exaggeration (my wife's), said Mennel
said so, said we were to throw the ergotine out of the window, said
I might live in England, etc. The simoom blew. It was wild weather.

Next day, being without word of Mennel (and so still!), I went
up to Brunton [5] on the chance. B. condemned me out of hand, and
says both lungs are affected seriously, and ordered me to the Alps
in winter.

Then I came here, which is a pretty nice place (and a lovely
journey), and I know nothing about anything, and as for Mennel,
His tricks they are vain, His ways they are dark, His whole little
game Is more than a lark.[6] In the words of his sacred Majesty King
George the Third, what—what, what—why, why, why? Can you
throw any light? Did they quarrel, or did the pirate sell my uncle,
or had he sold us, or did his courage collapse, and why did he bolt?

1. "Louis improves slowly but steadily, and by the beginning of June he is able
to go by easy steps to Royat . . . By this time cholera had appeared at Hyères, so
once more the tent had to be shifted; the pleasant home given up. So they decide to
come to London to have a consultation of doctors—they arrived on the 1st of July
[August? Cf. *Letters, 2, 227*] and Louis was looking better than I had dared to hope
though he was very thin and waxen looking. . . . Louis sees four doctors, two say he
may stay in England, one that he should return to Davos and the 4th that he should
go to Switzerland for two years. We all go to Bournemouth for a time and eventually
Louis makes up his mind to stay the winter there . . ." (*Diary*, pp. 342-3).

2. Playing on the name "Ernest Hart" (1835-98), fellow member of the Savile
Club; surgeon, oculist, and editor of the *British Medical Journal*. But RLS may also
have had in mind Henley's interest in Bret Harte. "If you see the *Athenaeum*,
and note a Bret Harte in it, remember that you know the author" (Henley to RLS,
undated, MS, Yale). Cf. n. 6, below.

3. See above, p. 141.

4. Dr. George Balfour.

5. Dr. Thomas Lauder Brunton, 50 Welbeck St., Cavendish Square, London; M.D.
Edinburgh, 1868.

6. Cf. Bret Harte, "Plain Language from Truthful James."

I am dull and have a cold; real dull. About *Old Glory* [7] I see much
to say, and, when I am less stupid, shall say it; but now? Unbroken
clouds extend.

Yours ever,

R. L. S.

Of Bournemouth, Davos, Torquay,

Mentone, Nice, Cannes, and Hyères,

Esq., Invalid.

MS, Yale.

Sunnington Rise, West Cliff Gardens,

Bournemouth [September 1884]

Dear Cherls,

A checkie—

Very small,

And a bill—

Very big.

Pray pay and we will see to meet it somehow. My finances are
strangely at sea, but there is a good time coming. As for how my
account stands, I have no notion; if it costs naething, ye micht let's
ken; if not, O not!

Yours,

R. L. Stevenson

Jaickson's grand. Yon was awfae aboot the litrytyur.

MS, Yale.

Wensleydale, Bournemouth, 4 October 1884

My dear Charles,

Herewith a chequy.

I was sorry to hear of your accident, but hope you are picking up
overhand. I have been detected in the felonious possession of many
yards of tapeworm; I was instantly arrested and the goods have
been restored to their maker, much good may they do him. The
worm was very like me in figure; in the face, there was only a family

7. A projected play by RLS and Henley.

resemblance. I may now say, and that gladly, that I have had every infamous complaint. 'Tis a strange world.

Yours,
THOMSON

MS, Yale. Letters, 2, 246.

Bonallie Towers, Branksome Park,
Bournemouth, 11 November [1884] [8]

My dear Charles,

I beg to inform you that I have already received Colvin's interest from him directly; I also beg to apologise for sinful delay about the enclosed receipt, which may still be interesting from an antiquarian point of view. I am in my new house, thus proudly styled, as you perceive; but the deevil a tower ava' can be perceived (except out of window). This is not as it should be; one might have hoped, at least, a turret bogshop.

We are all vilely unwell. I put in the dark watches, imitating a donkey with some success but little pleasure; and in the afternoon I indulge in a smart fever, accompanied by aches and shivers. There is thus little monotony to be deplored; and what might still weigh upon me, my wife lightens by various inexplicable attacks, now in the pleasant morn, now at the noon of night. I, at least, am a *regular* invalid: I would scorn to bray in the afternoon, I would indignantly refuse the proposal to fever in the night. What is bred in the bone, will come out, Sir, in the flesh; and the same spirit that prompted me to date my letter regulates the hour and character of my attacks. I am, Sir,

Yours,
THOMSON

MS, Yale. Letters, 2, 248. Addressed:
"Mr. Thomson (ex-precentar) care
of Charles Baxter Esq." etc.

[Bournemouth, 13 November 1884]

My dear Thomson,

It's a maist remarkable fac', but nae shuner had I written yon

8. Postmark.

braggin, blawin' letter aboot ma business habits, when bāñg! that very day, my hoast begude in the aifternune! It is really remaurkable; it's prōvidenshle, I believe. The ink wasnae fair dry, the words werenae weel ooten ma mouth, when bang, I got the lee. The mair ye think o't, Thomson, the less ye'll like the looks o't. Proavidence (I'm no sayin') is all verra weel *in its place,* but if proavidence has nae mainners, wha's to learn't? Proavidence is a fine thing, but hoo would you like proavidence to keep your till for ye? The richt place for proavidence is in the kirk; it has naething to do wi' private correspondence between twa gentlemen, nor freendly cracks, nor a wee bit word o' sculduddery ahint the door, nor, in shoart, wi' ony *hole an' corner wark,* what I would call. I'm pairfec'ly willin' to meet in wi' proavidence—I'll be prood to meet in wi' him, when my time's come an' I cannae doe nae better; but *if he's to come skinking aboot my stair-fit,* damned, I micht as weel be deed for a' the comfort I'll can get in life. Cannae he no be made to understand that it's beneath him? Gosh, if I was in his business, I wouldnae steer my heid for a plain, auld ex-elder that, tak' him the way he tak's himself, 's jist aboot as honest as he can weel afford, an' but for drink an' weemen an' a wheen auld scandals near forgotten noo, is a pairfeckly respectable and thoroughly decent man. An' if I fashed wi' him ava', it wad be kind o' handsome like: a pun'-note under his stair door, a bottle o' auld, blended malt to his bit mornin', as a teshtymonial like yon ye ken sae weel aboot, but mair successfu'.

Dear Thomson, have I ony money? If I have, *send it's* for the loard's sake.

JOHNSON

MS, Yale.

Bonallie Towers, Branksome Park,
Bournemouth, 16 November [1884]

My dear Charles,

Herewith receipt and thanks. I was much surprised and vexed to hear of the death of poor Magnus; [9] so I go on outliving people—

9. Alexander Magnus Retzious Simpson (*b.* 1852), brother of Sir Walter and Eva Simpson. "Have you heard of Magnus Simpson's death? It is most sad, and has affected me more than I could have imagined. Poor Eva. You know their house was just newly got up. . . . You will write to her, I hope. Wattie, to my dismay, *seems*

is it not strange? I am very sorry for Eva, but I do not see that I should write to her. I am on Walter's side in their dispute; [10] I think she has behaved badly. I wrote to her once and was not answered; and I have no desire to seek the renewal of an acquaintance where my own esteem is doubtful and which would not improbably find its solution in a quarrel. The death of Mag. really removes the last link that was at all likely to have brought us together. Of course you understand I have, and I wish, no quarrel; and if I had anything to say, as I most sincerely pity her isolation and bereavement, I might even stretch a point and write. But what is there to say? There is only one consolation that I know, and that as old as the Bible: that he is taken away from the evil to come. He is safe, now, from pain and dishonour. More I know not—nor any man. But it is probably well with him.

Please look up the papers you have about Hervey Osbourne's grave, find the address of the *marbrier,* take up your best French quill, and see that the concession is assured for some while longer.[11] This is *immediate;* please see to it. I would write myself to save posts, but have not the address.

On Thursday [12] I was 34; and Magnus I suppose in his grave! You might send me some details.

Ever yours affectionately,
R. L. Stevenson

MS, Yale.

CB to RLS

Edinburgh, 31 December 1884

Dear Thomson,

I feel I maun tak up ma pen to say Hoo's a wi' ye this last day o'

almost indifferent. He cannot really be so, I think, for heart is not wanting in the Bart" (CB to RLS, 13 November 1884).

10. CB's letter of 19 November 1884 confirms the implication of estrangement between Eva and Sir Walter. Cf. above, p. 84, and below, p. 299.

11. "The concession for Henry [*sic*] Osbourne's grave is dated 6th April 1876 and purports to be for 15 years, which would make the termination 1891. The words are *"concède pour quinze ans."* If you wish to make certain, the person to address is The Maire, Ville de Saint Germain-en-Laye. . . . But as far as I understand the matter, nothing requires to be done. But thae frŏgies! a buddy never kens wha' they may be at" (CB to RLS, 19 November 1884).

12. The 13th.

the year an' to wuss ye a' the gude things Prōvidence hes keepit frae masel the last twalmonth. Here's a' luck t'ye an' yer wifie tae, an' faither and mither an' a.

Eh man, this has been an awfu year wi me bōnds and imprisonment and a' kinds o' abüse. Am no' mysel ava, an' noo a'm on the tee tottle an' it's no pyin'. There's ower muckle o' the same, and I'm fairly on ma dowp.[1] Could ye no spare a trifle till an auld freend Thōmson. Ye'll mind yin or twa o' thae auld stories a ken aboot ye. Ye're still inside hangin distance, ye ken, but it's no likely that Peter Thōmson wad betray a freen excep under the pressure o' an awaukened conscience.

A five pun note wad see me on for a whilie.

Yours,

Jōhnson [2]

MS, Yale.

[Bournemouth, *ca.* 1 January 1885]

Dear Charles,

I send on to these birds to make new bargains owing to the errors. They haven't taken the trouble; so you just keep this copy, if you please, and make the corrections on the other and send it on for me to initial.

Guid New Year. Awful hurry.

Yrs ever,

R. L. S.

Henley seems better and worse.

MS, Yale.

Bonallie Towers, Branksome Park,
Bournemouth [January 1885]

Dear Charles,

Here's luck to you and all manner of good to all your friends and doings. I am in bed again, but no very bad, I think; and I hear

1. Butt-end.
2. Originally signed "Thomson."

Jaickson's no sae weel. Here is a bit chequie. Tak off what I'll like be owin' you, and send the lave fleein' back to Bournemouth, that's a man, for I'm needin' 't uncoly.

THOMSON

Also a bargain to keep.

MS, Yale.

[Bournemouth, January 1885]

Fair killed wi' correspondence. Here's the receptacle, or what dye ma' ca' it—receepy: sume dāmd French affair.

Henley's better, but awfu' doon in the mouth like; I kenna why. He just writes as dowie as can be thocht o'.

R. L. S.

Damn Teetottle, say I!

MS, Yale.

B.T., B.P., B., 27 January 1885

Dear Charles,

If Clark the printer [3] slings you a bill, for God's sake, meet it. It will not, I think, be for long, as I am in treaty with *P.M.G.* for *The Dynamiters*.[4] I am a machine of work, now Henley's gone.

Yrs ever,

R. L. S.

House Bought: [5] not a doit: whuskey consumed by Jaickson: wirra, wirra!

3. R. and R. Clark, who had printed "For Private Circulation Only," two plays by Henley and RLS: *Admiral Guinea* and *Beau Austin* (Edinburgh, 1884); this year they were to print a third, *Macaire*.

4. *More New Arabian Nights: the Dynamiter*, by RLS and Fanny, was published in April by Longmans, Green, and Co. The "treaty" with the *Pall Mall Gazette* apparently fell through.

5. "In February we buy a house at Welbourne for Louis called 'Sea View'—the name was at once altered to 'Skerryvore'" (*Diary*, p. 343). Cf. *Underwoods*, Poems xxxiv and xxxv. The house was a wedding present to Fanny from RLS's parents.

MS, Yale.

> Bonallie Tower, Branksome Park, Bournemouth,
> 30 January 1885

Charles Baxter Esq., W.S.

My dear Sir,

I beg to remark that if, in contradiction to every probability, you have returned the duplicate agreement to Messrs Longman,[6] you cannot do better than write to that firm and recover it. I have no doubt, on a proper representation of your error, they will kindly consent to repair it.

> Yours very faithfully,
> THOMSON

If you have not, what does all this mean? One of these is for me: that you retained. The other was for Longman: that I countersigned and sent to them. More I cannot say. I have written you already many * weeks ago, asking you to register the duplicate, as I thought that better than to delay further with Longman.

> R. L. S.

* I do not know the date—at the time of the affair. It appears I must file my letters.

MS (telegram), Yale.

> Bournemouth, 6 February 1885

Can you not bring down your wife with you Let us know if we may expect her

6. "Now then, for the third and last time: Where is that agreement with Longman about *Child's Garland?* Are you, or are you not, a man of biz? Do you, or do you not, reply to letters? Did you, or did you not, lie foully when you maintained at Monaco that your habits were more methodical than mine? And lastly, will you, or will you not, return that agreement?" (CB to RLS, 26 January 1885).

MS, Yale.

CB TO RLS

Edinburgh, 20 March 1885

Dear Johnson,

I sent yon pickle siller [7] you were speerin for yestreen. Ye're aye welcome 's lang as I hae a bawbee in ma pooch. Ye ken it's no like the time we wes borrowin three penny bits o' ilk ither and no aye pying back.

Man, I'm fair to the wa' noo. Ye mind I wes aye ettlin [8] at the law, hed aye a kin' o' hankerin for leetigation (Gōd knows 'ave hed ma bellyful syne), but that's no it. Weel, efter the cairds was done for an' a' got oot o' Dumbarton (dam yon Bailie tae hell) I thocht I wad tak to the law, and no to be a burden tae ma freens, I just wheeped up canty and cosy to Lunnon, but gosh me, they're ōn me aince mair, an' ye'll see in a swatch I cut oot o' the *Times* and sent to Jaikson to forward it ōn to ye, that the Law Society, as they ca' themsels (Gōds dam), hes been on til me. What to dae noo 's mair than a can ask or think.

Yours truly,
THOMSON

MS, Yale.

[Bournemouth] 24 March 1885

Dear Thomson,

It's extrōdnar: you an' me in a court of Law—a place 'at I swure I wouldnae pit ma fit in for the Queen hersel, and here we're baith in't; an' the extrodnar pairt of it is that I cannae weel mak' out the richts and wrongs of it. But you and me must hae been innycent: there's nae doobt o' that. They had me up yince in a multiplepindin'; I had seen ower muckle o' thae games, sae nae suner had I taken the aith than I said, "My loard," I says, "it's proper that I should tell ye, at the first off go, how it stan's. There's a wheen folk that has a prejudice on my chara'ter," I says, "but, my loard, whatever for that," I says, "I'm innycent." "Whae's accusin' you?" says

7. Bit of money.
8. Aiming.

he. "My loard," I says, "I div not know; and, my loard," I says, "I div not care." And I lookit roond the court like a lion. There was a wheen low writer lads that leugh; but the Judge, whae was a very decent spoken man (it wasnae Deas; it was yin I had never forgathered wi' afore—Muir,[9] I think, was the name of him), he up, and says he, "The gentleman," he says, "is labourin' under some mistak'," he says. "My loard," I says, "there's been ower monny o' thae mistak's in my case; there was the trust mistak," I says, "and there was the afeelyation mistak'," I says, "and the till mistak', an' the plate mistak', an' the French cairds mistak'," I says, "and now, to pit the tap to it, I'm accüsed o' multipplepindin![10] It's a thing," I says, "my loard, that I'm incapable of!" "My guid man," says he, "this is a ceevil case." "My loard," says I, "the're all ceevil by their way of it; but yince ye're in the Dōck, nae mair civeelity for puir Johnstone." The loard turned to an aaadvikate: "Mr. Trayner,"[11] says he, "cannae ye no get a better wutness?" "I'll try," says he, and tauld me to step doun; and I never heard nae mair of it! I've aften thocht sinsyne if I had aye been as bauld at the first off-gang, mebbe I wad hae had less injustice. But ye see I was mōrally convinced that this yin was a shaam, and whiles I wasnae sae clear. There's a wheen awkwardnesses in the warld, and mony things are unco sair to expleen. Nae doobt somebody had multiplepindit, but I'll tak my aith it wasnae me.

I'm muckle obleeged to ye for thon siller, and I remain,

Dear Johnstone,	Dear Thamson,
Yours,	Yours,
THAMSON	JOHNS'ONE

9. David Mure, Lord Mure (1810–91), Solicitor General, 1858–59; Lord Advocate, 1859; Lord Commissioner of Justiciary at the time of writing.

10. A stock joke among Scottish lawyers. In spite of its formidable name, multiple-poinding means merely a suit to determine which of two or more claimants is the true creditor, so that the debtor shall not be subjected to repeated claims. "Man, I fair pisht masel lauchin at the multiple pinding, an' so did the Gōdkin [William Mitchell, CB's senior partner]. Ye're just donnert; it's no a crime or a wad hae committed it masel lang syne; it's a fōrm o' law an' ye sweer onything 'at comes intil yer heed. Gōd kens wha' it's a fōr, but tha's hoo it is" (CB to RLS, 5 April 1885).

11. John Trayner (1834–1929), advocate; Sheriff of Forfarshire, 1881–85.

MS, Yale.

Bournemouth, 2 April 1885

My dear Charles,

I write out of a whirlwind. Please do this for me. Go down to
17 Heriot Row. If you have (as I think you have) the keys of my
business table, open it with them; if you have not, this is to authorise you to get a locksmith and have it opened. Messrs Denham and
Co., upholsterers, 10A N. St. Andrew Street, are to despatch the
table to Bournemouth, and I request you to put yourself into communication with them, getting them to help you if the locks have to
be opened, and letting them know as soon as the table is ready for
transmission. The papers etc. that you will find you had best clap
into a cheap portmanteau and send off here. There are also (or
were) in my old school playbox a lot of blank-books and some MS,
all of which should come too. Excuse apparent bluntness, time being on the hunt; and pray recognise the extreme delicacy of the
service I ask you to do for me.

Ever yours,
R. L. STEVENSON

Charles Baxter Esq., W.S

MS, Yale.

[Bournemouth, *ca.* 2 April 1885]

For Jaickson.
Dear Thomson,

It's grand: ye have the right lilt; ye have the real fire; man, ye're
a poet! I write this to our friend Jaickson, who will forward my
subscription, as there is a kind of a diffeeculty wi' my bankers:
purely temporary, but unco vexawtious.

Jaickson has nae kind of soul aboot him. When I read him my
Sculduddry[1] Sangs, whilk were thocht to be very bonny by abody
but the police, he seemed fine an' pleased wi' them; but it was—
O horror, Thomson—it was to BORRY! Ye will find mony seemilar
disap'intments in that c'reer of literature, to which ye now devote

1. Bawdy. See below, p. 205.

yourself, and which *I* have flang under my feet wi' scōrn. Onyway, ye have ae sincere admirer—

Your auld frien',

Dauvit Johnstone

P.S. I would be blythe o' a bit note: say 10 pund or, to mak a roond sum of it, and for convenience, 12 pund ten.

P.P.S. Mebbe thirteen would be simpler.

Later. I think, since ye're sae kind, we'll mak' it seventeen pund ten. It's a fine, handy, comfortable sum. Ye'll can draw a bill upon me.

Later still. Eh, man, ye're po'me's beautifu!

MS, Yale.

[Bournemouth, *ca.* 9 April 1885]

My dear Charles,

A thousand thanks for the admirable manner you have executed the task; I thought you would appreciate the delicacy when you opened a certain drawer and came upon my arsenal! These shall now go into the heaving deep, I guess.

I shall certainly and gladly do something for your Scotch paper.[2] You will have to tell me shape, space, manner of publication, whether story for one number or more, and all particulars of that sort, before I can really tackle the problem.

I expect to be able to remit money to you on Monday at latest, or Tuesday.

Yours ever in haste and some depression (for a good cause),

R. L. S.

2. "I have been thinking that some of your old Scotch stories might come in now for a magazine which is being started here, primarily to meet the falsehoods of the Liberation party, but also as a moderate-priced literary periodical for the Scotch Country Folk. I am a director of the company which starts it and which will be formed today. We shall pay about *Cornhill* prices, and I think Story may be editor. I wish you would think of this and let me know. Look at it not only from a pecuniary point, but from a patriotic one" (CB to RLS, 7 April 1885). Though called *The Scottish Church*, the magazine was not intended to be primarily a religious publication. It ceased to exist as a literary journal in December 1887; its editor, Robert Herbert Story, D.D., carried it on for a time as the *Scots Magazine*. RLS's only contributions were two poems printed in the April 1887 number, "A Lowden Sabbath Morn" and "Ille Terrarum" (reprinted in *Underwoods* later that year).

MS, Yale.

[Bournemouth, April 1885]

Dear Charles,

Could you oblige me with a cheque for £40? It will only be for a week, at the outside ten days. Here is the situation: I have about sixty pounds in the bank; a debt of some fifty that I ought to pay; my people are to pay me money to buy furniture in about a week; I shall get no more money of my own for 3 weeks or a month, depending on the promptitude of printers; and in the meanwhile must live. If you will make this advance, I am a skipper on the hilltops.

When are we to get into the dam house?

Yours excruciatingly,
THAMSON

MS (telegram), Yale.

Westbourne, Bournemouth, 21 April 1885

Been ill Shall write soon Perhaps today

MS, Yale.

FANNY STEVENSON TO CB

Skerryvore, Bournemouth [September 1885]

My dear Mr. Baxter,

A good deal of feeling has been occasioned by the disappearance of an individual known by several aliases, but passing in London under the name of William Ernest Henley. Any information as to his whereabouts will be most thankfully received by many anxious inquirers. Letters sent to your care have failed to elicit an answer. His friend—"pal" is I believe the vulgar word used between them —R. L. Stevenson is not so well as might be hoped, and seems to be in some anxiety as to the health and state of this William Ernest Henley, alias John Silver, alias etc., etc.

Imploring an immediate reply, believe me,

Yours sincerely,
F. VDEG. STEVENSON

MS, Yale.

FANNY STEVENSON TO CB

Skerryvore [September–October 1885] [3]

Dear Mr. Baxter,

Louis asks that you send what money you have of his. Day before yesterday he had another bad hemorrhage. This time it took place in the day. It was not so bad as the last, but sufficiently alarming. I am much depressed by the two coming so close together. The doctor actually tries to make me go away for a time as my nerves are altogether unstrung, but it would be much worse for me away. He wants me to go to Edinburgh for a couple of weeks, and says he will take care of Louis. I most certainly shall not. Anyone would be frightened—Sam was white as a sheet all that day, but I soon got over it. It is this appalling recurrence that upsets me. He is very cheerful now, though he was, for the first time, inclined to give up the fight, and thought of Davos. I hope England is not a fatal mistake. I could see nothing else to do with cholera yonder. Our love to all.

F. VdeG. S.

MS, Yale.

FANNY STEVENSON TO CB

Skerryvore, 8 December [1885]

Dear Mr. Baxter,

I return you Mr. Young's letter as you ask, but I am writing more particularly (and in great haste, as Valentin [4] is waiting to post my letter) to say that I wish *extremely,* as does Louis, that you would pay us a visit very soon. Not only should we be most delighted to get a sight of Mr. Johnson—Thompson—but there [are] a couple of matters of business that I think you should be consulted about, and that seem to me, at least one of them, of great importance. I think that Louis's father has been—what shall I say?—ill

3. "In the end of August Louis and Fanny go to Exeter for a little change and Louis has a bad illness there and cannot return home till Sept. 12th" (*Diary*, p. 344).

4. Valentine Roche, the French maid who served the Stevensons from Hyères to the end of the first South Seas voyage.

advised by his lawyer,[5] and—but it cannot be explained without meeting you. The point is that in a likely contingency I think you should appear as Louis's legal adviser.

Louis has written some Scotch verses that I think he will publish soon.[6] You will like them, I know. It is a kindly, homely dialect, heart-warm. Give our love to your wife, who hasn't seen us for so long that she must almost have forgotten who we are. Pray recall us to her memory; and *do* come. We want you for every selfish reason.

Most truly yours,
F. VdeG. STEVENSON

For how long a time is Mr. Young paid when he gets his fifty dollars? When was he paid last?

MS, Yale.

Skerryvore, Bournemouth, 14 February 1886

My dear Charles,

I have at last a moment to write to you; it is already my ninth letter this mortal day, and I have other two to write, so be lenient and try to be grateful.

First, business: I enclose 3 bills, which you might pay; £20 you might remit to me here; and I don't know, but I almost half think we might invest the hundred. I am afraid to do it; I know it will evoke sleeping bills, and I'll just have to sell again; and that indeed is why I have so long delayed. But if there is anything very good to do with a small sum like that, you might perpend and advise me.

So far so well. I am going, if you will allow me, to dedicate my next book to you. I think I ought to let you know because you are a damned professional man, and it might not suit your book. It's not indecent, nor irreligious: in fact it is a kind of a boy's story; and as far as it has gone, Henley and my wife and I all think well of it. What's mair, Sir, it's Scotch: no strong, for the sake o' they pork-puddens, but jist a kitchen o't, to leeven the wersh, sapless, fushion-

---

5. This is the first of a series of references to disputes over the settlement of Thomas Stevenson's share in the famous engineering firm. The only persons in Edinburgh who might be able to elucidate the affair are unwilling to discuss it.

6. *Underwoods*, Part II, In Scots, Chatto and Windus, 1887.

less, stotty, stytering South-Scotch they think sae muckle o'. Its name is *Kidnaaapped; or Memoyers of the Adventyers of David Balfour in the Year Seeventeen Hunner and Fifty Wan.* There's nae sculduddery aboot that, as ye can see for yoursel. And if you hae no objection, I would like very much to put your name to it.[7]

And now see here, I *long* to see "Brashiana." Do please send them to me. Remember I have never seen them but just a few at a time as I sent them, and I have a real homesickness for those children of my Muse. (Damn this hair! [8] Hurray! gone; why, now I am myself again.) Send me the copy, and I swear you shall have them again.

My wife is at Bath, and gives me good news of my father,[9] who is (she thinks) more hipped than hurt. She is not very well herself, but the change (by last accounts) had done some good. I have acidity beyond comprehension or belief: I am a bottle of vinegar with the heartburn; and my brain is a kind of chaste and spotless cotton wool. As I fear this letter well displays. Let me hear on all these my points. And believe me, my dear old man,

Yours affectionately,
ROBERT LOUIS STEVENSON

MS, Yale.

[Bournemouth, ca. 6 March 1886]

Dear Charles,

I know not what to say about that money (I had a dam dream that I had bust up); these Australian failures would rather shake the thing, wouldn't they?[1]

For God's sake, see about the boy's grave in Paris *at once;* I feel sure the concession runs near an end.[2] Believe me, the huntedest bugger in Christendie,

R. L. S.

7. "There is nothing in the world that could give me a greater pleasure than what you propose. I think it is a beautiful practice putting a friend's name on a book. It is like a handgrasp that lives forever. A book lives while we are dead, and it does seem something that the memory of a friendship which I think, my dear boy, has been singularly uncrossed by cloud should somewhere live embalmed in a kindly message from one to other" (CB to RLS, 16 February 1886).

8. In the pen-point.

9. Thomas Stevenson's mind was failing.

1. With reference to investments being managed by CB.

2. "To keep your mind easy about the concession I send you the paper. . . . The concession lasts for *15* years from 1876, so all is well" (CB to RLS, 8 March 1886).

Having been betrayed into a low expression, I will put a good many privates on the envelope.

MS, Yale.

[Bournemouth, 7 July 1886] [3]

Dear C. B.,

What has the account come to from the Clarks? [4] Suppose I came north, could you take in me and my wife for a couple of days? [5] Of course no foolishness or denners or the like. I have a leakage which nothing will stop apparently; so I cannot move yet awhile. But I am under orders to trip anchor when (and if) it does; and my heart is set on Kirkmichael of all places. Strathairdle [6] is an old flame of mine. What followed on the wars of the McGuinness's? [7]

Yours,

a dull dog,

R. L. S. [8]

  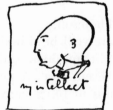

If I come, *tell no one.*

R. L. S. [9]

3. Postmark.

4. Cf. above, p. 157, n. 3.

5. "Your letter is like a rainbow in the sky. To be sure: my house is to be open all summer, and will be at your and your wife's service whenever you can come and for as long as you like. The secrecy of the grave shall rule over all" (CB to RLS, 8 July 1886).

6. Strath Ardle, Perthshire.

7. See above, Introduction, pp. ix ff.

8. The drawings were perhaps inspired by a portrait of RLS made at this time by the American artist, J. W. Alexander (see *Letters*, 2, 342).

9. Postscript on envelope.

MS, Yale. Letters, 2, *343.*

[Bournemouth, end of July 1886]

Dear Charles,

Doubtless if all goes well towards the 1st of August we shall be begging at your door. Thanks for a sight of the papers,[1] which I return (you see) at once, fearing further responsability. Glad you like Dauvit; but eh, man, yon's terrible strange conduc' o' thon man Rankeillor.[2] Ca' him a legal adviser! It would make a bonny law shoot, the Shaws case, and yon paper they signed I'm thinking wouldnae be muckle thought o' by Puggy Deas.

Yours ever,
R. L. S.

MS, Yale.

CB TO RLS

Some Dawmd Jile, a dinna ken the bluddy name o't,
but it's in Pawree! Pawree! falsely so ca'd,
30 September 1886

Ma deer Thōmson,

A'm share ye'll be thinkin a'm deed, but no, mair's the peety. Doon agen, man, doon again. A' flesh is girss an' the floor o' the feeld wuthereth awa'. A puir buddy hes na chancet noo 'a days, what wi polis an' bilies an ax o' pawrliment a' cuttin doon onest tho humble perfeshions. Well, man, eftir yon maist scawndawlus abortion (excuss a teknikawl alloosion) o' justis at Dumbarton (it wes nae mair me 'at did it sellin thame obschene cairds than oor grate and gude cheef Maister Gledstane himsel'), a mairchant in speshialities 'at 'a ken frae Pawris ses he to me ses he, "Man, Johnson, Pawris is the plaice for a man o' your stawmp. There's a' kin' o' thing intil Pawris—chantin'," ses he, "an' macaroni an' floor de rows an' a heap mair." Well, 'a thocht ontil it an' the lang an' the shōrt wis—to

---

1. "I send you, *but be sure to return them,* two documents for the fun of the thing: a copy of the 'Certification of the Behaviour of John McIntyre to Ardshiel and Alexr McNab' and Certificate of Ardshiell's death and buriall in France, 1757. I know your concern for these affairs will procure their safe return, as they are worth preserving" (CB to RLS, 22 July 1886).

2. See *Kidnapped*, chaps. 27 ff. The conduct of which Lord Deas would have disapproved was Rankeillor's and Alan Breck's in tricking Ebenezer Balfour into confessing his plot against David.

Pawris (Pawree the frōgies ca's it) 'a gangs. Weel, I dis gey an weel thare no' a bād plase ava' but kittle rale kittle, an' a hantle owre reddy wi' thair shootin' airons. But wi a bit practis at the savat, as they ca't, a handy bit dōdge a' maun alloo an' nōvel to *me* at leest, I warstled ōn, the Lōrd helpin as he aye dis thame 'at pits thare trust intil Hum. But gude kens I maun hae angered hum for it's come til an en' noo. I send you a paper wi' a accoont o' yin o' the *maist* blagyard pervarsins o' justis *'a*'ve seen in a' *ma* bōrn days. Dimbaurton wis bad eneugh, Gōd kens, but *here* wis *me,* Johnson, a 'onest scōtch man, afore a wheen o' the dawmdest frōgs I wadna demeen masel to ca' them frōgies 'at ever Gōd pit breeth in, a'snicherin an' lauchin an' kecklin an' that bluddy cōcky *Gōds dawm* it wis fair disgustin'. Man, a've aye been thinkin aboot ye an' the bōny days o' auld lang syne an' thae auld cōmunions on the green green hull side an' the blessed wurds o' sanctifeed grace at poored out o' Rev. Jōhn M'Cracken's lips sae often whan we wis bairns thegither. A aye think kind o' ye Thōmson, an' if a had a penny ye suld hae a bawbee ony time ye wis needfu. A'm awfu needfu enoo masel, man, an' wad thawnk ye kindly if ye wad send me fufty poonds to akoont o' the siller ye're ocht me. Ye'll mind on yon bit note o' han' for a hunner an' fufty. Ten Bawnk notes to Maister Murdux, Post ōfis, Pawree 'll fin' me share eneuch whan I get oot. Yer deer auld freen

JOHNSON

Thon's a' a dawmd lee aboot the fust, a dawmd bletherin perjired villin o' a dawmnd frog-eatin deevil o' a frogie. Gods Dawm.

MS, Yale.

[Bournemouth, 5 October 1886] [3]

Dear Charles,

The Alan Breck [4] has come and I am very proud of it. I am somewhat down just now—autumn, I think; and I hope soon to pull through. When are we going to see you?

Yours ever,
R. L. S.

3. Postmark.
4. Perhaps an acknowledgment, in the character of Alan Breck, of the dedication of *Kidnapped.*

MS, Yale.

Fanny Stevenson to CB

British Museum [November 1886] [5]

My dear Mr. Baxter,

Enclosed you will find the paper properly signed by Louis. He has been rather bad from that cold. As he went rapidly worse, Mr. Colvin yesterday telegraphed to Dr. Scott [6] of Bournemouth. Dr. Scott arrived last night, at nine; already his drugs have taken effect, and Louis is much better. If the improvement does not continue, he will come again on Saturday. He thought Louis very ill last night. Our first doctor, with a most touching faith, left everything to nature. Sam will be off in a fortnight to the West Indies. [7] Have you a rich uncle there, or anyone to whom you could give him a letter of introduction? I hear the two doctors coming at the same time, so with love to yourself and your wife, and to the Henleys who will be with you,

Believe me sincerely yours,

F. VdeG. Stevenson

MS (telegram), Yale.

Westbourne, Bournemouth, 22 December 1886

When do you come Stevenson

MS, Yale.

[Bournemouth, late 1886 or early 1887]

Dear Charles,

1st. Herewith a bargain.

2nd. Pray let me know whether there were plates of *Virginibus*

5. Dated by Colvin. "We go to Frankenloy on the 2nd Nov. having seen Louis in passing through London; he is ill at Mr. Colvin's and not able to return home" (*Diary*, p. 345).

6. Dr. Thomas Bodley Scott, RLS's physician at Bournemouth. See the dedication to *Underwoods*.

7. Lloyd was having trouble with his eyes and was planning the sea voyage in hopes of improving them.

Puerisque,[8] or only of the *Donkey* and *Inland Voyage:* this, if you can manage, by return of post, as much hangs upon it.

3rd. Will you agree to join the de Mattos trust? After all these years, at last Robertson has consented; [9] and I hope the same lapse of time has not changed your willingness. This would be a real service to me.

4th. I send a cheque from my father.

My life is one of no change, except rotten little variations of health, and that I am now able, and now unable, to work. A man who rarely passes the door can rarely have adventures. And to this hath that once wierd creature R.L.S. declined! When are you coming to see Skerryvore? I am,

Ever yours affectionately,
ROBERT LOUIS STEVENSON

MS, Yale.

[Bournemouth, April 1887]

Dear Baxter and Henley,

I dreamed I was with you in Edinburgh last night, and we discussed Rossetti—(why Rossetti?)—and I was wakened up by my own delight at my wit. Here is the witty remark, and damme, I think it worthy to be engraved on stone:

Henley, *je suis content de vous: vous
avez manqué de tact.—!!*

It is simply as great as the world!

Ever yours, both of you,
R. L. S.

Get and play the lovely "Rigaudon de Dardanus" by Rameau. It's de-lightful.

8. Reset and printed in 1887.
9. See above, p. 94.

MS, Yale.

Private and confidential

[Bournemouth, after 21 April 1887]

My dear Charles,

From the enclosed papers, I gather (1) that my cousin [10] is a very angry man and a very disagreeable correspondent, but (2) that the present state of the business is monstrous and must be arranged. Pray go to see Cheyne.[1] Niether my mother nor I approve of the state of the business, and we are willing to compromise, and anxious to improve Davie's position. I am quite willing myself to go I am sure as far as they would ask; I believe my mother is, too. She said, ere she left,[2] that she was willing to accept their proposal; but on this you must see herself. One thing you must tell Cheyne is that we have never understood the present contract till now. You go as from me for information: my mother has given me power to negotiate.[3] This whole business has made me really ill; I cannot compare all the papers: Davie's, for instance, I cannot reread. The statement of the history of the business is most misleading in all. But that doesn't change the fact of the present state.

R. L. S.

MS, Yale.

[Bournemouth, 29 April 1887]

My dear Charles,

Thank you for yours, the first decently supportable communication I have had in this matter. My idea is, first of all, to compromise; secondly, to compromise as fairly as we are able. I don't think my father should be worried, nor my mother, nor yet me; and I don't think we fight for anything important, as I think ill of my father's health. This gives you a free hand, I think; I will back up almost anything.

You misunderstand my attitude about Dick.[4] I have had worse suspicions of him than you have had, but I now think him, like other

10. David A. Stevenson, a member of the Stevenson engineering firm.
1. Probably Harry Cheyne (1845–1915), W. S. 1868.
2. Mr. and Mrs. Stevenson left Skerryvore for Edinburgh on the 21st.
3. The lower edge of the leaf is torn off. Two lines of writing may be missing.
4. James Dick, Thomas Stevenson's chief clerk.

folk, more essentially muddle-headed than anything else; if he acts partly in Brebner's [5] interest, I should not be surprised nor yet blame him. Brebner, on my father dropping out, is the stay of the business; there is no use blinking that, though we have little to do with it. It is D.A.'s lookout; and my love for D.A. is not at this present writing very eager. I am sorry I wrote to him as I did; I took more than my 24 hours, but temper would not quite blow off even then; I should have said nothing about myself. Since I have said what I did say, and since it is plain, I fear, that Mowbray [6] has tattled, you might I think find a chance to drop a hint to Cheyne of why the monstrous doctrine of my interest was broached. Not that it matters.

Your woodcuts are done and will go to you soon. I have been sorely tried with this affair: all these contentions are so damned ignoble; and I have a good lot on my mind too of which I cannot write, or not yet. It is a heavy season with me: a kind of garden of olives, in a small way; and I don't know quite whether I ought to be crucified,[7] which I suppose was one of Christ's troubles, nor yet whether I have the pluck to be, and that I suppose would be another. But I suppose (in the good old Scots phrase) I shall "get a clearness" at last; and meanwhile I am as cheery as possible, and not in bad health for me, and (to boot)

Yours ever affectionately,

R. L. S.

MS (telegram), Yale.

Westbourne, Bournemouth, 4 May 1887 [8]

If we come north this week can you take my wife and me in

STEVENSON

5. Probably Allan Brebner, B.Sc. (Engineering), Edinburgh, 1880.

6. John Thomson Mowbray (1808–92), W.S., Thomas Stevenson's business agent. He was the author of *An Analysis of the Conveyancing (Scotland) Act* (1874) and other legal works.

7. RLS, despondent and under the influence of Tolstoi, was seriously meditating martyrdom by going to Ireland to share the sufferings of a farm family named Curtin, who were being boycotted by the Land Leaguers. See Furnas, pp. 259 ff.

8. "On the 3rd of May he [Thomas Stevenson] is so ill that the doctors are anxious about him and I write to tell Louis who telegraphs to say that he is coming and he arrives on the 5th [*sic*]" (*Diary*, p. 346).

MS (telegram), Yale.

York, 6 May 1887

Arrive three thirty Can you meet us

LOUIS

*MS, Yale. Between May 1887 and May
1888 all but a few of the letters are
edged in black.*

[Edinburgh, after 13 May 1887] [9]

Dear C. B.,

The book found. My mother would much like to speak to you.
Could you look in this evening. I have come on traces of a deal
more money; so I hope all is right. I shall pack off the lot to Mowbray.

Yours ever,
R. L. S.

MS, Yale.

MRS. THOMAS STEVENSON TO CB

Skerryvore, Sunday 7 August [1887] [1]

My dear Mr. Baxter,

I arrived here last night and found Louis looking pretty well but
pale and thin; and today it is now 4 P.M. and he has never been
down stairs at all, so I fear he feels rather weak. I do trust that the
voyage may do him much good. All the Doctors agree that it is the
best thing for him.

9. Thomas Stevenson died on the 8th and was buried on the 13th of May.
1. "Louis has one cold after another and my brother advises him to go back to
Bournemouth, he also strongly advises him to try a complete change of climate for
a year and suggests either Colorado or one of the health resorts in India. They leave
on the 31st May and that was the last sight of Scotland that Louis ever had. After
consultation with Dr. Scott at Bournemouth Louis decided to try a complete change
of climate and fixed on America that Fanny might have an opportunity of seeing her
relations. Louis wished me to go with them. . . . I join them at 'Skerryvore' on the
5th [*sic*] of August and find Louis looking very delicate" (*Diary*, pp. 346–7).

Louis and Fanny are disappointed that you have never written to them about the very desirable tenants for the house that you mentioned to me. They would be very willing to give it at a cheaper rent to well recommended people. Has anything happened to make them change their minds? Louis wanted to write to you but he is too tired, so I offered to do it to save him trouble.

We are all anxious to hear how little Eddie is. I do hope that he has quite got over the attack and is in his usual again. We shall be glad if you can give us a line soon. We all unite in kindest regards to every one of you, and I am ever,

Yours most truly,
M. I. STEVENSON

MS, Yale.

Finsbury E.C., London [21 August] 188[7] ²

My dear Charles,

My foot is on the shore. The money sent is, if you please, to be put on deposit receipt—say £100 of it; the rest on current account for a cut and come again. Two quarters of Bob's allowance should be paid out of it this year; I am not very sure whether one is not already due. And at Christmass, please send £10 to Katharine for a Xmas present. Should Henley be in want of money, £30 (thirty pounds) are to be at his service at once at your judgement; and should there be any real press or any real benefit to be gained, again on your best opinion, £30 more: making in all £60. This makes more of course than what I had laid aside; but then you must lift the deposit receipt if ever necessary—or rather when necessary. I shall write today to Longman and Chatto to tell them your receipts will be sufficient for any money due to me.

With best love, and the kindest remembrances,

Ever, my dear Charles, your affectionate

R. L. S.

2. "On the 20th we all go to Armfield's South Place Hotel, Finsbury, which we find most comfortable. Louis says, 'This Hotel is just "Togers'"' where the Micawbers used to go.' A number of people came to say good-bye to us—Mr. James, Mr. Gosse, Mr. Archer, Mr. Henley—and Mr. Colvin stays Sunday night [the 21st] with us and sees us on board next day" (*Diary,* p. 347).

P.S. Will you inquire about my income tax? I have never received the assessment, and cannot make it out. Salisbury is the District Centre.

MS, Yale.

[Saranac Lake, New York, 20 October 1887] [3]

My dear Charles,

I see by your account (or think I see) that £30 went to Henley; but he has never said a word about it. Which way is it? Excuse this note: I am very busy and have a lot to write just now. I have upwards of £700 a year for 12 articles: [4] two of which I have already written. You see my mind is quite muddled.

Ever yours,

R. L. S.

MS, Yale. Letters, 3, 24.

[Saranac Lake, 18 November 1887] [5]

My dear Charles,

No likely I'm going to waste a sheet of paper.[6] It is all right about the £30: I only wanted to know; very likely some reference was made, but I had not remarked, or not received it, and I wanted to know. I am devilish glad it came handy: I fear he is having a bad time over the non-whiskey; well, it is a fine plucky business, and I am overjoyed. I would rather he had done this than a hundred pounds.

O, pay the income tax. I am proud to be so assessed. There is I believe no doubt about the money for the articles; but I have now calculated it so often that I have forgotten the original amount in dollars; but it is 25, or 30, or 35,000 dollars, and I believe the one

3. "A good many people recommend Saranac in the Adirondack Mountains where Dr. Trudeau, himself a consumptive patient, has started a sanitarium where much good has been done. . . . On the 29th [of Sept.] we hear that Fanny has taken a house at Saranac and we are to go at once" (*Diary*, pp. 350–1).

4. Commissioned by Edward L. Burlingame, the editor, for *Scribner's Magazine;* $3500 for the twelve articles, which came to include some of RLS's finest essays.

5. Postmark. Envelope marked "Private."

6. RLS had originally begun a letter to Scribner on this paper.

of these that comes nearest £700. Anyway it is first chop. I am offered £1600 ($8,000) for the American serial rights on my next story! [7] As you say, times are changed since the Lothian Road; well, the Lothian Road was grand fun too—I could take an afternoon of it, with great delight. But I'm awfü' grand, noo, and lāng may it last!

Remember me to any of the faithful—if there are any left. I wish I could have a crack with you.

Yours ever affectionately,
R. L. S.

I find I have forgotten more than I remembered of business. First, I just wish to remind you of Bob's allowance; it would be a beastly thing for him if it got late. Second, I wish you would look up my copy of the *Jekyll and Hyde* agreement; and if I have *reserved* the American rights, telegraph to me the word Reserved. But if, as I understand, they are not reserved, well, 'tis a beastly business, and you can let me know in course of post. Third, please let us know (if *you* know) for how much Skerryvore is let; you will here detect the female mind: I let it for what I could get, nor shall the possession of this knowledge (which I am happy to have forgot) increase the amount by so much as the shadow of a sixpenny piece; but my females are agog.

Yours ever,
R. L. S.

MS, Yale.

[Saranac Lake, 2 December 1887] [8]

My dear Charles,

This is a letter of the most disgusting nature.

Will you please send (as may be most convenient) four hundred and fifty (450) francs to Madame Vve. Chevillon, Gretz, par Nemours, Seine et Marne. It is on behalf of an historical character, Mrs. Osbourne; and that really disgusting person, O., pretended he had

7. *The Master of Ballantrae,* serialized in *Scribner's,* November 1888–October 1889.
8. Postmark.

paid it long ago [9] for the swaggerness' sake, and has led to this delay.

Also please send two pounds (£2) sterling to Messrs Willis and Trantum, Westbourne, Bournemouth. I write them by the same post explaining.

We have it jolly cold now and no mistake. Yesterday afternoon at 2:50, with a bright sun, the thermometer in the verandah stood at $+10°$; this morning it was at $-5°$. What it was during the night I know not.

We all keep better, after a kind of dwam.

Yours affectionately,

R. L. STEVENSON

Better put *"aubergiste"* on the letter to Mme C.

MS (cablegram), Yale.

Saranac Lake, 6 December 1887

Pay Henley Macaires [10]

STEVENSON

MS, Yale.

CB TO RLS

Edinburgh, 9 December 1887

My dear Louis,

I cannot tell you how welcome your last letter was. It smelt so of good health and spirits and was so like the olden times, and its news, especially pecuniary, were so good, that I felt inclined to go straight off and get drunk. I didn't, I'm sorry to say, for I know I ought to have done so, and I'm afraid you may be vexed at my want of feeling, but I think I did take an extra grog (or two) at night, so you won't mind, will you? I should not wonder you still feel much more really the Lothian Road roamer than anything else. Do you

9. The bill was for Fanny's board in 1877, when she was still Osbourne's wife.

10. Whatever royalties there were on *Macaire,* one of the unsuccessful dramas written jointly by RLS and Henley.

never look at your present self as a strange sort of middleaged person whose existence it is difficult to understand—and us so young, and just in from, or going out to, the "road." I don't believe it's really you or me that walks about now. The things have our names and a kind of mouldy likeness, but I know it's all a sham and that we really are only one-and-twenty and never will be anything else —till we trip over something that lands the mouldy likeness in the grave and perforce we must go in with it. Bad scran to it.

£1600! Well, well. I ought to nourish a secret grudge, I know, but I don't. I think I must be a very good person indeed. Find me another who in similar case never to himself hath said, "Dam the fellow! what right has *he* to get on like that?" No, clearly, I must be very, very good.

The *Pall Mall* of y'day describes your residence and prints your French menu, which amused me very much.[11] But it shows a danger: possibly some light-hearted *jeu d'esprit* might meet the same fate and astonish some of our friends!

I have never exercised the discretion you left me about the other £30 for Henley, not that it wouldn't have been acceptable, but there always comes a crisis now and then and I was reserving it for that. But it has occurred to me that it might be well invested in sending Henley to New York when the play gets there. If it made any hit, W.E. would be a lion, a lion would get work, and work would be paid, and there the lion might be able to stand on his own tail, and be happy for ever more. I think there's something in it. What do you say? Of [course] the lion *in posse* knows nothing of the second £30 and has not even the remotest suspicion of the possibility.

Now to business. I *wired* that *Jekyll and Hyde* was "not reserved"

11. The menu (*Pall Mall Gazette,* 8 December 1887) composed by RLS for the benefit of an overzealous lady reporter lodging at a neighboring sanitorium-hotel, reads:

Saranac Lake
Chateau Baker
Menu du 17 Novembre, 1887

Huitres au Batter	Sel
Fowl à la Barn-door	Poivre rouge
Pie à la Pie-crust	Vin rouge de Cantenac
Pain à l'Américaine	Eau de Fontaine de Saranac
	Visky Vierge

because I thought it better to settle the matter at once. Waiting a course of post when that involves weeks is always a worry.

I have arranged Bob's allowance thus: £10 on each of 15th May, 15 August, 15 November, and 15 February. The £20 you sent him I treated as for the first two terms, and then sent him £10 for Novr. a little in advance to stay the approach of a Tailor armed with a Solicitor.

Skerryvore is let till 22nd Feb. at the total sum of £109, 4. The tenant has the option of taking it on for another term on giving a month's notice. I think that's all you wanted to know, but I haven't your letter beside me just at present.

Continue to be well and happy, my dear Louis, none deserves it better. My love to all those that are with you, and believe me ever

Yours affectionately,

C. B.

Telegram *re Macaire* received and had attention.

Mitchell desires me to send the enclosed "work" of art.[1]

I just love *Memories and Portraits*. I think it beats everything yet.

MS, Yale. Letters, 3, 35.

[Saranac Lake, 12 December 1887] [2]

My dear Charles,

Will you please send £20 to Aunt Alan [3] for a Xmas gift from my mother. Moreover, I cannot remember what I told you to send to Katharine; but as God has dealt so providentially with me this year, I now propose to make it £20, too. They had better go separately, one from me, one from my mother. I beg of you also to consider my strange position: I joined a club, which it said it was to defend the Union; and I had a letter from the secretary, which his name I believe was Lord Warmingpan [4] (or words to that effect) to

1. "Body o the Lord" deleted.
2. Postmark. Envelope marked "Private."
3. Margaret Jones Stevenson, widow of RLS's uncle, Alan Stevenson, and mother of Bob Stevenson and Katharine de Mattos.
4. Actually John Horace Savile (1843–1916), Viscount Pollington; later (1899) Earl of Mexborough.

say I was elected, and had better pay up a certain sum of money, I
forget what. Now, I cannae verra weel draw a blank cheque and
send it to: Lord Warmingpan (or words to that effec'), London,
England. And man, if it was possible I would be dooms glad to be
out o' this bit scrapie. Mebbe the club was ca'd "the Union," but I
wouldnae like to sweir; and mebbe it was nae, or mebbe only words
to that effec'—but I wouldnae care just exac'ly about sweirin. Do
ye no think mebbe Henley, or Pōllick,[5] or sume o' they London
fellies micht mebbe perhaps find out for me? and just what the
soom was? and that you could aiblins pay for me? For I thocht I
was sae dam patriotic j'inin', and it would be a kind o' a come
doun to be turned oot again. Mebbe Lāng would ken, or mebbe
Rider Hāggyard:[6] they're kind o' union folks. But it's my belief
his name was Warmingpan, whatever.

> Yours,
> THOMSON
> alias Robert Louis Stevenson

Could it be Warminster?
Give us news of all your folk; a Merry Xmas from all ours.

MS, Yale.

[Saranac Lake, 25 December 1887][7]

My dear Charles,

This is Christmass his day and I drink your health and your
wife's, and your bairns's, with three times three.

Your letter came a few days ago, and many thanks for all your
answers; and truth and I think that I did pretty well with the
house!

But the object of this writing is altogether Xmassy. I want you to
lay out a matter of £5 for me on wine. Consult your wife: 'tis a
houseful of invalid ladies, very poor and very proud; Mrs. Baxter
may have riper views than I as to what is good for them. £5 on wine,
and (say) £2 on turtle soup and (if 'tis to be found) other invalid

---

5. Walter Herries Pollock (1850–1926), barrister and author. See above, p. 42 n. 2.
6. H. Rider Haggard (1856–1925), author of *She, King Solomon's Mines*, etc.
7. Postmark. Envelope marked "Private."

delicacies of that order. Act as for yourself; and, please, Mrs. Baxter, counsel the man, and don't let him send the materials for a spree but wh[at w]ill [8] do the ladies good; an[d,] it is still Mrs. Baxter I address, [if] you think my proportion of wine is [too g]reat, change it—I only make [it s]o great because it is so imper[isha]ble. And generally, when all [is d]one, and money laid out to the tune of £7 (seven pounds) exclusive of expenses, send the whole with such a nice letter as your Muse may inspire you with, or without a word if ye're sic a timber-treed dog as a' that comes to, to our staunch and excellent friend, Miss Adelaide Boodle,[9] Lostock, Westbourne, Bournemouth. I propose you should send a word, because I am so very anxious, if you or I should choose wrong, they might exchange again—of course at my loss. I write, telling her my views as to charging a house with extraneous and unwelcome goods; and I wish you to repeat the blow when they are sent, and beg a return, and offer an exchange, of what is no use to them.

Dear Charles, affectionately yours,

MS, Yale.

[Saranac Lake] 30 December 1887

My dear Charles,

I am more upset than I can well say by the collapse of the *Deacon Brodie* [1] business. I never built one farthing on it; but I cannot but fear that Henley did, and what to do for or about him is more than I can think. I think I shall telegraph you to let him have the coin, but I may not, because I think you would very likely do that anyway.

What adds to my discomfort is that I feel I have played a weak game with W. E. H. I have all along allowed him to sacrifice the plays to Teddy,[2] and I knew I was wrong, and I repent. My wife

8. Gaps made by excision of the signature.

9. Adelaide Boodle and her mother were the Stevensons' near neighbors, and most intimate friends, at Bournemouth. Numerous letters from RLS to Miss Boodle, whom he nicknamed "The Gamekeeper," have been published, and she recorded the friendship in *RLS and His Sine Qua Non,* New York, 1926.

1. *Deacon Brodie* had been acted with moderate success in Chicago, but its road tour was a failure.

2. Edward Henley, Henley's actor brother. A barroom brawl in Philadelphia had earned him some bad publicity.

writes me she saw Teddy in New York; he came seeking money, and was staying in a far more expensive hotel than we can afford, and had just sickened us all with his misconduct at Philadelphia. Since then he has been killed, I am bound to say I believe by a corrupt decision; but whether that decision would have been given or whether the papers would have let it pass had he not been so careful to make a public exhibit of himself some week before, that I very much doubt. It is no defence to the administration of justice in this dollar-ridden land, where if a man liked to stoop he may pick up literally what he pleases: I have myself had to refuse, unopened, an offer which I was told contained "more than I had ever dreamed," and that by a man who knew what prices I have had already.[3]

The point is: I have long groaned under this slavery to Teddy, a young man in whom I do not believe, and whom I much dislike. I have put up with it, as I put up with the whole [4] affair for W. E. H.'s sake; and I now bitterly blame myself. I find by W. E.'s letters how grossly Teddy has been deceiving him, for I have heard indeed different accounts of his success; and I see very plainly that this lad, besides making W. E. himself quite reckless of all other considerations, is bound to bring nothing but evil. I am pouring out upon you a sick heart. The first thing is to keep up W. E. H. against this disappointment. The next is that I must set my face against this whole Teddy business in the future, as I should have done frankly at first. He may be God Almighty's own individual and single man of genius, but by the splendour of the deity, he is not the man for me nor I for him; and O, to God, if W. E. had only never heard of him!

If you see a chance to blow cold on Teddy do so. He let out to my wife he has been letting W. E. support his wife even during this campaign; and the drunken whoreson bugger and bully living himself in the best hotels, and smashing inoffensive strangers in the bar! It is too sickening. The violence of this letter comes from my helplessness: all I try to do for W. E. (in the best way) by writing

---

3. Cf. the following entry in *Diary*, p. 359: "On April 2nd [1888] Mr. Bandmann, an Austrian actor who has brought out a new play of *Jekyll and Hyde*, comes all the way from New York to try to get Louis to accept some money from him, but as Louis has already authorised the other edition he does not see his way to do so."
4. Followed by an unidentifiable sketch.

these plays is burked by this inopportune lad. Can nothing be done? In the meanwhile I add another £20 to W. E.'s credit.

Yours ever affectionately,
ROBERT LOUIS STEVENSON

MS, Yale. Letters, *3, 45.*

[Saranac Lake, 2 January 1888] [5]

Dear Charles,

The £19, 14 was designed merely for my credit. You are the flower of Doers.

I hope my last about the Henley matter was clear to you for what it was: a screaming escape of steam by the safety valve. That that lad should hang round W. E.'s neck like a mill-stone—safety valve suddenly closed.

I have written W. E., mostly on indifferent matters; don't worry *him* about the safety valve.

Will my doer collaborate thus much in my new novel? In the year 1794 or 5, Mr. Ephraim Mackellar, A.M., late steward on the Durrisdeer estates, completed a set of memoranda (as long as a novel) with regard to the death of the (then) late Lord Durrisdeer and as to that of his attainted elder brother, usually called by the family courtesy title, the Master of Ballantrae. These he placed in the hands of John Macbrair, W.S., the family agent, on the understanding they were to be sealed until 1862, when a century would have elapsed since the affair in the wilderness (my lord's death). You succeeded Mr. Macbrair's firm; the Durrisdeers were extinct; and last year, in an old green box, you found these papers with Macbrair's indorsation. It is that indorsation of which I want a copy; you may remember, when you gave me the papers, I neglected to take that, and I am sure you are a man too careful of antiquities to have let it fall aside. I shall have a little introduction descriptive of my visit to Edinr.—arrival there, denner with yoursel', and first reading of the papers in your smoking room: all of which, of course, you well remember.[6]

Ever yours affectionately
R. L. S.

5. Postmark.
6. This proposed introduction to *The Master of Ballantrae* was not used after

Your name is my friend Mr. Johnstone Thomson, W.S.!!!

I still triumphantly support the whole family here on my American earnings alone! This is brave work, isnae't?

Enclosed the Peer's autograph, but I can't read it; and even he seems to have forgotten the name of the club!

The Lord Love You!

MS, Yale.

CB TO RLS

Edinburgh, 3 January 1888

Warmingpan! forsooth: a kin' o' swinler, if a'm no mistacken. He'll hae ca'it himsel Tōrington. See til the bit scrappie o' a paper 'at Henley sent tae me. So I ups and writes to Lōrd (sic a like Lōrd) Tōriton ceevil an' canty an' crouse an' freenly like this: "Man, Tōrieton, ye'll no mind me may be, but a kent ye weel at the schule; ye'll mind o' Eeton, I'm shūre" (ses I, no at I wes there exacly, but jist for a kin' o' introduckshun). "Weel, man, yon wes a gran time wi the boats an' the crucket ba' fawr be'er 'an the fute ba' div. Ye no think an' a mind yer deer mither cummin an' geein me a saxpence puir body an no ower mony between the baith o' us but noo wha sae gran's yersel! Ma certy [7] a secketary tae an' intil a Club nae less! Ye'll hawrdly ken yersel, but ye wes aye a clever chappie stick in til yer wark an ye'll get on, nae doot. Noo, ma bit mannie, jist tak a

---

all, but CB came through with the requested document: "Be it known to all to whom these presents shall come: I, John Macbrair, Writer to his Mātys Signet, in Edinburgh, hereby testify and declare that the within memorialls regarding the lamentable deaths of my Lord Durisdeer and his brother, the Master of Ballantrae (attainted in the Troubles) were placed in the custody and possession of me, as Doer for the said family, by myself and my predecessors for time immemoriall, by Mr. Ephraim Mackellar, A.M., sometime steward on their estates, the day and date hereof sealed on the back and foresides with the signets of the said Mr. Ephraim and myself, to remain in sure fence and keeping unopened for the space of one hundred years, full and complete, from the '62, in which the foresaid tragicall occurrences fell out; and thereto I bind myself and my executors and successors whomsoever upon my great oath, taking burden upon me for them. In witness whereof I have subscribit these presents (written by Andrew Johnstone, my servant, on one sheet of unstamped paper) at Edinburgh, along with the said Mr. Ephraim, before witnesses, the said Andrew Johnstone and Nicholas Clouston, Chairman, there, this   day of   1794. [Signatures]—Note. At this date diction was not more or hardly more archaic than now. The only variations were a few trifles in spelling. A 100 years before we might have had some fun" (CB to RLS, 23 January 1888).

7. **My word!**

keek in yer pass buke and see if there wes ane Stevison's gien in his name til the Club. Ye'll no ken him, he wesna at Eeton wi you and me na na far frae thāt, but still a decent buddie when sober, and maist parteeklar anxious to ken whatna Club he's pit his name tae. Nae doot he wad be a droppie the better at the time. Write shune and tell's and gie ma best luve to yer minnie [8] an yersel." Weel, Sir, the dawmed Swab's taen deil a bit o' notish and the mystery's still to be solvit, but he's no dune with Tamson yet. Peter's bāck's up, and a'll tear the secret frae the verra bottom o' his guts if a hae to swing for't.

Yon french deevil's answerit. Gey an cautious, puir bodie, she's waited till she "tooshéd" the siller afore writing. Sic like is a' frōg-ies. . . .

>   With all best wishes for the New Year to you all,
>   Ever yours affectionately,
>   C. B.

MS, Yale.

>   [Saranac Lake, 8 January 1888] [9]

Dear Chairles,

This being the Sawbbath day, I beg to request you to send £10 (ten pound sterling) to Dr. Barnardo his homes,[10] and believe me, Dear Chairles,

>   Ever sabbawtically yours,
>   ROBERT LOUIS STEVENSON

P.S. It might be sent in the name of "A Penny Novelist," and so continued annually, if my funds keep up.

MS, Yale.

>   Saranac Lake [21 February 1888] [1]

Dear Charles,

Enclosed signachers. I agree with all you propose in the matter of

---

8. Mother.

9. Postmark. Envelope marked "Private."

10. Thomas John Barnardo (1845-1905), who founded homes in which destitute children were educated and helped to migrate to the colonies.

1. Postmark.

the Scott letters.[2] And so they thocht naething o' ye in the Islands
and yere akchuated by the lowest envy again your auld Thōmson.
Damned! I haenae time and nae patience to correck your low
faults and vices, which grow upon [you] wi' your growth.

Yours afftely,

R. L. S.

MS, Yale.

Saranac Lake, Adirondacks, N.Y., U.S.A.,

25 February 1888

My dear Charles,

I am sorry to put you on a piece of business that will not I fear
be altogether pleasant. It is now Feb. 25th, and though I have
written to Mr. Mowbray and was then (I think about a month ago
—but do not bet on that) promised a speedy answer, my mother
and I know no more of how we stand or of what is doing than the
last day I spoke with you in Edinburgh. I do not like this way of
doing business—however like my own you may consider it; and I
cannot refrain from thinking that with a man so old and so negli-
gent as Mowbray, however sure I might be of his integrity, I should
require to make equally certain of his clerk's. Today, accordingly,
with my mother's full approval, I wrote a note to J.T.M., in which
by ingenious inattention to grammar I strove to veil my act of
insurrection, and of which I inclose you a copy. Please, therefore, on
receipt of this consider yourself empowered to beard the somnolent
lion, and by fair means or foul, and (as before) at any sacrifice of
my reputation whether for intelligence or good feeling, try to glean
for us some idea of where we are—and to see that we are all right.

I have been quite ill, but am now on the mend.

Yours ever affectionately,

ROBERT LOUIS STEVENSON

2. Perhaps a proposal to edit Sir Walter Scott's letters. If so, nothing came of it.
The letters were not edited until 1932.

[Enclosure] [3]

Saranac Lake, Adirondacks Mts, N.Y., U.S.A.,
26 February 1888

My dear Mr. Mowbray,

We are now so long without any definite news of how we stand in money affairs that I have thought it would spare you trouble to ask Charles Baxter to enquire and to become the medium of communication. I write to him to that effect by the same post, and I hope this will be found the simplest arrangement for all parties.

I have fair accounts to give of our party: my mother, who is about to go down to Boston for a day or two's change, has felt the cold a little, but seems now more acclimatized. As for myself, I detest but I believe I benefit by our incredible weather.

I trust you may be able to find something about my grandfather, my father, and my uncles: any old letters with the smallest tincture of familiarity that you may chance to have preserved I should like well to see and would willingly pay to have copied; and for any reminescences (as I wrote you before) I should be most grateful, if you could spare the time—but I know how difficult that is.

With kind regards, in which my mother heartily joins,

Believe me Yours very sincerely, R. L. STEVENSON

J. T. Mowbray Esq., W.S., 15 Northumberland Street, Edinburgh.

P.S. My mother begs me to say that we concur in whatever you shall think right as to the Castle Street and Blair Street houses.

R. L. S.

MS, Yale.

[Saranac Lake, 13 March 1888] [4]

Dear Charles,

Still I pour in floods of occupation on my doer. Fanny is always uneasy about the grave in St. Germain. It would be a good plan, it

3. A typed copy, presumably made by Lloyd Osbourne.
4. Postmark.

would be a kindness, to inquire; pray order a new cross at the same time.

Enclosed a letter for the archives, upon the terms of which pray be silent to *all*.

Ever yours,

R. L. S.

P.S. Also dunning letter from Pollington.[5] Since I have been committee-elected to the Athenaeum,[6] I burn to be out of it. If I can escape at once with honour and no loss of coins, let me do so; if not, let me escape with honour.

R. L. S.

MS, National Library of Scotland.
The first of the "Quarrel Letters,"
selections from which are printed in
Connell, pp. 113 ff.

HENLEY TO RLS

Private and Confidential

Merton Place, Chiswick W., 9 March 1888

Dear Boy,

If you will wash dishes, and haunt back-kitchens, in the lovely climate of the Eastern States, you must put up with the consequences. Very angry I was with you when I heard of it; and very glad I am to know that you've got off so cheaply. That attack of *The Newcomes* is a distressing symptom, it is true, but no doubt you'll get over it in time. But wash no more dishes meanwhile. 'Tis gay, 'tis romantic, 'tis Bohemian, 'tis even useful and cleanly; but it's too desperate a delight to be often yours.

5. See above, p. 180 n. 4.

6. "Rule II. Election by Committee.—It being essential to the maintenance of the Athenaeum, in conformity with the principles upon which it was originally founded, that the annual introduction of a certain number of persons of distinguished eminence in Science, Literature, or the Arts, or for Public Services, should be secured, a limited number of persons of such qualifications shall be elected by the Committee. The number so elected shall not exceed Nine in each year" (*Athenaeum. Rules and Regulations*, London, 1851, p. 7).

What a swell you are getting, to be sure! I shall address you in future as "R. L. S. Esq., M.A.," [7] or as "Dear M.A.," or as "Great, good, and just M.A.," or as "Illustrious M.A."—*enfin!* You have it, and you deserve it. Pollock [8] has it too, and doesn't deserve it. The difference is subtle, perhaps, but by an Intellectual M.A. it may, and doubtless will, be apprehended.

I am out of key today. The spring, Sir, is not what it used to be. It amuses, and distresses, me to hear your view of life. "Uncommonly like rot," is it? Have you only just begun to find that out, O Poet of "The Counterblast?" [9] These three years past I've been entertaining the idea, and it promises to master me. I've work in hand; I owe not more than a hundred pounds; I am beginning to make a reputation; my verse is printing [1] and promises well enough; other joys are in store, I believe; and I'd give the whole lot ten times over for—*enfin!* Life is uncommon like rot. *C'est convenu.* If it weren't that I am a sort of centre of strength for a number of feebler folk than myself, I think I'd be shut of it dam soon.

You will be bitterly disappointed in my *Dumas.* [2] I think I'll withdraw the dedication now. How am I to content you, wretch that you are? How, between two *Saturdays* and two *Art Journals,* [3] produce a decent piece of work of that sort? I should have three months clear for it at least; and I shall get only a day or so now and then.

I read *The Nixie* [4] with considerable amazement. It's Katharine's; surely it's Katharine's? The situation, the environment, the principal figure—*voyons!* There are even reminiscences of phrases and imagery, parallel incidents—*que sais-je?* It is all better focussed, no doubt, but I think it has lost as much (at least) as it has gained; and why there wasn't a double signature is what I've not been able to understand.

7. Since at least one biographer has missed the point, it should be noted that "M.A." means "Member of the Athenaeum," not "Master of Arts."
8. See above, p. 181.
9. See *Poems,* p. 158.
1. *A Book of Verses* (1888).
2. Henley had written an essay on Dumas, *Saturday Review,* 56 (1883), 594, which he later revised for inclusion in his *Views and Reviews* (1890); but he published no book on the subject.
3. Henley had given up the editorship of the *Magazine of Art* in 1886 but was advisory editor to the *Art Journal* and was reviewing regularly for the *Saturday.*
4. Fanny Stevenson's story, published in *Scribner's* in the March number.

Still no news of the *Deacon!* [5] The young man [6] is about the coolest hand ever dealt, I think. There's one thing pleasant to reflect about, however, and that is that, as you say, if the play has failed in N.Y., there's an end of it. I wish I knew. Better aff as aye waggin', ye ken! And it has been waggin' ower lang.

Louis, dear lad, I am dam tired. The Châtelaine's [7] away. The spring is spring no more. I am thirty-nine this year. I am dam, dam tired. What I want is the wings of a dove—a soiled dove even!—that I might flee away and be at rest.

Don't show this to *anybody,* and when you write, don't do more than note it in a general way, if at all. By the time you *do* write, you will have forgot all about it, no doubt. But if you haven't, deal vaguely with my malady. I wish you were nearer. Why the devil do you go and bury yourself in that bloody country of dollars and spew? And you don't even get better! *C'est trop raide.* And you are 4000 miles from your friends! *C'est vraiment trop fort.* However, I suppose you must be forgiven, for you have loved me much. Let us go on so till the end. You and I and Charles—D'A, and Porthos, and *le nommé* Aramis! 'Twas a blessed hour for all of us, that day 13 years syne, when old Stephen [8] brought you into my back kitchen, wasn't it? *Enfin—!* We have lived, we have loved, we have suffered; and the end is the best of all. Life is uncommon like rot; but it has been uncommon like something else, and that it will be so again—once again, dear!—is certain. Forgive this babble, and take care of yourself, and *burn this letter.*

Your friend,
W. E. H.

MS, National Library of Scotland.

RLS to Henley

[Saranac Lake, March 1888]

My dear Henley,

I write with indescribable difficulty, and if not with perfect temper, you are to remember how very rarely a husband is expected

5. See above, pp. 61 and 191.
6. Henley's brother Teddy.
7. Anna Boyle Henley, Henley's wife.
8. Leslie Stephen. See RLS to Mrs. Sitwell, February 1875: *Letters, 1,* 209.

to receive such accusations against his wife. I can only direct you to apply to Katharine and ask her to remind you of that part of the business which took place in your presence and which you seem to have forgotten. She will doubtless add other particulars which perhaps you may not have heard—such as that she refused to collaborate on my wife's version of the tale, and when she agreed it was to be written, asked that a copy might be sent her; she will also, I have no doubt, lend you the copy of her original story, from which you will be reminded how the matter stands.

I am sorry I must ask you to take these steps; I might take them for myself had you not tied my hands by the strange step of marking your letter "private and confidential." An accusation of this gravity, you must suffer me to say, should not have been made without leaving me free to communicate with Katharine. I wish I could stop here. I cannot. When you have refreshed your mind as to the facts, you will, I know, withdraw what you have said to me; but I must go further and remind you, if you have spoken of this to others, a proper explanation and retractation of what you shall have said or implied to any person so addressed will be necessary.

From the bottom of my soul I believe what you wrote to have been merely reckless words written in forgetfulness and with no clear appreciation of their meaning, but it is hard to think that anyone—and least of all my friend—should have been so careless of dealing agony. To have inflicted more distress than you have done would have been difficult. This is the sixth or seventh attempt I make to write to you, and I will now only add that I count upon your immediately applying to Katharine for the facts, and await your answer with the most painful expectation.

You will pardon me if I can find no form of signature; I pray God such a blank will not be of long endurance.

ROBERT LOUIS STEVENSON

MS, National Library of Scotland.

[Saranac Lake, 23 March 1888] [1]

My dear Charles,

I am going to write what I should not, and shall probably not,

1. Postmark. Envelope marked "Private."

send; but in the melancholy that falls upon me, I must break out at least upon paper. I fear I have come to an end with Henley. The lord knows if I have not tried hard to be a friend to him, the lord knows even that I have not altogether failed. There is not one of that crew that I have not helped in every kind of strait—with money, with service, and that I was not willing to have risked my life for; and yet the years come, and every year there is a fresh outburst against me and mine. If the troubles that have been brewed for me in Shepherd's Bush [2] had been taken out of my last years, they would have been a different season. And I have forgiven and forgiven, and forgotten and forgotten; and still they get their heads together and there springs up a fresh enmity or a fresh accusation. Why, I leave to them—and above all to Henley—to explain. I never failed one of them. But when they get together round the bowl, they brew for themselves hot heads and ugly feelings.

But then, as I say, I have known and suffered under [them?] long. I knew long ago how Henley tried to make trouble for me, and I not only held my peace, when I had the evidence, I willingly forgave also; for I understand all his nature, and much of it I love. And I would have gone on forgiving, too, or so I think, ad libitum; but unless this business comes to a termination I dare scarcely hope, it is what I cannot pass over; even as it is, the best reconciliation to be hoped will be largely formal. If this letter go, which I much question, and I am sure it had better not, I shall put you in no false position by calling it private; I shall only ask you to judge, and to be wiser in what you do with it than I am in writing it. It is hard for me to recognize my old friends falling away from me; whatever my defects I do not think they have changed; but I daresay I deceive myself and I have indeed altered for the worst. If I have not, some singular feeling springs spontaneously in the bosom of those whom I love. For God's sake don't let us . . . But hush upon that.

You will tell me this is another case of the tact of the elephant. I know it is or hope it is, but the tact of that animal applied to one's wife is a little difficult to stand.[3]

So much I must say, in case I send this. It stands on an accusation brought against my wife of a description to cut both of us to the

2. The suburb where Henley lived during most of his London days. Katharine de Mattos was one of the group to which RLS refers.

3. Deletion: "It is not [three or four words illegible] to forgive as time passes."

soul, couched—well that is nothing, and sent to me in a letter marked "private and confidential," with directions it was to be communicated to no one and immediately burned. The baseness of this special form of the anonymous letter, I feel sure he was unaware of, though I remember him branding the same conduct in another person—Gosse. Of course, it is not a thing to be respected; yet I have so far respected it that I have written to him, instead of to the principal, in the first place. I also still refrain from dwelling on the nature of the charge (it cuts especially deep as he had means of knowing exactly how it stood) until he shall have a chance of doing what he ought. But this much I do wish to say: to get an acknowledgement of the way in which the facts really are is my first purpose. And whatever you do, pray do nothing that may compromise my hope of getting this. You see why I do not mark this letter private; yet if you decide you should communicate any idea of its nature to Henley, pray at least consider this great need of our position.

I can't say it is anger that I feel, but it is despair. My last reconciliation with Henley is not yet a year old, and here is the devil again. I am weary of it all—weary, weary, weary. And this letter was (so the writer said) intended to cheer me on a sick-bed! May God deliver me from such consolations. I slept but once last night, and then woke in an agony, dreaming I was quarrelling with you; the miserable cold day was creeping in, and I remembered you were the last of my old friends with whom I could say I was still on the old terms. Dear Charles, either you are a very magnanimous fellow, or the others have not been very [4]—*coetera desunt.*

Since when I have dined and continue scribbling, and will say for myself that I am a stout friend and eager to help anyone. It seems to me that little feverish crowd expect too much from me and are (some of them) willing to repay too little—not that I have ever to my knowledge asked from them anything but some little attention to my feelings. I see that in the revulsion produced by this "private and confidential" of Henley's, and my fear of placing you in any false position to him, I shall have possibly deceived you as to my attitude and wish. I would infinitely prefer you should remain outside of this entirely: the last thing I desire for your sake,

4. "careful of" deleted.

for his, and for mine is that you should appear to know of it; and in the frame of mind in which I find myself, I have but one clear thought: the desire of wresting an acknowledgement of how the facts stand, and can offer—can certainly promise—no reconciliation. It will probably come to a smash; and I shall have to get you to give the poor creature an allowance, pretending that it comes from Hamilton Bruce [5] or—anybody but me. Desert him I could not—my life is all bound about these thorns; but whether I can continue to go on cutting my hands and my wife's hands is quite another question. I think, and I think, and when I recal all, although I see myself in a thousand ways unwise and (as my way is) sometimes harsh and often foolish with my mouth, I do seem to see a record of a not ungenerous friendship upon my side. The tale of the plays, which I have gone on writing without hope because I thought they kept him up, is of itself something; and I can say he never knew—and never shall know—that I thought those days and months a sacrifice. On the other side, there have been—I think there still are—some warm feelings; they have never been warm enough to make him close his mouth, even when he knew he could hurt me sorely, even to the friends whom he knew I prized: to you, I know not; to others, I do know, and have long buried the knowledge. I know the man; I loved him; I have shown it—even in the hardest trial, when I risked his anger on the drink business. I have not changed my thoughts of him, not even, I believe, my heart. Last winter, my illness was largely the work of his persistent unkindness. I thought it was over; it begins again in this staggering attack; and the bottom of my thoughts is, that we shall be better apart. The old intimacy is impossible, on the old terms.[6] I see not the call I have to pursue a friendship that is so fruitful of the cruellest pains to me, and that risks, if it has not already lost me, other friends.

I should be unjust to you if I did not say hastily and plainly and with the profoundest honesty that to you I believe he is a sincere friend: I never heard him speak of you except in terms of love. God forbid that my weak need to pour out my distresses should in

5. Robert T. Hamilton Bruce (1846–99), whose wealth derived from a chain of bakeries in Glasgow. He was a principal backer of the *Scots Observer* and the dedicatee of Henley's *Invictus*.

6. Deletion: "for if I could regain confidence [one or two words illegible]."

any way cloud the friendship of you two—remain [?] happy! But to me—whether by my own fault, or through some not quite un-natural jealousy, or from the influence of lesser persons—he has been of late so miserably changed that I have had little but bitter-ness from our acquaintance, and indeed I think I should rather call it our estrangement. About what it began I never knew. He assured me last spring it was through no fault of mine but because of mat-ters personal to himself, and I was so impressed by the depth and recentness of the estrangement that I was far from inviting further confidence. He so assured me, right or wrong, and for the first time, after more than a year, I had a day or so of genuine pleasure. It has not lasted long, this reconciliation. If the first quarrel (of which I never understood one word) was not my fault, God knows I think this one is not. But what exasperates me in this clique is that they foment these things in my absence. Since I left (I would not say it to them—I may to you) I think not one of them has had anything but money from me; and here again they have sprung up one of their little bitter cabals in my absence and my silence. It is a process essentially weariful, and I perceive no possible end to it but a judicious distance—no longer in space, which avails me noth-ing, but in heart, which will at least save me further lacerations. If I give the business up for a bad job and stand apart, I fear it is but a little I shall lose, and what I shall gain in peace I cannot estimate.

So far (sometimes I own in rising moments of irritation, on the whole in a miserable soberness) I have written. Whether to send or not, who knows? After this you are the last of my old friends to whom I dare pour forth a feeling. God! can it be my blame? Two of them have married wives who love me not: [7] there I may a little stand excused; and for Henley—well, a man is no judge in his own quarrel, yet I am strongly in error or I am on the whole on the right side of that account. It is damned hard not to weep, my boy, at this back-look; but I have better to do, and must be calm for others. I believe a little quite unconscious jealousy and the influence of a person who shall be nameless explains all. To you, I do devoutly be-lieve, he will be the old affectionate, fine, big heart of a fellow whom we have both loved. As for me—I despair. Thank you for

7. One of the wives was Lady Simpson; the other may have been Louisa Pyrland, whom Bob Stevenson had married in 1881.

paying Clark.[1] Traquair [2] will not call; the thing had been previously mismanaged.

Yours ever,

R. L. S.

P.S. I may deceive you on one point: with Colvin I have never had a cloud; it is *ad hoc* that I cannot write to him. I dare not complain to him of Henley, for I do not think—I am sure he does not really like the man. You, who do, whatever you may think of me or of his conduct, can make the due allowances; and my complaint will not injure Henley—for lord! we both know him!

And on another: I have used the phrase "principal." In case Henley should communicate with you and name names, do not be led to suppose that I think "the principal" [3] was aware of the affair. That would be to me an inconceivable meanness.

R. L. S.

Well, I send it. Take it for what it is: a very desolate cry!

MS, National Library of Scotland.

[Saranac Lake, 24 March 1888] [4]

My dear Charles,

I enclose a document for the archives; I sent you a wrong one the other day, but have not fished out the right. I sent you today a long wail, on which it occurs to me to add that in re-reading it I observed a lie. I said my ill-health of last winter was due to Henley: well, that was surely not so; but many a bitter hour, and a heaviness in my view of life, which I have not yet got rid of, came from that inexplicable estrangement. Also, there was a point I am not very sure if I succeeded in making clear, though it is of no real importance: I mean the reason why I must keep all this from Colvin. Because if Colvin knew, he would probably have no more to

1. See above, p. 157.
2. Ramsay Traquair, who was married to one of the sisters of RLS's mother. He had a son, William (the "Willie" of *A Child's Garden*), and a daughter, Henrietta Traquair Milne.
3. Katharine de Mattos.
4. Postmark. Envelope marked "Private."

do with Henley, and that is the last thing I wish. I have wondered
so much at people quarreling: I have always said, "Let 'em do what
they like, *I* won't quarrel"; and here I find myself considering the
worst.

By this time, I suppose you will have seen Mowbray [5] and found
out that he is (as he wrote me) more than willing to give up. I was
glad I had written, and written as I did.

I confess I am glad I wrote you yesterday, and even glad I sent the
letter. It has been a huge relief to me; and if it has been pain to you,
you must try to forgive me. Well, God bless us all—and Henley in
the front rank, though I think I will let Him bless him during my
discreet absence—for the future; and believe me, I feel shame to
write "yours affectionately" to you: it was so I used to sign to
Henley, and the dreadful part of a thing like this is that it shakes
your confidence in all affection and inspires you with a strange,
sick longing to creep back into yourself and care for no one. For
all that, I do care for you; and I do care for Henley too, and all his
fine spirit and courage and geniality and loyalty—though to me,
of these late days, he has not been loyal—and his rich temperament
which was a fund of pleasure to me, and all of which are now only
subjects of regret.

Yours affectionately,
ROBERT LOUIS STEVENSON

MS, National Library of Scotland.

MRS. THOMAS STEVENSON TO CB

[Saranac Lake, end of March 1888]

P.S.[6] I must add a line just to tell you that Louis keeps wonderfully well in spite of changes of temperature varying from 8° below
zero to 70° above within a week. One day was like summer with
dry pure air in spite of rivers of melting snow all around us—how
different from an Edinr. thaw! Louis had two walks and a drive that
day and was not too tired. Fanny started off on her journey to
California all alone last Monday,[7] and we have heard that she has
reached Chicago in safety. We all mean to leave this place in a

5. See above, p. 173.
6. RLS's letter, to which this is a postscript, is not recovered.
7. I.e. 26 March (*Diary*, p. 359).

fortnight or 3 weeks—we go first to New York, and our further movements are still shrouded in uncertainty. Lloyd and Louis are engaged to write a story [8] for the *New York Ledger,* a sort of American *London Journal* of a highly moral order. The proprietor [9] is a very wealthy man, who wishes to raise the literary tone. I hope Gracie and the little boys are all getting well through the spring weather and that your father is enjoying his dinner parties as usual. Tell him with my kindest regards that I valued his delightful letter very much and thought it was most kind of him to answer mine so promptly. I wonder where Jane and he will go this summer. We often long for a sight of you all.

M. I. S.

MS, National Library of Scotland.

RLS TO HENLEY

New York [end of March 1888]

My dear Henley,

I have received a communication from you per Huish.[1] I am sorry you took so strong a step, and that you cannot write to me yourself upon a point of business. However I must answer to yourself, as my answer involves a little blame. You have never sent me the names of those photographs.[2] I do not know what they represent, and I wish you would see to have this remedied. I am much behind with my work now, having been thrown out of gear; but if all goes as I hope, and the information comes, I should be able to tackle the matter early in July, which I hope will do.

I will say no more on my other matter; indeed I now somewhat regret my last; for if you feel so much disinclined to write, it is perhaps better for you to let it alone. On all this, judge for the best; and believe me—still and always, if I never saw your face again—

Yours affectionately,

ROBERT LOUIS STEVENSON

8. *The Wrong Box.*

9. Robert Bonner (1824–99), who had been introduced to RLS at Saranac on the 19th by S. S. McClure (*Diary,* p. 359). "To the public he sold the *Ledger* as cheaply as possible, three dollars a year, but to authors—he had a mania for 'big names'— he paid startling sums" (*Dictionary of American Biography*).

1. Marcus Bourne Huish (*d.* 1921), editor of the *Art Journal,* 1881–93.

2. RLS was to have written an article on the sculpture of Auguste Rodin.

MS, National Library of Scotland.

[Saranac Lake, 5 April 1888] [3]

My dear Charles,

I enclose a letter which I suppose to be (and have answered on that hypothesis) from one who once had the initials W.C.M.[4] It is touching.

Since I wrote you, I have been utterly miserable. A letter has come from Katharine, which shows the case (I fear) to be worse than ever. *Facts of the case:* Katharine made a story in which a person met a girl escaped from a lunatic asylum in a railway train. My wife proposed and offered her the idea of the girl being a Nixie. Katharine preferred her own, wrote it, tried it in all the magazines, was everywhere refused, and then wrote and told my wife she might go ahead with her Nixie, even asking (if it appeared) that a copy might be sent for. To my eyes I can conceive nothing simpler or more straightforward than the whole matter.

However, my wife's story does appear and has considerable success, Katharine's having been everywhere refused; and this wakes up (I suppose) the little devil of envy. Henley writes to me (as I told you) under seal of the strictest secrecy to say my wife's story is Katharine's, and that he is amazed her name does not appear. Now the original proposal of the Nixie by my wife took place in Henley's presence; therefore he knew better than he said. But it is possible—and I now fear it is probable—he does not know all the steps, and has indeed only been a hand gun for Katharine, who (as you doubtless know) has a great power in that quarter. For SHE now writes (and it is so that I consider I have now a right to mention the ground of the dispute) that she was totally unprepared to see *The Nixie* appear. Till I hear more I shall make no qualification; it looks like real treachery. Both she and Henley refer to this in the lightest manner, sandwiched among professions of kindness; and I need not remark how very small a degree of kindness it had required—supposing we were in the wrong—to have said nothing of so small a matter, nor how very little an amount of tact would have enabled them to understand how much pain they would give. But Henley at least knew pretty well, when he directed his letter to

3. Postmark.
4. Probably W. C. Murray. Cf. *Letters, 3,* 299.

be kept secret; there was nothing else in his communication that, by any contortion of sense, could have been private: [5] it was all protestations of friendship and news about his volume of poems. Now that I suspect there was a petticoat behind, Henley's conduct is more explicable, but the hope of any good result is much less. For if Katharine wishes, she can keep him to any mark.

I feel this business with a keenness that I cannot describe. I get on during the day well enough, only that whenever I think of it, I have palpitations. But at night! sleep is quite out of the question, and I have been obliged to take to opiates. God knows I would rather have died than have this happen.

I am going to write of it no more; if I get a satisfactory answer— how can it be one?—good and well. If not, I will simply communicate no more with either, and we must make some arrangement about an allowance to Henley. I cannot let the old boy go quite from me. It is well however that I cannot meet him just now: my sense of the unprovoked and mean nature of these insinuations is too strong. And it is just a year since the reconciliation, when I forgave him all—God knows how gladly and wholly—and felt a boy again to be reconciled to my old friend.

Pray pardon my pouring out to you. As I have said already, you are the only one to whom I can unbosom. Henley has his little crowd of swelterers, I fear. Alas! alas!

Events keep me quite apart from Simpson; of all my friends you and Colvin are the only ones that remain.

I believe I never explained to you why Traquair did not call: he was never instructed; it all came too late; and the poor soul was sold up—although I took steps by return of post.

Ever yours affectionately,

ROBERT LOUIS STEVENSON

I still do not mark this private, feeling as if I never dared do such a thing again; but I have disembosomed to you freely, and, above all, what is only suspicion you must conceive to be in confidence.

5. The "Private and Confidential" *may* have been written without thought of the passage about Fanny, since other parts of the letter are highly personal.

CB to RLS

Edinburgh, 5 April 1888

My dear Louis,

You will believe that your long letter of the 23d has distressed me very much. I can't bear to think of any estrangement coming between you and Henley, especially knowing as I do the profound affection and admiration he has for you, and how bitterly he felt before what he supposed was a diminution of your regard for him. For your position and feelings, my dearest friend, I must say I have the warmest sympathy. You have devoted more than a brother's love to the whole family; you have lavished freely upon them everything you had to give. And now when something like thanklessness and forgetfulness manifests itself, it is hard to bear. But that is only an element, as I understand it, in the present crisis. Of course I don't know what Henley has been writing to you, but that it was wilfully done to hurt you and your wife I cannot believe. If it were possible, then I too would feel I had lost a friend. No, it cannot be. You know well how I appreciate Henley's infinite capacity for blundering in matters of taste and discretion. It cannot surely be more than that? To take the heart from Henley would be to leave him very different from the man you and I have known and loved. It surely cannot be.

The fact is that these cursed plays have been at the bottom of all the mischief. I have never heard a grumble from Henley with regard to you except in that connection. He relied hopefully on them for money, and thought you little interested in them, and blamed you accordingly; but beyond that no word of adverse comment ever passed his lips to me. There is, I fancy, as you say, in his communications with you (for I'm sure no such thing appears in his talk or letters to others) a certain amount of jealousy. You have earned great success and fame and money, while he remains not only hard up but hampered by the misdeeds of the wretched Teddy. It's not unnatural. Poverty *is* a hard thing, but I think that I have noticed that it is a dangerous thing for a rich man as you now are, or seem to him, to give money; and I'm afraid that the recent gifts, which it gave you so much pleasure to suggest, and me to carry out, may have carried a certain gall with them. It seems to me a strange thing, but perhaps there is in human nature a mean place, which even unknown to one's self suggests a bitter contrast between success and failure, which the presence of pecuniary help emphasizes. Anyway, let him try his own feet; when his back is to the wall, as it will be, we must and will do something, and then the relief will come without *arrière pensée*.

Let us make allowances. Let us remember that the same stock which produced the worthless Ted, in whom he believed so long as the saviour of the family, produced him, and let us be thankful that the traits are so much modified. Let us remember the early associations, the early training and companionship,[6] that we may cease to wonder at the elephantine tact, by which euphuism [*sic*] one is compelled to admit one means occasional lapses from the feelings and conduct of a gentleman. My dear Louis, take *everything* into account, but don't let anything rankle till it leads to a split between two men who should be bound by every tie together that can unite human hearts. It is almost enough to make one weep to think that the last letter I had from him contained the proof of an Envoy addressed to me in his new *Book of Verses* which celebrated our ancient friendship (of the three) and aspired after a life-long continuance of it. You *must* see that you would break the man's heart if you split with him. He loves you, snarls at you, envies you—if you were his wife he'd beat you; but he cannot get on without you. And you must not kill him. Remember the great disadvantage of correspondence: how tones, looks, touches modify the words, while on paper you have nothing but the hard nib of a steel pen. Remember *everything*, Louis my friend, and forget, forget only to think of parting with one who would, I verily believe, give his life in your service. The family are bad influences for him. As you say, they Squat around the Bowl and inflame themselves till you seem to have done something awful, and then bang goes a letter. To you it must be unspeakably irritating, but to them and him it is only an escape valve, the steam is over, and he probably hobbles to the piano and thumps it with a smiling face as the notes recall some long gone antics, in which you play the leading part. I can see him as he sits there with nothing but love in his heart for you, and never dreaming for an instant that he has by some foolish complaint or quarrel been stinging you to the quick in the cold Adirondacs.

6. About eight words deleted.

No, no, it is not you who have changed, or if changed you are so for the better. And the assurance of your lasting feelings for me makes me doubly sure that if fault there be between you and Henley, it is not on your side. And here I must tell you—I think it will plead for him with you—that some years ago I used to dread that I was losing you, that our friendship must be a happy memory—one, true, that could never die, but which must for ever live in the past. You seemed so far removed, so many famous men and women courted you, so many new interests were ever opening for you that I felt sadly that I must be growing dim and shadowy indeed. I know now that I was morbid about it all. I know now how the days of your youth and the friends that were its companions never lose their interest for you. I know the steadfast love, which has seemed to me like that of a woman, but for a time I doubted and was sad. Then it was that Henley battled bravely: it was he who swore to me by all his gods that I was wrong, that you were as true as ever, that on your part there was no slackening of the bonds; and after many months I began to hope again. There is no shadow of doubt with me now. I believe I have in you a friend whose heart will beat true to mine till it ceases to beat at all, and if I know myself, I repay your affection with all that my nature holds. So you see that Henley has a claim. He maintained that I was nearer you than he was. How easy it would have been to cast a doubt! Here there was no jealousy at least. No meanness—only the loving resolve that nothing should come between you and me.

Think of everything: how much he owes you (there is pathos in that for *us*), how helpless he is, how brave and good he has been, how he has struggled and fought the world with disadvantages which most men would have fallen under; and once more let the old friendship creep in and the poor faults and smallnesses be forgotten. If you can only do this, it will be a happy day for me. I am hurrying home, so pray accept my love to your wife and yourself, and believe me always

Yours affectionately,

C. B.

You were right to write. These things *must* be gotten off one's mind.

MS, National Library of Scotland.

[Saranac Lake, 10 April 1888] [7]

My dear Charles,

I know you will curse the sight of my hand, but you are to consider I have no one else to pour out my troubles to in the world. And this affair hag-rides me. How I wish I had died at Hyères, while all was well with me! but now troubles thicken, and griefs.

I lay last night counting up my sins against these friends of mine, and I found some of them heavy enough, and my mouth was closed. But in the course of these self-depreciations, my mind started another hare, which vexes me. Last winter I was disagreeably affected to remember that a number of works in my own hand were in Henley's possession, that he might die any day, and these highly unprofitable exercises [8] might fall in the hands of his brothers. Therefore I wrote to Henley (it was in the worst of our estrangement) asking him to destroy them, and explaining it was partly in Lloyd's interest. I am sorry to say he paid no regard to my request. So much he confessed to me when we were reconciled; and as I was bent on reconciliation, I allowed myself no commentary on his conduct, only repeated the request. And now it came in upon me last night that he may just as well have disregarded my second request. And here I am quite stranded. I could never approach him now on the matter, and yet these foolish things are a thorn in my side. It has occurred to me that when next you meet Henley, you might be able to find out if they are destroyed; and if they are not, see that they are. I care damned little for what's left of my life (unless I could get to sea) but I do not want any who still value me to be pained when I am gone.

Unless I could get to sea! Ah, folk can't write letters to you there! And maybe I'll manage it yet; but it's the money that sticks us.

Talking of money, Teddy, his first communication to me since he has been here, wrote and asked me to support his company for six weeks! I offered in return to pay his and Grace's [9] passage back

7. Postmark. Envelope marked "Private."
8. The "Sculduddry Sangs" mentioned above, p. 161.
9. His "wife," thus described by Henley in a letter to RLS, 3 May 1884: "Did I

to England, and I suppose he won't be pleased. This young man is quite a hopeless character.

> Ever yours affectionately,
> ROBERT LOUIS STEVENSON

MS, National Library of Scotland.

[Saranac Lake, 10 April 1888] [10]

My dear Charles,

I have written you today already, and here I must write again, having found not only the paper for the archives announced before, but also a bill which should be paid, and having (forbye) received one from [you] which deserves answer. Bless God you acted as you did! and may the Lord lighten my poor befogged wits! It was Lord Pollexfen [11] I wished to withdraw from: the Athenaeum I think (as you think) it would be impudent not to accept; so pray announce my resignation to Lord Pollexfen (or whatever his name is —he used to live in Indy Street, didn't he no?) and try to pardon so hopelessly obscure a correspondent.

I do not wish to make this letter bitter to you, as all mine must be. I have lain awake night after night sorrowing to think of Henley receiving mine, and the hash it might make of his *Dumas,* and how it would dash the pleasure of his verses. But to pretend that one is not thinking of this is almost an unseemly affectation. Think of it I do; and when I don't think of it, start up to wonder what load is at my heart. But you at least ought to have been kept clear, and had I taken time, I would not have set pen to paper to you about this wretchedness; but at the first blow I had not the self-restraint. To

---

tell you Ted is married? . . . The bride is a nice little girl; a chanteuse, with a remarkable voice; very ladylike and pretty, and absolutely unprofessional; Grace the name of her." CB wrote to RLS, 23 September 1891: "our respectable friend Ted . . . has married another lady, never having been legally united to the Pedley, who is now, I believe, on her own hook, was here recently singing in some comic opera, and I have been told is under someone's so-called protection. A worthy pair, but he at any rate a damned blackguard." Both letters in Beinecke Collection at Yale.

10. Postmark. Envelope marked "Private."
11. I.e. Pollington (cf. above, pp. 180–1).

no one else have I referred, or do I mean to refer, to it; if I could only stop referring to it to myself, I would do yet.

Weel, weel, I didnae mean to girn [1] nae mair. Faur ye weel.

Yours affectionately,

R. L. S.

MS, National Library of Scotland.

HENLEY TO RLS

Merton Place, Chiswick W., 11 April 1888

Since the above was written, your last [2] has come in. I knew not whether to laugh or cry over it. Try the dates, however, and be resolved on one point: that the official letter was meant, not as an affront, but merely as a reminder. If I remember aright, it was written before there had dawned upon me any suspicion that my remarks upon the *Nixie-Watersprite* coincidences could possibly go near to turning our lives into separate tragedies. In any case, it was written, at my request, with a view to reminding you that you were down for the article, and that the sooner we had the copy the better we should be pleased, and with no other object whatever.

Do you remember an official letter addressed to Bob by the (then) editor of the *M. of A.*, and which, beginning "My dear Stevenson," struck cold to the heart of the recipient? You were able to reassure him on the point. Try and be as sagacious and far-seeing in your own interest as you were in his, won't you?

I want this to go tonight, so I will only say again, forgive me, and have faith in me yet. I am not ungrateful nor disloyal. Surely you should know that much of me by now? And the old affection, the old kinship, the old affinity (*enfin!*) is as living and dear as ever.

W. E. H.

P.T.O.

I forget the names of the Rodins. The bust of Hugo, the bust of W.E.H., the bust of J. P. Laurens,[3] the "Eve": I think these were of

1. Snarl.
2. Above, p. 199.
3. Jean Paul Laurens (1838–1921), French historical painter.

them. For the rest, I thought you'd write of what you saw in the round, and sent them merely as reminders of the general style.

MS, National Library of Scotland.

[Saranac Lake, 12 April 1888] [4]

My dear Charles,

I write mainly to inform you that as Henley has not written to me, I have written to him: [5] whether well or ill I know not, but putting the grounds of my annoyance honestly before him, which seemed to me (upon the whole) the best. I am in a frame of mind highly human: I wish I were dead and have no mind to die. The bottom wish of my heart is that I had died at Hyères: the happy part of my life ended there; since then I have never been well enough really to enjoy life, except for a day or two at a time, and I fear my character has suffered, and I know that troubles have grown upon me. Poor Henley!—well, and poor me!

It occurs to me that you may be puzzled (knowing my opinions) at my eagerness about having the verses destroyed. One word will explain it: the lad [6] has had scandals enough about his own father; it would be too bad if there followed one about me.

Yours affectionately,

R. L. S.

Charles, God knows I don't want to be hard, but in my heart I think niether I nor my wife have been kindly used; and to whole-sale concession there appears no end. If I could trace one step of my own that had a share in it, I would write and ask pardon; but *I* had done literally nothing when this shell burst suddenly upon my peace. Living in hope still, only wishing I had died before many things, I am

Yours perturbed,

R. L. S.

4. Postmark.
5. Not recovered.
6. Lloyd.

MS, National Library of Scotland.

[Saranac Lake, April 1888]

My dear Charles,

Herewith a codicil to my will. The idea having occurred to me that, if this job goes on, there may be war among my heirs, I thought it well to tighten up the screws in every particular. My mind has always troubled me a good deal that Henley is not mentioned; yet I could only leave him a legacy, which he would throw into the sea at once; and I hoped there would be peace among my heirs and friends, so that he would be helped in tight places. All this we must consider in time. I feel sometimes (when I do not think upon the circumstances) returns of hope. Angry with Henley I am not, for I think I follow all that passed; but I own I desire my life to be fortified from more of these assaults. And the trouble is (now that I have some hint of his principal's attitude) I fear the facts have all got rearranged in their heads, and they now probably believe devoutly the most wonderful legend of infamy on our side. Against this (if it be so) it is hard to see what to do. In my first letter to Henley I simply sent him to Katharine for the facts; I fear it was to a troubled source. But the truth is people go wrong continually —I own my blunder in this: they expect too much, and they grant and take too great freedoms from their friends; and when the frailty declares itself or the freedom is abused or resented, they forget their own share. I have made this trouble—in all innocence, which is a very poor plea—but I see if I had taken a better attitude, no word of it would have happened.

Yours affectionately,

R. L. S.

I got codeia and managed to sleep, but I have not yet been able to get back to work, and feel run down. Fanny safely arrived in San Francisco. My mother has written you about the business, for your trouble about which all thanks.

R. L. S.

MS, National Library of Scotland.

[New York, *ca.* 16 April 1888] [7]

My dear Charles,

God bless you for your letter: it is impossible to write more kindly to both W. E. H. and me; and God knows I wish I could just write and say I have forgot it all. I will enclose to you a copy of Katharine's letter. You are to observe first that no shadow of blame was thrown on her; so far from that I sent Henley to her that he might learn the facts, and I fancied she would have told them. That is a small matter. Suppose that I am insane and have dreamed all that I seem to remember, and that my wife has shamefully stolen a story from my cousin, was this the class of matter that a friend would write to me? God knows if I heard ill of Henley's wife, I should bottle it up in my heart from him, not write it to him in the midst of fulsome protestations of love; and so, I think, would you. He has written me since another letter [8] in which he tells me— what is perhaps very true—that I have cumbered him with my aid in the matter of the plays. I fear it may be so: it is painful to think; and his writing that to me (though I think it indicates a festering spirit) I can readily forgive. But does one friend write to another accusations against his wife? And such an accusation—a theft of money and of reputation? Of two things, one: either my wife is innocent, and then I suppose even my enemy would hold his peace? or she is guilty, and then, O surely almost my enemy would try to hide it from me! If this be friendship, I am not robust enough to bear it. If it be want of tact, it is strangely like want of heart. But the truth is, it is the old business; this is only one pebble (the plays was another) picked up to wound me with, in an access of concocted bitterness. A similar bitterness was concocted last year, and there will be another a year after. I write it in all soberness; and any pebbles I could have received—and have received—but not this heartless cruelty. You speak of his verses: the thought of that has been heavy on me; if I know my soul at all, I would do anything to

7. Postmark illegible. RLS and his mother left Saranac on 13 April, arriving in New York City on the 16th (*Diary,* p. 360). Envelope marked "Private."
8. Not recovered.

have delayed this trouble till his book was out. But friendship—
which I am sure he has had from me in his hours, and most sincerely too—friendship has surely some obligation of ordinary kindness; it is not a covert from behind which a man is to fill you with
injuries and reproaches and escape safe himself. I do not know
why I go on reasoning. He has sent me not a word. And whether this
be good or evil, I know not. It gives me at least time (which I
eagerly embrace) to delay. To Katharine's letter I can return no
answer. Her view of the facts is too radically different from mine;
we have no common grounds, even if we seemed to have a common
spirit; and though there came along with this two subsequent notes
in a somewhat different and not so pert a spirit, they still indicate a
belief which argues hallucination either on her part or mine; and
between 2 hallucinations what can be done? Accordingly I fold
my hands and wait. Henley may so write that I shall feel able to
pass it over, I do not know; but I shall insist at least that I am to be
no longer a pin cushion for his outrageous arrows, but shall be
written to, if I am written to at all, with some ordinary consideration for my feelings. It is of course quite true that Katharine's attitude absolves him of three parts of what I had against him, but the
fourth part that remains—that willingness to seethe up against me
and mine in my absence and that heartless willingness to wound
me—was, it seems, the part that I most keenly felt.

I am just off a journey, in New York City, very tired and very
bitterly welcomed by the enclosed; but yours, dear fellow, was a
consolation such as you can hardly fancy. I was shaking like a reed
when I began to read it; before I was done I felt calm. O, a little
kindness will go far—and yours was much, my beloved friend. And
what you say of him is all true. I know his merits, damn him! The
trouble is, he deceives himself: he does not love me any more. It is
only a habit with him now to be my friend; it has long been divorced from any regard to my feelings. You would think he would
have shrunk from wounding Gosse,[9] as he stabbed me! But not so.
He sends this charge, and sandwiches it with protestations, and
marks it private and confidential, and directs that I am to show it to

9. Gosse, in a letter to William Heinemann, 7 December 1894, speaks of Henley
as "a man who has shown me bitter enmity in the past," but goes on to profess ignorance of the cause (Evan Charteris, *Life and Letters of Sir Edmund Gosse*, 1931, p. 235.)

no one (so that my wife was not to know!) and to burn it; and follows it up with another, equally marked private and confidential for no possible reason but to take the sting out of the former marking, and in this second epistle expresses his belief that there is nothing which should affect our friendship—all this to my mind clearly pointing to a guilty sense of what he had done. So far I accuse; and I find such treatment hard to swallow.

And now, in the strictest confidence, to defend him. This business of the story was (I thought, at the time) silly. Katharine even while she consented—as she did to me with her own lips—expressed unwillingness; I told my wife so, and I asked her to go no farther. But she had taken a fancy to the idea, and when Katharine had tried her version and failed and wrote to tell us so, nothing would serve her but to act on this unwilling consent and try hers. Hers succeeded, and this was trebly vexatious to Katharine, as I clearly see. Now frankly she can do what she will with Henley; I have long suspected this, and I fear—perhaps so have others. Her view of the case, passion suppressing many of the facts, she has handed on to him. And certainly the conduct, if it were as she seems to think, would have been abominably bad. So my poor Knight Errant put lance in rest and charged—at me, though what I had to do with it I do not clearly know. But what will a man not do with a woman at his elbow. So, if you think me harsh in my judgement of his conduct, say so, and pray God you may convince me; but if you agree with my judgement, make still the allowance, and remember that it was all packed into him by an angry woman whom he admires— and what an angry woman is, we all know; and what a man is when he admires.

In all this I have not mentioned my wife. Her feelings you may imagine; and since it was in Henley's house and presence that she proposed to Katharine her version of the tale, and since no woman can make allowance for another woman's influence, she sees treachery in his conduct, where I see only *influence* on the one hand and *unkindness* on the other. It is possible I judge harshly; I have spared no pains to try to be just, but the quarrel is mine and the pain mine, and it is not likely that I see things as they are.

My dear Charles, this is I think the fourth letter I have sent you on this matter; those I have written and destroyed to you, to him, or to Katharine, are not to be counted. I have never had so heavy a shake.

Re Macbride [1] yer ain I think would be best. I enclose his.

Yours ever affectionately,

R. L. S.

[Enclosure] [2]

Dear Louis,

As Mr. Henley's very natural but unfortunate letter was written without my wish or knowledge, I have refused to let him go further in the matter. He had a perfect right to be astonished, but his having said so has nothing to do with me. If Fanny thinks she had a right to the idea of the story, I am far from wishing to reclaim or to criticize her in any way. At any rate I cannot be said to have done any wrong or gained anything by the matter, and I therefore refuse to be questioned about it or to let any one else be troubled any further; I am sick to death of the matter and the notion of any quarrel has made me feel quite ill. It is of course very unfortunate that my story was written first and read by people, and if they express their astonishment, it is a natural consequence and no fault of mine or any one else. I assume that you know me sufficiently to be sure that I have never alluded to the matter, even to friends who have spoken of *The Nixie*. I trust this matter is not making you feel as ill as all of us.

Yours affly,

(signed) KATHARINE DE MATTOS

This seems pleasantly put!

R. L. S. The copyist, for whose soul you are requested to pray.

MS, Yale.

CB TO RLS

Edinburgh, 27 April 1888

My dear Louis,

My only consolation throughout this business has been that I

1. Not identified.
2. Copy in RLS's hand.

have been able to share your pain and to know that but for your being able to pour out the whole thing to me it would have been harder to bear. I think if we could have been together it might have been easier for you. As it is, you know, my dear boy, that every sympathy of which I am capable is with you. I have been in London with Henley for some days and found him quite unable to appreciate the wound he had inflicted. Before I left, however, I had the satisfaction of hearing him say that he wished he had never put pen to paper on the subject—and so do I, most devoutly.

Your analysis of the Defence I believe to be accurate. To the Influence add Liver, from which he has been suffering much, and you will find enough to disorder a man's judgment. Let us give these two as much weight as we can.

Throughout the whole business I have not hesitated to tell him that I thought his position indefensible. I still think so, but I think that of K. worse. A man is led on the ice, however unwarrantably; the leader should not let him drop through the first hole. But there is not much use in discussing the question. With a little common sense and a touch of generosity all this would never have been. But to say or think Henley is disloyal is as far off the mark as to deny the moon under eclipse. He has strayed under Influences; we shall yet welcome him back. Believe me, my dear Louis, it will be so.

The present point is, however, that I have taken both your interests into my hands. Any continuance of a correspondence at present would be a hollow sham; even if the "Subject" were avoided, a Presence would remain which could never be dispelled in writing. And therefore, for the sake of all of us, I have obtained from Henley, and ask from you, an agreement that all direct correspondence shall cease between you for a period of six months and shall not be resumed without my leave. Trust me in this. I am doing what I see is the only course. I hope you will agree. Nothing in life is more fatal than the gradual growing of the misunderstanding which comes of a half-hearted correspondence.

It is in pursuance of this agreement that Henley has not written. I send you a note from him to me, however, which contains a message you ought to have, and there is this further message which I quote: "I read the *Deacon* last night. I want you, when you write to Louis, to tell him that I told you I think (I *do*) it contains his best work. I had no idea how good it is. I have decided to print it, together with a selection from the American criticisms, and send it round." That is the message, and in a line today he presses me not to forget it.

In this connection it will not be altogether without a grain of amusement that you will learn that *Teddy* has cast Henley off! Henley wrote him with a full and free opinion of his recent conduct, and the reply comes to the mother after weeks of silence that he will have nothing more to do with H. or the *Deacon!* For pure sheer unadulterated impudence beat me that if you can. The one good thing is that Henley's eyes are at last thoroughly open about Ted, and I think we shall not hear much more of that unmitigated scamp.

I must add a few lines from Henley's last. "I am absolutely unconscious of any offence to him of any kind since he quitted these shores. I have been in great trouble more than once, and trouble makes one selfish. But there has been no more estrangement than that, and no disloyalty either." All this, my dear, I sincerely think to be true. Do you try to think so too. In time I believe you will. Mind I make no excuse for, palliate in no way, the manner of that communication, for which I see no defence, but let us still keep forgiving, and one of these days Time, which heals all things, will bring a consolation for this wound also. How I wish I could do or say something to console and cheer you. It was indeed much to know that my letter had come not unkindly to you, but it is unbearable to think of you, with all your true loyal love for every friend, fretting, and sleepless, and suffering as you are doing. Words are powerless: what can I do or say? Nothing: I must just pray for the best for you all. You know that I would spare nothing in the world to save you a moment's grief—and here I am, helpless. My dear, I will say no more now. But believe me ever yours affectionately,

C. B.

The *History of Mexico* [3] is in my hands and absolutely safe. There are certain things which I cannot allow to die, and shall copy without a clue to authorship. The rest shall go burn. Keep your mind quite easy about this.

Have attended to the Cross business.

3. An early, unpublished "shocker"—novel, inspired by a challenge of friends.

MS, National Library of Scotland.

[Union House, Manasquan, N.J., 7 May 1888] [4]

My dear Charles,

I return herewith the bill and codicil. And about all this affair on which I have been wearying you with intemperate letters, I wish to say that I put myself in your hands without reserve. A man is no judge in his own quarrel; I cannot change the fact that I have been hit hard, but I can keep that to myself, and I will *do* what you say, for I am sure it will be just and kind. My wife, to whom I sent on your letter, was equally affected with myself. It is strange when you think what a couple of heartless drunken young dogs we were, that we should be what we are today: that you should so write, and I so accept what you have written. Remember it when your bairns grow up: youth is but a scuffle.

Ever yours,
ROBERT LOUIS STEVENSON

MS, National Library of Scotland.

HENLEY TO RLS

Merton Place, Chiswick W., 7 May 1888

My dear Lad,

Your letter is heart-breaking, and I do not know how to reply to it, for it convicts me (I now see) of a piece of real unkindness, unworthy of myself and our old true friendship. You may blame me in the bitterest terms you will for the cruel blunder I made in opening my mind to you, and I shall not complain, for I deserve them all. I should, I know now, have said nothing; and I shall never cease from regretting that I gave you this useless, this unnecessary pain.

You must not believe, though, that I struck to hurt. I did not. I thought the matter one of little consequence. It seemed right that you should know how it looked to myself, and that there might well

4. Entire dateline in CB's hand.—". . . we arrange to go to Manasquan, a place on the New Jersey Coast recommended by Mr. Low [see below, p. 323]. On 2nd May we all go to the Union House, a summer boarding house which we have all to ourselves at present" (*Diary*, p. 360).

be the end of it. I was elbows deep in the business from the first, and I had (I thought) a right to make remarks. It was surely as well (I reasoned) that you should hear of certain coincidences from me as from another quarter. That I had any feeling of unfriendliness is what I want now explicitly to deny. It is your mistake, dear lad, to imagine that I've ever been any other than your true friend and servant. I have not; I could not. Twice before (I want you to remember) you have put this same charge upon me: each time, as you know, to my astonishment. In this case, as in the others, I can truly say the amazement is the same. How much greater the distress has been I leave you to judge.

All this, and more, I should have said long since, but I could not answer your first letter. It put me (as it were) into the dock, and I preferred to keep silence till I could speak on the old footing and in the old terms. Now I can do that, I make haste to own that I spoke without a full sense of the regard that was due to you, and that I beg your forgiveness.

The good Charles was with us not long since, and our talk ran much on you. I doubt not that he has written, and told you all he could, and that you know ere this why I have not spoken and how I—we—have felt. Let me add that neither he nor you can know how grievous the estrangement has been to all of us, nor what a relief it is to us to think that it may now be at an end.

Forgive me if I write no more. I am far from well, and there are many things for which I am perplexed. And do not doubt me again, if you can help it. Life is short enough and cruel enough, as it is; and you and I, dear Louis, should know better than to waste the good that is in it—the good that we have made for ourselves—like this.

Ever your friend,
W. E. H.

His [5] original position carefully saved throughout; (1) and yet I gave him my word as to certain matters of fact; (2) and yet the letter (in consequence of this) can never be shown to my wife; (3) and yet, even if he still thinks as he did, I think a kind spirit would have even lied.

R. L. S.

5. A note in RLS's hand at the top of Henley's letter.

MS, National Library of Scotland.

[Manasquan, N.J., 9 May 1888] [6]

My dear Charles,

This word to acknowledge your last, though I had practically answered it before it came, so swiftly do great minds jump! My dear friend, your letters have really carried me through this miserable passage; so do not think you can do nothing, when you have done all.—I had read Besant's article in *Longman's Mag* [7] ("The Endowment of the Daughter") and meant to endow Katharine's daughter in this way, advancing her the capital against her ultimate share in my estate; then, when I got to New York and found her letters, I shied, fearing chiefly misapprehension; but the other day, thinking after all the child had done no ill, whether I or its mother had, I wrote and proposed it to K. If she should agree, I shall get you to look into it. I fear the child is already 12, and so the premium will be grown greater or the period of payment must be delayed proportionally. It would possibly save time if you glanced into it (a chance arising) in the meanwhile.

Yours ever affectionately,

R. L. S.

MS, National Library of Scotland.

FANNY STEVENSON TO CB

236 Taylor Street, San Francisco, Cal.
[received 29 May 1888]

Dear Mr. Baxter,

I have been trying to recall the will I made when I was ill in Switzerland. Somehow I feel doubtful about it; I was so very ill at the time that I hardly knew what I was about, and cannot remember it. To make assurance doubly sure, and considering the uncertainty of life, I thought I would just make another. I shall speak to Mr. Young on the subject. I write this that you may not think I am entirely out of my mind—as certainly I might well be under the circumstances. I do not see how it is possible for me to return to

6. Postmark.
7. Walter Besant's article appeared in *Longman's*, *11* (1888), 604.

England after the disgrace that has been put upon me by Louis' friends. Had Henley only been satisfied with making the charge to me, I should have been bound to say nothing to Louis on account of the ill effect of such a thing upon his health. As it is, they have nearly, perhaps quite, murdered him. It is very hard for me to keep on living! I may not be able to, but must try for my dear Louis' sake. If I cannot, then I leave my curse upon the murderers and slanderers. I had done them nothing but kindness, ever, nor surely had Louis.

Since this horrible untrue charge has been made against me, I have received not one letter from all those I considered my friends in England. That is very natural. I was a foreigner, and they knew nothing about me but what they saw on the surface. I can do without them, though it is very bitter. I gave up my own country and my own friends for Louis, and God knows, and I almost think you will believe me, I was sincere, I loved them all. The hardness of it is that Louis has brought this upon me—for him, I mean, not me; that through his friends I should be ashamed to show my face in England is what breaks his heart. I think it is almost better that we were both out of such a world. I never go to bed now but I am tempted sorely by the morphia and the arsenic that stands by my bed. I have always had courage before, but I feel beaten now. They say that one is supported by the consciousness of innocence. That is not true. Were I guilty—though of such a thing I could not be— I should brazen it out. It's the injustice—the injustice that eats my soul. How can anyone believe that I could rob my dearest friend, the one upon whom I was always seeking to heap benefits. If Jenkin [8] were alive he would—alone amongst them all, I fear—know without proof that I could not be a thief. It seems like a strange nightmare that such a thing could befall me. Louis always said that my worst point was my devilish pride. Perhaps God means that it should be humbled. Every day I say to myself can this be *I, myself?* really I, myself? Nothing that I have said here shall I say to Louis. Unless I become quite mad, in which case nothing will make any difference. If it so happens that I must go back to perfidious Albion, I shall learn to be false. For Louis' sake I shall pretend to be their friend still—while he lives; but that in my heart I can ever forgive those who have borne false witness against me—!

8. Fleeming Jenkin (cf. above, p. 91).

While they eat their bread from my hand—and oh, they will do that—I shall smile and wish it were poison that might wither their bodies as they have my heart. Please burn this letter lest it be said that I was mad when I made my will. Those who falsely (knowing it to be false) accuse me of theft, I cannot trust to be honest. They may try to rob my boy after they have murdered us. I can leave clear proof of my sanity in the clearness with which I am managing affairs. I have authorized Mr. Young to submit to me plans and prices for five cottages, each calculated to rent at 25 dollars per month, on the Oakland place; the money to build them with may be raised on a mortgage, but as here I should have to pay 8 per cent for it, I imagine it would be better to raise the money in England upon Skerryvore. The rents can then go to pay off the debt, after which Lloyd can have the rest. I am also, at Louis' request, negotiating for the charter of a yacht. Tomorrow I am to see different men and calculate the expense that I may telegraph Louis a clear statement. This yacht is a deep sea vessel, and we will—if we go—sail to the South Seas. I loath the thought. In fact I hate the hateful world. I hadn't had so much happiness, and the time is not long—why should they so wickedly take away the little I had? I tried to give them some. Are all English people like that? Are you like that? No, how could I have forgotten in my bitterness the one true man I believe in, Sidney Colvin—no, thank God, *he* will not fail me. There is comfort in that.

F. VdeG. Stevenson

MS, Yale. Letters, 3, 67.

Union House, Manasquan, N.J.,
but address to Scribner's [11 May 1888] [9]

My dear Charles,

I have found a yacht and we are going the full pitch for seven months. If I cannot get my health back (more or less) 'tis madness; but of course, there is the hope, and I will play big. We telegraph to you today not to invest £2,000; and I now write to ask you to send same sum *quam celerrimum* to our account at Messrs John Paton and Co., 52 William Street, New York.

9. Postmark.

In reference to Henley's note, I am at a loss how to answer. You had better answer for me: as you judge it likely whether I would communicate such matter as he seems to think his letter contained —although I could never find that it did—to anyone except yourself. I will stand by your judgement and your answer. This shows me how wise you were to prevent correspondence.

If this business fails to set me up, well, 2,000 is gone, and I know I can't get better. We sail from San Francisco, June 15th, for the South Seas in the yacht *Casco*.

With a million thanks for all your dear friendliness,

Ever yours affectionately,

ROBERT LOUIS STEVENSON

MS, National Library of Scotland.

FANNY STEVENSON TO CB

236 Taylor Street, San Francisco
[15 May 1888] [10]

Dear Mr. Baxter,

Already the hands that dealt me the cruelest blow are held out to be filled. I am not surprised, except that the time is so short. The only thought my generous Louis has is to do all he can to help them; I wish to ask you to see that he does not do wild and rash things, nor make promises that in a cooler moment he might not feel inclined to make good. He wrote something about some sort of an annuity for Katharine's child. Would it not be better to give what money she requires directly? And as it is needed? I have very little faith in these new-fangled annuity affairs, and it would be foolish to run the risk of losing a large sum of money only to save Katharine any embarrassment she might feel in receiving it after what she has done. As for me, I am not likely to change in my feelings of resentment. The injury can never be condoned nor do I ever wish to see England again. Indeed, if I can help it, I never shall. It is most probable that I never shall. Every penny that goes to them, any of them, goes with my bitterest ill will. When an injury is done to Louis his whole thought is what good he can do them in

10. Postmark. Envelope marked "Private."

return. He is very near being an angel. Still, not even he can understand what this has been to me. Were you disbarred for dishonor-
able conduct through your friend's treachery, and you innocent,
and he knowing it—that is the nearest thing to it. You would feel
that you were destroyed, as I feel that I am.

Yours,

F. VDEG. STEVENSON

MS, Yale. Envelope marked "Private."

MRS. THOMAS STEVENSON TO CB

Manasquan, 19 May [1888]

My dear Mr. Baxter,

I wonder what you think of this sudden change of plans and our
start off to the Pacific? How nice it would be if you could join us
for a time. It seems greedy to have a yacht all to ourselves. Louis is
greatly delighted with it, and I do trust that he may improve in
health and be able to do some work on board so that the cruise may
be self-supporting. We hope that the £2,000 may very soon be returned to capital again and meantime would like £1,000 to be
taken from Louis's money and one from mine.

I am writing a line to Mr. Mowbray to tell him that I shall not
in future trouble him with any business letters but just write to
you and let you consult him when it is necessary.

I leave Heriot Row in Mr. Liston's [1] hands, but shall tell him to
apply to you in case of need. I can quite understand keeping interest off the £500 a year to be paid by the Business, but surely
£100 a year is *very* good interest. I wish we could have a few investments on the same scale. Kindly enquire about this as I do not like
to trouble Mr. Mowbray about it.

Our next address is c/o Mr. J. D. Strong, 236 Taylor Street, San
Francisco, California. When we get there Louis will send you a list
of our future chances to get letters, and you know how welcome
they will be when we are so far from all our friends. It is a thought,
to go quite beyond the reach of news! I wonder where you will
all be going this summer. I trust you will all have a happy time

1. Not identified.

and that dear little Eddie will keep strong. With kindest regards to all at Rutland Square and Rothesay Place,[2]

Believe me ever yours most truly,

M. I. STEVENSON

MS, National Library of Scotland.

[Manasquan, 22 May 1888] [3]

My dear,

I have had a sore mail.[4] You were right; and Henley should not have written. I send you his letter, and I must ask you somehow or other to get me out of the task of answering it. I will say frankly this tread of the elephant's foot is too heavy for me. You will observe that [5] my delicacy in never referring to my wife's miserable position is construed (I must suppose) as a tacit condemnation; that to me, a married man, he writes a letter of reconciliation which I could never dare to show my wife! I have been even using my wife ill, by my treatment of this matter, but this passes the measure. Henley and Katharine may make their peace with *her* if they are able. I am weary of trying to think and plan, and suppress letters, for their sake; not one thought do they give to me. And you must try to explain to him that for his sake and mine, I must simply not be supposed to have received the enclosed specimen of correspondence. Explain to him also, if you are able, that when a man in a matter of this description does not dwell on his wife's feelings, the suppression does not imply that she is dead. But I feel he will never understand.[6]

O, I go on my journey with a bitter heart. It will be best for all, I daresay, if the *Casco* goes down with me. For there's devilish little left to live for. And don't think me ungrateful, my dear; God bless you, for your kindness and your wisdom. And would God I had had your letter before I wrote. For this wooden incapacity to under-

2. The home addresses of CB's father and CB respectively.
3. Postmark. Envelope marked "Private."
4. "On the 21st Louis gets some worrying letters which upset and depress him very much and he stays much in his bed" (*Diary*, p. 360). One is the letter from Henley, 7 May, above, p. 216; the other is the note from Katharine de Mattos enclosed in the present letter, below, p. 227.
5. Eight lines of MS deleted.
6. Several words deleted.

stand any feeling that can inspire one word of my correspondence
or one act of my life is the severest blow of all.

By the same mail I had a pencil note from Katharine, also enclosed, along with my answer. I do not know whether it is that I
am "weary of well-doing." [7] I think not. I think I perceive that I
injure these people by treating them with too great delicacy, which
they misconstrue—and what drives me wild, misconstrue to the
disadvantage of my wife.

O, Henley's letter! I cannot rise from it. What does the man
think? Has he ever met a human being on his way through life?—
Well, well, here I am writing all night again, with all my reams
of work in hand, and within 9 days of leaving for San Francisco.
This business has been my headstone; I will never be reconciled to
life. O, I speak wildly—but it will never be the same to me. Katharine has behaved in a manner that I shall leave herself to qualify if
she please; Henley, poor devil, seems unable to understand a
single impulse of my heart or a single necessity of my position; he
seems also quite unable to believe my plain word. [8]

Well, I mean to beat the wind. I *will* have a good time on the
Casco. It means a hard heart; well, harden it, O Lord! and let's be
done.

Lord, man! I can't help loving him either. I would give a leg
that this were blotted out, and I could sit down with him as of
yore. [9] Does he suppose my wife *enjoyed* this business? God, what a
want—what a corpse-like want of thought for others this displays!
Don't you see me going to my wife and showing her this letter,
and—read it!

Truly, I have found in myself wonderful things, but I believe in
my widest flights of unconcern for my neighbours, I never flew
one-third of this. But the affair is back in your hand. The trouble
is, dear Charles, and this I feel wretched about: they will have to
put off Rodin [1] to next year. I lost more than a month over this
business. I had this chance of a schooner, which I thought I might
enjoy—and I mean to, if the devil's in it—and which might do me
good; and I am in dreadful arrears. I have still two articles which
must be done in eight days, a feat I know not how to accomplish:

7. II Thessalonians 3:13.
8. Six lines of MS deleted.
9. Four lines of MS deleted.
1. See above, p. 199 n. 2.

and in short—the Rodin must go over to next year. For I cannot
do it on board.

Next day: the horrible part here begins
Of other business—I have the pretty complete certainty that the
£2,000 will carry me well through my seven months. What you
have in hand, and what we may hope you shall receive in the interim from publishers, Skerry V. etc., may thus collect, and should
amount to something ere my return. If I come back in any health
I should make another £300 in six months by finishing my novel,
The Master of Ballantrae. Pretty soon after, Lloyd and I should
have one of our ships at the harbour mouth. And they should go
far to keep us for the year, so that (what I am particularly anxious
to manage) the *Casco* letters may go towards repayment of the
capital now borrowed. I shall think it unlucky if I cannot get from
10 to 15 hundred out of them, and this should go (or a great part of
it should) toward the hole made in capital. I now find myself in debt
to my heirs, for I scarce think myself entitled to decrease the little
stock.

But now there remains the question of buying the deferred annuity for Katharine's child. I do not think this quarrel should be
allowed to interfere with that design, which seems to me highly
desirable. At the same time I mean the expense to fall on Katharine's share of what I have left to her. I wish you would inquire into
the thing. After this letter of mine, it is unlikely we shall have
further correspondence; nor unless she chooses to own the truth,
do I much desire it. So if you find, at the child's present age, the
thing to be possible and not too expensive, you had better just
manage it for me personally, and send me a little codicil by which
I can reduce Katharine's share in a proportion. I think, considering
all things, it could scarce seem mean if I added the amount to
Lloyd's? He at least is a comfort to me; and in all this trouble, he
and yourself are my only stand-by's. My wife feels the thing too
bitterly to be much help—she had a very strong affection for
Katharine; and I have to steer my own course often much against
her will, though of course as she is in S.F. I am playing off my own
bat. Lloyd approves of the letter to Katharine; we both feel it is impossible I should continue to appear to accept this unfair usage of
my wife, and that I have done as much in the way of hanging off,
and giving Katharine a chance to do the right thing spontaneously,

as the oldest friend has any right to ask. It is just possible this
business will delay my sailing! At least today work is once more
impossible.

As to Henley's letter, then, you will try to explain to him, as
kindly as you can, what it appears to me are its defects, and how
from the nature of these defects, it is better I should not be supposed to have received it. I cannot describe with what disappointment I read it, but upon this you will not dwell. My plan, in not
receiving it, and not answering it, is to keep the door open for the
return of friendship. I could not write to him myself,[2] and point
out to him the position in which he leaves me as to my wife, because I am too proud to do so, and because if I tried I should but
open the wound. I lay the burthen, then, upon your shoulders,
and should I receive any letters from W.E.H. before I have heard
from you, I shall act upon your original proposal and send them
to you unopened.

He says he was "in the business from the first." He was in it
enough to have known a little more, as I reminded him, were he not
under an influence which I fear is (just now at least) an evil one.
But it is true: I know how easy he is to lead.

You will hear from me again ere I sail, my dear Charles—I trust
in better spirits.

I cannot say I think I act harshly. I am trying to do the best for
all. The Lord knows there is in my soul this morning no hatred
and no anger; a very weary disappointment, a dread of the future,
and a doubt of all—that is my sentiment. With my voyage in front
of me—the dream of a life realised—I must still say, Would God
I had died at Hyères! I have never been well enough since then to
enjoy life as I once did; I have had a considerable success, which is
a disappointing circumstance in life, believe me; and—well, now,
I feel as if I were moving among bladders. For either I am a very
unjust judge, or I am being hardly used by those whom I loved and
tried to serve.

Your kindness, your countenance, and the affection you show to
me, my dear, has been of the most incalculable support, and I
thank you again and again, and am—O, I hope—

Ever yours,
R. L. Stevenson

2. MS, "to himself."

Because I say nothing of my wife's position and my wife's feelings, you at least will not misunderstand me. There are things of which a man cannot write, but dear God, that he must feel. And think of my wooden Henley! I shall never get an answer to this before I am on the sea—if all goes well. Better address to Scribner's, and I shall hear at our first *escale*.

R. L. S.

To my wife, I shall (God forgive me) pretend that your plan has held all the time, and that I have not communicated with Henley. So here you see I am still tricking and lying for him, and he cannot think once of my position. It is indeed disheartening. Words cannot describe my wearyness of life. And it seems it would have been so easy for Henley to have made his letter presentable! Lloyd is in a great state of doubt too: hating to go to sea without a friendly hail! to Henley, and yet not knowing how or whether.

Some of the first of this letter, being the usual steam escape, I have deleted in a cooler moment.

R. L. S.

[Enclosure]

That was best. I am afraid to speak or breathe. There is devilry in the air.

K. DE M.

This precious scrap is all she says when I sent her, as sole answer to her former letter, the information that I should never tell Fanny of it, and enclosed a message from Fanny—I now forget its terms—to the effect that letters might be misunderstood and we must not judge K. in the meantime. If there is not even thanks, I must explain it to myself as hopeless. Poor woman, she has put her foot in it deep, but this stubborn pride in wrong-doing can lead only to greater misery in the end. I do not envy her night thoughts!

[Enclosure] [3]

Dear Katharine,

You say 'that was best.' I thought it best for you. But is that all you have to say? Have you no thanks to make me for an act which I

3. A typed copy, presumably by Lloyd Osbourne.

own I thought generous? I suppressed a letter which deeply affected my wife's character from the person most concerned; a letter which, if I know anything of life, there is no other human being but myself who would have even tried to pardon; a letter of which (permit me to remind you) you were so much ashamed that you followed it up with two vague notes of apology and deprecation. Up to this moment you have never had one word of reproach from me. I must say now it had been 'best' if you had called to memory, when Henley came to see you, that which I myself so vividly remember. By so doing you might have saved me a friendship of which I have great need; and you would have saved yourself, when your better nature speaks, cruel reproaches. But it would have been better still if you had found it in your generosity to respond to my wife's message, which I was surprised to receive from her, which I was rejoiced to send on to you, and which I am now cast down to find has elicited no answer in your heart.

So much I will say; for I find that my silence is misconstrued, and it is necessary to be frank. I know, and you know, how you have used my wife. I know, and you know,[4] how when this matter came up you failed me with Henley. I know, and you know, how you wrote in answer. I know, and you know, how, as soon as you had sent the letter off, your heart misgave you. I know, and you know, how I have sought to spare you till today. I now remind you nakedly of the truth. I do not know how to say what I wish to say. There is always a door open: it is never too late to say, I have sinned—if not for others, at least for oneself. God knows my heart is heavy enough with my own offences to make me sicken at the thought of seeming harsh. But I counsel you, if you wish peace of mind, to do the right thing, and to do it now.

Your old friend and cousin,

ROBERT LOUIS STEVENSON

MS, Yale.

[Manasquan, N.J., 26 May 1888] [5]

My dear Charles,

I shall just have to ask you to write no more about this affair

4. Transcribed by Lloyd: "You know, and I know"; corrected by RLS.
5. Postmark. Envelope marked "Private."

for a while; I can open no more letters that bear upon it. It has quite smashed me, and I am beginning to fear I may loose my cruise after all, which would be hard on Lloyd.

I cannot sleep; I can never get the thought out of my head. I had the most hideous revulsion after writing so sternly to Katharine, and it was three days before I could forgive myself. But even now, when I am more sure that I did right, and the only thing right, my heart is wretched. I was not meant to punish sinners.

Of course I am sure you will make it right in time with Henley, but do not let me hear for awhile. I could not bear another disappointment. Really, something would happen.

I wish you would be prepared to pay £10 *per mensem* to Young the San Francisco man. It is an allowance to Belle,[6] which I have been paying myself; but if I go the voyage, I shall have to pass on the duty to him, and tell him to draw on you. He will communicate with you when I have seen him. I am also about to give a little charge to Miss Boodle [7] to look after our Mary Ann,[8] and if she finds it necessary to help the family, pray give her what she may require.

I am, my dear fellow, the most purely unhappy card on ground— or so my egotism thinks, when there are (I daresay) a thousand who might envy me.

Ever yours affectionately,
R. L. S.

P.S. We leave Monday, if I shall be able—a dreadful doubt which I keep to myself, but I *am* doubtful.

MS, Yale.

Lloyd Osbourne to CB

St. Stephen's Hotel [New York], 1 June [1888]

My dear Charles,

R.L.S. recovered with utmost promptitude and despatch, and tomorrow we leave in fairly good trim on our voyage. The doctor, last night, was very encouraging about him; [1] says voyage is just

6. His stepdaughter, Isobel Osbourne Strong.

7. See above, p. 182.

8. Mary Ann Watts, the Stevensons' housekeeper at Bournemouth.

1. "On the 28th we go to New York, meaning to start for San Francisco on the 31st but the weather is damp and cold and Lou takes sore throat. We send for

the thing—Pacific especially, and he has but little doubt but that Louis will return an able-bodied sort of person. There is nothing the matter with him now, and all he wants is to turn over a new leaf, and enjoy himself in the open air.

I have a detective camera—an affair you wear over the region of your heart—taking people without their knowledge. I have had very good success with it. I shall send you, from time to time, my proofs. I shall try to send them all, and you might keep them, as the "Earl and the Doctor's" [2] fate was to lose all their portable property. I should be able to get some very good results: beautiful young women surf-bathing, etc., and views illustrative of the customs and manners of the country.

With ever best wishes (I am writing by gas-light, and my time is limited),

Yours ever,

LLOYD OSBOURNE

MS, Yale.

CB TO RLS

Edinburgh, 6 June 1888

My dear Louis,

Doubt as to where, or when, or if ever you will get this damps the ardour of the letter-writer, but I must send a word on the chance. I fully share your disappointment. The key of his position, or rather his attitude, is found in the phrase, "I thought the matter of little consequence." I really do think he did—till I shewed him that to accuse a person of being a liar and a thief without a shadow of evidence was a matter of very grave consequence indeed. I do not think that this simple elemental idea had ever crossed his brain. As for K., she is really too steep. If there *has* been bad behaviour, hers has certainly been not the least, and I regard her as the wicked

Dr. Cleveland who attended him at Newport in Sept.; he throws off the cold very quickly and the doctor is delighted with the improvement in him since he saw him last. We get leave to start on our great journey on Saturday, the 2nd June" (*Diary*, pp. 360–1).

2. *South Sea Bubbles*, by the Earl and the Doctor (New York, 1872). The Earl, the author of the book, was George Robert Charles Herbert, 13th E. of Pembroke (1850–95); the Doctor was George Henry Kingsley (1827–92).

mainspring of all this distress. I am not yet disposed to take a favourable view of the endowment scheme, and I want you to let it simmer for a little. I know you so well that I quite understand the impulse of your mind not only to return good for evil, but even to repay an aggravated wrong by an exceeding benefit. Yet one may go too far. All I ask is just to consider it a little more, till the time when the peace and rest of your sea life have eased the fever and misery of these later days. The children will not be quite unprovided for, and I do think you have nearer and very much kinder people to consider. But *all* I say is give the thing a little more time, and then I will acquiesce in anything you determine on.

I have today re-invested the proceeds of the Union Steamship Co.; 4 ½ per cent is the best I could get, and I have been progging up Dick to get a statement of the business, which he promises this week.

With love to you all,

Ever yours affectionately,
C. Baxter

MS, Yale.

Yacht Casco, Oakland [25 June 1888]

My dear Charles,

Here I am in my berth, and pretty sick. I cannot recover from this affair, though crossing the continent picked me up for the time, and I long to get to sea. Shall I ever return? I have no great mind to see England any more, I must confess, but time is a great healer.

I wish you would tell Henley how heartily I have enjoyed his verses. My wife and I were both rejoiced to see him at last do something worthy of himself, as I do think this volume is; some of the pieces are as good as I want to see, both old friends and new. If I write woodenly, it is simply because I have no spirit and am very weary and out of sorts; but I read the book with sincere emotion and am to quote one in an article.

And now business: First, we are going to build houses on the Oakland property; the money could be raised here on the houses, but this at eight per cent, which is absurd; and I wish you would communicate with Young and send him my other thousand for this purpose. It should be a good investment itself, and besides it will turn what has been an expense into a source of profit. He is to write you himself.

2nd. Please communicate with Colvin as to his insurances: I am to help him (if needful) to keep them up, and this of course is to be done; *however I may have to raise the money to do it with.* Any step you find necessary, I approve beforehand.

Good bye, my dear old fellow. We all send you the kindest wishes, and whether or not we ever meet again, you stand near in my heart.

It is easy to send a last word to you, but just in case of accidents, I wish to send one to W.E.H. also. These words will do: "Auld Lang Syne." To Katharine, if I come again no more, I send these: "It is never too late to repent and make amends." But these are of course only testamentary.

Good bye to yourself.

Yours ever affectionately,
ROBERT LOUIS STEVENSON

I am going to have a job to manage to enjoy myself, but I'll try!

Second Sheet.

Since this (continual wild porridge of affairs delaying us still) your letter to Fanny and yours to me have come. I thank you for both. I agree with you as usual; do no more about this endowment till I have time to be a man again, for I own there is in the proposal an ugly spice of vengeance.

I have arranged with Young to call on you for as little as possible, preferring to keep some ready money, even if I have to pay dearer on the mortgage. He will write; but I do not fancy he will ask more than £600 or less than £400. Whatever he wants let him have; it is a sound investment, I believe. I was delighted to hear we were out of the shipping business, for which I have less taste than none.

I was rejoiced you agreed with me. I have no natural taste for harshness, and to return an apology cut me to the soul. But I was very certain I was right all the same; and indeed such a letter could not have been shown to my wife—she would never have forgiven it and she would have been right. A strange suspicion which I cannot—or rather will not—write hangs over this affair, and may a little more excuse Henley if it be correct; but I would fain not believe it. *When* we meet we may speak of it.

You should have seen us counting over the ship's specie today: *Treasure Island* wasn't a circumstance.

My wife and I both owe you very much, dear man, and are not ungrateful. You can imagine what a shatterer it was for her—or perhaps you scarcely can. She had a special fondness for K.; she was indeed stabbed in the house of her friends.

I am a little better; the blood has stopped again, and I hope when I am fairly at sea, I may get rested.

Ever yours affectionately,

R. L. S.

MS, Yale.

FANNY STEVENSON TO CB

San Francisco [25 June 1888]

Dear Mr. Baxter,

Tomorrow we leave,[3] and I have just a moment to drop you a line before we start. I am afraid I wrote you wild letters, though I really knew what I wanted to say. I *did* then feel uncertain as to whether I had any friends left or not, except Colvin, of whom I always felt sure. You had been Henley's friend first, and how far you had gone with him in his views I did not know. May I say that it is sweeter balm to my soul that you still believed in my integrity because of the evidence than for reason of any friendship? And that I may still call your friendship mine is more to me than I can explain to you. At the time I wrote to you I was in bodily ill health as well as mental, and I was greatly depressed in spirits. Dr. Chismore,[4] Louis's old doctor, and a very clever man, found it necessary to operate on a tumour in my throat. He had partly removed the thing when he discovered that a large artery was involved and any further use of the knife would be followed by the gravest consequences. So there was nothing to be done but an attempt at ab-

---

3. According to *Diary* (p. 361), they settled aboard ship on the 26th, were towed to North Beach on the 27th, and out through the Golden Gate on the 28th.

4. Dr. George Chismore (1840–1907), 920 Market St.

sorption. I was very skeptical at first, but I now believe that it is going to be successful. At any rate I can see him again when we come back this way, and then if it must come out whether or no, he is the only man I care to have touch me with knives.

Our yacht is really lovely. We have a Japanese cook who speaks French, German, and English, and cooks like an angel; his name is Cousina.[5] We have a very good Captain,[6] and are prepared for any and every accident and emergency. Every atom of the stores from whiskey to the sailors' tobacco was selected by myself. I was delighted with the idea of Mrs. Stevenson being sent out to order "seventy pounds of the cheapest plug chewing tobacco." She, Mrs. S., seems greatly pleased with San Francisco, and has been about to see all the sights. Valentin is madly in love with every Chinaman she sees, and threatens to marry Cousina. Louis is now very tired, but even at that, better than he was in England. He has had one hemorrhage, not very bad, since he has been in America. Certainly his health is a very different sort of thing in this country, let the climate and weather be what they may.

I think you were quite right in letting the endowment business rest. Louis's first impulse is to do something madly generous to them who despitefully use him, but I find it well not to act too quickly, as his views are apt to change when he grows cooler and it is too late. I can see, in this case, that he thinks he had been in too great haste. There is certainly no harm in letting the affair simmer till we return.

I have arranged with Mr. Young to have four cottages built on my land here, the most of the money for building to be raised by mortgaging the place. Louis at first thought of mortgaging Skerryvore, as the rate of interest is so high here—8 per cent, but Colvin may want what we can get on that. I am as anxious to give all that I can, or all that I have, to my friends as Louis is to give to his enemies. Louis's plan looks nobler, but is it really? Is it not better to give with love than scorn? In the latter case you humiliate the receiver, and you can hardly help the reflection, "What a fine fellow am I!" Of course I do not mean shut your hand while your enemy starves, but do not choke him by force with plum cake.

We have taken the yacht for an indefinite period, though we have

5. Cousina quit at the Marquesas and was replaced by Ah Fu.
6. Captain A. H. Otis.

paid for seven months. The first port where we may really expect to get letters is Honolulu. Please let us hear from you there: "to wait for yacht *Casco,* General Post Office, Honolulu, Sanwich Islands." And now goodbye, and may God bless and keep you safely and happily—you, and all those you love.

Most truly yours,
FANNY VDEG. STEVENSON

MS, National Library of Scotland.

KATHARINE DE MATTOS TO RLS

[1888]

I know this can never get better, but perhaps nothing can make it worse. So do listen when I once more assure you of my entire ignorance that Mr. Henley was writing. If I had wished to write or to speak to anyone on the subject, I could have done it myself, but I never had any wish to do so. How well Mr. Henley knows this he has perhaps told you. The letter in which I tried to do so was returned to Mr. Baxter. I don't think I exaggerate when I say I was maddened with despair when I read your letter which taxed me with a dreadful preconceived plot. I can only myself know how impossible it would have been to me to do such a thing. How deeply sorry I am it is useless to try to say, and impossible not to remember all your past kindness, which has now turned into life-long distrust of me. If I have failed to understand anything said to me at Bournemouth or put a wrong construction on things, I am more grieved than ever, but I cannot say it has been intentional.

KATHARINE DE MATTOS

MS, Yale. Letters, 3, 77. Note by CB:
"Recd 22 July 1889."

Yacht Casco, at sea, near the Paumotus,
7 A.M. 6 September 1888 with a dreadful pen

My dear Charles,

Last night as I lay under my blanket in the cockpit, courting sleep, I had a comic siezure. There was nothing visible but the southern stars, and the steersman there out by the binnacle lamp;

we were all looking forward to a most deplorable landfall on the morrow, praying God we should fetch a tuft of palms which are to indicate the Dangerous Archipelago; the night was as warm as milk; and all of a sudden, I had a vision of—Drummond Street. It came on me like a flash of lightning; I simply returned thither, and into the past. And when I remembered all that I hoped and feared as I pickled about Rutherford's [7] in the rain and the east wind: how I feared I should make a mere shipwreck, and yet timidly hoped not; how I feared I should never have a friend, far less a wife, and yet passionately hoped I might; how I hoped (if I did not take to drink) I should possibly write one little book, etc. etc. And then, now— what a change! I feel somehow as if I should like the incident set upon a brass plate at the corner of that dreary thoroughfare, for all students to read, poor devils, when their hearts are down. And I felt I must write one word to you. Excuse me if I write little: when I am at sea, it gives me a headache; when I am in port, I hear my diary crying, "Give, give." I shall have a fine book of travels, I feel sure; and will tell you more of the South Seas after my few months than any other writer has done—except Herman Melville perhaps, who is a howling cheese.[8] Good luck to you, God bless you.

> Your affectionate friend,
> R. L. S.

Love to Henley and Simpson. And Bob, if you see him.

MS, Yale. Letters, *3, 80.*

> Taiti (as ever was) [15 October 1888] [9]

But then, my dear Charles, I have seen nothing of it, having been in bed ever since I left Fakaravu, in the Low Archipelago. This illness, which has been pretty sharp and is now leaving me very slowly, has done one good thing. Since those miseries, I have never felt myself, and now I begin to recover. I thank God I shall soon have some news of all I love: in the first rank of whom I need not tell you my poor Henley is.

You will receive a lot of mostly very bad proofs of photographs,

7. See above, p. 88.
8. RLS had been introduced to Melville's work by Charles Warren Stoddard, during his first stay in San Francisco. "Howling cheese" is a term of compliment.
9. Postmark. Envelope marked "Private."

the paper was so bad. Please keep them very private, as they are for the book. We send them, having learned so dread a fear of the sea that we wish to put our eggs in different baskets. We have been thrice within an ace of being ashore; we were lost(!) for about twelve hours in the Low Archipelago, but by God's blessing had quiet weather all the time; and once, in a squall, we cam so near gaun heels ower hurdies that I really dinnae ken why we didnae athegether. Hence, as I say, a great desire to put our eggs in different baskets, particularly on the Pacific (aw-haw-haw) Pacific Ocean.

You can have no idea what a mean time we have had, owing to incidental beastlinesses, nor what a glorious, owing to the intrinsic interest of these isles. I hope the book will be a good one; nor do I really very much doubt that—the stuff is so curious. What I wonder is, if the public will rise to it. A copy of my journal, or as much of it as is made, shall go to you also; it is, of course, quite imperfect, much being to be added and corrected; but O, for the eggs in the different baskets.

All the rest are well enough, and all have enjoyed the cruise so far, in spite of its drawbacks. We have had an awfae time in some ways, Mr. Baxter; and if I wasnae a verra patient man (when I ken that I *have* to be) there wad hae been a braw row; and aince, if I hadnae happened to be on deck aboot three in the mornin', I *think* there would have been *murder* done. The American Mairchant Marine is a kent service; ye'll have heard its praise, I'm thinkin, an' if ye never did, ye can get *Twa Years Before the Mast* by Dana, whaur forbye a great deal o' pleisure, ye'll get a' the needcessary information. Love to your father and all the family.

Ever your affectionate friend,
Robert Louis Stevenson

MS, Yale. Letters, 3, *86.*

Tautira (The Garden of the World),
otherwise called Hans-Christian-Andersen-ville,
[Papeete, 10 November 1888] [1]

My dear Charles,

Whether I have a penny left in the wide world, I know not nor shall know—till I get to Honolulu, where I anticipate a devil of an

1. Postmark.

awakening. It will be from a mighty pleasant dream at least, Tautira being mere Heaven.

But suppose for the sake of argument any money to be left in the hands of my painful doer, what is to be done with it? Save us from exile, would be the wise man's choice, I suppose, for the exile threatens to be eternal. But yet, I am of opinion—in case there should be *some* dibs in the hand of the P.D., i.e. painful doer, because if there are none, I shall take to my flageolet on the high road and work home the best way I can, having previously made away with my family—I am of opinion that my aunt, Mrs. Alan Stevenson, should have her money from my mother: £20—twenty pounds. I am of opinion Miss Adelaide Boodle should have her box, like last year, at the same figure, and I am of opinion that if W.E.H. and his are in the customary state, and you are thinking of an offering, and there should still be some funds over, you would be a real good P.D. to put sume in with yours and tak' the credit o't, like a wee man! I know it's a beastly thing to ask, but it after all does no earthly harm, only that much good. And besides, like enough there is nothing in the till, and there is an end. Yet I live here in the full lustre of millions: it is thought I am the richest son of man that has yet been to Tautira. I!—and I am secretly eaten with the fear of lying in pawn, perhaps for the remainder of my days, in San Francisco. As usual, my colds have much bashed my finances.

Do tell Henley I write this just after having dismissed Oli the sub-chief,[2] in whose house I live, Mrs. Oli, and Pairai, their adopted child, from the evening hour of music, during which I Publickly (with a k) Blow on the Flageolet. These are words of truth. Yesterday, I told Oli about W.E.H., counterfeited his walk, counterfeited him playing on the piano and the pipe, and succeeded in sending the six feet four there is of that sub-chief somewhat sadly to his bed, feeling that his was not the genuine article after all. Oli is exactly like a Colonel in the Guards. I am, dear Charles,

Ever yours afftly,

R. L. S.

2. Political name: Ori à Ori; real name: Teriitera. See Furnas, pp. 322–5.

MS, Yale. Letters, 3, *88. A continua-*
tion of the preceding letter, though
written on a separate leaf.

Tautira [10 November 1888]

My dear Charles,
   I forgot:
   Mrs. Mary Ann Watts and her credit on Willis and Trantum,
the same, please, as last year; if you haven't Mary Ann's address,
Miss Boodle will manage it. Our mainmast is dry-rotten, and we are
all to the devil. I shall lie in a debtors' jail. Never mind: Tautira is
first chop. I am so besotted that I shall put on the back of this my
attempt at words to "Wandering Willie." If you can conceive at all
the difficulty, you will also conceive the vanity with which I regard
any kind of a result; and whatever mine is like, it has some sense
and Burns's has none.

R. L. S.

Home no more home to me, whither shall I wander?
   Hunger my driver, I go where I must.
Cold blows the winter wind over hill and heather;
   Thick drives the rain, and my roof is in the dust.
Loved of wise men was the shade of my roof-tree,
   The true word of welcome was spoken in the door.
Dear days of old, with the faces in the firelight,
   Kind folks of old, you come again no more.

Home was home then, my dear, full of kindly faces:
   Home was home then, my dear, happy for the child.
Fire and the windows bright glittered on the moorland,
   Song, tuneful song, built a palace on the wild.
Now when day dawns on the brow of the moorland,
   Lone stands the house and the chimney stone is cold.
Lone let it stand, now the folks are all departed,
   The kind hearts, the true hearts, that loved the house of old.[3]

3. Cf. *Poems,* p. 256.

MS, Yale. Letters, 3, *112.*

[Honolulu] 8 February 1889

My dear Charles,

Here we are at Honolulu, and have dismissed the yacht and lie here till April anyway in a fine state of haze, which I am yet in hopes some letter of yours (still on the way) may dissipate. No money, and not one word as to money! However, I have got the yacht paid off in triumph, I think; and though we stay here impignorate, it should not be for long, even if you bring us no extra help from home. The cruise has been a great success, both as to matter, fun, and health; and yet, Lord, man! we're pleased to be ashore! Yon was a very fine voyage from Tahiti up here, but—the dry land's a fine place too, and we don't mind squalls any longer, and eh, man, that's a great thing. Blow, blow, thou wintry wind, thou hast done me no appreciable harm beyond a few gray hairs! Altogether, this foolhardy venture is achieved, and if I have but nine months of life and any kind of health, I shall have both eaten my cake and got it back again with usury. But man, there have been days when I felt guilty, and thought I was in no position for the head of a house.

Your letter and accounts is doubtless at S.F. and will reach me in course. My wife is no great shakes: she is the one who has suffered most. My mother has had a Huge Old Time. Lloyd is first chop. I so well that I do not know myself—sea bathing, if you please, and what is far more dangerous, entertaining and being entertained by his Majesty [4] here, who is a very fine, intelligent fellow, but O, Charles! what a crop for the drink! He carries it, too, like a mountain with a sparrow on its shoulders. We calculated five bottles of champagne in three hours and a half (afternoon) and the sovereign quite presentable, although perceptibly more dignified, at the end.

Valentin [5] leaves us here, to mutual glee. Stop her private wages, and be ready (when she applies) to give her her little stock. It has been the usual tale of the maid on board the yacht.—This reminds me, I believe I poured forth my sorrows over my captain in your ear. Patience and time have quite healed these conflicts; we do what we want now, and the captain is a trusted friend. It *did*

4. Kalakaua I (1836–91), King of Hawaii.
5. See above, p. 164.

require patience in the beginning, but the seed has borne a most plentiful crop, and we feel quite proud of our tame captain, and (as I say) really like the man.

I have very little time by this mail, so hurry all I can. I was overjoyed at the news of the Henley Baby; [6] it should go far to heal that household. I have no word from him, and shall not try to write in the midst of my scurry. He little understands the harm he did me; but I am sure, upon all our cruise, the number of times we—all of us—longed for his presence would show it was no change of liking for him that we feel. For all that, time has not diminished my fear of him, and I doubt if I ever desire to correspond again. As for Katharine, I had an answer to my appeal, which settled that matter; I do not wish to see her. All these clouds, and the extraordinary health I enjoy and variety of interests I find among these islands, would tempt me to remain here—only for Lloyd, who is not well placed in such countries for a permanency, and a little for Colvin, to whom I feel I owe a sort of filial duty. And these two considerations will no doubt bring me back—to go to bed again—in England. I will write again soon, and beg for all news of the Henleys and all friends and beloved enemies.

Yours ever affectionately,

R. L. S.

MS, Yale. Letters, *3, 119; Clement
Shorter,* Letters to Charles Baxter.

Honolulu, [8] [7] March 1889

My dear Charles,

At last I have the accounts: the doer has done excellently, and in the words of Galpin,[8] "I reciprocate every step of your behaviour." Only upon one point would I protest, in *re* my mother. (1) The house is hers; she might live in it if she chose and pay no rent to the trust; therefore, if she lets it, the rent is hers, and (in my contention) the trust has nothing to do with it. But (2) suppose you have some argument I do not follow which disposes of No. 1, I can-

6. Margaret Emma Henley, born 4 September 1888, died 11 February 1894. Cf. Henley's poem, "When You Wake in Your Crib."
7. Postmark. Envelope marked "Private."
8. One of the publishers of the *Magazine of Art.*

not see how you are to charge her with the rent received for the use of the house during the winter *before* my father's death. It was let then to meet extra expenses in the South; the extra expenses were incurred by my father; why, then, is my mother to be charged with the covering sum? I see no answer to that, anyway. And still, if I am dull and there should be a reason, I should like to make up my mother's money to what it was. Possibly we had better wait to decide this till we meet, so that I can make sure I follow.—The £5 and £20 paid on account of my mother is all right: let it slide. I used to embezzle from her: turn about is fair play.

Quite right you were, of course, about Bob, Henley, and the book of verses. Let Bob's interest slide: it's only an annoyance to him and bookkeeping for your clerks; to me it would not make the change of a hair. I send a letter for Bob in your care, as I don't know his L'pool address,[9] by which (for he is to show you part of it) you will see we have got out of this adventure—or hope to have—with wonderful fortune.[1] I have the retrospective horrors on me when I think of the liabilities I incurred, but thank God I think I'm in port again, and I have found one climate in which I can enjoy life. Even Honolulu is too cold for me, but the South Isles were a heaven upon earth to a poor catarrhal party like Johns'one. We think, as Taheite is too complete a banishment, to try Madeira. It's only a week from England, good communications, and I suspect in climate and scenery not unlike my own dear islands; in people, alas, there can be no comparison. But friends could go, and I could come in summer; so I should not be quite cut off.

Lloyd and I have finished a story, *The Wrong Box*. If it is not funny, I'm sure I don't know what is. I have split over writing it. Since I have been here, I have been toiling like a galley slave: three numbers of *The Master* to rewrite; five chapters of *The Wrong Box* to write and rewrite; and about five hundred lines of a narrative poem [2] to write, rewrite, and re-rewrite. Now I have *The Master* waiting me for its continuation—2 numbers more; when that's done, I shall breathe.

This spasm of activity has been chequered with champagne

9. Bob Stevenson had been appointed professor of art at the University of Liverpool.

1. See *Letters, 3,* 114.

2. "The Feast of Famine."

parties. Happy and Glorious *Hawaii ponoi nana i kou moi* (Native Hawaiians, dote upon your monarch!)—Hawaiian God save the King. (In addition to my other labours I am learning the language with a native *moonshee*.[3]) Kalakaua is a terrible companion: a bottle of fizz is like a glass of sherry to him; he thinks nothing of five or six in an afternoon as a whet for dinner. Look here: Van Laun,[4] Edmonstone,[5] Charles Mackay,[6] and Sam Bough[7]—he could have taken all four, one up, another down; as for you, you poor creature, he could settle you before breakfast. You should see a photograph of our party after an afternoon with H.H.M.: my! what a crew! The proud drunkenness of Lloyd, the soppy swan-neckery of R.L.S., my mother—let us draw a veil till you see it.

Yours ever afftly,
ROBERT LOUIS STEVENSON

I enclose one of many Income Tax things I have received. What's wrong?

My dear friend, This is only to show that my heart is in the right place, though my body is not. It, alas, should [be] in Tautira with my well-beloved "savages," as they are fond of calling themselves. I am really better than I have been for some time. I *believe* the thing in my throat is gone, though I am nervous about it, and imagine that it is coming back when it is not. Louis is wonderful, and Lloyd is quite the literary man. It was very saddening to hear of poor Mrs. Henley's [8] death, and most unexpected. I hope she passed away with as much comfort as one may. She had not too much in life. I had meant to write to Anna,[9] congratulating her on the new acquisition, but somehow I can't write letters. My love to you all.

F. VdeG. S.

3. Joseph Poepoe.
4. Henri Van Laun (1820–96), teacher of French and author.
5. Not identified.
6. Journalist and minor poet (1814–89); father, out of wedlock, of Marie Corelli.
7. Scottish landscape painter (1822–78). For RLS's first meeting with him see *Letters, 1,* 29 ff.; and for RLS's obituary notice, *Academy, 14* (1878), 530.
8. Emma Morgan Henley, Henley's mother.
9. Anna Boyle Henley, his wife.

MS, Yale. Letters, *3, 138.*

Private

Honolulu [12] [1] April 1889

My dear Charles,

As usual your letter is as good as a cordial, and I thank you for
it, and all your care, kindness, and generous and thoughtful friendship, from my heart. I was truly glad to hear a word of Colvin,
whose long silence has terrified me; and glad to hear that you condoned the notion of my staying longer in the South Seas, for I
have decided in that sense. The first idea was to go in the *Morning
Star,* missionary ship, but now I have found a trading schooner, the
Equator, which is to call for me here early (*D.V.*) in June, and
carry us through the Gilberts. What will happen then, the Lord
knows. My mother does not accompany us; she leaves here for home
early in May, and you will hear of us from her, but not I imagine
anything more definite. We shall get dumped on Butaritari, and
whether we manage to go on to the Marshalls and Carolines, or
whether we fall back on Samoa, Heaven must decide; but I mean
to fetch back into the course of the *Richmond* (to think you don't
know what the *Richmond* is!—*the* steamer of the Eastern South
Seas, joining New Zealand, Tonga Tabu, the Samoas, Taheite, and
Raratonga, and carrying, by last advices, sheep in the saloon!)—
into the course of the *Richmond* and make Taheite once again on
the home track. I take my backgoing son-in-law [2] along with me.
This family has been a sore trouble to me, but Joe is a good photographer, and the idea is to get up a diorama and let Lloyd lecture,
and try to start a little money, honestly got, for this Skimpolian
household. Joe is a loveable fellow, but I tell you, and you know,
I would rather have to deal with D. A. Stevenson [3] (in view of your
last news) or Paganini MacKnight [4] than one of these truculent
fools who do not know the meaning of money. It is heartbreaking;
but there—the burthen is on the back, and the diorama is an
honest and hopeful pitch to lighten it. What think ye?

The picture of the *chatelaine* passing away in a dwam of mater-
nal vanity over what strikes me as a portly and really personable

1. Postmark.
2. Joseph Strong.
3. See above, p. 172 n. 10.
4. Not identified.

infant has been going round the family all evening (the steamer came in but an hour or two ago) with rapture. A more dramatic work I never saw; and though it's the kind of thing that tempts a man to chaff, it did my heart good. Long may the babe flourish! And to think of it in South Howard Place! I was born in plain Howard Place, with none of the points of the compass, myself, and it did my business. I wonder: I have always had a little fear of that corner of Edinr; Warriston Park is raither a Boggy Bit, isn't it not, Mr. Johns'one? or üsed to be?

Would I like to see the *Scots Observer*? [5] Wouldn't I not? But whaur? I'm direckit at space. They have nae Post Offishes at the Gilberts, and as for the Car'lines! Ye see, Mr. Baxter, we're no just in the punkshewal *centre* o' civ'lization. But pile them up for me, and when I've decided on a address, I'll let you ken, and ye'll can send them stavin' after me.

A propos of D. and T.S.,[6] I hear this with miserable feelings. It is a wretched business; I pray God it may not go so far as a case. If I were the only person to consider, I could cry quits now, rather than so damned a scandal should smirch my name; but of course I have no right to interfere with my mother, and no will to cut up what is the hope of all the family as well as of my folk; for I guess the Alans [7] will get nothing from that crew, and they will always take something under my testament.

O—and another thing. As to the Young debt.[8] It was never intended to chivvy Young, and if he has left his family in difficulties, niether my mother nor I would like the family chivvied. Pray deal with them in all gentleness.

You will keep up my charities please this year as last: the Xmas boxes and sich, and I have told Miss Boodle to apply to you in case the Watts family come to remediable grief. Act for me *tanquam Bonus P.F.*[9] as usual; also *Bonus* P.D., or painful doer.

You shall hear from me again by next mail, I hope with clearer details. And I am meanwhile,

Ever your affectionate
R. L. S.

5. The first issue of the *Scots Observer*, edited by Henley, appeared 24 November 1888.

6. David and Thomas Stevenson, i.e. the firm.

7. See above, p. 180 and n. 3.

8. Not identified; but not E. B. Young of San Francisco.

9. Pater Familias?

MS, Yale.

[Honolulu, 27 April 1889] [1]

My dear Charles,

I forget if I have made my plans clear to you. They stand thus:

We should leave Honolulu early in June, per trading schooner *Equator* for the Gilbert islands. Our subsequent movements, which are quite in the air, will be most briefly indicated by this post office guide: Letters: c/o H.B.M. Consul, Apia, Samoa, "to await arrival" up to September incl.; c/o H.B.M. Consul, Papeete, Tahiti, "to await arrival," up to December inclusive; c/o E. B. Young, S.F., Cal., thereafter.

I wish you would register the title *The Pearlfisher* [2] for me. It is for a story Lloyd and I are on—the gaudiest yarn—and I have a dreadful fear someone will burk the name, as has happened to me once before with *Robin Run-the-Hedge.* [3]

I am off work and go to Hawaii for ten days for a change, to a home of the King's; he says one man can speak English. It is on the Kona Coast, where the King is perpetually engaged on a treasure chase. Old Kamemeha [3a] the 1st (or 2nd, I forget which) sold gin to the pirates, and his female chamberlains buried the proceeds in a cave upon that seaboard; but alas! there are many hundred caverns there, and the chamberlains died game. Hence, *sa majesté actuelle revient et reviendra toujours bredouille.*

A pretty touch of seaman manners: the English and American Jacks are deadly rivals. Well, after all this hammering of both sides by the Germans, and then the news of the hurricane [4] from Samoa, a singular scene occurred Sunday before last. The two church parties, *sponte propria,* fell in line together, one Englishman to one American, and marched down to the harbour side like one ship's company. None were more surprised than their own officers. I have seen a hantle of the seaman on this cruise; I always

---

1. Postmark.
2. The story which later appeared, in truncated form, as *The Ebb-Tide.*
3. *Robin-Run-the-Hedge,* by Annette Lyster, London, Simpkin, 1884.
3a. I.e. Kamehameha.
4. The famous Apia hurricane had occurred 15 March 1889. Three American warships, *Trenton, Vandalia,* and *Nipsic,* and three German, *Adler, Eber,* and *Olga* were sunk or beached. Only the British *Calliope* had enough engine power to escape in the teeth of the gale.

liked him before; my first crew on the *Casco* (5 sea lawyers) near
cured me; but I have returned to my first love.

I must say farewell, as the night draws on and I must be on "the
eight seas" tomorrow.

Ever yours,

R. L. STEVENSON

MS, Yale. Letters, *3, 140.*

[Honolulu, 10 May 1889] [5]

My dear Charles,

I am appalled to gather from your last just to hand that you have
felt so much concern about the letter. Pray dismiss it from your
mind. But I think you scarce appreciate how disagreable it is to
have your private affairs and private unguarded [6] expressions getting into print. It would soon sicken anyone of writing letters. I
have no doubt that letter was very wisely selected, but it just shows
how things crop up: there was a raging jealousy between the two
yachts, our captain was nearly in a fight over it. However, no more;
and whatever you think, my dear fellow, do not suppose me angry
with you or Coggie; [7] although I was *annoyed at the circumstance*
—a very different thing. But it is hard to conduct life by letter, and
I continually feel I may be drifting into some matter of offence, in
which my heart takes no part. Please reassure Coggie.

I must now turn to a point of business. This new cruise of ours
is somewhat venturesome, and I think it needful to warn you not
to be in a hurry to suppose us dead. In these ill-charted seas, it is
quite on the cards we might be cast on some unvisited or very rarely
visited island; that there we might lie for a long time, even years,
unheard of, and yet turn up smiling at the hinder end. So do not
let me be "rowpit," [8] till you get some certainty we have gone to
Davie Jones in a squall or graced the feast of some barbarian in
the character of Long Pig.

5. Postmark.

6. MS, apparently "unregarded."

7. CB and Coggie Ferrier had released for publication a letter from the Stevensons in the Marquesas. The Stevensons had met there a British yacht, the *Nyanza,*
belonging to the Dewar family of distillery fame, and had commented on its ugli-
ness as compared with the trim lines of the *Casco.* Hence repercussions in Scotland.

8. Sold at auction.

I have at last heard from Colvin; he must have had a real bad turn. I gather I have had a touch of the same; overwork brought on a very distressing attack of blood to the head, so that I could scarcely see, scarcely understand what was said to me, and presented by way of face a purple expanse only enlivened by a pair of white lips. I trust mine has drifted off without further harm. I hope Charcot [9] will get him round. I will back you up, of course, as I have said so often, in anything it may be possible to do for him. It is already cheering we have been able to do something.

I have just been a week away alone on the lee coast of Hawaii; the only white creature in many miles, riding 5½ hours one day, living with a native, seeing poor lepers shipped off to Molokai, hearing native causes and giving my opinion as *amicus curiae* as to the interpretation of a statute in English: a lovely week among God's best—at least God's sweetest—works, Polynesians. It has bettered me greatly. If I could only stay there the time that remains, I could get my work done and be happy; but the care of a large, costly, and no' just preceesely forrit-gaun family keeps me in vile Honolulu, where I am always out of sorts, amidst heat and cold and cesspools and beastly *haoles*. What is a *haole?* You are one, and so, I am sorry to say, am I. After so long a dose of whites, it was a blessing to get among Polynesians again, even for a week.

Weel Charles, there are waur *haoles* than yoursel', I'll say that for ye; and I trust before I sail, I shall get another letter in a vein of more content and with more about yourself.

Ever your affectionate friend,
R. L. S.

It is strange to think: during all these months when I have been in postal range, till this letter of Colvin, you are the only one of my old friends who has written to me. When I seemed to feel in your last that you too were a little irritated, this came home to me sharply. I see partly where I have been to blame; yet I think it is rather hard measure; and perhaps if you will consider this isolation, and how very annoying it is never to be able to write a careless word lest it should find its way into the newspapers, you will be inclined to make more allowance.

9. Jean Martin Charcot (1825–93), pioneer in psychopathology.

MS, Yale.

[Honolulu, 7 June 1889] [1]

My dear Charles,

The last mail we are likely to receive has come in, and I fear I am to go away with your last (pardon me) a little shirty letter for farewell. Well, it can't be cured, but I would fain hope your painful feelings will blow over, and indeed I think you will come to see I was right (as to the matter; in the manner I daresay I was very far amiss), that I have a perfect right to object to the publication of private letters, and that whether the public wants to read them or not is nothing to the purpose. To the public I may be an object of unwholesome curiosity; to my private friends I would like to remain a private friend like any other, and to enjoy the priviledge of writing in confidence. It may seem hard to conceive, but I like my doings being published just as little as you would.—Ah, you say, and you are going to write a book about them!—Even so, Charles; but then I shall choose for myself.

I have at last definite news of Colvin, which alarms and distresses me. If I had had it in time, I would have given up this cruise and come home. Pray remember, if ever he should be in want of help, *you are to strain my credit to bursting, and mortgage all I possess or can expect,* to help him. I hope this is strong enough; if I return to find myself deep in debt, I shall be only pleased if it was done for Colvin. All other directions as before.

I shall draw a new will in case we all go down, and file it here in the consulate.

The address till further notice is to be care of R. Towns and Co., Sydney, where I wish you would send me a flageolet of the best description with all needful appliances. The one I have is very inferior: it is a D, as I should rather like the new one to be. I hope it will last the cruise, but it is already split, is very hard to clean, and the keys do not unscrew, so that a small accident may *put out my pipe.* The voice, flageolet, guitar, and taropatch make up our band; a magic lantern with scripture pictures is the attraction for the eye. We shall give them several Hawaiian songs, *Freut euch des lebens, Il segretto,* Carnival of Venice, Nights of Seville, etc.; and if the natives are not pleased, you bet the performers will enjoy

1. Postmark. Envelope marked "Private."

themselves.[2] Another thing we shall want out at Sydney is full advertisements and price lists of *really fine* magic lanterns. The idea is to begin the panorama there, and when it is ready, carry it to some of the islands in style, and get more stuff for it, thus making it feed itself. Can you send us these two, then: (1) A-1 flageolet (2) price lists of A-1 magic lanterns for public performances, full rigged for cities and metropolises; and receive the benediction of the Island Nights [3] Entertainment Troup. Walk up, ladies and gentlemen! Wish we had Henley here: bet he could learn to sing second; besides we could put him in a glass case, as a specimen *Beritani*.[4] The object of the present show is to take the place of the yacht as something to interest and amuse the natives.[5]

MS, Yale.

Honolulu, 16 June 1889

My dear Charles,

Herewith a certified copy of my new will necessitated by fresh risks and obligations. I wish to say I have since re-read your last, and withdraw, with apologies, the epithet "shirty" applied to it. It was, on the other hand, a wise and careful letter—wisely cold; only the coldness shocked me, for God knows I have enough of it now from old friends. But I quite appreciate the spirit in which you wrote, and I hope you will forgive the dulness that made me fail to understand it at the first.

I am going on here with my complicated burthens: to give poor Joe Strong (a very annoying, loveable man) a square start in life. His debts have proved less and his assets more than was feared, but the expense of the whole experiment is staggering. I have sent £200 to R. Towns and Co. in Sydney to dole out to Belle and the child; in case anything unforeseen should happen to delay us beyond expectation, they, Towns and Co., are to communicate with you; and of course, Belle and the boy must not be left in trouble. My health keeps incredibly good: for the last six days I have been from five

2. Deletion: "Now you see what a thing it is: you don't suppose I want all that published."
3. MS, originally, "Teriitera Variety."
4. Britisher.
5. Not signed.

to eight hours in continual business, much of it very annoying, some downright painful, and am fairly fit today on the back of it. Our schooner is now due and we are fairly ready to get away. To all our chronies now on land, we cards prepared for sea send salutations. I trust all is explicit; and I do hope my new books will sell, for this is a tight place to pass, and if I can pass it, and the lecture and panorama pays, I shall feel safer for the future. We have sickness and doctors' bills and a nurse on our back foreby—which I could have gladly spared. But my books have been amazingly profitable this last year, and I make hay, with rather morbid eagerness, while the sun shines.

June 18th

On June 17th, my wife twice saw you come into the *lanai,* once before 12, and once before four P.M. Do not mention this, as it most likely means only a passing state of health: the doctor thinks it nothing out of the way in her condition; yet I am superstitious enough, or anxious enough to be superstitious, to pass you on the dates. You had a very severe expression. We have all been very much annoyed and wearied, but things are plainer now, the schooner is overdue by some days, she cannot be long now, and then to sea! I am very tired today and do not feel like much correspondence, and I have a good many letters before me. But perhaps I can add a word later on; and perhaps indeed I may be still many days here. *Aita te pahi*—no ship—being an old word of ours in Tahiti and likely to be an older friend ere we are done with sea faring.

19th

I inclose a scrap written many months ago, which I found in packing: it was a curious evocation under the circumstances, and I faintly remember how it impressed me. I lie writing this in the balcony of the Hawaiian Hotel, having been fired out of my own house by general colds; I am mighty quiescent—the reaction after days of conflict—and still *aita te pahi.*

19th. The *Equator* is at the buoy. Farewell!

Yours ever,

R. L. S.

MS, Yale. Letters, 3, *171.*

Apia, Samoa, 28 December [1889]

My dear Charles,

By a providential error on the part of the postmaster I received yours of 3rd June on my arrival here, and was more pleased and more ashamed of myself than words can describe. I am extremely sorry that any petulance of mine should have put you to so much distress; and yet I well understand it, having myself watched in a similar manner and with the same sleepless nights 2 and perhaps 3 friendships go to Hell, as I honestly consider, without fault of mine. However, yours was a nightmare only. I hate this letter-publishing racket, and am inclined to squall when it comes my way; but I would no more make a quarrel about any such innocent indiscretion and purely personal annoyance than I would—I lack a simile—the thing at least is not in me, and I only deeply regret that my usual loudness and shrillness should have given you so much distress. I tried to re-read your letter this morning, and I could not bear; I hate so to see this waste of tissue caused by me.

The rest of this letter I ask you to make known to my mother, as I shall not have time to write again to her. Our cruise in the Gilberts was a rough time in a good many ways; so was the voyage down. Poor Joe on his arrival here was condemned and sent off at a few hours' notice to Sydney, whither, in case of the worst, Fanny and Lloyd will go next Sunday by the *Lubeck*—if Fanny is able, but she also is far from well, and I do not think I shall allow her. It is very difficult to see what is the right thing. All I am sure of is that I must stay. I cannot return till I have seen either Toga or Fiji or both; and I must not leave here till I have finished my collections on the war: a very interesting bit of history, the truth often very hard to come at, and the search (for me) much complicated by the German tongue, from the use of which I have desisted (I suppose) these fifteen years. The last 2 days I have been mugging with a dictionary from five to six hours a day; besides this I have to call upon, keep sweet, and judiciously interview all sorts of persons— English, American, German, and Samoan. It makes a hard life, above all as after every interview I have to come and get my notes straight on the nail. I believe I should have got my facts before the end of January, when I shall make for Toga or Fiji. I am down right in the hurricane season, but they had so bad a one last year, I don't imagine there will be much of an edition this. Say that I get to Sydney some time in April, and I shall have done well, and be in a position to write a very singular and interesting book, or rather two: for I shall begin, I think, with a separate opuscule on the Samoan Trouble,[6] about as long as *Kidnapped,* not very interesting, but valuable and a thing proper to be done. And then hey! for the big South Sea Book—a devil of a big one, and full of the finest sport.

This morning, as I was going along to my breakfast a little before 7 reading a number of *Blackwood's Magazine,* I was startled by a soft *"Talofa, alii"* (Note for my mother: they are quite courteous here in the European style, quite unlike Tahiti: *alii*=gentleman=*ariie* in Tahitian) right in my ear; it was Mataafa[7] coming from early mass in his white coat and white linen kilt, with 3 followers behind him. Mataafa is the nearest thing to a hero in my history, and really a fine fellow: plenty sense, and the most dignified, quiet, gentle manners. Talking of *Blackwood*—a file of which I was lucky enough to find here in the lawyer's—Mrs. Oliphant[8] seems in a staggering state: from *The Wrong Box* to *The Master* I scarce recognise either my critic or myself. I gather that *The Master* should do well, and at least that notice is agreeable reading. I expect to be home in June. You will have gathered I am pretty well; in adition to my labours, I suppose I walk five or six miles a day, and almost every day I ride up and see Fanny and Lloyd, who are in a house in the bush with Ah Fu.[9] I live in Apia for history's sake with Moors, an American trader.[10]

6. *A Footnote to History.*

7. Ablest—and hence most distrusted by the Germans, British, and Americans—of the three contenders for the high chieftainship of Samoa.

8. Margaret Oliphant Oliphant (1828–97), prolific novelist and author of biographical and historical works. She was presumably the anonymous reviewer of *The Wrong Box* and *The Master of Ballantrae* in *Blackwood's Magazine, 146* (1889), 255, 696.

9. The Chinese cook, shipped in the Marquesas on the *Casco* cruise, had remained with the Stevensons through the *Equator* cruise also.

10. Harry Jay Moors, ablest, wealthiest, and best informed of the non-German traders in Samoa. His wife was a Samoan. He later wrote *With Stevenson in Samoa,* Boston, 1910.

Day before yesterday I was arrested and fined for riding fast in the street, which made my blood bitter as the wife of the manager of the German Firm [1] has twice almost ridden me down, and there seems none to say her nay. The Germans have behaved pretty badly here, but not, in all ways, so ill as you may have gathered; they were doubtless much provoked, and if the insane Knappe [2] had not appeared upon the scene, might have got out of the muddle with dignity. I write along without rhyme or reason, as things occur to me.

This of Joe Strong's illness and probable death is a serious consideration: it means a certain adition to my cares, no doubt of that; and suppose him to die, what the mischeif am I to do with The Widow? Poor Joe, he was a great annoyance, even to the last. On Apemama, after some miserable misconduct, I had to take all the photographic business out of his hands. And yet he was so gentle and pleasant that I never felt my affection shaken, even in our rows; I could far better have parted from his wife. Singular story: on Apemama, the only person who wore shoes was Joe: all the rest of us and all the natives went barefoot; well, the print of a child's foot shod, and shod very neatly, was continually to be observed about our sleeping house, and we have traced it accompanying Joe's footprints right across the island and along the beach. It is all very well to say you are not superstitious, but I kept the fact religiously from Joe, who never observed it, and when we came here I did fully expect to hear that Austin [3] had been ill or else was dead. No such news having come, I presume my ghost story is a foozle like all the genuine ones. But still it's an odd circumstance, and hard to explain.

I hope from my outcries about printing you do not think I want you to keep my news or letters in a Blue Beard closet. I like all friends to hear of me: they all should, if I had 90 hours in the day and strength for all of them; but you must have gathered how hard worked I am, and you will understand I go to bed a pretty tired man.

Tomorrow (Monday, I won't swear to my day of the month—

1. Deutsche Handels und Plantagen Gesellschaft für Süd-See Inseln zu Hamburg —the "Long-Handle" firm which, with the backing of the German Imperial government, aimed at, and almost achieved, a monopoly of Samoan trade.

2. For details see *A Footnote to History*.

3. Austin Strong.

this is the Sunday between Xmas and New Year) I go up the coast with Mr. Clark,[4] one of the London Society missionaries, in a boat to examine schools, see Tamasese,[5] etc. Lloyd comes to photograph. Pray Heaven we have good weather: this is the rainy season. We shall be gone 4 or 5 days, and if the rain keep off, I shall be glad of the change; if it rain, it will be beastly. This explains still further how hard pressed I am, as the mail will be gone ere I return, and I have thus lost the days I had meant to write in. I have a boy, Henry,[6] who interprets and copies for me, and is a great nuisance. He said he wished to come to me in order to learn "long explessions." Henry goes up along with us, and as I am not fond of him, he may, before the trip is over, hear some "stlong explessions."

I am writing this on the back balcony at Moors', palms and a hill like the hill of Kinnoul looking in at me; myself lying on the floor and (like the parties in Hendel's song)[7] "clad in robes of virgin white." The ink is dreadful, the heat delicious, a fine going breeze in the palms, and from the other side of the house the endless, angry splash and roar of the Pacific on the reef, where the warships are still piled from last year's hurricane, some underwater, one high and dry upon her side, the strangest figure of a ship was ever witnessed. The narrow bay there is full of ships: the men of war covered with sail after the rains, and (especially the German ship which is fearfully and awfully topheavy) rolling almost yards in, in what appears to be calm water.

Samoa, Apia at least, is far less beautiful than the Marquesas or Tahiti: a more gentle scene, gentler acclivities, a tamer face of nature; and this much aided for the wanderer by the great German plantations with their countless regular avenues of palm. The island has beautiful rivers, of about the bigness of our waters in the Lothians, with pleasant fords and waterfalls and overhanging verdure, and often a great volume of sound, so that once I thought I was passing near a mill, and it was only the voice of the river. I am not specially attracted by the people: they are courteous, pretty chaste, but thieves and beggars, to the weariness of those involved. The women are very attractive and dress lovely; the men purpose-

4. Rev. W. E. Clarke.

5. The second (Mataafa being the first) rival of the German-supported Malietoa for the high chieftainship.

6. Henry Simele, who became one of RLS's most trusted aides at Vailima.

7. Air from *Theodora* (1749).

like, well set up, tall, lean, and dignified. As I write, the breeze is brisking up; doors are beginning to slam, and shutters; a strong draught sweeps round the balcony; it looks doubtful for tomorrow. Here, I shut up.

Ever your affectionate,

R. L. STEVENSON [8]

MS, Yale. Letters, 3, *179.*

Norddeutscher Lloyd, Bremen,

Februar [9] den 3en 1890,

Dampfer Lübeck zwischen Apia und Sydney.

Hooray for the Deutscher [9] Lloyd!

My dear Charles,

I have got one delightful letter from you, and heard from my mother [1] of your kindness in going to see her. Thank you for that; you can in no way more touch and serve me. I wish Henley had gone. I wish too he would have done with biting heels: an old friend's heels are a poor diet. Ay, ay, it is sad to sell 17; sad and fine were the old days. When I was away in Apemama, I wrote 2 copies of verse about Edinr and the past, so ink black, so golden bright. I will send them, if I can find them, for they will say something to you, and indeed one is more than half addressed to you. This is it.

To My Old Comrades [2]

Do you remember—can we e'er forget?—
How, in the coiled perplexities of youth,
In our wild climate, in our scowling town,
We gloomed and shivered, sorrowed, sobbed and feared?
The belching winter wind, the missile rain,
The rare and welcome silence of the snows,
The laggard morn, the haggard day, the night,
The grimy spell of the nocturnal town,
Do you remember?—ah, could one forget!

8. Signature cut out, supplied by CB with the note: "Original sent to Miss Hampson, Platt Cottage, Manchester"; later purchased by Mr. Beinecke and restored to MS.

9. Written in German script.

1. Who had returned to Edinburgh to attend to the dismantling and sale of 17 Heriot Row.

2. Printed under the title "To My Old Familiars" (*Poems*, p. 268).

As when the fevered sick that all night long
Listed the wind intone, and hear at last
The ever-welcome voice of chanticleer
Sing, in the bitter hour before the dawn:
With sudden ardour these desire the day.
     (Here a squall sends all flying)
So sang in the gloom of youth the bird of hope;
So we, exulting, listed and desired.
For as in the palace porch of life
We huddled with chimaeras, from within,
How sweet to hear! the music swelled and fell,
And through the breach of the revolving doors,
What dreams of splendour blinded us and fled!
    I have since then contended and rejoiced;—
Amid the glories of the house of life
Profoundly entered; and the shrine beheld:
Kindlier it glows and brighter than we dreamed!
Yet when the lamp from my expiring eyes
Shall dwindle and recede, the voice of love
Faint insignificant on my closing ears,
What sound shall come but the old cry of the wind
In our inclement city? what return
But the image of the emptiness of youth?

So as in darkness, from the magic lamp,
The momentary pictures gleam and fade
And vanish, and the night resurges—these
Shall I remember, and then all forget.

They're pretty second rate, but felt. I can't be bothered to copy the other.[3]

The magic lantern job is given up. Impossible to make Joe Strong work, however little; and now his health is gone, and it would be cruel to try. With all that, he is so extravagant that I despair of supporting him. Yet the fool is thoroughly loveable: he has every good quality that I don't possess, and none that I do; and it's scarce too much to say that I despair of being able either to desert or to support, either to leave or tolerate the man. In some ways, the world goes cross with the luckiest: J.D.S. and his wife

3. See *Poems,* p. 270.

and family are the worst in the lot today. Lloyd was to have gone to Cambridge; now, seeing me saddled with this mule-load of struggling cormorants, he seems to be about refusing to go. I respect the impulse, yet I feel I shall, and should, oppose the decision. It seems written, I shall never save; well, the best for him is to get equipped for his own battle after I am gone.

Meanwhile, I have bought 314½ acres of beautiful land in the bush behind Apia; when we get the house built, the garden laid, and cattle in the place, it will be something to fall back on for shelter and food; and if the island could stumble into political quiet, it is conceivable it might even bring a little income. I have paid one half of it. The other is due in six months; and if by any accident I should fail in meeting it, H. J. Moors of Apia will draw on you personally for the amount: $10 currency per acre—at $7 to the £1, 157¼ acres; I leave *you* to reckon. It makes about £200, by my count, which is more interesting than exact. We range from 600 to 1500 feet, have 5 streams, waterfalls, precipices, profound ravines, rich tablelands, 50 head of cattle on the ground (if anyone could catch them), a great view of forest, sea, mountains, the warships in the haven: really a noble place. Some day you are to take a long holiday and come and see us; it has been all planned.

With all these irons in the fire, and cloudy prospects, you may be sure I am pleased to hear a good account of business. I believed *The Master* was a sure card; I wonder why Henley thinks it grimy. Grim it is, God knows, but sure not grimy; else I am the more deceived. I am sorry he did not care for it; I place it on the line with *Kidnapped* myself. We'll see as time goes on whether it goes above or falls below.

In seven days now I shall have my flageolet—I trust it isn't a clarinet, as you wrote, for I could neer blaw it. I die for it, my own being now quite dumb, and a bloody instrument at the best. I'll give you quarter of an hour of it once, in memoriam of one Sunday afternoon in Rutland Square, and you shall return my laughter. God, I laugh at the recollection! I trust I may be able to amuse you as exquisitely; but alas! the flageolet is an easier instrument. The duffer is only effete and uninteresting; he cannot be so wild, so inspired as on the oboe.

I agree with you, I doubt Barnardo [4] a little; I'll look into it,

4. See above, p. 186.

when home. Excuse the iron stupidity of this letter: it is the movement of the steamer, so different and strange to me after 20 months
on small schooners; the day besides is squally, and I have had mis-
adventures with the ink pot. We are tearing fast southward into
cold weather, and O, my! how shall I like it? 'Tis a thing that remains to be seen.

Thank you particularly for asking of my wife's throat; there are
no symptoms of return, thank God. I believe she means to add a
word or two to this. Our voyage (we are the only passengers on
this big ship) is delightful: captain a charming fellow, weather delightful, table generous, excellent light table wine at 1/-!, really
nothing bad except the coffee. Long life to the Norddeutscher
Lloyd! This boat loses 20,000 marks a trip; at least it loses it like
a gentleman. Will you allow me to observe that the world is (at this
time and for once) *not* too much with me?

Ever your affectionate
R. L. S.

I take this blank corner to add a warmer expression of my thanks
for your friendship; so much has fallen away, death and the worse
horror of estrangement have so cut me down and rammed me in,
that you and Colvin remain now all in all to me; and Colvin I cannot but fear is sore stricken. I beg of you, dear old friend, to take
care of your health physical and moral; you do not know what you
become to me, how big you bulk; you must not measure it by my
mean letters, nor by anything that I shall ever say; you remain alone
of my early past, truer now than ever, and I cling to the thought of
you. Hard thoughts I sometimes have of others, God forgive me; I
cannot get farther yet than that half ugly word of pardon, and
even so, said with a grimace; I prefer to think of two that have stood
by me, you and Colvin, with a warmth that grows ever greater.
When we talk you shall tell me, and I will try to learn, where I
have been in fault with the others; I will take hard words from you
and believe hard judgements, but not by letter, please, only when
we meet.

My dear friend, or may I say as Louis does, My dear Charles?

I add a few wandering words to my husband's letter. I am very
very sorry that you thought so much of the small affair of the letter.

I wish it had never been spoken of. When friends are so widely separated it seems a waste to dwell upon such things as momentary annoyances. Friendship, as I take it, is something like marriage. A quick word here or there means nothing, and passes, not to be thought of again. I think it is something to be proud of that Louis has arrived at nearly forty years and still keeps one friend of his youth, and another of his early manhood. It is *not* a scant allowance. And even of dead friendships there is always a tender memory. As for me, I can never enter that enchanted garden of the past: I came too late, and I fear one of my sex would not have been admitted. But now I trust you will be willing that the gate of the present may be opened to me, and though there may be no butterflies to chase, nor pots of gold to dig for at the foot of rainbows, I may still find some pleasant flowers growing there: heartsease, and forget-me-nots, and such homely plants, and I know there are many quiet nooks where one may rest and warm one's heart in the sunshine. You will let me in?

In return I offer you all that is to be found in "Vailima," otherwise the Samoan plantation. I say plantation because of literary feeling for the word; at present it is only bush, but full of the most glorious possibilities. I cannot keep my mind long upon any other subject. What a day it will be when the Stevensons come out to meet you at the steamer, our flower-crowned Samoan boys singing as they row. And when we return, on the beach shall be waiting saddle horses, and a buckboard (you have yet to learn what a buckboard is, but you will like it when you do know), and a crowd of black boys to take your impedimenta of civilization. While you are mounting your steed, half clad (yet perfectly clad) *houris* will gather to bid you *kalofa*.[5] Then away we dash between fragrant lime hedges, through a little native hamlet where the dogs bark and my friends there call "kalofa" as we pass, into the somber forest, out again, and only twenty minutes from the beach, and here we are at Vailima, the place of the five rivers. It is not possible to go on: the prospect becomes too dazzling for mortal eyes. I will only hint that an original dance, and a song expressly for the occasion shall be sung and danced in your honour, and for you shall the succulent pig, the delicious fei, and the delicate young leaves of the taro be baked in the earth oven. Begin to think upon it now,

5. A variant of *talofa* ("my love to you").

for come you must. Even though you will not open that little gate to me, but leave me outside to gaze longingly through the palings, Vailima, as the Spanish say, is yours. You see, after all, how little worth is the friendship I offer when I put in that saving clause, "as the Spanish say." At least you see I am frank, and if you lift the latch you know to whom and what, and there can be no misapprehension.

I am extremely glad you liked *The Wrong Box*. I could not but feel a little alarmed when I thought of what liberties the authors had taken.[6] I believe Lloyd was the one really responsible for that, so please put it down to the bold rashness of youth; though I noticed an expression of relief on his stern countenance when I told him there was no sign in your letter of hostile intentions. You may, however, be biding your time, in which case you will soon have him.

I cannot conceive what Mr. Young has been doing all this time about the cottages. I see from a letter Mrs. Stevenson has from Valentin that they are not even begun yet, or weren't in January. He may be waiting for the rainy season to pass, but why did he then not write and say so? Valentin's money you sent her, by the way, was a present and not back wages, but that is a trifle.

The weather here is abominable, and the criminal stamp very strong upon the faces of the passers-by. Louis likes the town, but I don't. I pine for my Islands, and my Islanders. It is a sudden drop to fall from the society of kings to that of the descendants of— "Sydney ducks."[7] Long ago I once found myself next at table to a person who remarked that he was born in Sydney. "Then do tell me," said I, in all innocence, for I supposed them to [be] something of the nature of "Bombay ducks," "what *are* Sydney ducks?"

Louis has written a song for Tembinoki,[8] the king of Appemama, which he means to publish in the *Scribner* with a portrait of his magnificent majesty, other photographs such as his "matted men" dancing, and a flag I designed for the Island.

And that reminds me, a ship has just arrived from the Gilberts and I must get letters and presents ready for her return. This vessel,

6. The caricature of CB as Michael Finsbury.

7. Convicts.

8. "The House of Tembinoka," first collected in *Songs of Travel*. See *Poems*, p. 272.

the *George Noble,* brings word that the schooner *Tiernan,* on which we very nearly took passage, has been wrecked off Butaritari. Had we taken her instead of the *Equator* we should have been aboard at the time of the wreck. She was caught between two squalls and lost eleven native passengers and all her cargo; nothing was saved. Even had we escaped with our lives, Louis's papers and all our photographs would in all probability have gone to the bottom. And we thought her so much safer than the *Equator.* It seems almost miraculous that we have returned no worse than we have: myself a little broken down by the hardships of the voyage, Lloyd with what they call here by the reassuring name of "bush rot," but Louis I may say *well.* God grant that the British Isles may respect the work of their Southern sisters.

As to poor Joe Strong it was to be sooner or later, and the sooner the better for him and all connected with him. It sounds hard to say this, but I do not mean it that way. There are few people towards whom I feel more tenderly than towards Joe, but we know, as he knows himself, that he is better out of it. All I ask is that the crossing may be made without pain or fear; and that I believe may happen. If he faints, there can be no return, and I trust that may be the way of it. It seemed almost cruel to ask the doctor, as we have just done, what we should do if he appeared to be on the point of fainting. He is a sweet, engaging, aggravating creature, refined, artistic, affectionate, as weak as water, living in vague dreams. One needs to be a millionaire to support him, and a philosopher to love him. We're not the one, but I think something of the other, and we do love him. Lloyd, who is living with the Strongs, partly for economy, partly for discipline, and partly to keep his thumb upon them, is much broken by it. When I go to the house he clings to me as he did when he was a baby in arms. Though the table at their boarding house is better than ours, the bread is as dust in his mouth, and the meat and vegetables are no more than shadows to him. He has now, however, got his typewriter, and to that he holds fast and as it were anchors himself by it, it being the only thing on the premises that gives any sense of security and stability. And that reminds me that just lately his eyes have got a little better, which is what we had no right to hope for. For one thing he had his ears pierced, and went through the Islands in earrings. Another factor I believe to be the sunlight. As to myself, as Louis tells you, I have had no recurrence of that tumor; my sister, the second younger to myself,[9] is I fear in much worse case. A tumor in her throat is choking her, and it is feared that a surgical operation may be fatal. If I had only known in time to send her to my San Francisco doctor!

I shall send off to Mrs. Stevenson another lot of diary which runs on until I was too ill for want of wholesome food to write any more. If you care to see it it is at your service. I was a little taken aback when I found that Henry James had seen the other, but it was my vanity only, for I had written in so pell mell a fashion that I was a little ashamed of it. The facts, however, were all right.

Most affectionately yours, with much love to your wife,

FANNY VDEG. STEVENSON

MS, Yale. Letters, *3, 189.*

Union Club, Sydney [7 March 1890]

My dear Charles,

I did not send off the enclosed before from laziness, having gone quite sick and being a blooming prisoner here in the club and indeed in my bedroom. I was in receipt of your letters and your ornamental photo, and delighted to see how well you looked and how reasonably well I stood. Again consider the problem in the enclosed. I *believe*—but have yet to consider Samoan prices—that a thousand pounds or at the outside 1250 should erect my house in its first and imperfect state. I am sure I shall never come back home except to die; I may do it, but shall always think of the move as suicidal, unless a great change comes over me, of which as yet I see no symptom. This visit to Sydney has smashed me handsomely; and yet I made myself a prisoner here in the club upon my first arrival. This is not encouraging for further ventures: Sydney winter—or I might almost say Sydney spring, for I came when the worst was over—is so small an affair, comparable to our June depression at home in Scotland.

I need not say, my dear Charles, that all you have done for Bob and Henley exactly pleases me. You have nothing to do with either: you acted according to my instructions in making both the loans,

9. Elizabeth Vandegrift Patterson.

whereof no more, an you love me. I must tell you that the Strongs have been behaving excellently. Joe still lives, but in great and unceasing danger; Belle has been a kind nurse to him; both have lived all this while on their allowance, and not made one penny of debt. I cannot tell you how encouraging this is, and how it reconciles me with life.

The pipe is right again; it was the springs that had rusted, and ought to have been oiled. Its voice is now that of an angel; but Lord! here in the club I dare not wake it! Conceive my impatience to be in my own backwoods and raise the sound of minstrelsy. What pleasures are to be compared with those of the Unvirtuous Virtuoso.

Yours ever affctly,
The Unvirtuous Virtuoso,
ROBERT LOUIS STEVENSON

MS, Yale. Note by CB: "Sending original of Father Damien pamphlet."

Private and confidential

Sydney, 12 March [1890]

My dear Charles,

Enclosed please find a libel: [1] you perceive I am quite frank with my legal adviser; and I will also add it is *conceivable* an action might be brought, and in that event *probable* I should be ruined. If you had been through my experience, you would understand how little I care; for upon this topic my zeal is complete and, probably enough, without discretion.

I put myself in your hands, for Henley's sake,[2] not for mine. My case is beyond help. This leaves tomorrow the 13th; two weeks later, day for day, it will be followed by presentation copies, which, for all purposes of action, is publication quite enough, is it not? Thus you will have no power to save me, and can, with a light conscience, follow my desires. That is to say: 1st. If you think Henley should try the gamble, you will let him have it. 2nd. If you think Henley shouldn't, you will kindly see whether the *Times,*

1. *Father Damien: An Open Letter to the Reverend Dr. Hyde,* first published in pamphlet form in Sydney.
2. Henley published the *Letter* in the *Scots Observer,* 3 and 10 May.

Scotsman, or other leading paper will touch it. 3rd. If none of them will, see if Chatto will issue it as a pamphlet. N.B. *Of course in no case will I receive any emolument.* Or, if, in your good judgement, you see any other reputable means of publication, I set you free to adopt it.

On the probabilities of action, a barrister here whom I consulted, one of the leaders, said, "Have you used any epithets—any epithets, you know? coarse expressions? No? Not called him 'Hell-Hound'? nor 'Atheist'? No? O then, there's nothing in it?" Which is funny, but unhappily not true. What's more to the purpose, his colleagues in Honolulu, whom I know, would probably—I think certainly— dissuade him with eagerness. But then there is the Boston Board of Missions—they may be a low lot, I don't know them from Adam— and the trouble may come from there. I own I cannot see what they would gain, unless revenge. But then sectarian animosity does not reckon, and there is no question, I may find myself nipped between conflicting churches. You must weigh this in considering for Henley. I don't want to give him a serpent for a fish—no offence to eels. On the other hand, you, better than I, can judge if the thing would be apt to help him. It seems to me rather a spirited piece; but of course I am the last to know, and all of us here, knowing Dr. Hyde personally as we do, are perhaps apt to consider it more pungent than it can appear to the outsider. He is a large, dark, smooth, grave, personable man; carries his blue ribbon like a decoration; and looks as though you might have encountered him in Queen Street, arm in arm with Dr. Phin.[3]

Much love,
ROBERT LOUIS STEVENSON

MS, Yale.

[Sydney, 20 March 1890]

My dear Doer,

You will receive along with this a document in which you are trustee. It seems elaborate, and dodgy; I trust it is also, as it looks to the layman, perfectly efficacious.

---

3. Rev. Kenneth Macleay Phin (1816–88), D.D. Edinburgh, 1869; leader of the Assembly for many years; Convener of the Home Mission Committee, 1869–88.

I will inclose here Moors's last letter in which you will see how things go upon Vailima—Stevensonia, as he calls it—and what you may look for in the way of drafts. I think you will agree it is a very kindly letter. The man himself is a curious being, not of the best character; has been in the labour trade as supercargo; has been partner with Grossmühl, the most infamous trader in these waters, the man who is accused of paying natives with whist counters; has settled down at last in Apia, where everyone owes him money on mortgage, where his business is both large and growing, and where he took a great though secret part in the late war. I was forced to be his guest, rather against my will, for his looks, his round blue eyes etc. went against me, and the repulsion was mutual. However we both got over it, and grew to like each other; and it's my belief he won't cheat me. He is highly intelligent; tells a story well and from a veracious understanding: of all the scores of witnesses I examined about the war, H.J.M. was the only one whom documents invariably corroborated, and also (although the most open enemy of the Germans at the time) appeared to suffer from no bias in the retrospect. He is married to a Samoan, whom he treats kindly, and his oldest girl is in the States at school. I draw you this portrait because the man is necessarily a feature in my business life and has the marring of many of my affairs. You may wonder I should become at all intimate with a man of a past so doubtful, but in the South Seas, any exclusiveness becomes impossible; they are all in the same boat, or with exceptions so few that they are scarce worth mention. The character of my solicitor for instance is extraordinary; and it was perhaps chiefly as a choice of evils that I left my power of attorney with H.J.M. At the same time, he is a man of so strong an understanding, and is so well-to-do, that personally I am not the least alarmed.[4]

MS (cablegram), Yale.

Sydney, 10 April 1890

Return Islands four months Home September

4. Not signed.

MS, Yale.

[Sydney, 10 April 1890]

My dear Charles,

I have been quite knocked over; go back islands four months, pick up again; sail today, don't know where. Sealed orders, but I know some of the islands from slips: Suwaruu,[5] Christmass, Penrhynn, Apemama, and Tapituea:[6] what else?—O, nine: *all these I have no right to mention!* they are surprised, so keep 'em secret. And I daresay to you they are all Greek and Hebrew. Persons with friends in the islands should purchase Findlay's *Pacific Directories:* they're the best of reading anyway, and may almost count as fiction.

We are leaving today, April 10th; gone 4 months; we should be back here August 10th. I'll expect a long letter, and a state of accompts, care of Towns. Good by, just now. I must not write more: still weak and groggy.

Yours ever afft,

R. L. S.

Only Lloyd, Fanny, and I go. We leave the Strongs here under custody of a bank (where the wild teller grows). Joe still alive, but pretty weedy.

MS, Yale.

Janet Nichol, at sea, off Upolu [20 May 1890]

My dear Charles,

This is to let you to wit that the voyage has had the old effect; and whereas I went on board, out of bed, at Sydney, and not fit to take a drive, let alone to go on a journey, a fortnight after I was ashore and cutting about on Savage Island, and having my pockets —(*proh pudor*) and my trouser pockets—picked of tobacco by the *houris* of that ilk, and sitting prating with missionaries, and clambering down cliffs to get photographs like a man of iron. We have a good ship, though truth! she rolls, a good table, and the best sort of shipmates.

5. I.e. Suwarrow (Cook Islands).
6. Tabiteuea (Gilbert Islands).

I say, please let me find at Sydney a statement of my account; I expected it every mail, and it has damped me horrid not to know how I stand. Also you might order me the *Saturday Review* from 1st April on. The address at Sydney will be as of yore. I thought I was to get the *Scots Observer,* by the way? and I know I didn't.

In making out the deed of gift, the Oakland property was forgotten, I cannot think how. And I am going to try to get that put through at Apia.

I may then add a word or two. In the meanwhile, dear Doer, I am as you know very well,

Your affectionate

Louis

MS, Yale. Letters, *3, 199.*

Hotel Sebastopol, Noumea [August 1890]

My dear Charles,

I have stayed here a week while Lloyd and my wife continue the voyage in the *Janet Nicoll;* this I did partly to see the convict system, partly to shorten my stay in the extreme cold—hear me! with my extreme! *moi qui suis originaire d'Edimbourg!*—of Sydney at this season. I am feeling very seedy, utterly fatigued, and overborne with sleep; I have a fine old gentleman of a doctor who attends and cheers and entertains, if he does not cure me; but even with his ministrations I am almost incapable of the exertion sufficient for this letter, and I am really, as I write, falling down with sleep. What is necessary to say I must try to say shortly.

Lloyd goes to clear out our establishments; pray keep him in funds, if I have any; if I have not, pray try to raise them. Here is the idea: to install ourselves, at the risk of bankruptcy, in Samoa. It is not the least likely it will pay (although it may), but it is almost certain it will support life with very few external expenses. If I die, it will be an endowment for the survivors, at least for my wife and Lloyd, and my mother, who might prefer to go home, has her own. Hence, I believe I shall do well to hurry my installation. The letters are already in part done; in part done is a novel for Scribner; in the course of the next twelve months I should receive a considerable amount of money. I am aware I had intended to pay back to my capital much of this; I am now of opinion I should do foolishly. Better to build the house and have a roof and farm of my own, and thereafter, with a livelihood assured, save and repay, than to go on, living expensively and paying back capital which makes only a modest return. I am in hopes you will share this view. The price of the house will be considerable; my expenses have to be faced before we have cattle, feed, and vegetables. On the other hand, once faced, there is my livelihood, all but books and wine, ready in a nutshell; and it ought to be more easy, and it would be certainly (by all the laws of arithmetic) less expensive, to save and to repay afterward. Excellent, say you, but will you save? and will you repay? I do not know, said the Bell of Old Bow. But, on the other hand, will you tell me how much I shall lose, if I delay building my house and mounting my plantation, and must live at heck and manger,[7] paying three prices for one, after I have paid back the money, and while I economise, under this drain, the fresh capital necessary for the installation? It seems clear to me.

Have you paid back what I owe to Simpson? Please guide Lloyd all you can. We see him go, Fanny and I, with sinkings. He is not —well—not a man of business.

The deuce of the affair is that I do not know when I shall see you and Colvin. I guess you will have to come and see me; many a time already we have arranged the details of your visit in the yet unbuilt house on the mountain. I shall be able to get decent wine from Noumea. We shall be able to give you a decent welcome, and talk of old days. A propos of old days, do you remember still the phrase we heard in Waterloo Place? I believe you made a piece for the piano on that phrase. Pray, if you remember it, send it me in your next. If you find it impossible to write correctly, send it me *à la réccitative,* and indicate the accents. Do you feel (you must) how strangely heavy and stupid I am? I must at last give up and go sleep; I am simply a rag.

The morrow: I feel better, but still dim and groggy. Tonight I go to the governor's; such a lark—no dress clothes—24 hours notice—able-bodied Polish tailor—suit made for a man with the figure of a puncheon—same hastily altered for self with the figure of a bodkin—front flaps of coat descending to pudenda—sight inconceivable. Never mind: dress clothes, "which nobody can deny,"

7. I.e. in great fullness.

and the officials have been all so civil that I liked niether to refuse
nor to appear in mufti. Bad dress clothes only prove you are a grisly
ass; no dress clothes, even when explained, indicate a want of
respect. I wish you were here with me to help me dress in this
wild raiment, and to accompany me to M. Noel-Pardon's.

My dear Charles, it is a very poor affair to (what is called) succeed. My faults, whatever they were, were taken very easily by my
friends till I had (what is called) succeeded; then the measure was
changed. What I have gained is an invitation to the governor's in
New Caledonia; what I have lost, you can see in what I wrote last
night, when I mentioned you and Colvin—and you two only. Even
Bob writes to me with an embarassment which communicates itself to my answers. Our relation is too old and close to be destroyed;
I have forgiven him too much—and he me—to leave a rupture possible; but there it is—the shadow. I bore you with these regrets.
But I did not ever care for much else than my friends; and some
they are dead etc., and I am at the end of the world from what
remains; gone, all are gone. I cannot say what I would not give, if
there came a knock now at the door, and you came in. I guess Noel-
Pardon could go begging, and we might burn the £200 dress clothes
in the back garden for a bonfire; or what would be yet more expensive and more humourous, get them once more expanded to
fit you, and when that was done a second time, cut down for my
gossamer dimmensions.

I hope you never forget to remember me to your father, who has
always a place in my heart, as I hope I have a little in his. His
kindness helped me infinitely when you and I were young; I recall
it with gratitude and affection in this town of convicts at the
world's end. There are very few things, my dear Charles, worth
mention; on a retrospect of life, the day's flash and colour, one
day with another, flames, dazzles and puts to sleep; and when the
days are gone, like a fast-flying thaumatrope, they make but a single
pattern. Only a few things stand out, and among these, most
plainly to me—Rutland Square.

I don't know if it will cut you to the heart as it does me, but the
Boehm flageolet has gone (presumably with the heat) out of tune.
A, B♭, B, C, C♯ have all run together: C♯ certainly flat, and most
of the others I think sharp; all at least run into "pie," and the pipe
smiles in the face of the performer. I dare not play now: it is bad

enough to play inconceivably ill; when the pipe itself is out of tune, the offence is capital.

I believe I show in these words that I am not quite so much out of gear as I was last night; yet I still struggle with somnolence and make but an imperfect fight of it, and when I walk it is still on aching legs. Possibly the long voyage, and so long ship's food, explain my state; but I feel unusually useless. My loneliness has a certain pleasure. Ever, my dear Charles, your affectionate friend

ROBERT LOUIS STEVENSON

On my arrival at Sydney, I shall doubtless find a letter. This is to be ready before, and to go first of all, should there be mail on the move.

P.S. Just returned from trying on the dress clo'. Lord, you should see the coat: it stands out at the waist like a bustle, the flaps cross in front, the sleeves are like bags.

MS, Yale.

RLS TO ANDREW CHATTO

Union Club, Sydney [August 1890]

Dear Mr. Chatto,

The letter to Dr. Hyde is yours, or any man's, I will never touch a penny of remuneration.[1] I do not stick at murder; I draw the line at cannibalism; I could not eat a penny roll that piece of bludgeoning had gained for me.

I believe you will soon receive sheets of a thin book of ballads from Scribners.[2] Pray put it in the hands of Clarke, Edinburgh; see that the American spellings are removed, see that "O!" is always "O!" and never "Oh!", and bring it out, if you please, on the same terms as *Underwoods*.

With good wishes—(I daresay Mr. Osbourne will call on you and give my news)—I am

Yours sincerely,

ROBERT LOUIS STEVENSON

address Apia, Samoa

1. The *Letter* was brought out by Chatto and Windus this year as a pamphlet, and the royalties sent to the Leper Fund.
2. *Ballads*. See RLS to E. L. Burlingame: *Letters, 3, 203.*

Copies of *Ballads,* please, to
  Sydney Colvin, British Museum
  Theodore Watts,[3] (*Athenaeum?*)
  George Meredith,[4] Box Hill, Dorking
  Charles Baxter, W.S., 11 S. Charlotte St., Edinburgh
  H. B. Bailden,[5] Princes Street, Edinburgh
  Prof. R. A. M. Stevenson, 16 St. Leonard's Terrace, Chelsea
  W. E. Henley, *Scots Advertiser* [6] Office, Thistle Street, Edinburgh
  George Saintsbury Esq.[7] (?), *Saturday Review?*
  Edmund Gosse, Delamere Terrace W.
  Ori a Ori,[8] Sous chef de Tautira, Tautira, Tahiti
  Tati Salmou,[9] Chef de Papara, Papara, Tahiti
  Madame la Princesse Moe,[1] Papeete, Tahiti
  H.M. the King of the Hawaiian Islands,[2] Honolulu, Oahu, Hawaii
  Six to myself.

                                                              R. L. S.

MS, Yale.

                              Vailima, Apia, Samoa [14 October 1890] [3]

My dear Charles,
  Good morning to you from a new address. This is but a note to say
that [I] breakfasted the other morn with my freemason portrait of

3. (Walter) Theodore Watts (later Watts-Dunton) (1832–1914), novelist, poet, and
critic; a lifelong contributor to the *Athenaeum.* See *Letters, 2,* 347.
  4. RLS had met Meredith at Box Hill in 1878. See *Letters, passim.*
  5. Henry Bellyse Baildon (*d.* 1907), poet, essayist, editor; lecturer on English
Language and Literature at University College, Dundee, and St. Andrews; author of
Robert Louis Stevenson: A Life Study in Criticism, 1901. Their friendship began in
1864, when, as schoolboys in Edinburgh, they together started a magazine called
Jack o' Lantern. To Baildon's acknowledgement of the gift, RLS replied: "Glad the
Ballads amused you. They failed to entertain a coy public, at which I wondered; not
that I set much account by my verses, which are the verses of Prosator; but I do know
how to tell a yarn, and two of the yarns are great" (*Letters, 3,* 285).
  6. A slip for *Observer.*
  7. George Saintsbury (1845–1933), literary critic and historian.
  8. See above, p. 238.
  9. High chief of the Tevas.
  1. "Princess" Moë, a high chiefess.
  2. Kalakaua. See above, p. 240.
  3. Postmark. Envelope marked "Private."

yoursel in front of me, and with inexhaustible joy fared on the familiar traits and strange equipments. I have no view but that I shall soon see you somehow.

I imagine you should soon get some money from McClure-away,[4] but it depends on the run of my work, which is just now very complicated and goes now this way and now that: three big jobs all under way, and the divil himself knows which to turn to first. *The Wrecker* the most pressing, the letters most remunerative, and as the way is, *The Pearl Fisher* the most tempting.

If you think my proposed dealing with Lloyd hard on the young man, relax it; I know well that a little free head in youth is worth all the corn that can be stacked for age. Be, as heretofore, the Judicious as you are the Painful Doer, and do not forget the

Done

who is more of a

Dun

R. L. S.

This place is heavenly, but up to now, the home of Short Commons and Hard Work; Plain living and High Words (levelled at tresspassers and idling labourers) are the main crop hitherto. Better luck in the future. I must go round and rail at my boys, à la farmer. Adieu.

R. L. S.

MS, Yale.

[Samoa] 6 November 1890

My dear Charles,

I have drawn on you today at 30 days in favour of H. J. Moors for £200. All my money is to go to you from the letters, so you should soon be in high funds. I have done this to get the profit on the dollar, instead of receiving it here; and it is better it should

---

4. Samuel Sidney McClure (1857–1949) had founded the McClure Syndicate in 1884, and through the Syndicate—the pioneer organization in its field—was currently marketing the serial rights to RLS's letters from the South Seas. A blend of Mulberry Sellers and Sam Slick, McClure appears as Jim Pinkerton in *The Wrecker*. References—frequently exasperated—to him are frequent in the letters from this point on.

pass through your hands at any rate. I have no time for more. Very busy and pretty well, but there's a lot to do, and little time to turn round, and a lot of nincompoops to boss.

Yours ever,

R. L. S.

MS, Yale.

[Samoa, 6 December 1890]

My dear Charles,

I wonder if you ever receive any of my letters. I see you miss many; and I have myself lost so much that I now take the precaution of registering. This is disagreeable matter. I have at least received word from Lloyd: one letter—others are lost I suppose. From it I gather that Henley has not been to call on my mother. I have taken a good deal from Henley for myself and my wife, for a wife counts on the same plane as her husband; this treatment on an old lady, recently bereaved and very lonely, I refuse to pass over—the supplies are stopped. He may go and beg from whom he pleases; no threepenny piece of mine goes near him. His disloyalty as a friend has long been very plain to me. What a picture, when in the midst of our trouble, I send McClure to him [5]—McClure who had heard from us nothing but Henley's praise—and the uncivil fellow receives my guest with dispraise of myself; and what a contrast is the conduct of McClure, who never breathed a word in betrayal of Henley, and continues to give me news of him as though all were well, so that I only hear of this by a back way. And yet that is what I have been accustomed to accept, and accepted. The treatment of my mother stands on a different base: it is so cruelly small to an old woman very much alone. I have a

5. To offer him employment. "Before I sailed for London, Stevenson gave me letters to a number of his friends there—Baxter, W. E. Henley, Sidney Colvin, R. A. M. Stevenson, and others. I found most of Stevenson's set very much annoyed by the attention he had received in America. There was a note of detraction in their talk which surprised and, at first, puzzled me. Henley was particularly emphatic. He had a double grievance: that a nation whom he despised as a rude and uncultivated people should presume to give Stevenson a higher place than he held in England, and the personal jealousy which he later voiced in his own writings. He believed that his own influence upon Stevenson's work was not sufficiently recognized" (S. S. McClure, *My Autobiography*, New York, 1914, p. 193).

loyalty to her also; he has chosen to strike me there, and I am done with him for time and for eternity.

You will kindly communicate to him the enclosed scrap of paper; on second thoughts I will post it myself. Here are the terms: "The man who did not care to call upon my mother returning alone and bereaved to the empty roof of my father, is—in the name of him dead and of her living—dead to me forever. Farewell." *Explicit Amicitia*. My mother also did not tell me; everyone seeks to spare me pain, save Henley alone. But he has given me the last pang. Should he write to me, I will enclose his letter unopened. I have supped full of him. What would my father say, ye Gods, if he could but know? I think he—W.E.H.—had some entertainment in his time in that poor house. The fire is a little cold; he might have made a visit of digestion to the widow, now when the mirth has ceased.

I am so moved with living rage that I can think of nothing else. You seem to be doing as I would have you, to judge from Lloyd's letter. A thousand thanks. I do not think this breach should make you think me variable in my affections. Change the thing: suppose your father were dead, you in a far part of the world, your mother returning alone to Rutland Square, and I keeping camp unmoved in Heriot Row. Would you accept such conduct? I know you better. And yet, if I have tried you—and I fear I have—it has not been as Henley has tried me. It was an ill day for me when I saw him; all that was pleasant in the past but augments my bitterness this hour.

I am, my dear Charles,

Yours ever affectionately and gratefully,

R. L. S.

Next day

Of course the first note is condemned; I give you a copy of the substitute: "I hear you have not thought fit to call on my mother since her return. I think my father tried to make you welcome in that house. He is gone, the house is empty; it would have been very fit you should have paid your respects to his widow. Perhaps if you had called to mind some of the past, you would have thought it kind to visit my mother. Had I been so indifferent, we should never have met. I will say no more; I do not wish to part in harshness from so old a friend and one bound up with the memories of so

much joy and sorrow. But let the parting, if you please, be final.
R. L. S."

I have no more anger; I am simply weary of the incubus. He must
feel it strange after all to receive, and to have earned, such a farewell in that city of Edinburgh, where I made myself no sluggish
friend to him.

MS, Yale.

[Sydney, 26 January 1891]

My dear Charles,
    Caught on the hop by mail. Paper enclosed signed. My view as
to the business is this. Let Davy [6] say what his view was when he
signed the agreement, and if that be anyway reasonable, accept it.
If he will not do this, or flies too high, will he agree to an arbiter?
or to a friendly A.B. suit? [7] If to none of these things, I authorise
you (in the last resort) to take it before the courts nakedly. My
mother,[8] I think rightly, objects to this authorisation; let us rather
have a full report first with copies of the deed and correspondence.
    Please remember to register this and all other letters of the least
importance: so many otherwise miscarry.

Yours ever,
R. L. S.

MS, Yale. Letters, 3, 279.

S.S. *Lübeck,* at sea [11 March 1891]

My dear Charles,
    Perhaps in my old days I do grow irascible—"the old man viru-
lent" has long been my pet name for myself—and I daresay you
were inclined to exclaim at my surprising outburst from Apia.
Well, the temper is at least all gone now. Time is good at lowering
these distemperatures; far better is a sharp sickness, and I am just
(and scarce) afoot again after a smoking hot little malady at Sydney.
And the temper being gone, I still think the same. "Better a finger

6. David Stevenson.
7. An arbitration suit.
8. Who had just returned from Scotland. RLS was in Sydney to meet her.

aff as aye waggin'." For some years it has been rather a one-sided friendship. I have had few occasions to speak well of him; I am sure I have lost none. I know of more than one that he has had, and siezed, to speak *not* well of me; and even at the antipodes these things leak out at last. You will tell me he does not mean them, that he talks much and loud, that his bark etc. That was all very well when our friendship stood upon four legs; in those days I let him roar his fill like the young lions. When (thanks to another, not to him) it began to stand on three, a different bearing was required. Since then I have spoken of him with Lloyd often, he will have told you how; and I have written of him to you, to no one else: these were priviledged communications. He has not confined himself to such. During the same period we have had not much occasion to serve each other; I do not believe that we have either of us lost many; I do not think so meanly either of him or me. Then he had an occasion: he had not long before lost his mother, I had lost my father, she her husband; she went to a desolate home, where you attended, helped, and comforted her like my good trusty friend; he never paid her a call. I may be wrong, but if this be friendship, I prefer the other thing. We have not our parents for ever; we are never very good to them; when they go, and we have lost our front file man, we begin to feel all our neglects mighty sensibly. I propose a proposal. My mother is here on board with me; today for once, I mean to make her as happy as I am able, and to do that which I know she likes; you, on the other hand, go and see your father, and do ditto, and give him a real good hour or two. We shall both be glad hereafter. I send your father my love—in no merely verbal sense; charming old gentleman, I wish I could see his clever face!

As for Henley, what a miss I have of him. The charm, the wit, the vigour of the man haunt my memory; my past is all full of his big presence and his welcome, wooden footstep. Let it be a past henceforward: a beloved past, without continuation. I had a letter from him the other day in which he signed himself "my old friend." I accept the phrase: I am his old friend; I was, not am, his friend. The affair is ended, the record closed, without ill will on my side and without irritation. I believe I see him without prejudice; I believe I know what arguments he can bring forward in his own defence. They leave me very cold, for this reason: that I do not think he should have argued. But I grant them valid, a fair set off. He may win the cause then; I am quite satisfied if I lose the half friend. The only pity is it was not earlier.

Thence I turn to the more cheerful subject of pipes. The pipe sent, a Boehm flageolet, is awfully difficult, and its difficulty was not lightened by the fact that the tutor was all wrong. However I have made it all out, and it has a mighty pretty note, far better than a piccolo, above all in the low notes. I wish you to order me another, and two cases—no case was sent with the last, and two turn-screws—no turnscrew was sent, and a packet of pads; also two mother-of-pearl mouthpieces; I live in endless fear of breaking a spring and being silenced. Should you see any easy and good flute duets, you (or your friend) might send them also; for I can usually take the upper part, and the ordinary D flute-flageolet can generally take the second, and so we have music.

Please remember always to register when you write; masses of my letters are lost and masses of yours: Sydney is a jawhole. For instance—I need not bother with instances: such is the grim fact, and must still be borne in mind.

Yours ever,
R. L. S.

MS, Yale.

Consulate General of the United States of America,
Apia [writing from Tutuila], Samoa
[March] 189[1]

My dear Charles,

I have had to draw a bill on you for £150. This was suddenly forced on me by a rise in silver on the beach; it is hard the Republican party should oppose a copyright bill against my books with one hand and with the other raise the currency against my draughts so far away as Apia beach. But I believe (to be more just) they even promoted the copyright bill.[1]

I had not meant to draw until I heard you were in funds, but I think you should be by now. I hope you will remember to register your letters, or I may never receive them.

I write you from Tutuila, where I am on a trip with the Ameri-

1. Congress had finally, in 1891, passed the first international copyright bill.

can consul,[2] and tomorrow or next day we sail for Manu'a, the least known group about Samoa. It is a lovely spot, a lovely morning; we go tonight to a big feast and dance at the next village; yesterday I walked to the top of the island. It was desperate hot at first; then it rained cats and dogs; and the road was steep to mount and slippery to descend. To crown all, when I got to the summit, the valley had twisted so that I could not look back on the bay we had left, and the trees grew so thick on the steep other side that I could catch but glimpses of the further shore and sea. It may be six to eight hundred feet we climbed, in a continuous wood of palms, forest trees, and tree ferns, and crossing and recrossing a stream; the road a good road for Samoa, but in the upper part of course a mere ladder of roots and rocks.[3]

MS untraced. Letters, *3, 316.*

[Vailima] Tuesday, 19 May 1891

My dear Charles,

I don't know what you think of me, not having written to you at all during your illness. I find two sheets begun with your name, but that is no excuse. . . . I am keeping bravely; getting about better every day, and hope soon to be in my usual fettle. My books begin to come; and I fell once more on the Old Bailey session papers. I have 1778, 1784, and 1786. Should you be able to lay hands on any other volumes, above all a little later, I should be very glad you should buy them for me. I particularly want *one* or *two* during the course of the Peninsular War. Come to think, I ought rather to have communicated this want to Bain.[4] Would it bore you to communicate to that effect with the great man? The sooner I have them, the better for me. 'Tis for *Henry Shovel.* But *Henry Shovel* has now turned into a work called *The Shovels of Newton French: including Memoirs of Henry Shovel, a Private in the Peninsular War,*[5] which work is to begin in 1664 with the marriage of Skipper, afterwards Alderman Shovel of Bristol, Henry's great-great-grandfather, and end about 1832 with his own sec-

2. Harold M. Sewall (1860–1924), Consul-General; Minister to Hawaii, 1897.
3. Not signed.
4. James Bain, bookseller, 14 King William St., Strand, London.
5. Not completed.

ond marriage to the daughter of his runaway aunt. Will the public
ever stand such an opus? Gude kens, but it tickles me. Two or three
historical personages will just appear: Judge Jeffreys,[6] Wellington,
Colquhoun Grant,[7] and I think Townsend the runner.[8] I know the
public won't like it; let 'em lump it then; I mean to make it good;
it will be more like a saga.

Adieu.

Yours ever affectionately,

R. L. STEVENSON

MS, Yale.

Vailima, Sunday, 20 June 1891

My dear Charles,

Your hand was a welcome sight. But I think in the pressure of
arrears, you must have let a point slip. £890 in hand, you say, but
nothing of the house; has the house money gone down to that?
Well, I shall know when your bill comes. It is so exceedingly
difficult and anxious to finance our establishment that I am going
to ask you to get one of your clerks to send me monthly my ballance;
I do not mind details, only the result and a note of large payments
to account. This will be a great help and pacifier. We trust we are
nearly through not only the worst of our expenses, but what has
bothered us far more, the currency famine. I have been driven at
last to import gold from Sydney. I shall probably hear from you as
to my big bills next month. I still think the money should be
raised; it is so needful I should have a credit in Sydney.

I have written to McClure thus: "It seems your agent in England
is retaining 25/100 of the *Black and White* money; [1] I remember
nothing of this in our bargain, which is not at hand, suppose it in
consequence to be an oversight, and have to ask you to rectify it."
I have an idea this will bring things to a hearing. Our recollection
is 10/100, but my papers are in too huge a disorder to let me look
for the bargain with any hope of success. It would probably take
days and I have no days to spare.

6. George Jeffreys (1648–89), 1st Baron Jeffreys of Wem; Lord Chief Justice, 1682;
Lord Chancellor, 1685; conductor of the "Bloody Assizes."

7. (1780–1829). A lieutenant-colonel in intelligence in the Peninsula.

8. A famous Bow Street runner.

1. For the British serial rights of the South Seas Letters.

I have drafted this month 132 pp. of my MS: 66,000 words; and out of all that toilful scriving only four letters and two chapters of *The Wrecker* go to press! It is not a life for a hog; but thank God even at this pitiful and costly rate, four months should see me shut of both these nightmares. This rate of production is worthy of my early beginnings, when I used to write the matter of a volume to produce a 5 guinea *Cornhill* essay. Only one thing is changed, my power of enduring work; it has been common for me to write seven and eight hours, and that with no other inconvenience than extreme fatigue.

Fanny, I am rejoiced to say, is better. We make a big and rather a pleasant party up here, and all my spare time is spent in making (or rather marring) music. How often have I not thought of you and your oboe! But we have easier instruments, though some of my upper notes would raise a smile. I fear this is a dreadful poor letter, but business so overrides us at this critical hour, you must excuse my incomparable dryness.

Yours ever affectionately,
ROBERT LOUIS STEVENSON

I have asked Lloyd to try and give you my news. You say nothing of the Henley affair, from which I gather you disapprove. Well, you are very likely right; it makes a damned hole in my life: I am always thinking of things I want to say to him, but *que voulez vous?* he wore me out. I have no ill feeling, plenty of kind ones, but no desire to go back into that doubtful medium. By the way, we ought to decide on the property of our sketch plays.[2] *Hester Noble,* being very largely mine and founded on an old play of mine, I think should come to me. I must go on another sheet, I see. *The King of Clubs* was mainly his, and should go to him. *Ajax* and *Honour and Arms* remain, and by my memory were fairly equally contributed to by both. I will do as you say: either give him these, or toss up for 'em, you and he. The rest I do not remember to have been of much account. Do what he wishes. But I think some sharing should be done, as we put a good deal of thought into these drafts, and it is hard we should both be shut out of our own. Besides I was thinking Henley might have a chance after the *Beau,*[3] and one of these

2. None of these sketched plays was ever completed.
3. *Beau Austin* had finally been produced—by Beerbohm Tree at the Haymarket

might please him. I have named *Hester Noble* because it was so very largely mine and I have been always tempted to make a story of it. But should you find he likes it himself, I will gladly cede it. Do not let him think me indifferent (which I am not), but sound him and give way. I place myself in your hands. You might mention casually I had been reading our old plays, and thought *Macaire* the footiest rot, and was bowled over by *Admiral Guinea* and shed tears. I had clean done forgot it was so good. And I declare, with decisive cutting and powerfully acted, the blame thing would have a chance.

O I do not possess a copy of the last act of *Deacon Brodie* as rewritten and would like that. I have never even seen it since it was copied.

Yours ever,
R. L. S.

Flageolet to hand: A-1.

MS, Yale.

[Samoa] Saturday [15] ⁴ August [18]91

My dear Charles,

Yours received with the account to my huge relief. Had it come by last mail I should have taken a change; but I had to send Fanny away alone two days before the mail came in. I trust she will have

---

Theatre, London, November 1890—without much success. "Beerbohm Tree called here yesterday. Him and me is pals, and he've persuaded me to dine with 'im tomorrer and go see *The Dancing Girl*, which 'e've told me 'e 'ave made money by and laid aside for the first time, so 'e may perdooce hartistic werks at a lost in time to come, but wich 'Enley are that mad at 'im not playin' *Bo Orstin* at a lost, so before 'e cum, 'Enley, 'e sez, 'e won't go to see 'im play the *Bo,* and spile 'im all to rot wen 'e do perdooce it, wun night or two, but wich the joak his, that 'e ain't perdoocin the *Bo* at all, but like a nasty lo acter, perfers to rake hin the filthy looker wich 'Enley 'e despiges hof, excep in the koat tale of 'is ('Enley's) frends. And then the next joke is that after abusing Tree like a pickpocket, and letting the beauteous George Moore befoul him (over his own name) in the *Journal,* Henley now writes me proposing a meeting with Tree, who has of course heard all that H. has said about him. *He,* however, is quite good-natured about him, laughs, and said yesterday to me in a solemn manner, 'The fact is I don't *think* he's quite responsible'! What would H. have said? What yells and roars!!" (CB to RLS, 23 September 1891).

4. Dated by RLS: "August ?th (16th?) 91"; Saturday was the 15th.

profited. The money we sent her off with left us with forty pounds in the bank, which, at this distance from my base and in my then state of uncertainty as to how we stood, was somewhat thrillingly perilous. All's well that ends well; and the possibility of reaching the end of this ruinous year without disaster makes me smile.

I was relieved to find you did not too severely blame me *re* Henley; vexed to find he had got in trouble with you also.[5] I do find his arrogance surprising, and being (I am told) a somewhat arrogant bird myself, I should be a judge. I cannot but think there must be much whiskey in that head.

I read your Church Association with great interest, dear Senator of the Red Cross; did not the Free Mason suggest some of the plan? I thought these upper bugs who could go and vote in country chapters smellt of the level and the mallet, Brother Charles. Your portrait and thrilling masonic biography delighted us all beyond measure. Would I were a mason and tippled in a lodge—and all the other masons attended in obeissance—O would I were a mason, deep in masonic dodge.

I trust by the time you receive this, you will be much the better for your voyage.[6] Music goes on here daily from about 12:30 till 2. The pianist has recently deserted; but the flute, B♭ clarionet, and Boehm flageolet have made great advances in the gavotte from *Don Juan* (Gluck) and a lively, *classical* (?) and *original* (??) setting of *The Marseillaise.* Our next is to be the Minuet from *Alceste,* I think. I now approach my upper D without alarm; I will not say so much about E. The flutist [7] has got quite a lip and does not blow sharp more than about one day in seven. And the clarionet begins to show some rudimentary notions of time. He has twice fallen out and come in again on the right beat, which (to one of my experience in conducting) is the beginning of hope. I am now going to prepare a piece with a lot of cross rests, and when we can

5. On 2 May Henley told Charles Whibley that "C.B. has gone over to the enemy." Henley's biographer comments: "It was neither a very notorious nor a very prolonged abandonment. Charles Baxter was far too sagacious—far too fond, as well, of both Will and Lewis—to act in a blatant and melodramatic fashion. Perhaps he tired, for a time, of Henley's insistence on reopening the scars. Perhaps 'Lacrimae Rerum' [Henley's poetic version of the estrangement] was a little too much for him to stomach" (Connell, pp. 213–4).

6. CB was taking a holiday in Sweden.

7. Probably Joe Strong; the clarinetist appears to have been Lloyd (see below, p. 290).

play that, I shall feel hopeful in earnest. But the clarionet is not industrious *every* day, and is liable to despair; then the flute and the flageolet encourage him tenderly. You should hear us blowing solemnly through the "pie" stages, before the clarionet has siezed any idea of the beat—it is wonderful; and the flute and I generally keep together, which is no joke when the powerful blasts of the clarionet are showered upon us at random.[8]

Excuse this gabble. But the band is my chief diversion in these wretched revolutionary days. We are going to dine today with the Chief Justice; [9] he is a very nice fellow, but (like all our other officials) about as fit for his post as—Johnny Adam [10]—I do not mean to hint from the same causes. We sit and pipe on a volcano, which is being stoked by bland, incompetent amateurs untaught, I fear unteachable.

Your affectionate

R. L. S.

I confess myself with a confession. H.'s conduct to my mother was only the last straw. I had been nettled and worried for years before by his strange attitude behind my back, and though I forgave, I could not truly forget. It seems it's all right about the 25 p c and McClure; it was a special case about England and very silly on my part.

R. L. S.

MS, Yale.

[Samoa] 15 September [1891]

My dear Charles,

I drew another bill on you yesterday for £250. Had the mail come in with the news of your credit having reached Sydney, I need

---

8. "About the music, of which you write so flattering a tale, I am wondering, for you don't specifically say, if the selections I ordered from London ever arrived. . . . I am glad, very glad, that orchestra is, and is likely to remain, at least 17,000 miles away. It may perhaps ascend as a sweet savour to heaven—they ain't partickler thar, but oh it must be fearsome to listen to. Forgive me, I still remember my own efforts upon the oboe and its effect upon *you*. What then—but no, I will drop the subject" (CB to RLS, 23 September 1891).

9. Conrad Cedarcrantz, a Swede appointed as a compromise candidate by the three rival powers.

10. See above, p. 38.

not have done so; but I had to. 'Tis in favour of Hayhurst, Gurr, and Co.,[11] and I hope to the Lord you can meet it; I should think money would be coming in. Next month I shall have a story [12] ready which should bring in some cash. I only write to make this confession, and to remain

Yours ever afftly,

ROBERT LOUIS STEVENSON

Dilapidator

MS, Yale.

HENLEY TO CB

11 Howard Place, Edinburgh, 17 September 1891

My dear Charles,

Thanks—many—for the communication of Stevenson's proposals and ideas.

I think it fair that he should know, in respect of *Beau Austin,* that the effect of it was neither failure nor success: only an immediate disappointment. The truth is, that we—you and I that is, and especially you—were let in. Tree produced the *Beau* as a stopgap: he was under contract to produce *The Dancing Girl* at a certain date, and he was ready with nothing else in the meanwhile, so he put us on. It was an excellent stroke of business—for *him;* but it has not advanced the interests of the Henley-Stevenson combination in any way. We made some pounds apiece, it is true; but there have been no offers for country rights, and none for American; nor (tho' I hear that Tree has bought the dupes, *let*) has our manager repeated the experiment. No doubt, the thing will have its day; but for the present there is nothing for us but to wipe it up and say no more about it.

All this means that I am indifferent—absolutely—to the fate of the projected plays. There is not the slightest chance, as I think, that anyone of them would touch the actor-manager heart. And if there were, I should think twice (and more) before I ventured to condescend to such a crowd as the "élite of the British Theatre."

---

11. For a first-hand account of these acquaintances and their relations with the Stevensons, see *Our Samoan Adventure,* by Fanny and Robert Louis Stevenson, ed. Charles Neider, Harper and Brothers, New York, 1955, pp. 120 ff.

12. *The Beach of Falesá.*

Moreover, I do not believe myself complete enough to push through a play alone. Please signify all this to Stevenson, and add that, so far as I am concerned, he can do as he pleases with those drafts. I don't know where they are, nor what is their condition, nor anything about them. I should like to try and write the *Ajax*, for the fun of the thing; and if we had an actor, I would do my best for *Honour and Arms*. But even here my sentiment is purely Platonic. Let him do with them, to be brief, as he will. I make no other condition than this: that, if he take on another collaborator, he makes no sort of mention of me.

As for those at present in existence, I send you *Deacon Brodie*, as it was played in the U.S.A.; he can have more copies if he wants them. Also, Nutt [1] (and Nutt is not alone in this) is anxious to publish the *Théâtre* of W. E. H. and R. L. S. The passing of the American Copyright Act has halted the pirate, I believe (for I haven't had time to go into the question), and Pinero, Jones, and the rest are coming out as men of letters at 3/6 apiece. I think we might go in and scoop them as dramatists who can at least be read; and if he will, I shall be happy to lead the adventure. There is no occasion to print *Macaire*, since he objects to *Macaire;* and for the other three, they can be published (1) singly in a limited edition (Walter Blaikie [2] has produced an exquisite sample page), (2) singly for all the world and his wife to buy and read, and (3 and 4) singly or in bulk in (a) a limited or (b) a general edition. It is for him to decide. I shall but note that, in the event of publication, I should like to sweep away the stage directions—at all events, to restrict them to the essential—and print the plays as Congreve printed his: as pieces of English, and no more.

Yours Ever Affectionate,
W. E. H.

MS, Yale.

[Samoa] 14 October [1891]

My dear Charles,

This is painful-doery with a warrant. I send you herewith a story:

1. Alfred T. Nutt (1856–1910), Henley's London publisher.

2. Walter Biggar Blaikie (1847–1928), Chairman of T. and A. Constable, publishers, Edinburgh.

The Beach of Falesá. I have asked McClure to make you an offer for serial rights. If he offer less than £500, I am disinclined to accept; if less than £400, I refuse point blank. You should hear from him almost at once, and if he does not come to the scratch, it will be a fine problem what to do next. I believe it will be best to have it out as a small volume through Cassell's and Scribner's; [3] I refuse shilling touch, and incline to half-a-crown, but will accept two shillings if the Cassells force it: terms as usual, and better take some money down if I am behindhand, as I fear I must be. The Scribners must just please themselves as to price etc.; these conditions are for England.[4] I fear we shall miss Christmass with it, or it will be a near thing if we catch it. I don't know though, you should get it early in November; it might still be doable. But then of course the volume is a gamble; and it might be worth while to find out what Lippincott would offer, or even Arrowsmith. I will of course sell nothing but serial rights; and these emphatically not for less than £400. I prefer the naked gamble to that. Even before you hear from McClure, you might make inquiries. But remember if McC. offers £500, it is his, even if you have found better, as I have offered it to him for that. Awfully sorry to bother you with this; but McC. is so little of a businessman and so much of a splasher, that I do not care to send him the copy direct. My hope is, he will give the sum asked, and there will be no more bother.

I am rather involved in politics to my regret, but we have had larks here that I could not hold the candle to. I expect I shall figure in *The Times* [5] about the time when you recieve this. You may hear of [6]

Glad to hear you are to have a holiday. Nothing like the sea. Hope you will come back like a young lion.

R. L. S.

3. It was published as a separate volume by Cassell and Co. *ca.* July 1892, and later as the first story in *Island Nights Entertainments* (1893). It was also serialized in *Illustrated London News,* 2 July–6 August 1892, under the title *Uma.*

4. This sentence added in margin.

5. In a letter, dated 12 October and published 17 November, the second in a series of letters to the London *Times* attacking the administration of Samoa. They are reprinted in the Vailima Edition of RLS's works: *26, 374* ff.

6. Sentence breaks off.

MS, Yale. Letters, *3, 363.*

[Samoa] November 1891

3 encl.—by George there's going to be 4!

Dear Charles,

I have just written one enclosure with an eye to Henley, another will go from my mother and me anent the trust, and now here's between's twa.

1. I don't mean you to *send* me any money: it would only break my heart; I wanted your bookkeeper to send once a month a rough statement of my balance. However, there came, with this of yours, niether coin nor yet statement! so I'm still in the mud. I draw on you today for £200 in favour of Hayhurst, Gurr, and Co. You should be able to meet it easy, I believe. Unless you really send the money away! I must have expressed myself ill indeed! However, there is no help for it now, and I hope it is a mere passing misapprehension, that will be already cleared up.

2. I wish you to take steps to have me released from the Fowke and de Mattos trusts. Humphrey Jones, C.B. (with whom you had better communicate at 24 Carlyle Mansions, Cheyne Walk, Chelsea) gives me to understand that my co-trustees are willing and eager to be shut of me. So I suppose, under the circumstances, it will be a matter of form.

3. Haith! I believe that's a'. By this time, I suppose you will have heard from McClure, and *The Beach of Falesá* will be decided for better for worse. The end of *The Wrecker* goes by this mail— an awfae relief. I am now free and can do what I please. What do I please? I kenna. I'll bide a wee. There's a child's history [7] in the wind; and there's my grandfather's life [8] begun; and there's a histy of Sāmoa in the last four or five years [9] begun—there's a kind of sense to this book: it may help the Sāmoans, it may help me, for I'm bound on the altar here for anti-Germanism. Then there's *The Pearl Fisher* about a quarter done; and there's various short stories in various degrees of incompleteness. Deil, there's plenty grist, but the mill's unco slaw! Tomorrow or next day, when the mail's

7. Not executed.

8. *Records of a Family of Engineers,* a fragment, first published in the Edinburgh Edition of RLS's works (*18,* 1896, 187 ff.).

9. *A Footnote to History: Eight Years of Trouble in Samoa* (1892).

through, I'll attack one or other, or maybe something else. All these schemes begin to laugh at me, for the day's far through, and I believe the pen grows heavy. However, I believe *The Wrecker* is a good yarn of its poor sort, and it is certainly well nourished with facts; no realist can touch me there, for by this time I do begin to know something of life in the XIXth century, which no novelist either in France or England seems to know much of.

You must have great larks over Masonry.[1] You're away up in the ranks now and (according to works that I have read) doubtless design assassinations and kiss—I believe it is the devil's arse? But I am an outsider, and I have a certain liking for a light unto my path which would deter me from joining the rank and file of so vast and dim a confraternity. At your altitude it becomes (of course) amusing and—perhaps—useful. Yes, I remember the L.J.R., and the constitution, and my homily on Liberty, and yours on Reverence which was never written—so I never knew what Reverence was. I remember I wanted to write Justice also, but I forgot who had the billet. My dear papa was in a devil of a taking; and I had to go out to lunch—to meet the Wigans [2] at Ferriers—in a strangely begrutten [3] state, which was *infra dig.* for a homilist on Liberty. It was about four, I suppose, that we met in the Lothian Road—had we the price of two bitters between us? questionable!

All you say of Henley I feel; I cannot describe the sense of relief and sorrow with which I feel I am done with him. No better company in God's earth, and in some ways a fine fellow, a very fine one. But there has been too much hole-and-cornering, and cliquing, and sweltering; too much of the fizz and cackle of the low actor lot; and of late days, with all sorts of pleasant and affecting returns of friendship when we met, too much and a too visibly growing jealousy

1. " 'Tis a strange craft, and the more interesting the more you see and know; for years after I joined it, I saw nothing in it; now I see everything. Would it were like other human institutions worked more in accordance with the spirit. But I must not prose to you, who are "a Profane," as we politely term those who are not of us. I should like some day to "make" you. You would enjoy it. The L.J.R. was curiously enough not altogether dissimilar. Do you remember the fatal ritual I invented, and the *awful* scene that followed on its discovery? I still remember meeting you in the Lothian Road and hearing the terrible news that fell from your blanched lips. I also remember a sensation as if my knees were melting. That was the way terror affected *me*" (CB to RLS, 23 September 1891).

2. Not identified.

3. Tear-stained.

of me. It made my life hard; now it leaves it a good bit empty. *Et puis après?* So they both died and went out of the story; and I daresay young fellows short of a magazine article in the twentieth century (if our civilisation endures) will expose the horrid R.L.S. and defend and at last do justice to the misused W.E.H. For he is of that big, round, human, faulty stamp of man that makes lovers after death. I bet he has drunk more, and smoked more, and talked more sense, and quarreled with more friends than any of God's creatures; and he has written some A-1 verses—talking of that—man alive!— —

4. Your bookseller—(I have lost his letter—I mean the bloody maid has, arranging my room—and so have to send by you)—wrote me a letter about Old Bailey Papers. Gosh, I near swarfed; dam'd, man, I near hand dee'd o't. It's only yin or twa volumes I want: say 500 or 1,000 pp. of the stuff; and the worthy man (much doubting) proposed to bury me in volumes. Please allay his rage, and apologise that I have not written him direct: his note was civil and purposelike. And please send me a copy of Henley's *Book of Verses;* mine has disappeared.

Wednesday

My mother is to give me an order for £100 (her bond), so that makes only £100 you'll have to meet on my bill.

The orchestra is better at a distance no doubt; and Lloyd sometimes quacks on the clarionet in a manner to bring blood; but it's great fun.

R. L. S.

MS, Yale.

[Samoa, December 1891]

My dear Charles,

No word from you, and there need be little in mine.

1mo. A man, D. C. Doig,[4] 175 Bond Street, London, writes to ask me to give my name to a committee for a statoot to Sir Walter. I write and give my name, and announce "a frugal subscription." Will you please send it to him. How much would you give, if you were me? Would £5,5 be shabby? Judge and act.

4. Presumably of William Doig and Co., fine art publishers, 174 New Bond St.

2nd. Baron Tauchnitz will soon write to you, I believe. We have been corresponding, and I can't be bothered with it any longer. If he makes a decent offer accept him. Try and screw him up to £50 a volume; I think that would be good. £40 I think he should give; and at £40 I am willing to bind myself to give him all my books, if he is willing to bind himself to take them all.

All well but Fanny, who goes not very robustly.

> [Yours affectionately,
> ROBERT LOUIS STEVENSON] [5]

MS, Yale.

[Samoa, December 1891]

My dear Charles,

1st. As to Henley, I am quite willing to put myself entirely in his hands as to publication, non-publication, and whole or partial publication. Just what and how he likes. I have no intention of writing any of the plays; but of *Hester Noble* I wish to make a short story some of these days for a collection. The others I expect him to use or leave as he wishes. I request him to write for me a statement that I may use *Hester Noble,* as explicit as mine here. He has all the papers in a portfolio; if there ever was a sketch of *Hester,* I should be obliged if he would send it me.

2nd. About Runciman's [6] family, I am not surprised. Whatever I can do, I wish to do. I am going to draw on you for £200, and to charge you with a Xmas hamper for Miss Boodle, and I am going to ask Miss B. to get a goose for Mary Ann Watts. If after that is through, you have £20 to my credit, let it go to Mrs. Runciman; if you have £50, let £30 go to her. Or if the thing is being more sensibly managed, and a fund could be administered, I would willingly subscribe £20 a year for five years. Surely ten others could

5. Complimentary close and signature cut out, but supplied by CB, with the note: "autograph given with portrait to Speculative Society Dec. 1892."

6. James Runciman (1852–91), journalist and teacher. He was associated with Henley in the days of *London,* but was later estranged. Henley's obituary comment in the *Scots Observer* was: "Of James Runciman, just dead in the prime of life . . . it is enough to say that he was a writer and journalist of brilliant parts, great promise, and some performance." On 17 September Henley had written to CB: "We're making a subscription for Runciman's widow and children—left destitute, I am sorry to say. I hope that Stevenson will bear a hand" (Beinecke Collection).

be found to join me in this, and it would give the babes a chance.*
If none of these schemes can be managed, I place myself in your
hands as I have so often done before; be thou my almoner! But I
have written what I should prefer.[7]

* If this could be arranged I would advance my quota if needful
to 25 or even 30; but £200 a year is certainly ample, and she
should certainly be able to do with £150. I inclose a letter for
Mrs. R.

MS, Yale.

[Samoa] January 1892

Dear Charles,

I am at work on a short tale, *The Go-Between*,[8] which I estimate
at 30,000 words; but remember, I do not bind myself as to the size
—that is my guess: might be longer, might be shorter. I have announced the fact to the Ed. *Illust. Lond. News,* who wanted a summer story, and referred him to you. If he doesn't seem to rise to the
occasion, there is Scribner, A. P. Watts,[9] and McClure all to be
tried. I hope to send the most of it next mail. 'Tis a prettyish tale
—or should be: Haddington Coast, Whitekirk Parish, *temp* 182–,
love story. As a bystander, I suggest not less than £500 for serial
rights.

R. L. S.

By the way, I can give evidence in Simpson's case.[10] At a very
early date he told me of the Scotch marriage; I am inclined to believe either in '74 or '75. It was not later than '76, that I could
swear to, I think; but I am still labouring to piece things together
rightly. If this can be of service, I suppose the Deputy Commissioner here (Western Pacific Act) would be the right person to take
my evidence, and he living on the spot, it should cost but little.

R. L. S.

7. Signature cut out.
8. Never finished.
9. Alexander Pollock Watt (*d.* 1914), agent for most of the leading authors of the
day.
10. It would appear that Simpson had contracted an irregular Scottish marriage
several years prior to his formal one. Cf. below, p. 299.

MS, Yale.

[Samoa] 31 January 1892

My dear C. B.,

I had a strange rambling dream about you last night, in which I am sorry to say you figured in a divorce court and turned out to be the heir of a Highland family—Campbell of Glenure, in fact. My emotion, as I sat in court, was so extreme that I woke up; and then I thought your claim to the estates and name was scarce valid. It was this: that the late Campbell was the illegitimate son of— *proh pudor!*—your excellent father! But the judge was delighted with the case, and divorced you, and changed your name to Charles Baxter Campbell, and served you heir in Glenure—all in one advice, which was quick work. He mentioned, in his decision, that twenty ancient highland targets hung in your (highly illegitimate) ancestral halls.

McClure is bothering about *The Beach of Falesá,* and as I want no bother, I have told him to take it or want it. Should he choose the latter, you will receive the copy close on the heels of this, when I believe the best way will be to give it to Cassells to publish in a small volume, as I believe I suggested before. It will come in well about Easter, and though I never thought that a good publishing season, it pleases the publishers, who are supposed to know. I again repeat my opinion that it should be bound and sold at half-a-crown. Should Cassells hesitate, take it to Charles Longman, who will jump at it, or I'm mistaken. At 250 words to the page it will make close on 130 pp.: a little volume truly.

Feb. 1st

I have just received a letter from Cassell and Co., in which they seem to speak of taking the serial rights themselves and to prefer holding off for other stories to make a larger volume. I think this chimerical: two of the proposed stories have already telescoped into a proposed longer one, which will be a volume itself. And unless Cassell and Co. choose to pay at least £400 for the serial rights —supposing McClure to throw up—it must come out as a volume. I enclose herewith a plan, which should be added to the volume, and this is the dedication:

To three old shipmates among the islands:
Harry Henderson,[1]
Ben Hird,[2]
Jack Buckland,[3]
their friend,
R. L. S.

You are to understand that this appearance in book form is what I would prefer. Only the lust of gold and the tightness of the money market makes me hesitate. And even so, I am not sure that I shall not lose in the long run. I fear the P.D. has a bad time, and will try not to load him again with such disagreeables. But this year of house-building and plantation-making was necessarily a dear one, and I reached for cash down where I could see it. Have just had the Bloo-ming Influenza and lost a month: poor start for the year. No scrape of the pen from you or Colvin this mail, which seems mangy but is doubtless susceptible of explanation.

My influenza will explain nothing going to Henley. I have received his *Lyra Heroica* [4] and was knocked of a heap to find myself Lyring Heroically, which I thought beyond expectation. It was good of him to stretch a point for his old friend. The book is in many ways excellent; I found many brave old friends—the chief joy of such a collection—and made some new. He may well be proud of it, but I had rather in these days see another volume of his own. However, that will be coming, and should be good. I have remarked one or two fine pieces—and one very fine—in the *Journal.* As to his finances, I dare not ask. But I repeat my promise to try all I can to help him. I think you know pretty well how I feel: few things in my mishandled life make me sicker than the thought of that breach. And yet I bore much, as God sees me. And yet I know in the original quarrel it was not he who was to blame directly: he was only to blame indirectly, by having corridor'd, and stewed, and Shepherd's-Bushed, till he prepared the state of mind which brought the mine to an explosion. Well, he managed

1. Partner in the Sydney firm of Henderson and Macfarlane, owners of the *Janet Nichol,* in which the Stevensons made their last Islands cruise.
2. Supercargo of the *Janet Nichol.*
3. A "remittance man," the original of Tommy Haddon in *The Wrecker.*
4. An anthology edited by Henley, who had included RLS's "Requiem."

to be his own enemy and mine, but I should not wish him to lose, if I can prevent that.[5]

MS, Yale.

[Samoa, 30 March 1892]

My dear Charles,

Herewith the documents signed. Do I understand our paper properly? It means that of the land and house the destination passes to Fanny, but not of the furniture and plenishings; so that, if she died before me, the heritable property would go by her will, but the moveables would be held for me. This is how I read it; pray tell me if I am wrong.

There seems a strong feeling against *Falesá* for a volume, so I consent to withhold it till there are more. God knows when that may be. I hope this is a privileged communication, but I must tell you I fear the solvency of the Great McClure must be a-totter. This will leave me in a dreadful hole, for I have no idea my money will have been kept separate as he proposed: the being is too Pinkertonish [6] for that. I can net a thousand pounds inside the year, and have *David Balfour* besides ready for sale; and besides, there must be dropping profits on the essays, *Wrecker,* and (perhaps, to a tune of shillings) on the Samoan war.[7] But this leaves seven or eight months to be crossed, and aweel I wot I cannae see the mere poasibeelity o' the thing. It looks as if I might have to overdraw on you considerably; it is merely impossible to stop our expenses here, and though I might reduce my staff, that would be unwise. I would not get the boys again, and to train new ones costs both fash and siller. Kindly turn this in your head, and tell me (by return if you can) what I had best do to "pass the centres." It is annoying when I had got my house built and much of my plantation made, and everything was so well balanced, to have another fellow's carelessness rob me of my reward. But there is no use fretting. And I don't see why we should not get through.

5. Not signed.
6. See above, p. 273 n.
7. *A Footnote to History.*

Burlingame [8] has directions to send you slips of the hurricane [9] for Henley. It is a failure, which I could kick myself for having to publish *tel quel.* A writing or two more and I could have made a good thing, but time flies, and the book must be out by July. Tell W.E.H. I only send it him to keep my promise, but shall be nowise ill-pleased if he decline the golden opportunity. It is such stuff as we should have told each other in old Bristo days to take away and rewrite.

I am greatly overdone with literature and affairs. With love,
[Ever yours affectionately,
ROBERT LOUIS STEVENSON] [10]

MS, Yale. Letters, 4, *42.*

[Samoa, 27 April 1892]

My dear Charles,

I have just written the dedication of *David Balfour* to you, and haste to put a job in your hands. This is a map of the environs of Edinburgh *circa* 1850 [*sic*]. It must contain Hope Park, Hunter's Bog, Calton Hill, the Mouter Hill, Lang Dykes, Nor' Loch, West Kirk, village of Dean, pass down the water to Stockbridge, Silver Mills, the two mill lades there with a wood on the south side of the south one which I saw marked on a plan in the British Museum, Broughton, Picardy, Lieth Walk, Lieth, Pilrig, Lochend, Figgate Whins. And I would like a piece in a corner, giving for the same period, Figgate Whins, Musselburgh, Inveresk, Prestonpans, battlefield of Gladsmuir, Cockenzie, Gulane—which I spell Gillane, Ficha, Dirleton, North Berwick Law, White Kirk, Tantallon Castle and Castleton, Scougal and Auldhame, the Bass, the Glentiethy rocks, Satan's Bush, Wildfire Rocks, and, if possible, the May. If need were, I would not stick at *two* maps. If it is but one, say *Plan to Illustrate David Balfour's Adventures in the Lothians.* If two, call the first *Plan to Illustrate David Balfour's Adventures*

8. Edward Livermore Burlingame (1848–1922), editor of *Scribner's Magazine,* 1887–1914.

9. The hurricane chapter of *A Footnote to History.*

10. Complimentary close and signature cut out, but supplied by CB, with the note: "signature sent with portrait presented by me to the Academy July 1892."

about the City of Edinburgh, and the second *Plan to Illustrate David Balfour's Adventures in East Lothian.* I suppose there must be a mapmaker of some taste in Edinr; I wish few other names in but what I have given, or few as possible. As soon as may be, I will let you have the text, when you might find even some amusement in seeing that the maps fill the bill. If your mapmaker be a poor creature, plainness is best; if he were a fellow of some genuine go, he might give it a little of the bird's eye quality. I leave this to your good taste. If I have time I will copy the dedication to go herewith; I am pleased with it. The first map (suppose we take two) would go in at the beginning, the second at Chapter XI. The topography is very much worked into the story, and I have alluded in the dedication to our common fancy for exploring Auld Reekie.

The list of books came duly, for which many thanks. I am plunged to the nostrils in various business.

Have drawn on you this 27th of April for £150 in favour of A. Crawford and Co., San Francisco.

Yours ever,

R. L. S.

MS, Yale.

[Samoa, received 29 June 1892]

Dear Charles,

No time remains to me till the mail goes. I send you this list of copies for the Samoa History. Because I have not yet heard if the Cassells take it. It is now all in the hands of Scribner's and must be before the public *instanter;* if a despatch or two, even a cablegram or three, be needful, stick not at the expense; it would be deplorable to have taken all these pains and be too late.

Glad to hear you had come to an agreement with McC. What a lark their blushing virtue is!

Yours ever,

R. L. S.

MS, Yale. Dictated to Belle Strong.

Vailima Plantation, Upolu, Samoa,
20 June 1892

My dear Charles,

Yours of 29th April to hand. Please draft and send us a codicil to my wife's will giving me a life rent in case of her decease, or if you think it safer, draw a new will embodying the change. Then you could effect a change in the position of John Lloyd,[1] making him, instead of co-executor with me, alternative executor to succeed on my decease. I think it is all right about McClure.

Ever affectionately yours,

R. L. STEVENSON [2]

MS, Yale.

CB TO RLS

Signet Library, Edinburgh, 1 July 1892

My dear Louis,

You may remember this accursed abode of sin and misery; think of me still wandering about it—the old weary grind just the same to look at, but how changed! A "proof" is on, everybody excitement, counsel primed, witnesses ready with their lies, agents in a fuss, but no Puggy Deas,[3] no Johnny Adams,[4] no R.L.S. nor other *joyeux compagnons* to laugh at the dreariness of the whole blooming bag of tricks. All the companions who remain, sheriffs or M.P.s or Lord Advocates or, worse, middle-aged W.S.'s with families intent upon accounts of expenses and no fear of God but only of the Auditor before their eyes. Alas I am indeed a Wearywarld: I care for nobody and nobody cares for me, and in the middle of infinitely more than I ever deserved I have not even the heart to be decently grateful. Such is the Painful Doer of today. Edinburgh does me harm: I am never well in it; the one earthly happiness I can think of is to look for the last time upon its walls. As a memory it would be charming; as a reality it leads, I am afraid, only to drink or the Private Asylum or both.

1. A friend of Sam Osbourne and Fanny; Lloyd Osbourne was named after him.
2. Signed by RLS.
3. See above, p. 143.
4. See above, p. 38.

I told you Lady Simpson and Flo. Fitzg. had been presented. As I expected, they were blown upon, but you will never guess by whom. There is one Mrs. Clifton, a kind of cousin of the Simpsons' mother; I don't suppose you ever knew her. Impelled by a sense of Duty to Her Queen, she denounced Lady Simpson as an ex-mistress of six years standing, an adventuress, and a liar, and Flo as her illegitimate child.[5] This in a letter to the Lord Chamberlain, adding that the brother and sister *"at whose request she wrote"* felt deeply pained at the insult offered to Her Majesty by one of their family. Unexpectedly to them no doubt the Lord Chamberlain's office furnished us with a copy of their letter, and it was put to Eva and Willie [6] whether they adopted it, which they did! Can you conceive anything more vile? Well, there has been an awful shindy, and I have done what I could to help, but of course it wasn't much. The decision will be made known, I believe, today or tomorrow, but I cannot hope for any good result. One may say and truly that the step was a foolish one, but really my sympathies are all with Etta [7] now. She has stood up under the thing with an amazing pluck and good temper worthy of anyone's admiration. Here was the *London Journal* romance of years successfully crowned: she received at Court, and really well accepted in *very good* Society—such as you could hardly credit—and the whole castle tumbles to pieces in a night at the touch of the wicked fairy's wand. It is a tale hardly to be believed. There will of course be a sequel. . . .

Ever affectionately yours,

C. BAXTER

MS, Yale. Letters, *4, 88. First half dictated to Belle Strong.*

Vailima Plantation, Upolu, Samoan Islands
[18 July 1892]

My dear Charles,

Enclosed is the slip filled up.[8] I shall try to remember the set

5. The exact relationship between Lady Simpson (Anne Fitzgerald Mackay) and Florence Fitzgerald remains obscure. In a letter to RLS, 28 December 1886, Sir Walter Simpson describes "Flo" as "a girl staying here who has an insatiable appetite for young men to dinner . . ." (MS, Yale).

6. William Simpson (*b.* 1850), Sir Walter's younger brother.

7. Presumably Lady Simpson.

8. The enclosure is a note to CB from William Adamson, lithographer and

of Samoan stamps; [9] but look here, if I forget this time, keep me up to the mark in future.

Awfully glad you have got a good man for the *Davy Balfour* maps. As for your news of the presentation of Lady Simpson of Strathavon, the whole family fell in swaths about the apartment; but man, why didn't ye no send us the *Gentlewoman?* [1] You will never be forgiven until this is done. An irate amanuensis here interrupts with a countenance deformed with fury and says, "Why don't you tell him there is no book stall in Apia?"

Perhaps you will understand our situation better if I tell you this. I have been now for some time contending with powers and principalities and I have never once seen one of my own letters to the *Times*. So when you see something in the papers that you think might interest the exiles of Upolu—how much more if you see anything that you know will convulse them, like my lady's picture in the *Gentlewoman*—do not think twice: out with your saxpence, and send it flying to Vailima.

Of what you say [2]—amanuensis called to the cookhouse—of the past, eh, man, it was a queer time, and awful miserable, but there's no sense in denying it was awful fun, and life?—yes, sir, it was deadly living. Do you mind the youth in Highland garb and the

---

engraver—doubtless the mapmaker referred to in the present letter. He writes that he has made a copy of the "enclosed letter" (RLS to CB, 27 April 1892, above, p. 296) and that he hopes to submit a rough draft (of the map) in a few days.

9. "The children, who (as well as all the rest of both families) are very [well], thank you immensely for the princely supply of Samoan stamps just received. The ½ stamps especially are sufficient to make a collector's fortune" (CB to RLS, 15 November 1892).

1. "Lady Simpson of Ballabraes, presented by Mrs. Smith, had a magnificent train in rich cream brocade arranged from left shoulder with plumes of feathers; cream duchesse satin petticoat trimmed in festoons of chiffon and feathers; diamond ornaments. Miss Florence Fitzgerald, presented by Lady Simpson, was much admired" (*The Gentlewoman*, 4 June 1892, p. 764). "I don't know if I told you that Lady S. presentation was cancelled (but *not* Flo Fitzgerald's), and there has been much distress in consequence" (CB to RLS, 3 August 1892). By "cancelled" is presumably meant "stricken from the rolls or records."

2. Letter continued in RLS's hand.

tableful of coppers? Do you mind the SIGNAL of Waterloo Place? Hey, how the blood stends to the heart at such a memory! Ha'e ye the notes o't? Gie's them—Gude's sake, man, gie's the notes o't; I mind ye made a tüne o't an' played it on your pinanny; gie's the notes. Dear Lard: that past.

Glad to hear Henley's prospects are fair; his new volume [3] is the work of a real poet. He is one of those who can make a noise of his own with words, and in whom experience strikes an individual note. There is perhaps no more genuine poet living, bar the Big Guns. In case I cannot overtake an acknowledgement to himself by this mail, please let him hear of my pleasure and admiration. How poorly Kipling compares! K. is all smart journalism and cleverness: it is all bright and shallow and limpid, like a business paper—a good one, *s'entend;* but there is no blot of heart's blood and the Old Night; there are no harmonics; there is scarce harmony, to his music; and in Henley—all of these: a touch, a sense within sense, a sound outside the sound, the shadow of the inscrutable, eloquent beyond all definition. The first *London Voluntary* knocked me wholly.

Ever yours affectionately, my dear Charles,

ROBERT LOUIS STEVENSON

Kind memories to your father and all friends.

MS, Yale. Dictated to Belle Strong.

Vailima, 11 August 1892

My dear Charles,

Herewith please receive a considerable portion of *David Balfour.* McClure has been behaving in a particularly annoying and shilly-shallying manner. His own old unsolicited offer was sixteen hundred pounds for serial rights. I am now done with the bargaining, and place it in your hands. In my belief, sixteen hundred is a fair figure, and I should propose (while leaving you discretion) to refuse anything under fifteen hundred. Suppose Samuel to fail in reaching this figure, my advice would be to put the whole affair *quo ad* serial rights in the hands of A. P. Watt,[4] to whom, instead

3. *London Voluntaries.*
4. See above, p. 292.

of your idea of sealed offers, I feel rather inclined to intrust those books in the future for which I have not otherwise arranged.

Apropos of *The Beach of Falesá* I reply to you, although I believe it's through Colvin I have received the proposal. You will kindly communicate to him my answer. *The B. of F.* is *simply not* to appear along with *The Bottle Imp,* a story of a totally different scope and intention, to which I have already made one fellow, and which I design for a substantive volume. If on the other hand Cassell shall choose to publish it by itself, I would remind the lot of you that this was my own original proposal, which I have seen no reason to change, and which I should be rather glad to see come in operation.

As for the news about Etta, I only wish there were any possible means of communicating directly to herself my sympathy. I think it is really one of the most dastardly things I ever heard of, and I am now rather a connoiseur in dastards. I cannot remember whether I told you last mail the news of our domestic revolution— talking of dastards.[5] I shall enclose in this the papers from the Consulate [6] to be added to the archives. Doubtless anyway you will have heard some details through Colvin. But what in God's name could have happened to Eva? The animosity of women is always an extraordinary study. And when I remember that I once seriously dreamed of marrying that underhand virago my heart wells over with gratitude.

The beginning of your letter was exceedingly dreary and bad reading. You say you care for nobody, which I take the liberty of denying, and that nobody cares for you, to which I take the freedom to present the lie direct. However that humour is no doubt long blown by; and I can assure you if I had written during some of the pleasing episodes of the revolution—say no longer ago than last Thursday when I was chewing the bitterness of its last episode, I might have appeared to you almost as weariful a creature as you

5. ". . . we found Joe Strong out in various misdeeds: robbing the cellar and store-room at night with false keys. In revenge, when he found that he was discovered, he went round to all our friends in Apia and spread slanders about Belle. We turned him away and applied for a divorce for Belle, which was got with no difficulty, as he had been living with a native woman of Apia as his wife ever since he came here—an old affair begun when he was here before. . . . Louis was made sole guardian of the child, who has been sent to Nelly [Sanchez] to school" (Fanny's journal: *Our Samoan Adventure,* ed. Charles Neider, p. 185).

6. "These never came" (CB).

showed to me. And believe me the worst of what can have been troubling you can have been but a flea bite compared to the mouth-deep mires in which our family has been wading for six weeks. I wish I could say it was quite over, but owing to mismanagement on our side the unwelcome presence is likely to be continued on our island. The worst of it at least *is* over, and I do not believe that there is remaining in the hand of Fortune any such disgusting drug to be again administered.

Glad you saw Colvin. I wish you would tell me how you thought him looking. You and he are the last of the Romans, and it appears that one of these Romans must be rapidly aging. At least I hear by the means of an Academy schoolboy that "an old gentleman to whom I dedicated all of my books" recently presented the rector with a choice of two of my photographs.[7] If this be really you, and I cannot see who else it could refer to, it is enough to cure us all of existence.

> I remain,
> My dear old gentleman,
> Your ancient tottering but
> Faithful friend,
> ROBERT LOUIS STEVENSON [8]

P.S. When *Falesá* comes out in the *Illustrated* or wherever it is, do please send us a copy.

I am drawing on you by this mail at fifteen day's sight for two hundred and fifty pounds in favour of H. J. Moors. I presume with all these irons in the fire this should be no inconvenience. I must say I wish to goodness there were some way of my knowing vaguely how I stand. I draw bills like Elijah on the ravens. Now I seem to be let in for the addition to my house. It is no choice of mine—and I dislike it. But Lloyd has no room, and my mother objects vigorously to any partial improvement. With a bland trust in the ravens I shall probably go ahead; and if this induces my Doer to tear his hair, my best excuse is that I send herewith one hundred and forty-seven pages of *David Balfour* and trust that the rest shall follow by the next mail or that after. They say Faith is the chiefest of the

7. "*I* was the old gentleman. I saw the picture the other day on the wall of the Big Hall and it does everybody credit. It is an enlargement of the Boston one, which I think the best of all" (CB to RLS, 15 November 1892).
8. Signed by RLS.

virtues; it is at least one which a poor Maroon in the South Seas has to exercise beyond the warranty of prudence. See how it stands. I have this house in view; I know not how my accounts stand; if I wait and ask you, the house will be built, or else the season over, before I can possibly receive any reply. I do not say it is remediable, I only faintly bleat that it is inconvenient. I also hollowly mutter that it might lead to a catastrophe. Perpend.

Herewith in 3 envelopes 147 pages of *David Balfour*.

R. L. S.

MS, Yale.

[Samoa] 12 September 1892

My dear Charles,

Herewith *David,* Chaps. XXII to XXVII. The end should come next mail: about as much again.

I have drawn on you for £103, thirty days, for the German Firm. And I have to announce well beforehand a possible heavy expense. I am signing a contract for the new wing of Abbotsford: [9] £600 when the roof is on, £600 when complete. Of this my mother is to find £500, which leaves £700 for me. The first bill should probably fall to be drawn in December; I think it would be well on the whole to provide for the whole £700 before the end of February.

At this stage, I went out to suggest to my mother that she should write to you about her £500, and found her ungenially vague. It is particularly she who wants the house, and I immediately brought her to a more compliant temper by refusing to go on with it, unless the £500 was definitely promised for Jan. or Feb. This she has done, and I hope she can keep her word. The new house is a dam folly and (to me) a dam annoyance, for I wanted a rest and a holiday, which was all planned and has just had to be given up. But the new house without my mother's promised contribution would be a common fraud. So please, look out.

I am a little bothered about my will, but rather than change it, I am going to leave a private letter to Lloyd: the point to be con-

9. I.e. Vailima.

sidered being my little ward.[10] He leaves by this mail for school in California. The man Strong still decorates the beach. We met him two days ago; cheerful; but it's little we care if they let us sleep on in the house which his absence has brightened. The cursed thing is letting the child go to him, and be talked at and through and wept upon, and sent home again with dashed spirits and a damaged loyalty, and to have our mouths closed by—what?—Being Gentlefolk, I guess.

There was no word from you last mail; I suppose it miscarried. However, I must be well-to-do, I fancy: which is the magnum bonum—maximum, in my strategically false position here, with Abbotsford going the way Abbotsfords have to go. But don't blame me. The tale is this: Lloyd has no room; I wished to build him a cottage ad interim; and my mother, who saw it would postpone, perhaps prevent, the rest of the house, objected.

Yours ever,
R. L. STEVENSON

MS, Yale. Dictated to Belle Strong.

Vailima, Samoan Islands, 7 October 1892

My dear Charles,

The deuce and all—here have been nearly two months and not a word from you, and now turns up your letter of [   ] via Sydney! I hope to goodness we can manage to avoid this the next few months. The whole of *David Balfour* should now or in a few days be in your hands—I trust in time. To tell you the truth I am most unhappy that I have got embarked in the building of this new house, and I know there is going to be the deuce to pay to get to the year's end. As if all were not enough, it seems I am in for a libel action. An accursed ruffian, a missionary by the vile name of Arthur Claxton, of whom I narrated semi-anonymously a pleasing anecdote in the *Footnote to History*,[1] has taken the thing amiss. I am fighting it

10. Austin Strong.
1. "About the same time there occurred an incident, upon which I must be more particular. *A* was a gentleman who had long been an intimate of Mataafa's, and had recently . . . more or less wholly broken off relations. To him came one whom I shall call *B* with a dastardly proposition. It may have been *B's* own, in which

just now by merely procrastinatory measures, having retained both the lawyers. As we are both British subjects it can go first before the Consul here as Deputy Commissioner, thence to Fiji to the High Commission Court, and thence, alas, to the Privy Council. It will scarcely escape your powerful intellect that this may come to something short, not to say sweet. I am not really troubling about it, because when all is done it can never be more than a pecuniary cast-back, and I am not ashamed of anything that I have done. At the same time, in conjunction with the new house it makes not at all the kind of year that I like to look forward to, and I wish you would sit down and thoroughly consider my financial position. Is there anything that I can do to meet this sudden strain? Please let me know by return all that you can to give me a clear view of the prospects at home and any suggestion you can make as to what I could be doing to raise the wind. It is too intensely annoying that I should have been kicked into the new house at such a period, when I might otherwise have faced the missionary and all his works with composure.

The exact nature of the man's action I cannot find out. The story told of him in the *Footnote* is the A. and B. story of the man who proposed a treachery to the American Consul, and I *suppose* it is on that issue he means to attack. I have never yet received any copy of the book and seem to have lost the proofs of that part, so that I cannot be certain of what words I used; still I believe I shall have a good chance to come scatheless, as the truth of the story can be proved and proved again. It is at the same time possible that he may intend to take action on a private letter to himself [2] in which I said I must either break relations with him or cease to respect myself. On this, since I was unguarded enough to show a copy of it to one of the man's colleagues, I fear his action would be better

case it was the more unpardonable; but from the closeness of his intercourse with the chief justice, as well as from the terms used in the interview, men judged otherwise. It was proposed that *A* should simulate a renewal of the friendship, decoy Mataafa to a suitable place, and have him there arrested. What should follow in those days of violent speech was at the least disputable; and the proposal was of course refused. 'You do not understand,' was the base rejoinder. '*You* will have no discredit. The Germans are to take the blame for the arrest.' Of course, upon the testimony of a gentleman so depraved, it were unfair to hang a dog; and both the Germans and the chief justice must be held innocent" (*A Footnote to History*, 1892, pp. 293–4). "*A*" was Harold M. Sewall, the American consul.

2. Now in the Beinecke Collection.

grounded. But the real trouble is this: the man being a missionary will get any amount of subscriptions to carry on the law-suit and I suspect very few to pay the expenses in case he should lose. So that I imagine in the end R.L.S. must pay the piper. I will keep you posted month by month on all new developments.

I am quite of opinion that twenty per cent is a very handsome payment from a publisher; and I confess that since I have a little studied the subject, the bulk of the complaints against that very uninteresting class of men seem to me either groundless or grossly exaggerated.

Suppose that I am not wrong: that it will be difficult for you to meet the bills announced to you for the building of the new house, and that you agree with me as to the possibility of a serious expenditure immediately impending from the law-suit, I wish, so as to avoid possible delay, to put myself entirely into your hands. In that case any bargain that you can find to make for me I will accept. If time be of its essence, try to get the time as long as possible; but if it has got to be short, I shall have to fill the bill. Understand, any sort of work on any sort of terms and at any humanly possible period. The one thing I cannot have happen is to get altogether stuck, and as I am particularly well and working very easily the chance is a good one. Of course all this is written in a vast ignorance as to the state of my affairs, but I hope you will manage in your answer to make that entirely plain to me.[3] I see that my account in Sydney is already far lower than is wholesome— and I fear I must ask you to feed it. I do not like to say with how much, for I know so little of how I stand, but if it be at all feasible, I should like to have three hundred pounds at least paid into their English branch. The name of the bank, I suppose you remember, is the "Bank of Australasia."

Yours ever,
R. L. STEVENSON [4]

3. ". . . the next business is the house. You will know by this time that there need be no trouble about that. My trouble is that there will require to be a very large production to keep up present expenditure, and that is of course a matter of health. It cannot be imprudent to overhaul all unnecessary expense and get the place as soon as possible into a source of profit. This is not Preaching. It is only the Prudent Forelook of the Painful Doer" (CB to RLS, 15 November 1892).

4. Complimentary close and signature in hand of RLS; letter continued in hand of Belle Strong.

Oct. 10th. I enclose a more formal note to yourself, so that you may use it if you think best to Labby.[5] No farther developments in the Libel Suit. The Mission Committee will not sit until after the mail has left, but I think I may almost venture to announce its decision beforehand. It will do its best to prevent the fellow Claxton from going on with the Libel Case. If I understand his position rightly, that best will be of no avail. Somehow or another, by hook or by crook, he is got to place himself before the public in some kind of light of martyrdom, however cheap. A suit against me (whatever its result) is the readiest advertisement at the man's hand, and I shall be much surprised if he does not seize and use it for all it is worth.[6]

I trust you are not neglecting to register your letters. It is a terrible annoyance not to hear from you,[7] and a considerable source of anxiety not to hear of the arrival of *David Balfour*.[8] We should all be in bonny blankets if that gentleman were lost. With regard to the proposal made above, if you consider my financial position compromised or likely to be so, I should recommend your addressing yourself to A. P. Watt. The man has been dying to have a cut at the joint who now addresses you; these six years at least he has plagued me with advertizements, and for the first start I think he would be certain to do wonders.

Fanny's codicil I fear you will have to wait for till next mail. Her foot makes it impossible for her to go down to Apia, and the newspaper-reporting fiends have made it at least difficult for the Consul to come to us. I do not know where you got the notion that S. S. McClure is my agent. He is not so and, except for a specific purpose

5. Henry du Pré Labouchère (1831–1912), journalist and politician; founded *Truth,* 1876.

6. "Then comes the Libel business. I shall look for more news of this. It ought to be vastly interesting, and if all goes well, not too expensive. If you could only get into prison about something, it would be the cheapest advertisement in the world" (CB to RLS, 15 November 1892).

7. "Now please to understand that although I am not all I should be in writing to you, it is not that I am neglecting things on this side, where everything I think at the present moment is in perfect order. But I have an inordinate difficulty in writing to such a distance. The thousands of miles loom like a blank wall in front of me, and I cannot see over them. So if a stumbling block comes in the way, I trip and lose a mail. But I promise reform" (CB to RLS, 15 November 1892).

8. ". . . the whole of *David Balfour* is safely in Cassell's hands, and . . . after no end of correspondence and considerable worry I concluded a contract with McClure on the footing of £1600 for serial rights" (CB to RLS, 15 November 1892).

long since extinguished, never was so. I do not like to prophesy, but
I shall for one be extremely astonished if he ever is so again.
I inclose a curiosity.

R. L. S.[9]

MS, Yale.

[Samoa, 10 October 1892]

My dear Charles,
You are advised that Mrs. Sitwell [10] will be buying a cloak for
Fanny and will draw on you for not over £6.

Yours ever,

ROBERT LOUIS STEVENSON

MS, Yale. Dictated to Belle Strong.

Vailima Plantation, Samoan Islands, South Seas,
4 November 1892

My dear Charles,
The luck that pursues us is extraordinary. Of all letters, yours
are not those I wish to miscarry; and yet it seems as if I were never
to hear from you more. This mail indeed brought me an envelope,
and its contents were highly interesting, but had nothing to do to
business. It was your note written apparently when you were about
to sail for Sweden and enclosing your delicious letter to Robert
Simpson.[11] I wish I had your gift—I have appeared rather freely
lately as an insulting letter writer, but I do not consider I am fit to
black your shoes. Let me congratulate you in particular on your use
of the apparently inoffensive expression "Mr. William Simpson."
Whatever you do be sure and let me have the fullest possible re-

9. Last sentence and signature in hand of RLS. The "curiosity" is doubtless the
"disclaimer of Mr. Angus McClean" mentioned below, p. 316.

10. See above, p. 31, n. 8.

11. Son of Alexander Simpson, Sir James Young Simpson's brother. A lawyer
(he had the charge of Sir James' legal affairs), he appears to have been handling
the case against Lady Simpson for his cousins Eva and William. "I had an *idea* that
my letter to R. R. Simpson was pretty 'steep,' but I was hardly prepared for the
high compliments addressed to it by you! I don't think we shall do much more, if
anything, about the case. We have exhibited them to themselves as they really are,
and given them a big fright" (CB to RLS, 16 December 1892).

ports of the case, which I shall follow with the most intense interest. What do you yourself think the truth about Eva? For old sake's sake I would like to think she had nothing to say to it, and the discrepancy between Mr. and Mrs. Clifton leaves ground for hope in the matter. Where the devil did they fish up the petty officer and his wife? [1] Surely the position of Mrs. Clifton is a particularly bad point in their game. She strikes me as about the last person in this world to suffer personally from any mismanagement of Her Majesty's drawing room; and the fact that they could get no more congruous hand gun casts a strong suspicion on the truth of the story.

I had hoped that the letter would contain an acknowledgment, if not proofs, of the first instalment of *David Balfour*. It seems I had hoped too much. Apropos of *David Balfour*, I received from McClure a letter *re* your telegram. It was in his worst—that is most excited, incoherent, and offensive—vein; I have answered it and give you here a few extracts from my answer. "If you are at all annoyed at what has happened you must blame yourself. You were incapable during all these months of reaching any definite and feasible arrangement with myself. I have had in consequence to hand you over to Mr. Baxter, and with him you must manage to agree as best you can. I ought not to close this without saying that the step taken by Mr. Baxter seems to me to have been highly proper for an agent in his position. I am far from thinking that you had any thought but to deal with me as generously as the circumstances permitted. I only know, and direct your attention to the fact, that you have so managed to deal with me as that every mail in the last nine or ten months has been a fresh source of trouble, ambiguity, and distress, and that I am determined there shall be no more of such unnecessary annoyances in my life."

The fact that I never hear from you leaves me in the most horrid ambiguity as to my position. But since my last rather despairing letter one source of alarm has been practically removed. At the suggestion of the Missionaries I submitted my case and led my evidence before their committee here, for their directors to decide upon. This was done in direct defiance of the opinion of my solici-

1. "Clifton was a commander of the Granton Revenue Cutter for some years, and his wife was a second cousin, I think, of Sir James. She is a notorious slanderer, and she was at the bottom of the scandal wh. caused so much distress at the time of Sir James' Professorship. She was then, I think, denied the house, but Eva has for some reason or other stuck by her" (CB to RLS, 16 December 1892).

tor in Apia, so I think I ought to justify myself a little to my doer at home. I must first confess that I would have taken a considerable risk to oblige the decent Missionaries, and to spare the Mission, which is doing a respectable work, the hurt of a public scandal. We went into the affair with a pledge on either side that the matter should not go before a court of law. I am well aware this pledge can be broken—what matters it? It is all pure gain to me. If Claxton go at last before a court of law, he will go there with another stain upon his name. If he take me before a court, I shall at least have gained time, and the house may be finished and (please God) paid for before the law-suit begin. As for my contrary pledge to apologise if the Directors give the point against me, I am not so bitterly averse to apologising. Indeed I think I prefer apology to payment, and if I can get out of this affair, which looked so black to me a little while back, at the cost of an infinitesimal personal humiliation, I think I shall be on the side of the laughers.

The wood for my new palace—damn it—has begun to arrive. A few very apathetic black boys are at this very moment pretending to carry it up and pile it on my lawn. If the work go no better than it goes now, these bills of which I advised you in my last may perhaps not reach you before February. But this is not what I expect. I expect rather that the first bill will leave by the Dec. steamer, and should therefore be presented to you by the beginning of the year, and that the second will follow it about a month later. I trust there will be no bother about meeting them, and I am reminded that since so many of your letters have gone astray, the same thing may very possibly occur to some of mine, and then it will be only proper I should recapitulate here the essence of the business. Each bill is to be for £600. Of the twelve hundred, which thus falls to be raised, 500 is to be met by my mother, and I sent you her authority in my last to raise it for her at any price. The fact is it's at her request that I have plunged at this moment into such extravagance, and I refused to go on with it as soon as she talked of any delay in paying her share.

I have heard no more from you as to the map for *David Balfour* —a subject on which some news would be very welcome. What was the "story" you told me of—I suppose in one of the lost letters— and which Henley is soon to "send out"? [2]

2. "The 'story' you speak of must, I think, be a proposal on behalf of the *National Observer* for a short serial, which I was desired to submit to you. I can't

In [3] my doubt as to my finance, I enclose to you a list on the Army and Navy Coop. catalogue. If we can afford to make this order just now—I mean if you can afford to pay for it—*it will save money,* as we have to buy bad wine dear in driblets or go without—which is unpleasing and *infra dig.* If we could get the Carton and the Rauenthaler alone, it would be one great want satisfied. And perhaps you could meet these and the bins if not the other. The Rebello Valente I should scarce care to have you order at all, unless you could taste it. I have no use for port unless it is *old* and *dry,* and spotted this on the list for its age. Perhaps you may know of an *old, dry, light* wine yourself. Our number in case this order falls to be made is 67017. The list is on the outside of this sheet.

Good bye.
Yours ever,
R. L. S.

Carton (No. 17) at 56/– 4 doz.
Rauenthaler at 40/– 4 doz.
Heidsieck's Dry Monopole (No. 10) at 52/6 4 doz pints.
Rebello Valente (No. 120) at 90/– 4 doz.

———

1 wine bin, single, to hold 3 doz., doors, sides top and *back,* painted, at 8/–.
1 wine bin, single, to hold 6 doz., no frills at all—at 12/7.

———

Long sea freight for the bins.

MS, Yale. Letters, 4, *151. Dictated to*
Belle Strong.

Vailima, Upolu, Samoan Islands,
1 December 1892

My dear Charles,

I am sending off by this mail a bill for seven hundred pounds in favor of the German Firm. The extra hundred pounds I beg to

---

say I had much faith in it, as I fancied you could sell anything of the sort to a much better purpose outside. But Henley is, I understand, writing to you by this mail on the subject. I can hardly see how the *Observer* could afford to pay anything that would make it worth your while to supply them with a story" (CB to RLS, 16 December 1892).

3. Continued in RLS's hand.

apologise for and explain. We have at the present moment an exceptionally good chance to get specie; and as the account just received from your firm had relieved all my bitter anxieties, I at once went off at score on the other side and made myself a present of a hundred pounds in cash. But the three hundred pounds ordered to the Sydney Bank must be now upon the way, and I hope I can promise you a breathing space for some time to come.

In order to show how serious I am in this, I proceed to direct a fresh expenditure: Miss Boodle's Xmas hamper. This you know what to do about. But Mrs. Watts' Xmas goose I seem to have lost the hang of. How was it managed anyway? Did you send the money to Miss Boodle? Whether you did or not, that would be a good way. And whether by hook or by crook and whether I am a bankrupt or a millionaire, Miss Boodle has to have her hamper and Mary Ann Watts her goose.

I have had from McClure a copy of your correspondence with his brother, which was nearly the means of my dissolution. Only I do want you to make two or three considerations. In the first place McClure is not a dishonest man, although his shambling hand-to-mouth expedients might any day tip him over the margin into the penitentiary. In the second place he has put a vast deal more money into my hand than ever I had before, his offers having been the first thing to make me raise my charges. In the third place he is so far right in his description of the original bargain for *David Balfour*. He made that offer and I accepted it. What has led to the present trouble is some nine months of intolerable correspondence in which he tried to get all sorts of set-offs for himself. In the fourth place I would advise you if possible to avoid actual hostilities with the little man, whom you may still find useful.

As thus. Now that I understand you are going to make me pay something at least for all your trouble, I propose in any case of the least difficulty to plump the business right into your hands. As soon as I hear that you are agreeable to this arrangement I shall refer everybody to you and be done with this three month-answer-and-reply business for ever. Apropos—I have a novel on the stocks to be called *The Justice Clerk*.[4] It is pretty Scotch: the grand Premier is taken from Braxfield[5] (oh by the bye send me Cockburn's

4. Later, *Weir of Hermiston*.
5. Robert Macqueen (1722–99), Lord Braxfield; Lord Justice Clerk, 1788; the "Hanging Judge."

Memorials), and some of the story is—well—queer. The heroine is seduced by one man and finally disappears with the other man who shot him. Now all this, above all after our experience with *Falesá*, don't look much like serial publication; if the worst comes to the worst we shall of course do without that. But it has occurred to me that there is one quarter in which the very Scotchness of the thing would be found a recommendation and where the queerness might possibly be stomached. I mean Blackwood. And I think it might be perhaps worth while to sound the Blackwoods on the subject. I had sworn a great oath they should never have anything of mine, but there is no sense in cutting your nose off to spite your face. You will understand of course it is only the serial rights I offer them. I am not going to burden myself with another publisher, having about three too many already. Should there be any chance of their coming down like gentlemen, I would send you a specimen of the stuff for exhibition as soon as I had any ready.[6] Mind you, I expect *The Justice Clerk* to be my masterpiece. My Braxfield is already a thing of beauty and a joy forever, and, so far as he has gone, *far* my best character.

As usual I had no letter from you this mail—either you or the P.O. must have gone to the Devil. However, there was a very welcome one from the firm, which I acknowledge separately. I trust next mail may bring me something from yourself. Never forget to remember me to your father even if I forget to mention it myself; he [is] always much in my thoughts, and I look back with gratitude to all his kindness to an intolerable boy with whom you used to walk penniless in the Lothian road. I dare say if we met now we could manage to scrape up our three ha'pence apiece, or even to go the length of brandy for the Dutch nigger. Have you forgot that monumental blackguard? And was it to both of us, or only to me, that he made his obliging commercial offer?

We are all decently well, and the new house, as you will gather

6. "I've seen Bill Blackwood, who is staggered at what I've asked him: £2,000 for the serial rights. You see, an old humdrum house has no machinery for selling these all over the world. But here is the sort of idea that he ettles at: To pay £2,000 for the *Magazine* rights *and* an edition of say 3 or 5,000. I say, not good enough, and I'll see what better can be done. Besides, Bill Blackwood's money comes in slow and not sure. But in any case I think you should at once send on a specimen. And for goodness sake do retain something that you could replace it from in case of shipwreck or fire" (CB to RLS, 20 January 1893).

when you see the bill advised, is already roofed and in the painting. It's a lovely house—though I say it that designed it. But then on the other hand I am paying for it and may surely be allowed to find consolation where I can.

Yours affectionately,
ROBERT LOUIS STEVENSON [7]

Second Thought.

I wish Pitcairn's *Criminal Trials* [8] *quam primum*. Also, an absolutely correct text of the Scots judiciary oath. [9]

Also. In case Pitcairn does not come down late enough, I wish as full a report as possible of a Scotch murder trial between 1790–1820. Understand, *the fullest possible*.

Is there any book which would guide me as to procedure in the following points?

The Justice Clerk tries some people capitally on Circuit. Certain evidence cropping up, the charge is transferred to the J.C.'s own son. Of course in the next trial the J.C. is excluded and the case is called before the Lord Justice-General. Where would this trial have to be? I fear in Edinburgh, wh. would not suit my views. Could it be again at the Circuit Town? [1]

ROBERT LOUIS STEVENSON [2]

Dec. 5th

P.S. Dear Charles,

Here is the Devil's news: it seems our Oct. mail has been de-

---

7. Signed by RLS. Continued on a separate leaf in Graham Balfour's hand.

8. Robert Pitcairn (1793–1855), *Ancient Criminal Trials in Scotland*, etc., Edinburgh, 1833.

9. "The oath in criminal cases is the same as in civil trials: viz. 'I swear by Almighty God, and as I shall answer to God at the Great Day of Judgment, that I will tell the truth, the whole truth, and nothing but the truth'; but in case you may find a use for it, I enclose a copy of the oath administered to the *jury* in criminal cases. [Enclosure:] Jury Oath. You fifteen swear by Almighty God, and as you shall answer to God at the Great Day of Judgment, you will truth say, and no truth conceal, so far as you are to pass on this assize" (CB to RLS, 16 December 1892).

1. "I have asked Graham Murray to give me an idea of the course wh. would be followed in the case suggested by you, and I shall send anything he gives me on at once; but I think you may assume at once that the second trial could certainly take place in the country, and that there is no necessity for bringing it to Edinburgh" (CB to RLS, 16 December 1892).

2. Signed by RLS. Continued in the hand of Belle Strong.

stroyed by fire crossing the plains. I don't know if it all went, but if mine to you is among the number of the lost, it contained the end of *David Balfour,* a disclaimer of Mr. Angus McClean,[3] a lot of business which has fortunately answered itself, and a request to have three hundred pounds paid into my account to the Bank of Australasia. It could scarcely have been a more unfortunate mail altogether: nine important letters gone. I shall of course set myself at once to reproduce the end of *David Balfour,* though the devil of it is I do not quite remember where the second installment ended and the third began. (Have found out in further study of the Invaluable Register.)[4] If by any accident this letter should have survived, I wish you would cable to me. Here is the entry from the register: "Sent Oct. 12th Chas. Baxter, including end of *David Balfour;* another[5] re Angus McClean and Chidley, libel mentioned, proposal made to raise the wind if necessary per A.P.W., £300 ordered to Bank of Australasia." This will enable you to identify it beyond mistake. Also, I have on my register[6] a letter: "Edmund Church, Solicitor, inclosing deeds re Dora's trust." My aunt will know Mr. Church's address. For God's sake find out if these have miscarried also. The cable had perhaps better include Sidney Colvin. It might run, "All" or "Church, Colvin" or "Church" or "Baxter," and I will understand the word "lost." I see there was a longish letter to Cassells also. If I receive the word "None," I shall understand that none are lost of these four: yours,

3. In his letter of 3 August 1892 CB had written to RLS: *"Read enclosures from Truth and say if you wish your name still to appear as a backer of Angus Maclean?"* The enclosures, though missing, were doubtless the articles in the 5 May and 14 July numbers dealing with Maclean, the latter of which reads in part: "From a circular received so lately as Friday last, I learn that Mr. Angus Maclean is still touting busily for ten-and-six-penny subscribers to his preposterous 'British and Foreign Association.' Considering the fate which has befallen W. J. Morgan and has colleagues, I confess that I am surprised to see Maclean still pursuing this game, and I trust that as soon as the 'International Society of Literature, Science, and Art' is disposed of, the Public Prosecutor will turn his attention to this cheap imitation of it. In preparation for that event, I would again ask the following gentlemen whether Maclean has their permission to represent them as honorary members of his concern, and whether they seriously think that they are justified in allowing him to do so" (*Truth, 32,* 1892, 69). RLS is one of fifteen named. Cf. also the 11 August number (*32,* 1892, 290).

4. Interpolation in RLS's hand.

5. Dated 7 and 10 October: above, p. 305.

6. The words "on my register" are a correction in RLS's hand of the original reading, "lost."

Colvin's, Church's, Cassell's. I have a glimmer of hope, because I believe the registeredies traivel in a airn safe.[7]

MS, Yale. Letters, 4, 160.

[Samoa] 28 December 1892

My dear Charles,

Your really decent letter to hand. And here I am answering it, to the merry note of the carpenter's hammer, in an upper room of the New House. This upper floor is about done now, but the Grrrrrreat 'All below is still unlined; it is all to be in varnished redwood. I paid a big figure, but do not repent: the trouble has been so minimised, the work has been so workmanlike, and all the parties so obliging. What a pity when you met the Buried Majesty of Sweden—the sovreign of my Cedercrantz [1]—you did not breathe in his ear a word of Samoa!

> O sovreign of my Cedercrantz,
> Conceive how his plump carcase pants
> To leave the spot he now is tree'd in,
> And skip with all the dibs to Sweden.
> O sovereign of my Cedarcrantz,
> The lowly plea I now advantz:
> Remove this man of light and leadin'
> From us to more congenial Sweden.

This kind of thing might be kept up for a Lapland night—"Let us bury the great Joke." [2] Shade of Tennyson, forgive!

I am glad to say you can scarce receive the second bill for the house until next mail, which gives more room to turn round in. Yes, my rate of expenditure is hellish. It is funny: it crept up and up, and when we sat upon one vent, another exploded. Lloyd and I grow gray over the monthly returns; but every damned month there is a new extra. However, we always hope the next will prove less recalcitrant; in which faith we advance trembling.

The desiderated advertisement, I think I have told you, was

7. "Your October mail duly arrived, as you ought to be made aware of by the telegram I have sent you" (CB to RLS, 20 January 1893).

1. See above, p. 284. Cedarcrantz quit in defeat in 1893.

2. Tennyson, "Ode on the Death of the Duke of Wellington."

mighty near supplied: that is, if deportation [3] would suit your view; the ship was actually sought to be hired. Yes, it would have been an advertisement, and rather a lark, and yet a blooming nuisance. For my part, I shall try to do without.

O, by the way, Colvin would like to have a finger in the pie, and I believe about proofs, forms, etc. he would be very useful and relieve you of all sorts of distasteful little higgling details. If it seem well to you, will you make use of him? Of course in all the financial part you will be absolute and single.[4]

By the by, no one has thought fit to send me *Atalanta;* [5] and I have no proof at all of *D. Balfour,* which is far more serious. I have mentioned this to Cassell, but if you are in communication, jog somebody up. How about the *D.B.* map? As soon as there is a proof, it were well I should see it to accord the text thereto—or 'tother way about, if needs must. Remember, I had to go much on memory in writing that work. Did you observe the dedication? and how did you like it? If it don't suit you, I can try my hand again.

Yours ever,

R. L. S.

Nota Bene: My mother leaves on Sunday the first. Make a favour of it to Readman [6] to let him give up the house in June, when his month is up. So as that my mother shall get to dismantling it and be done. You had better get 17 on folks' books for sale immediately. If you can arrange this with Readman for June, my mother should

---

3. RLS's activity in Samoan affairs had caused him to be threatened with deportation, not by the Germans but by Sir John Thurston, British High Commissioner of the Western Pacific, who was in consequence reprimanded by the Colonial Office. A Mr. Sketchly of Levuka, Fiji, described Thurston to Fanny as a "typical self-made man," adding that he had called Sir John, to his face, "an ignorant, arrogant, swindling humbug" (Fanny's journal: *Our Samoan Adventure,* pp. 102–03).

4. "I think with you that Colvin should certainly be asked to do the editing work, but as you will see from *The Isle of Voices* business [CB had sold the story to the *National Observer* just when Colvin was about to give up the attempt to serialize it], he is not much use at selling. And it would, I think, be the best plan to send all MSS *here:* in the first place I am in touch now with all the necessary people, and after I have made the bargain and arranged for the cash business, Colvin can start in and do his part" (CB to RLS, 22 February 1893).

5. A British magazine for girls, in which *David Balfour* was being serialized (December 1892–September 1893).

6. Tenant of 17 Heriot Row since Thomas Stevenson's death.

be able to give delivery by the end of July. As she is harried with packing, she will probably not write herself, so accept this as from her.

ROBERT LOUIS STEVENSON

P.S.[1] Dear C.B. Liqueurs arrived and are first rate. How does the price go? L.O.

P.P.S. I have made a compromise with the firm, and consented, in view of their general obligingness, to pay half the money still due, so that I advise you of a bill for £300 (three hundred pounds) sterling. I enclose a People's Palace racket; if you think well, it might be attended to. I have asked James to write to you direct, and perhaps you had best expect his communication.[2]

R. L. S.

MS, Yale.

[Samoa, 8 January 1893]

Dear Charles,

Three letters from you this month. Well done, thou good and faithful. The presentation [3] sounds strange and touching in my ear;

1. In Lloyd Osbourne's hand.

2. "London, 11 November 1892. Dear Sir, I believe you take an interest in Boys, and that being so I venture to write on their behalf to ask you if you will present our Library with a set, or two sets, of your works, in which they greatly delight, and which get worn out so soon that we are constantly being obliged to purchase new copies, and that out of a limited income; so that if you will come to our rescue, we shall be more than grateful—Appreciative. I am Sir, Yours faithfully, M. S. R. James, Librarian." The People's Palace was a polytechnic institution in East London, founded, in part, as a result of Sir Walter Besant's statement (in *All Sorts and Conditions of Men*) of the need for education and recreation in that district. "I have sent the People's Palace books. The Librarian writes that he thinks you would be pleased to see yourself in rags. Your books of adventure are most popular with his constituents" (CB to RLS, 22 February 1893).

3. Of RLS's portrait to the Speculative Society. "The Spec presentation was a great success. Forty-seven members present and almost all in evening dress. I made the presenting speech; the Sec. moved the thanks of the Society, wh. was seconded by Graham Murray, and spoken to by Charles Guthrie. The function was quite brilliant" (CB to RLS, 16 December 1892).

but you do not tell me where I hang. Am I within eyeshot of Mc-
Bean?[4] Lord, lord! these be long memories, distant thoughts. Poor
McBean, too! Lord, lord, and had he lived, he might have been—
another John Wardrop Tawse,[5] perchance; and why not? I am sincerely affected by this—what shall I say?—friendly thought. And
Murray and Guthrie and Dalmahoy[6] there? God, sir, it's fair
rideeculous!

I believe I shall have no business to trouble you with, save to
announce a bill of £300—the last instalment on the house. For to
the Principal of the R.A.L.[7] I have replied direct, placing myself
with confidence in his hands. The delightful idiots and their Academy! I quite look forward to signing myself H.P.R.A.L. They will
be my only letters, strange for a man of that ilk!

Graham Murray's note,[8] re venues, was highly satisfactory and
did me all the good in the world. Thank you too for the Jury Oath,
which was quite new to me, and I may possibly use.

I have a great need for *Dr. Syntax's Tours* and *The Dance of
Death*—cuts by Rowlandson.[9] I wonder if they could be got out

4. "The 'portrait' is hung with great *éclat* next door to Sir Walter in the big
hall. You would hardly recognize the place now. Hall and lobby alike are hung
all round with pictures of the old members, and even Macbean looks comparatively
bright with the new associates" (CB to RLS, 16 March 1893). A marble plaque,
originally placed on the wall of the lobby, now over the door of the library, is
inscribed:

To the Memory of
WILLIAM MACBEAN
who died while Secretary of the Speculative Society
12th August 1842, aged 19.
His Official Services
commanded the Society's gratitude.
His amiableness its affection.

(*History of the Speculative Society, 1764–1904,* pp. 28–9.) Cf. the dedication to
Kidnapped.

5. See above, p. 109.

6. James Alexander Dalmahoy, W.S.; Secretary of the Spec, 1877–78, President,
1878–79; M.A. Edinburgh; lieutenant-colonel commanding the 1st Midlothian Royal
Garrison Artillery (Volunteers).

7. A proposed Royal Academy of Letters, of which RLS was apparently invited to
become Honorary President.

8. See above, p. 315 n. 1. The letter is in the Beinecke Collection at Yale.

9. *The Tours of Dr. Syntax* (1809–21) and *The Dance of Death* (1815–16): texts
by William Combe (1741–1823) and illustrations by Thomas Rowlandson (1756–
1827).

of No. 17, and sent to me by post? I hate to risk losing them, but they would really be of great use to me for a story that I have in hand. So would, if you chanced to see such a thing, or hear of it, any book on fashions, manners, what you will—but specially fashions, on which I am to seek, for 1810–20, and in particular for *1814 as ever was.*[10] I seem to have two books concentering on that year in spite of fate, fortune, or my own free will. They are

The Justice Clerk	*in gremio*	bloody serious
and		
Saint Yves	one third drafted	pretty light.

R. L. S.

MS, Yale. Dictated to Belle Strong.

Private and confidential! ! ! ![11]

Vailima, 8 January 1893

My dear Charles,

I have just had a turn of influenza, and being taken with rather a bad rigor in the middle of the night, fell into the usual train of repentant reflections—the result of which please consider and put aside for future reference.

In case of my death I want money to be made of it for my more or less innocent and attractive family. The method I propose is this: let all my correspondence be called in. I will append a list of the most likely people to this letter, but as I have done a good deal of scattering correspondence, a general advertisement in the papers with a request to literary journals to copy had better be resorted to. The *pièce de resistance* would probably be my long monthly budgets to Colvin,[1] though I have no doubt a good many

10. "Colvin is sending out some fashion stuff for the period. I also am sending later on two or three volumes of the *Belle Assemblée* (which is English notwithstanding its name), a fashionable Society Journal of 1810 to 1820 or thereabouts. It has coloured fashion plates and contains, I think, a fair presentation of the 'manners' of the day, which I think is what you want" (CB to RLS, 16 March 1893).

11. In RLS's hand.

1. Published separately as the *Vailima Letters* (1895).

amusing or characteristic extracts could be made from earlier
periods. I protest wholly against any idea of a biography. The circumstances of my pleasing career render this impossible.[2] At the
same time, a certain introduction (say by Colvin) might be suitable,
and perhaps a few reminiscences by different friends, which would
serve to fill up gaps. Now I think it is only due to Colvin to be the
formal editor of this book, yet you know very well that there are
reasons why I could not have my past correspondence go through
his hands. Therefore I propose that you should be charged with
the collection of the matter. It will all come into your hands, and
to save you any trouble in the matter I propose you should pass it
all over into those of my cousin Graham Balfour, to whom I write
by this mail advising him of the arrangement. When he shall have
made his selection, he can return it to you, and you send it on to
Colvin. In this way I believe we ought to be able to parry any un-
pleasantness. Colvin's own letters I think you should offer him the
choice of excerpting for himself. Of course you will ask him to do
the preliminary sketch. My dear boy, I have rarely felt more
humiliated than in the thought that I have to take all these pre-
cautions. As I have not the slightest intention of dying on the
present occasion, you will have time to reply to this and criticise

2. Cf. the codicil to RLS's will, dated 10 October 1885 (Beinecke Collection):
"This is a codicil to my will, revoking so much as is inconsistent with the text. If
my wife shall find herself able and willing to undertake my life with her own hand,
I desire that this shall be left to her, and should so have arranged it from the first
if I had not understood her to refuse; at the same time I request her to allow my
formerly designated biographer, W. E. Henley, to give his own account of matters
that he knows best, and to share emoluments with him in a proportion. I beg
Henley, suppose my wife shall desist from her present profession of willingness
to execute the task, to carry along with him in his work the counsels of my wife
and of my friend Sidney Colvin; and I beseech him to remember that whereas I do
believe an entertaining and not unuseful book may be made of my biography, it is
never worth while to inflict pain upon a snail for any literary purpose; and that
where events may appear to be favorable to me and contrary to others, I would
rather be misunderstood than cause a pang to anyone whom I have known, far
less whom I have loved. I add that the autobiographic fragments left, as they were
written in the extreme of sickness and low spirits, are to be used as material—and
not published, as they now stand, to be a shame to me. This I have now written
without erasure the tenth day of October, 1885, and here sign myself

ROBERT LOUIS STEVENSON.

"Should all these proposed designations fail, and my papers come into the
hand of any other biographer, I beg that he too, whoever he may be, will conform
to the principle laid down above.

R. L. S."

my arrangements, and I may as well suggest to you an idea that Fanny entertains: that I might now call in my letters and excerpt and arrange them for myself. I fear this would not only seem very strange conduct in a man of my age, but would lead to awkward questions of property. Doubtless when I am dead, my letters belong to my heirs; but as long as I am alive, do they belong to me? However, if this plan were feasible it would doubtless be much the best. Of course it would only apply to private friends, and there could be no advertisement possible.

List of people who may have letters of mine.[3]

Colvin.

Yourself.

Simpson.

My mother.

Mrs. F. Sitwell?[4]

Will H. Low.[5]

Cosmo Monkhouse?[6]

Gosse.

Meredith?

Henley.

Bob.

Aunt Alan.

Catherine?[7]

Mrs. Virgil Williams.[8]

Mrs. Charles Fairchild.[9]

Miss Boodle.

The Taylors.[1]

3. The names of Gosse and Meredith, and the question marks, are in RLS's hand. No letters to "Aunt Alan" have ever been published; two or three fragments of those to Dora Norton Williams are quoted by Anne Roller Issler in *Happier for His Presence,* Stanford, 1949.

4. See above, p. 31 n. 8.

5. Will Hicok Low (1853–1932), American painter and illustrator, whose friendship with RLS dated from his Barbizon days.

6. William Cosmo Monkhouse (1840–1901), poet and critic.

7. I.e. Katharine (de Mattos).

8. Dora Norton Williams, who, with her artist husband, Virgil Williams (*d.* 1886), was RLS's best friend in San Francisco during the winter of 1879–80.

9. The Fairchilds were prosperous Bostonians, who, before they had met RLS, commissioned the famous Sargent portrait, and who entertained the Stevensons at Newport in 1888.

1. Sir Henry and Lady Taylor, friends and neighbors in Bournemouth.

Now just taking the above list of names, do you think it would
be possible to apply Fanny's idea? Or do you prefer the other? Please
consider and reply.

ROBERT LOUIS STEVENSON [2]

MS, Yale. Letters, 4, *173.*

[Samoa, 1 March 1893]

My dear Charles,

I have had the influenza, as I believe you know; this has been
followed by two goes of my old friend Bloodie Jack, and I have *fefe*
—the island complaint—for the second time in two months. All
this, and the fact that both my womenkind require to see a doctor,
and some wish to see Lord Jersey [1] before he goes home: all send
me off on a month's holiday to Sydney. I may get my mail, or I may
not: depends on freight, weather, and the captain's good nature—
he is one of those who most religiously fear Apia harbour: it is
quite a superstition with American captains. (Odd note: American
sailors, who make Britishers' hair gray by the way they carry canvass,
appear to be actually *more* nervous when it comes to coast and
harbour work.) This is the only holiday I have had for more than
2 years; I daresay it will be as long again before I take another.
And I am going to spend a lot of money. Ahem.

On the other hand, you can prepare to dispose of the serial
rights of *The Schooner Farallone:* [2] a most grim and gloomy tale. It
will run to something between *Jekyll and Hyde* and *Treasure Island.* I will not commit myself beyond this, but I anticipate from
65 to 70,000 words. Could almost pledge myself not shorter than
60,000, but won't. The tale can be sent as soon as you have made arrangements; I hope to finish it in a month—six weeks, bar the

2. Signed by RLS.
1. Victor Albert George Child-Villiers (1845–1915), 7th Earl of Jersey; Governor
of New South Wales, 1890–93. In August 1892 his wife, the Hon. Margaret Elizabeth
Leigh (*d.* 1945), had almost caused an international incident by accompanying RLS
on a visit to the deposed Mataafa, on which occasion the Countess had masqueraded
as RLS's "cousin," Amelia Balfour. "The Jerseys have been and gone, trailing
clouds of glory over the island. . . . They were a selfish 'champagne Charley' set,
with the exception of the daughter, Lady Margaret . . . Lady Jersey tall and
leggy and awkward, with bold black eyes and sensual mouth; very selfish and greedy
of admiration, a touch of vulgarity, courageous as a man, and reckless as a woman"
(Fanny's journal, 23 December 1892: *Our Samoan Adventure,* pp. 185–6).
2. I.e. *The Ebb-Tide.*

worst accidents, for certain. I should say that this is the but end of what once was *The Pearl Fisher,* which we had sold the rights of to the *New York Ledger* through Pin[3]—look at that—through Mc-Clure for £1,000. This bargain is off, owing to the blooming conduct of the *Ledgerites;* but McC. in rather a handsome way—he can be handsome, though as a business man he is a weasel, a snare, and as annoying as the itch—maintained the offer. Under all the circumstances, it seems to me it would be right to let him have the refusal of it. But see: I had promised that my book was to be as long as *Kidnapped* (in its old form it would have been longer than *The Wrecker),* and in its present form I will not promise that it shall be as long as *Treasure Id.* This may make a difference. There is a peculiarity about this tale in its new form: it ends with a conversion! We have been rather tempted to call it *The Schr. Farallone: A Tract by R.L.S. and L.O.* It would make a boss tract: the three main characters—and there are only four—are barats, insurance frauds, thieves, and would-be murderers; so the company's good. Devil a woman there, by good luck; so it's pure! 'Tis a most —what's the expression?—unconventional work.

The rule of these matters is now in your hand, so I shouldn't stick my nose in, beyond posting you as to our position with McClure. I suspect we are in honour, if not in fact, bound to him; and seeing the yarn has so changed and shortened, I should not be surprised if he wished some easing of terms. In that case, I would suggest leniency: between you and me, it's the kind of story that may very well disappoint—might even raise howls.

I regret to confess I have to advise you of a bill for £200 to the Germain Firm.[4]

MS, Yale.

CB to RLS

Edinburgh, 16 March 1893

My dear Louis,

Your letter under answer is dated 8th January and was received here on 6th March, the chief subject being the disposal of your correspondence in the event of your death. With all your points:

3. I.e. Pinkerton (see above, p. 273 n.).
4. Not signed.

viz. Colvin's editorship, and the necessity of a selection being made, and that through Graham Balfour's intermediation, I cordially agree; and as far as I am concerned, I have taken steps to secure that all your letters should, in case of my death, pass at once into his hands. There is no doubt that the preservation of letters is in some ways apt to become a grievous burden, but on the other hand their destruction may become a great injustice. How many cases of miserable gossip and surmise might not have been made plain, and even creditable, if the original documents were still to the fore! The trouble is their custody, when one's own care for the reputations of one's friends is necessarily removed, and only the prying eyes and prurient curiosity of strangers remain to be gratified. I think that, in my case, I have made as secure arrangements as humanly can be made to see that while nothing of value is destroyed, everything shall remain in safe keeping, until it may seem necessary for any reason of importance to refer to the documents in the original.

Although no doubt your own selection would be the most satisfactory, I don't think the scheme of collecting your letters now practicable. There is a great difficulty in persuading people to make such a search, and a great delicacy in asking them to part with documents which, for many reasons, they naturally value. Add to this, that a selection made by the writer from his own correspondence is naturally to some degree suspect. One feels that here is what the man would wish us to see him, and the picture is not convincing. A selection even by the friendliest hand (not his own) must be infinitely more valuable, if only for the fact that there we shall have him as he painted himself from year to year, and not the conscious effort at an *apologia pro vita sua* which even the most candid self-made selection would inevitably have the appearance of. . . .

Ever affectionately yrs,

C. BAXTER

MS, Yale. Letters, 4, *179. Note by CB:*
"None of this is to go to Cassells."

[Samoa, 16 April 1893]

My dear Charles,
Yours of 22nd Feb. and 16th March to hand.

I seem to have led you on the ice, and I do not know how to ask you to forgive me. I have no short story ready,[5] and I fear am unable to prepare one for the mail. However, as I am in receipt of a letter from the editor, in which he says he will take my story, *whenever it comes,* I trust this will do no harm. I shall try to be more careful in the future. I see you are pitching in.[6]

It is understood that Colvin has nothing to do with the Business.
" "   "   " Baxter " "   " "   "   " Proofs.
      Est'ce clair?

About *The Justice Clerk,* I long to go at it, but will first try to get a short story done. Since January I have had two severe illnesses, my boy, and some heart-breaking anxiety over Fanny, and am only now convalescing. I came down to dinner last night for the first time, and that only because the service had broken down and to relieve an inexperienced servant. Nearly four months now I have rested my brains, and if it be true that rest is good for brains, I ought to be able to pitch in like a giant refreshed. Before the autumn I hope to send you some *Justice Clerk,* or *Weir of Hermiston,* as Colvin seems to prefer; I own to indecision. Received *Syntax, Dance of Death,* and Pitcairn, which last I have read from end to end since its arrival with vast improvement: what a pity it stops so soon! I wonder, is there nothing that seems to prolong the series? Why doesn't some young man take it up? How about my old friend Fountainhall's *Decisions?*[7] I remember as a boy that there was some good reading there. Perhaps you could borrow me that, and send it on loan; and perhaps Lain's *Memorials*[8] therewith, and a book I'm ashamed to say I have never read, Balfour's *Letters.*[9]

Inclosed you will find a codicil to my will. It is hateful having to do this, but there are internal reasons that make me think it needful. If you think the will had better be reconstructed, do so. By the way, Graham suggests that I have probably an English

5. "I have made a contract with the *London News* for *The Go-Between* at £500" (CB to RLS, 22 February 1893). Cf. above, p. 292.

6. "like a little man" deleted.

7. Sir John Lauder, Lord Fountainhall (1646–1722), Scottish jurist and Lord of Session, *The Decisions of the Lords of Council and Session from June 6th, 1678 to July 30th, 1712,* Edinburgh, 1759–61.

8. Probably Malcolm Laing, *History of Scotland from the Union of the Crowns . . . to the Union of the Kingdoms* (1800).

9. Sir James Balfour of Kinnaird, *Letters and State Papers during the Reign of James VI,* ed. James Maidment, 1838.

domicile; on consideration, I believe that must be so; so you had
better keep that in view. You see there is no Samoan domicile; I
am not in Samoa, *quoad* the law: I am in the Western Pacific under Sir John Thurston.[1]

I agree with your decision as to the letters. I feel quite sure if I
don't live until my vogue is quite over, there is money to be
picked up after I am grounded. Much of my correspondence to
Colvin must be really interesting.

O—now see my profound wisdom in saying don't quarrel with
the little man, Pinkerton *alias* McClure—I receive at last, after
twice dunning, my accounts from Charles Scribner's Sons to Febry
1st. In this they plead guilty to having sold 2,000 in sheets to
Canada, for which they credit me $155. Then we approach the
States, and behold they have sold 4866 copies to fifty millions of
people who used to have ten, 12, and even 15 editions of my books
produced for them simultaneously; of course that was cut-throat
overproduction, but 5,000 is not good enough. I propose never to
be in account again with any born American. I shall write them
that they must buy *David Balfour* outright (I trust the American
copyright has been looked after properly), and if they won't come
down with the dust, I'll try McClure. My whole income in the
states came to 1720; I'll send you the document, though; not the
individual slips: they are too bulky, and only annoy anyway.

It is funny about the three names they couldn't find for *D.
Balfour:* [2] no landsman ever thinks of looking at a chart, and these
names are on every chart, and in every pilot book. What a charming graceful note from George Barclay! [3]

I [4] have just held a council of war, with the result shown in the
enclosed copy of letter to Burlingame. I have reached this ulti-
matum with difficulty; I am not even sure that my position in the
matter is wholly honorable; and I see I shall require to give you a
pretty full history of my relations with Messrs. Scribners. My introduction to them was like a burst of sunlight. At last I got *some*
money from the States! Under these circumstances, and there being no legal status upon either side, the business has gone on in

1. See above, p. 318 n. 3.
2. See above, p. 296.
3. Not identified.
4. Continued in Belle Strong's hand.

the loosest possible manner. When a new book was on the stocks, I mentioned it in the course of ordinary correspondence; and when it was ready, they brought it out. There has never been a bargain signed between us: all was a matter of understanding. On the passage of the Copyright Bill I however wrote and announced that I required a higher per cent in royalty. This they granted for future works, apparently with the understanding (which was not wholly without justification) that any work already mentioned in our correspondence had been offered by me and accepted by them on the old terms. Legally, therefore, it should seem that I was quite free, and so were they—that I was quite free to take *David Balfour* where I please, and they to cease paying royalties on my past works. This is the least of my troubles: it appears they did not amount last year to more than a hundred pounds, and this with exceptionally good sales of *Across the Plains* and *A Child's Garden*. The point is, am I bound in honour? One thing of two: either their returns are dishonest, or they're publishers so incompetent that I should be a buzzard and a stock to let them wreck me longer. I am sure McClure would make a spirited offer for the copyright of *D.B.*, but what I would really like is to put that work in the hands of Mark Twain,[5] to whom I shall write by this mail an obscure letter preparing him for a possible communication from you. The points you are to consider then are: 1st. Am I free in honour to shake the Scribners? 2nd. Suppose they do not offer a sufficient sum, should you try McClure or Harper for another sum down; or 3rd. Should we delay the book a little and put it in the hands of Mark Twain?

For my own part I should be very well pleased to get 1500 or even a thousand down, and there is no doubt that the money down would be welcome this year. For the future I think it would be well to get into relations with Mark Twain. His address is Hartford, Connecticut.[6]

I hope to goodness I have managed to get this out reasonably clear, my head being in a far from clear state. It should not be forgotten that it will be of advantage in the future to have *Kidnapped* and *D.B.* in the same hands—not of course that I should profit

5. RLS was of course unaware that Mark Twain's firm, Charles L. Webster and Co., was joining the other bankrupts of 1893.
6. Address in RLS's hand.

directly, but always bear in mind that the proper handling of an author's books as a whole is his best and really his only good advertisement.

April 17th. Here is another thing in which you can perhaps help me, though I don't want it to be in any way a trouble to you. Not being able to trace my descent beyond a very little way back, I have taken it into my head to trace the surname itself. It promises to become much more interesting than I had thought. For instance, I have collected out of Pitcairn quite a large number of appearances of Stevensons from North Ayrshire, Westlothian and Berwick, and Perth; also one appearance of a MacSteen, which is very suggestive. These appearances give us at least an idea of the distribution of the Clan. I have found two lairds in the time of Mary: Stevenson of that ilk and Stevenson of Hirdmanshiels, both apparently substantial men. Query, whether barons? Whether both in the east country? And what became of them? These are questions which *somebody* in Scotland should be very easily able to answer. With the premature stopping of Pitcairn, I am left gaping. Hence my demand for Fountainhall. But perhaps experts could suggest some other works to dig in. You see my idea is to make this a first chapter of my family history, giving an idea of the very small importance of the clan, of the sort of stations in society they occupied, and wherever the case is interesting in itself or characteristic of the time and country, briefly telling the story. I have come by accident through a correspondent [7] on one very curious and interesting fact: namely that Stevenson was one of the names adopted by the MacGregors at the proscription. The details supplied by my correspondent are both convincing and amusing, but it would be highly interesting to find out more of this. It has crossed my mind that perhaps some young man may be pursuing researches for some purpose of his own in the records of the 17th Century. If there be such a one, he could be of great service to me with very little trouble to himself by keeping his weather eye lifting for the name of Stevenson. The place where any Stevenson dwelt and the trade that he followed would be always welcome in themselves, and of course if there were any interesting story in which he was mixed up, it would be pure gold.

7. Macgregor Stevenson, of New York.

I say, go gently with the Scribner question; it is a case of ca' canny! I believe.

R. L. STEVENSON [8]

[Enclosure] [9]

Vailima, 16 April 1893

My dear Burlingame,

You must have expected me to be shocked by the figures in your account to Feb. 1st, and you will be quite prepared for a change of basis. It is too late of course to make any change as to *Island Nights Entertainments,* though I shall ask you to keep me informed as to its sale from time to time as you shall be able. In regard to *David Balfour* please communicate at your earliest convenience with Charles Baxter Esq. W.S., 11 South Charlotte St., Edinburgh, Scotland, to whom I have now transferred my whole business, and make him an offer for the American copyright of that work.

I think I should tell you that in England *The Wrecker* has already brought in about four thousand dollars. It may of course be impossible to do as well as this in the States, but my name is worth something, if only as an advertisement; and in view of the offers I continue to receive from other persons, I should not think it fair to myself to sacrifice any more of my books upon such terms, and it would not be fair to you to allow you to suppose the contrary.

I should be glad to know what arrangement you made with Messrs Cassel as to the sheets sold to Canada. In my ignorance the affair seems of doubtful legality. But I have no doubt you can make this clear. I am yours sincerely,

(signed) ROBERT LOUIS STEVENSON

8. Last sentence and signature in RLS's hand.
9. Typed copy, presumably by Lloyd Osbourne.

MS, Yale.

FANNY STEVENSON TO CB

[Samoa] 21 May [1893]

My dear Charles,

Any form of words that I could use seem to me no more than a mockery; I know in my heart that there is no consolation for such a loss: [1] it is the tearing up of the roots of life. I find that I can say nothing. Only this, dear friend: come to us if you can. At least it would be a break and a change. You and Colvin are the last of Louis's old friends, all that is left of his youth. I cannot think that you know how dear you are to us and how we long to have you here. Do try and come. Everything is so different that it will give you, so to speak, a breathing spell in another world. You may arrive in the midst of war, but all the better for that; there is no danger to speak of, but plenty of wholesome excitement.

Ever your true and affectionate friend,

FANNY VdeG. STEVENSON

MS, Yale.

[Samoa, 17 June 1893]

My dear Charles,

I had no idea last month of the extent of your calamity. You have now before you one of the hardest battles possible, and I hope you will fight it like a man for the sake of your children and in the sight of Gracie, as we like to think. One thing I feel very strongly —you may say it's no business of mine, but I hope you won't, for I wouldn't like to think so—that is, your going into rooms. I was thinking how it would be with me: if, at our age, and with our habits, I was suddenly returned to the empty life of chambers, to live and sleep and waken there alone; and I found my heart draw back. I think it not fair and not right, and I tell you plainly, I do not see you standing it. When I lived alone in San Francisco, I found I must never have a drop of anything to drink in the house, for in my black isolation and gloom I could not measure what I was taking; how much worse, by the mere enumeration of years

1. The death of CB's wife, Grace Stewart, 24 March.

elapsed, will your case not be? I *think* you should return to live with your father; if that must not be, I *am sure* you should try to find someone to live with, and from my knowledge of you, I should rather suggest an acquaintance than a friend, some lean, cold, rugged, prejudiced old J. T. Mowbray kind of fellow with whom you would never be too intimate but on terms of courtesy and amused respect till the end. I know it is easy to talk away here; and I know how difficult it must be to carry out. But, my dear Charles, that idea of the empty lodging is a temptation of the evil one. Scott did it—you are not Scott—it will kill you.

Are your things to be sold off? What a dreadful laceration! [2] (And there I wrote something from dreamland!) I wonder if there is any way I can help you? Let me know. I feel sure from the rags of information in my Australian paper that you have taken too black a view of the Bank, and that things will come out a good deal better before all is done. As for the business, that has a dreadful sound indeed, but I can scarce believe it; pray keep me posted, if more should occur, or threaten.

Sunday, 18 June

I inclose a letter from A. P. Watt, which I have neglected. I have referred him to you, and you can refer him in turn to Colvin if you cannot be bothered with it yourself. Pray dismiss my business from your thoughts. The only thing I want is to be sure that codicil in favour of Mrs. Strong is in order. I wish you would send me also an abstract of my will. I am beginning to think twice about sending so much of my money—I mean my father's money—to Bob and Katharine.[3] My own people are going to be poor enough; and really R. and K. are the most indifferent and unfriendly people in the world.

Please consider what I say in the beginning of this.

I am now become teatotal and anti-tobacco, from necessity. I take brandy in my coffee at lunch, and (sometimes) a little brandy before turning in; and I am trying hard (but not very effectually) not to smoke. This has become necessary—I don't know why, and

2. Deletion: "Please get an artist [?] to have the two Canaletti [two or three words illegible] for me, and have put upon the [word illegible] the Gift of."

3. According to Henley (Connell, p. 298), the "Alans"—Bob, Katharine, and their sister—ultimately received one-quarter of the Thomas Stevenson patrimony; the rest, with all personal property, was left to Fanny and her children.

I hate it, but my sufferings otherwise are horrid. I don't know if it will last, and hope not.

I trust you will have better news for me in your next. Believe me,

Always your sincere and affectionate friend,
ROBERT LOUIS STEVENSON

MS, Yale. Letters, 4, 234.

[Samoa, 19 July 1893]

My dear Charles,

I return herewith Arnot[4] (which unfortunately I already possessed) and Balfour's *Letters,* to see what you can get for them. I wish in exchange *Life of Stair,*[5] life of Carstairs,[6] Wodrow's *Analecta,*[7] and life of Grierson of Lag,[8] and *Memoirs* of General Hugh Mackay.[9]

I have heard from Scribner's: they are to offer £1200, which is quite sufficient, and I am overjoyed to be so quit of the thing. I am still unfit to work, so cannot say what will come up first, or when anything may come up. *St. Ives,* I know, is postponed for a good few months, for I have come to one of my regular sticks in it. *The Justice Clerk, The Young Chevalier,* and [1] another! I must not say any more upon that head, as I am always preparing fresh disappointments for you. I daresay from precaution I may as well send the cablegram to you, though the Scribs having climbed

4. Hugo Arnot (1749–86), historical writer, *Collection and Abridgement of Celebrated Criminal Trials in Scotland* (1785).

5. Andrew Henderson, *The Life of John, Earl of Stair,* etc. (1748).

6. R. H. Story, *William Carstares: A Character and Career of the Revolutionary Epoch,* etc. (1874).

7. Robert Wodrow (1679–1734), ecclesiastical historian, *Analecta, or Materials for a History of Remarkable Providences, Mostly Relating to Scotch Ministers and Christians,* Edinburgh, 1840.

8. A. Fergusson, *The Laird of Lag: A Life Sketch,* Edinburgh, 1876. Sir Robert Grierson (1655?–1733), persecutor of the Covenanters, was the original of Scott's Sir Robert Redgauntlet.

9. *Memoirs of the War Carried On in Scotland and Ireland, 1689–1691,* Edinburgh, 1833. Mackay was defeated by Claverhouse at Killiecrankie, 1689; died, 1692.

1. Deletion: "*The Killing Time* [two or three words illegible] but I must wait till I can see my way. I wish I could call the thing *The Sweet Singer* but I fear I cannot; reams of human interest printing."

down makes it scarce necessary. But what a confession is their offer of £1200! I felt more than justified in what I had done. I have had, as you know and as you will see by their letters, which I enclose for your enlightenment, a former alarm with them, in which I came off victor in a very fine style. They are still weeping over the business, but I care not: Dip them where Stinchar flows! [2]

I am in hopes, with this house off my hands and paid for, and *The Island Nights*—which however will scarce prove a great success, I see—and *Catriona* [3] coming on, that I should live this year within my means like a gentleman of liesure. We are in the thick of war—see *Illustrated London News*—we have only two outside boys left to us, nothing is doing, and *per contra* little paying. And I calculate *I.N.E.* £200; *C.* in England £800; *C.* in the States £1200 = £2000. Back Rights + *I.N.E.* in States = ?? But boldly say, about £2500 altogether, or including That Grimy Work, *The Ebb Tide*, £3,000, or thereby. My expenses are paid to May, I think. Eight months should not come to more than £1600, but call it £2,000, and there can scarce fail to be a balance on the right side. This rainbow dream consoles me exceedingly.

I wholly concur with your remarks on both syndicating and the Cassells. I should never wish to thirl myself [to any one. But *if I understa]nd* [4] *aright* Hamer's [5] letter to be an offer of £1500 down [for on a 25%] royalty, I think it may be considered. Suppose we got 1,000 from the magazines: that would be £2500 down: no bad, and at least a hope that they would someday or other think themselves recuperated and begin to pay royalties again. Yes, I'm rather in favour of Hamer and a magazine, but we must keep ourselves free. You see, even if they offered me a really attractive salary, I would not take it: I could not bind myself to produce, nor yet to produce what either they or the public would think good. And to bind myself *without* a permanency would be madness.

I see I have overlooked the packing in my account, but I guess it can't much exceed the two thou.

I am clear for a new will. Bob never answers my letters, Katha-

2. Cf. Burns, "Behind yon hills where Stinchar flows."
3. The title eventually chosen for *David Balfour*.
4. Gaps made by excision of signature; text supplied by CB, who apparently could not read, or recall, the word left blank.
5. Not identified.

rine does not correspond, and I mean distinctly to use a pruning knife upon that side; of course my father's expressed wish binds me to do something, and something I must do. But I am far more bound and far more concerned to do well by Lloyd, and something for Belle and the child. I wish you would send me notes of the last will, and I will try to draft a new one upon fairer terms. Colvin's proposed visit to Ceylon I hope he can change to one here or to Honolulu; I am wholly averse to such an expense. My life here is dear; but I can live within my income for a time at least— so long as my prices keep up—and it seems a clear duty to waste none of it on gadding about. I am writing him on the subject. My life of my family fills up intervals and should be an excellent book when it is done, but big, damnably big.

My dear old man, I perceive by a thousand signs that we grow old and are soon to pass away—I hope with dignity; if not, with courage at least. I am myself very ready, or would be—will be— when I have made a little money for my folks. The blows that have fallen upon you are truly terrifying; I wish you strength to bear them. I can understand your desire to escape from Edinburgh; it must be hard, indeed, to stick there under such circumstances. But where? and how? I could not understand about the business; try to tell me what you meant. It was not in this letter, but the one before, about drawing out and leaving Mitchell in. It is strange: I must seem to you to blaze in a Birmingham prosperity and happiness; and to myself, I seem a failure. The truth is, I have never got over the last influenza yet, and am miserably out of heart and out of kilter. Lungs pretty right, stomach nowhere, spirits a good deal overshadowed; but we'll come through it yet, and cock our bonnets. I confess with sorrow that I am not yet quite sure about the *intellects;* but I hope it is only one of my usual periods of non-work. They are more unbearable now, because I cannot rest. *No rest but the grave for Sir Walter!* [6] O, the words ring in a man's head.

6. Cf. Lockhart's *Life of Scott,* 17 July 1832.

MS, Yale. Dictated to Belle Strong.

Vailima, Samoa, 14 August 1893

My dear Charles,

Yours of 7th July to hand. All quite satisfactory. Will you kindly hand over the enclosed to Mr. McPhail, for whose notes I was very much obliged.[7] No doubt *D.B* has been financially a tremendous success. Please do not forget about my will: I am very anxious to revise it. Sorry the visit cannot come off. Please excuse scrawl.

MS, Yale. Letters, 4, 244.

[Samoa and aboard the *Mariposa*, September 1893]

My dear Charles,

Herewith goes my will to you. Will you please send us a copy of Fanny's? I must get all this taut and done with. Of course this goes as a stopgap and to hold the fort until you shall send me a revision.

And here is a job for you. It appears that about 1665, or earlier, James Stevenson $\left\{{\text{in} \atop \text{of}}\right\}$[8] Nether-Carswell, parish of Neilston, flourished. Will you kindly send an able-bodied reader to compulse the parish registers of Neilston, if they exist, and go back so far? Also could any trace be found through Nether-Carswell? I suspect it to have belonged to Mure of Cauldwell. If this be so, might not the Cauldwell charter chest contain some references to their Stevenson tenantry? Perpend upon it. But clap me on the judicious, able-bodied reader on the spot. Can I have really found the tap-root of my illustrious ancestry at last? Souls of my fathers! what a giggle-giggle-orious moment!

I have drawn on you for £400 to the D.H. and P.G.[9] Also, I have written to Tauchnitz announcing that I should bear one-half part

7. "I send some notes about the Stevenson names which appear in Scotch historical documents. They have been compiled by Mr. J. R. N. McPhail, who is one of our best juniors at the Bar and son of the F.C. [i.e. Free Church] Minister of Pilrig" (CB to RLS, 7 July 1893).

8. I.e. either tenant or owner of.

9. The "German Firm" (see above, p. 254 n. 1).

of his fines and expences, amounting to £62,10.[1] The 400 to the
D.H. and P.G. includes £160 which I have laid out here in land:
Vanu Manutagi—the vale of crying birds (the wild dove)—is now
mine; it was Fanny's wish, and she is to buy it from me again when
she has made that much money.

Will you please order for me through your bookseller *The
Mabinogion* of Lady Charlotte Guest [2]—if that be her name—and
the original of Cooke's *Voyages* lately published? [3] Also, I see announced a map of the Great North Road: you might see what it is
like; if it is highly detailed, or has any posting information, I
should like it.

This is being finished on board the *Mariposa* going north. I am
making the run to Honolulu and back for health's sake.

No inclination to write more.

As ever,

R. L. S.

MS, Yale.

Sans Souci Seaside Resort, Waikiki, Honolulu, H.I.

[25 October] 189[3]

My dear Charles,

Sorry that I have not been able to keep my promise, and have
spent all this extra money! Have been sharply ill, but better. I say,
for God's sake, go and see the party who wrote the enclosed,[4] and
see with your eyes if anything can be done for him. He has sent
me quite a handsome volume, which, if nothing else be practicable, you might at least pay for. Fanny [5] and I leave on the 26th for
Samoa, thank Heaven! I am tired of fudging around here.

R. L. S.

1. Tauchnitz had been fined by the German government for reprinting *A Footnote
to History*.

2. Lady Charlotte Elizabeth Guest (afterwards Schreiber), *The Mabinogion: from
the Llyfr Coch o Hergest, and Other Ancient Welsh Manuscripts*, etc. (1849).

3. *Captain Cook's Journal during His First Voyage Round the World . . . a
Literal Transcription of the Original MSS*, etc., ed. Captain W. J. L. Wharton (1893).

4. A letter to RLS from James Hunter, a "ticket-writer" in Edinburgh, sending
an illuminated book of RLS's verses, designed and executed by himself, and request-
ing RLS's aid in getting better placed.

5. Who had come to Honolulu to bring RLS back home.

MS, Yale.

[Samoa, 6 November 1893]

Dear Charles,

Of course let John Horne Stevenson [6] have a proof of the introduction. I daresay you will have entrusted to his care the search.
It is really interesting now; we may get to something. I quite agree
with you as to the repairs. Graham Balfour has my will going
home to you. You must see if it's anyway right. Cassell's proposal
is all very well, but where are we to get £2,000 for the serial
rights? The only three American magazines that can afford to
pay [7] damn an English circulation out of hand, being really quite
as much English as American.

I enclose a card of Count de Douville-Maillefeu [8] recomending
one Dieppe of Abbeville as a purveyor of *table* Bordeaux. Will
you put yourself in communication with him; consult him as to
what sort of wine he ought to send for the voyage to the tropics,
and send me off a barrel (via Auckland, will be best) *quam
primum*. Dieppe might likewise send me directions about bot-
tling. Tell him I hope this may lead to permanent relations; I am
dying of bad claret—literally. As one grows up in years, the wine
must be good.

Books have arrived from Johnston: [9] many thanks. You will
have met with the abominable blow of my draft from Honolulu;
my little three weeks sail took seven weeks to conclude and, as
Fanny came up to look after me, cost a mint of money: teach me
to go gallivanting! [10]

MS, Yale. Letters, 4, 262.

[Samoa, 6 December 1893]

"Oct. 15, 1685, at Privy Council, George Murray, Lieutenant of
the King's guard and others, did, on the 21st of September last,

6. Edinburgh genealogist—not a relative—who finally set RLS on the right track
in his hunt for ancestors. See *Letters, 4,* 259.

7. *Century, Harper's,* and *Scribner's.*

8. Count Angilbert de Douville-Maillefeu (*b.* 1868), Chevalier of the Legion of
Honor, Councilor-General of the Dept. of La Somme. His estate was the Château de
Valna, near Abbeville, Somme.

9. W. and A. K. Johnston, booksellers, Edinburgh and London.

10. Not signed.

obtain a clandestine order of Privy Council to apprehend the person of Janet Pringle, daughtr to the late Clifton, and she having retired out of the way upon information, he got an order against Andrew Pringle her uncle to produce her . . . But she having married Andrew Pringle her uncle's son (to disappoint all their designs of selling her) a boy of 13 years old"—But my boy is to be 14, so I extract no further.

Fountainhall I, 370

Nov. 6, 1685. It appears Pringle of Clifton was alive after all,* and in prison for debt; and transacts with Lieutnt Murray, giving security for 7,000 marks.

I, 372

*No, it seems to have been *her* brother who had succeeded.

My dear Charles,

The above is my story, and I wonder if any light can be thrown on it. I prefer the girl's father dead; and the question is how in that case could Lieut. George Murray get his order to "apprehend," and his power to "sell" her in marriage?

Or, might Lieutenant G. be her tutor, and she fugitive to the Pringles, and on the discovery of her wherabouts, hastily married?

A good legal note on these points is very ardently desired by me: it will be the cornerstone of my novel.

This is for—I am quite wrong to tell you, for you will tell others, and nothing will teach you that all my schemes are in the air, and vanish and reappear again like shapes in the clouds—it is for *Heathercat*,[1] wherof the First Volume will be called *The Killing Time,* and I believe I have authorities enough for that. But the Second Volume is to be called (I believe) *Darien,* and for that I want, I fear, a good deal of truck:

> *Darien Papers* [2]
> *Carstairs Papers* [3]

1. A fragment, first published in the Edinburgh Edition (*26,* 1897, 91 ff.).

2. *The Darien Papers: Being a Selection of Original Letters and Official Documents Relating to the Establishment of a Colony at Darien by the Company of Scotland Trading to Africa and the Indies, 1695–1700* (1849).

3. *State Papers and Letters Addressed to William Carstares . . . Relating to Public Affairs in Great Britain, but More Particularly in Scotland, during the Reigns of King William and Queen Anne,* Edinburgh, 1774. Cf. above, p. 334.

Marchmont Papers [4]
Jerviswoode Correspondence [5]

I hope may do me. Some sort of general history of the Darien affair (if there is a decent one, which I misdoubt) it would also be well to have: the one with most details if possible. It is singular how obscure to me this [decade of Scots history remains, 16]90 [6]– 1700: a deuce of a want of light and [grouping to it! However, I believe I sha]ll be mostly out of Scotland in my tale: first in [Carolina, next in Darien. I wan]t also—I am the daughter of the horseleech truly—"Black's new large map of Scotland," sheets 3, 4, and 5—a 7/6 touch. I believe, if you can get the *Caldwell Papers*,[7] they had better come also; and if there be any reasonable work—but no, I must call a halt.

Also wanted by the family: *Lost in Samoa,* [8] evidently a boy's book, and must be rich reading.

And for the Lord's sake, order another case of liqueurs: *Eau de Vie de Dantzig* and *Oranges Amère,* same as last year, per Wyand Focking.[9]

Later

I inclose the application signed. You see I have now the name of the farmer Nether Carsewell, and besides I have a whole new lot of enquiries as to Hew Fulton and his family.—Yes, G. Balfour has the will—or I suppose you have it now.—I fear I shall have to draw on you again for those daughters of the horseleech,[10] the German firm, for £500 at least.—I fear the song looks doubtful, but I'll consider of it, and I can promise you some reminiscences which it will amuse me to write whether or not it may amuse the public to read of them. But it's an unco business to supply deidheid coapy.—Well, my dear lad, in the matter of my mother, I understood as you did, but what can I do? She pressed me most unduly, this house was built for her, and it seems she has walked

4. *A Selection from the Papers of the Earls of Marchmont . . . Illustrative of Events from 1685 to 1750,* ed. Sir G. H. Rose, 1831.
5. *Correspondence of George Baillie of Jerviswood, 1702–1708,* ed. G. E. M. Kynynmond, Earl of Minto, Edinburgh, 1842.
6. Gaps caused by excision of signature; text supplied by CB.
7. *Family Papers at Caldwell, 1496–1853,* Glasgow, 1854.
8. By E. S. Ellis (1890).
9. Wynand and Fockink, Dutch firm.
10. Proverbs 30:15.

off whistling. But you know *Ce que femme veult, Dieu le veult,* and a man cannot argue with his mother about coins. And anyway, I now understand her recent letter, in which she talks of paying me a higher board! She has taken the rue herself, and I would rather leave it so. As for her will, damn her will. She forced me to build this house without consideration of her will.—Your news of W.G.S. is very painful; of course I had long seen his mind was going or gone.[1]—Many thanks for your most excellent and entertaining letter and for the good news that you are to stay with your father.—Fanny's will received and will be attended to soon. I am in an awful hurry, largely because the mail day has changed, and I find myself with four and twenty hours, instead of four days as I had counted on.—No doubt we must just give up the name of *Northern Lights,*[2] but I'll try and trick them yet. I'll see if I can't find some licit combination.[3]

Dear C. B.

I had near forgotten. Will you get a copy of all my works—or stay! let's be merciful—all the fiction, *V. P'que, Mem and Portraits, Across the Plains,* and have them all bound in some fairly elegant manner with (say) "H.H. from R.L.S." on the side of each, and despatch them by slow freight prepaid to Henry Henderson [4]—Damn his address; I'll send it you next mail.

MS, Yale. Letters, 4, *280.*

Dictated [5]

Vailima, 1 January 1894

My dear Charles,

I am delighted with your idea,[6] and first I will here give an

---

1. "After three months' silence a business letter arrived yesterday from Walter Simpson (London), the writing and phrasing of wh. indicate complete restoration. Pray God it may be so" (CB to RLS, 21 February 1894).

2. Presumably the title being considered for the family history. It had been used in 1876: *Northern Lights: Pen and Pencil Sketches of Modern Scottish Worthies.*

3. Signature cut out.

4. See above, p. 294.

5. To Belle Strong.

6. The Edinburgh Edition of RLS's works.

amended plan and afterwards give you a note of some of the difficulties.

[1.] Romances

I   *Treasure Island*
II   *Prince Otto*
III *Black Arrow*
IV   *Master of Ballantrae*
V   *Wrecker*
VI   *David Balfour* Vol. I
VII *David   "   Vol. II*

2. Stories and Fantasies

I   *Arabian Nights (Suicide Club, Rajah's Diamond, Dynamiter)*
II   *(Jekyll and Hyde, Olalla, Thrawn Janet, Markheim, The Merry Men)*
III *Will o' the Mill, Treasure of Franchard, Providence and the G., Sieur de M., Lodging for the Night, Pavilion on the Links*
IV   *Island Nights Entertainments. Ebb Tide.*

3. Prose Works

I   *Inland Voyage, Donkey, Silverado,* and the 1st paper from *Across the Plains*
II   *Virginibus Puerisque, Memories and Portraits,* and the other papers from *Across the Plains*
III *Studies,* and *A Footnote to History. Father Damien(?)*

4. Verse. 1 vol.

The first difficulty comes in about arranging the short stories. The devil seems to have mixed these. Thus *The Dynamiter* is in Longman's hands while *The Suicide Club* and *The Rajah's Diamond* belong to Chatto. *Jekyll and Hyde* is Longman's and the stories that ought to go with it are Chatto's. If this could be arranged, I should be very much obliged to both these gentlemen and prepared to make some sacrifice. For instance, you propose two-thirds to one-third to Chatto on the 1st volume: we might reverse the terms, the half of it belonging to him. Vol. II: I suppose the best plan would be to pay Longman a royalty. Vol. III: only *Will o' the Mill* and *The Treasure of Franchard* belong to me. Good terms would require to be given to Chatto. He will be the hero of all this section.[7] I do not know but it would be a good plan to have these volumes bear his imprint.

You see I am proposing a much denser setting of the miscellaneous prose than you did. It would be quite impossible on the scale of a library edition to make single volumes of these little kickshaws. As it is, we get three substantial and well distinguished volumes out of it. You see I have queried the name of *Father Damien.* I quite agree that it is one of my best works, but I am kind of wae for Hyde. It may be a question whether my *Times* letters might not be appended to the *Footnote,* with a note of the dates of discharge of Cedarcrantz and Pilsach.[8]

I am particularly pleased with this idea of yours because I am come to a dead stop. I never can remember how bad I have been before, but at any rate I am bad enough just now—I mean as to literature; in health I am well and strong. I take it I shall be six months before I'm heard of again, and this time I could put in to some advantage in revising the text and (if it were thought desirable) writing prefaces.

I do not know how many of these might be thought desirable. I have written a paper on *Treasure Island,*[9] which is to appear shortly. *Master of Ballantrae:* I have one drafted. *The Wrecker* is quite sufficiently done already with the last chapter, but I suppose an historical introduction to *David Balfour* is unavoidable. *Prince Otto* I don't think I could say anything about, and *Black Arrow* don't want to. But it is probable I could say something to the volume of *Travels.* In the verse business I can do just what I like better than anything else and extend *Underwoods* with a lot of unpublished stuff. Apropos, if I were to get printed off a very few poems which are somewhat too intimate for the public, could you get them run up in some luxurious manner so that blame fools might be induced to buy them in just a sufficient quantity to pay expenses and the thing remain still in a manner private? We

7. "I don't anticipate any insuperable difficulty in all this. Leave the terms to me" (CB to RLS, 21 February 1894).

8. Baron Senfft von Pilsach, President of the Council of Samoa.

9. Contributed to *The Idler* (London) as one of a series of articles by popular writers, and collected in *My First Book* (London, 1894), edited by Jerome K. Jerome.

could supply photographs for illustrations, and the poems are of Vailima and the family.[1] I should much like to get this done as a surprise for Fanny.

The Ebb Tide is a matter on which you in England must judge. I am indifferent; if you think it is being successful in this magazine, you can publish it. If you think it is not, keep it for the works.

Please tell Mr. Mitchell that I may not have time to acknowledge his note before the mail goes and in the meanwhile that Wallace [2] has been tilting at a quintain, the report of the speech being deplorable.

Now I must give you a little rather hopeful news of Vailima. One Spaats,[3] a German, has made—or is making, for he still hangs in the wind—an offer of five cents a bunch on the ground for a thousand bunches of bananas monthly. If he sticks to it we shall put in 30 acres of bananas at once and off the bad bunches we shall be able to feed pigs innumerable. The German is thinking of making a tramway to Vailima.

Have [4] written to Colvin about "Romances."

R. L. S.

Edinburgh belongs to Seeley; if it could be got from them, it would go into the Travel volume. But I don't know. I think Seeley will stand out—they were never obliging about it—even, as I thought, a little niggardly. Can't get a name for that third section! There must be a good name, too, but it eludes me.

MS, Yale. A copy by CB, enclosed in his letter to RLS of 21 February 1894.

SIDNEY COLVIN TO CB

[7 February 1894]

Now as to the projected edition:—I have been consulting Bain,[5] a very experienced bookseller among the class of Steven-

1. See *Poems*, pp. 313 ff.
2. Not identified.
3. Not identified.
4. Letter finished in RLS's hand.
5. See above, p. 279.

sonian admirers, and he, thought not enthusiastic about the scheme, thinks it would answer, and the edition sell, *provided* the size of the volumes were only a moderate 8vo—not a great big "Library" edition, and that the price of each did not exceed 10/– (to be sold to the trade at 8/–) or at the very most 12/–; and even this, he thinks, it would be difficult to ask unless in addition to the very choicest type, paper, etc. there were some special embellishments,[6] in the way of head and tail pieces or the like. This I am inclined to think too. I give you his view for what it is worth.

As to the arrangement of the matter, I had written to R.L.S. by last mail suggesting that the *Inland Voyage* and the *Donkey* should make one vol. of travels (his own suggestion [7] for this section seems to me to crowd the matter far too much); and that a second volume might very appropriately be made if he chose, out of *The Amateur Emigrant* and *The Silverado Squatters. The Amateur Emigrant* would include the suppressed ocean passage which would need some recasting, etc. (I have sent him out my old proofs in case he catches on to the idea), as well as *Across the Plains.*

My further suggestion was that *Picturesque Notes on Edinburgh* should go in one volume, with a pick of the distinctively Edinburgh essays out of *Memories and Portraits* and *Across the Plains;* leaving the remainder to make up a separate volume, or possibly to be grouped with *Virginibus Puerisque.* Then his grouping of *Familiar Studies* with the *Footnote to History* seems to me quite out of it: the former might well stand alone (it is long), and the *Footnote* volume to be eked out with *Times* letters, or (*better*) picked passages from the unreprinted *Black and White* letters. Further, I think the Fleeming Jenkin Life should certainly come in the series, making a volume perhaps with the account of his grandfather, if he goes on with it.

As to the query about explanatory prefaces, for God's sake let there be none of them. Strictly historical notes to *David Balfour*

6. *"Note as to embellishments.* Colvin forgets that I propose to proceed by way of subscription and not by ordinary sale at all. The value of the edition will be its exclusiveness, and simplicity its feature. Type, paper, everything of the finest excellence, but bound in plain cloth with paper label backings like the edition of the Waverly Novels we all used to know once, printed I think about '36 or so, and if I remember aright Cadell had something to do with it. 'Embellishments' to be decent must be costly, and to my mind won't add a cubit to our stature" (CB).

7. "I sent Colvin your letter. C.B."

by all means, if he wishes it much (having regard to recent controversies); [8] but the trick of picking the sawdust out of the puppets before the eyes of the world is a disastrous one, which (as I am glad to find you also think) we should all do our best to discourage. The thing he has just written about *Treasure Island* would simply destroy the interest of the book, to any intelligent or imaginative reader, if it appeared by way of preface. Please join with me in begging that there may be no such public dissections (I suspect a McClure inspiration), and in your edition let the romances stand alone, with their original prefaces.[9]

MS, Yale. Note by CB: "This in an-
swer to mine of 22d January."

[Samoa, 28 February 1894]

Dear Charles,

The mail coming four days too late gives me no time to do more than run through yours and answer questions.

1°. There is no chance for Clement Shorter.[10] He must content himself and learn to be quiet like a wearied child.

2. Books arrived. Thanks.

3. You did right about Miss Boodle,[1] but a letter must have missed, as I wrote and ordered Miss Boodle and the goose for Mary Ann Watts. I wish this had not missed, but it was done.

4. Harry Henderson is already an old friend.[2] *Vide* dedication of *Island Nights*.

8. CB's letter to RLS of 22 January 1894 includes a clipping from the *Evening Dispatch,* 20 January, dealing with a controversy between RLS and Mr. Fraser-Mackintosh over a characterization in *Catriona.*

9. "In this prayer I heartily concur. The proposed papers might form a chapter of autobiography, and an interesting one, later on. C.B."

10. Clement King Shorter (1857–1926), editor, critic, and biographer. He edited *Illustrated London News,* 1891–1900, and was presumably trying to get a serial from RLS. See above, Introduction, p. xvii.

1. "I took it upon me to send your Xmas box to Miss Boodle, and whether you intended it or no, I think when you read her letter you will be pleased that I did so" (CB to RLS, 22 January 1894).

2. "Instructions about volumes for Henry Henderson have my attention. You are to send me his address. I shall take care that tho' not expensive the binding is as smart as is consistent with good taste! I suppose this is a new friend?" (CB to RLS, 22 January 1894).

6. Bravo for 17. You did well.[3]

You say nothing about Grahame Balfour, to our disappointment. We hear he is coming out again soon.

Ever yours,

R. L. S.

MS, Yale. Dictated to Belle Strong.

Vailima, Samoa, 26 March 1894

My dear Charles,

1. Received bills of lading for Wynand Fockink, and wine from No. 17.

2. I am glad to hear you have arranged for the publication of *The Ebb Tide*.[4] Colvin (between ourselves) is a bit of an old wife, and has so often predicted that a book would be my ruin in January, and by July defied me to do anything as good, that I have ceased to pay very much regard. I am sorry, however, if I understand you right, for one point. You say "McClure is giving two hundred down on a royalty of 20 per cent." These are good terms, but I had never meant McClure to be my book publisher. He was always begging me to give him a book; I always steadily refused to hear of it; and if he has told you something else, he should be confronted with his lie. This is just to repeat my former error of disseminating my books among several publishers. I really mean to keep them all for the future in the hands of one; and I am not at all certain that I should not do better to give up my liberty openly, and sell myself outright to Cassells. You might think of this.

3. I propose that you should take Mr. McClure in hand upon another matter. He is publishing for Fanny a series of articles [5] for which he agreed to pay *au fur et à mesure*. I need scarce tell you

3. "Your mother will tell you that 17 Heriot Row is sold. We got £3800, a big price as times go . . ." (CB to RLS, 22 January 1894).

4. "Looking to the holiday and the absolute necessity of keeping up funds, we have decided to publish *Ebb Tide* as a volume. Colvin don't like, but other people do, and even if they don't like it when they have bought it, you are too well established for it to do any harm. I personally think some of it magnificent, but then I am one of the outcasts who love *The Wrecker*. I have asked Scribner £600 for it, and McClure is giving £200 down on a royalty of 20%. This with £600 previously is not bad business" (CB to RLS, 21 February 1894).

5. Apparently in newspapers; not traced.

we have as yet received nothing. Not only that, but such of them as we have seen have appeared in a mutilated state, with receipts, which were an essential feature, left out. Now I wish you to arrange with him on two points. *First*—money. My wife wishes to receive this money herself; and we had arranged with McClure to send it direct. That had better be changed. You will receive the money from him and send it on to her as it arrives. *Second,* as to the MS. We intend to produce them in book form when they have done appearing; and it is absolutely essential, in view of his mutilated publications, that he should be reminded that he must finally produce the MS entire. It is really a cookery book, and he has published the plums and left out the cookery. I need not remind you that I have a weakness for McClure, confound him! And I wish you to go about these necessary huntings with not more than the necessary rigour.

4. *Pentland Rising.*[6] Your proceedings are approved and applauded.

5. I have unhappily mislaid the copy of your firm's letter to my mother and cannot quite recall the dispositions proposed.[7] But whatever they were, I am sure they were perfectly fair.

6. You will get, as otherwise advised, a pretty heavy bill in favour of the German Firm. I must draw upon you also in favour of Messrs Gordon and Young (E. B. Young) of San Francisco for £200.

7. This is certainly a heavy draft. But I have a word of hope. I had fully intended sending you by this mail the first hundred pages of *St. Ives*. This cannot be, owing to the infernal conduct of Chas. Scribner's Sons in not sending me a book. I estimate it at about 115,000 words, and some of it shall certainly be sent to you next

6. RLS's first printed work. "You will remember this little pamphlet printed by Elliott [see above, p. 11 n. b] in 1866. It has been quoted for some time in London catalogues at £5,5, but I don't know that any sales have taken place at that figure. There was a *trouvaille* of some 50 copies here lately, however, and I am gradually disposing of them. I sold the first the other day for £3,3. I did not of course give any guarantee as to quantity. I merely said the price is £3,3: take it or leave it. I shall see that a sufficient reserve is kept, but we may as well get three guineas a piece for the surplus as not" (CB to RLS, 21 February 1894).

7. "Your mother has been here and has approved of the proposals I put before her in the letter (a copy of which is enclosed) regarding the distribution of removal and repairing expenses. I trust they will meet your views, and in any case I think they are logical and founded on principle. I therefore recommend them to your acceptance" (CB to RLS, 21 February 1894).

mail. I am puzzled as to the best method of disposal. I always had an idea of Scribner's for *St. Ives*. Perhaps it might be well to try the *Pall Mall Magazine,* or let Cassells have the run of the whole thing, if you think better. The full title is *St. Ives: The Adventures of a French Prisoner in England.*

8.[8] I inclose a Rev. Mr. Beeching's[9] letter, for which I beg a favourable answer, but I regard this as entirely your attribution.

9. Of Henley I cannot speak. It is too sad.[1] I never envied anyone more than I did him when he had that child, and it proved—or seemed to prove—healthy. Alas! I might have spared my envy. After all, the doom is common to us: we shall leave none to come after us, and I have been spared the pain—and the pleasure. But I still sometimes wish I had been more bold.

10. Desire plan very much, by the intervention of your excellent bookseller, to have *Faithful Contendings Displayed*.[2] *Faithful Contendings Displayed,* to try to be more legible, and Choderlos de Laclos's *Liaisons dangereuses*. I believe I must now take to ordering all my books through your bookseller. Of course I don't want Choderlos registered: he is published at 2 ffs. in Paris.

Sleep in peace. Adieu. The mail goes.

R. L. S.

MS, Yale. Letters, *4, 300.*

Dictated[3]

Vailima, 17 April 1894

My dear Charles,

I *St. Ives* is now well on its way into the second volume. There remains no mortal doubt that it will reach the three volume standard. And I propose that you offer it to Cassells.

8. Continued in RLS's hand.

9. Rev. Henry Charles Beeching (*b.* 1859), Rector of Yattendon, Berkshire, 1885; B.A. Oxford, 1883; minor poet.

1. "Poor Henley has had great disasters. He has lost his beautiful little girl, and the *Observer* has changed hands, the purchaser becoming editor. How it is that misfortunes never come but in troops!" (CB to RLS, 21 February 1894).

2. *Faithful Contendings Displayed, Being an Historical Relation of the State and Actings of the Suffering Remnant in the Church of Scotland . . . from 1681 to 1689 . . . Collected and Kept in Record by M. Shields,* etc. (1780).

3. To Belle Strong.

I am very anxious that you should send me

1st. *Tom and Jerry,*[4] a cheap edition.

2nd. The book by Ashton—the *Dawn of the Century* I think it was called [5]—which Colvin sent me, and which has miscarried, and

3rd. If it be possible, a file of the *Edinburgh Courant* for the years 1811, 1812, 1813 or 1814. I should not care for a whole year. If it were possible to find me three months, winter months by preference, it would do my business not only for *St. Ives,* but for *The Justice Clerk* as well. Suppose this to be impossible, perhaps I could get the loan of it from somebody; or perhaps it would be possible to have someone read a file for me and make notes. This would be extremely bad, as unhappily one man's food is another man's poison, and the reader would probably leave out everything I should choose. But if you are reduced to that, you might mention to the brute who is to read for me that balloon ascensions are in the order of the day.

4th. It might be as well to get me a book on balloon ascensions, particularly in the early part of the century.

We are trying a complete rearrangement of our affairs here in Vailima, the old order having practically broken down. I am dividing the yearly expenses into shares, so much to Lloyd, so much to Belle, with permission to swallow all that they can save.

II And apropos of that, Mrs. Strong has twenty-five pounds of savings which she has given me to—as a—I didn't [6]—to invest for her as you should think fit. I don't know whether it would be best to put it in a savings bank or to invest it otherwise, but you will know. There is also the question of her earnings as my amanuensis. This is a movable feast, and I have thought it better that I should communicate to you every mail the amount she has earned for the past month. This month it is already four guineas (nothing off for bad spelling). This makes already twenty-nine pound four shillings; and I shall let you know what the full sum amounts to before the mail closes. Accordingly, every month you will please pay into Mrs.

4. Pierce Egan, *Life in London, or The Day and Night Scenes of Jerry Hawthorn and His Elegant Friend Corinthian Tom* (1821).

5. John Ashton, *The Dawn of the Nineteenth Century in England: A Social Sketch* (1886).

6. Marginal note by Belle Strong: "Please excuse marks of agitation in this letter —it is entirely the fault of the Amanuensis."

Strong's credit, wherever you may prefer to have it, the sum that I shall advise you.

20 April [7]

III At last, this book has come from Scribner, and alas! I have the first six or seven chapters of *Saint Ives* to recast entirely. Who could foresee that they clothed the French prisoners in yellow? But that one fatal fact—and also that they shaved them twice a week—damns the whole beginning. If it had been sent in time, it would have spared me a deal of trouble.

IV Awful sorry about H.H.'s address: I put the card in, for it is gone and I remember doing it perfectly; it must have slipped out before the sealing, and, worse luck, I have not got it now—that was my only copy. I could walk to his place of business if I were in Sydney—but the name of it! [8] Well, I must try to fish it out on the beach, as best I may.

V I read with fear and elation your charming proposal.[9] I wonder if I have enough popularity to float it; I doubt, no. But if you can pull it off, here's to ye!

VI Pray pay no attention to Lloyd's wine order this mail, and order us instead the [1] same case of wine as we had last year: Burgundy, Champagne, and Rauenthaler.

VII See most carefully to prevent any of Brenan's [2] cursed illustrations ever appearing again. The same remark applies to the unhung ruffian who made a public ass of himself in *Today*, or whatever it is called.[3] I warn you to be careful of this, in particular about Brennan, for I know how McClure pushes him.

8th. I have had a letter from Dr. Scott Dalgleish,[4] 25 Mayfield Ter-

7. The letter continues in RLS's hand.

8. Henderson Macfarlane and (cf. above, p. 294 and n. 1).

9. "I would propose issuing [the Edinburgh Edition], of course at fixed intervals, now a Romance, now an Essays, now a Poems—without previous knowledge of the subscribers, so that there would at each issue be a little flutter of surprise" (CB to RLS, 21 February 1894).

1. Belle Strong's hand resumes here.

2. C. Brennan, illustrator of *The Beach of Falesá*.

3. *The Idler*. To understand RLS's emotion, one must see the black-and-white drawings, allegedly portrait sketches, which accompanied the *Treasure Island* article (see above, p. 344, n. 9).

4. Walter Scott Dalgleish, M.A., LL.D. (1834–97), editor (Thomas Nelson and Sons) and author; Edinburgh correspondent of *The Times*.

race, asking me to put my name down to the Ballantyne [5] memorial
commitee. I have sent him a pretty sharp answer in favour of cutting down the memorial and giving more to the widow and children. If there is to be any foolery in the way of statoots or other sickening trash, please send them a guinea; but if they are going to take
my advice and put up a simple tablet with a few heartfelt words,
and really devote the bulk of the subscriptions to the wife and
family, I will go the length of twenty pounds if you will allow me
(and if the case of the family be at all urgent), and at least I direct
you to send ten pounds. I suppose you had better see Scott Dalgleish
himself on the matter. I take the opportunity here to warn you that
my head is simply spinning with a multitude of affairs and I shall
probably forget a half of my business at least.

9th. I have drawn on you for £120 in favour of George Dunnet Jr.
of Auckland. This is a for a holiday to Lloyd, who is very much
in want of it and goes for a month's skating to the South Island of
New Zealand.

10th. The Amanuensis has by this time risen to £4,10; that, with
what she is sending you to invest, makes £29,10. If it will at all sim-
plify investment, you can carry it to £30, and she will remain my
debtor till next month in the sum of 10 shillings.

Well,[6] the remainder of my business will not return to me, and
must just be passed over. Good bye, old man! A thousand thanks
for your kindness to my mother. I shall put in yours a letter of a
kind to Henley; it was all I could pump up. What is he doing
now? Is there any chance for him? the wretched animal!

Yours ever,

R. L. S.

MS, Yale. Letters, *4, 303. Dictated to*
Belle Strong.

Vailima, Samoa [*ca.* 18 May 1894]

My dear Charles,

I have received Melville's [7] report and the very encouraging docu-

5. Robert Michael Ballantyne (1825–94), author of many books for boys.
6. Letter finished by RLS.
7. Andrew P. Melville; see RLS's letter below, p. 358.

ments that he encloses. It would really seem to be going ahead. I am sending Colvin some copy. And I have no doubt he will see to my having proofs in time. But the point is, now that the Edinburgh Edition takes shape, that I should try to tell you what I really feel about it. In the first place, don't put in any trash. I would rather die than have *The Pentland Rising* foisted upon any reader as my idea of literature. See my letter this mail to Colvin.[8] In the second place, my dear fellow, I wish to assure you of the greatness of the pleasure that this Edinburgh Edition gives me. I suppose it was your idea to give it that name. No other would have affected me in the same manner. Do you remember, how many years ago I would be afraid to hazard a guess, one night when I was very drunk indeed and communicated to you certain "intimations of early death" and aspirations after fame? I was particularly maudlin, and my remorse the next morning on a review of my folly has written the matter very deeply in my mind; from yours it may easily have fled. If anyone at that moment could have shown me the Edinburgh Edition, I suppose I should have died. It is with gratitude and wonder that I consider "the way in which I have been led." Could a more preposterous idea have occurred to us in those days when we used to search our pockets for coppers, too often in vain, and combine forces to produce the threepence necessary for two glasses of beer, or wander down the Lothian Road without any, than that I should be well and strong at the age of forty-three in the island of Upolu, and that you should be at home bringing out the Edinburgh Edition? If it had been possible, I should have almost preferred the Lothian Road Edition, say, with a picture of the old Dutch smuggler on the covers.

I have now something heavy on my mind. I had always a great sense of kinship with poor Robert Fergusson [9]—so clever a boy, so wild, of such a mixed strain, so unfortunate, born in the same town with me, and, as I always felt rather by express intimation than from evidence, so like myself. Now the injustice with which the one Robert is rewarded and the other left out in the cold sits heavy on me, and I wish you could think of some way in which I could do honour to my unfortunate namesake. Do you think it would look

8. Dated 18 May: *Letters, 4,* 306.

9. This feeling of spiritual kinship with Fergusson and Burns—"Scotland's three Roberts"—was repeatedly expressed by RLS.

like affectation to dedicate the whole edition to his memory? I think it would. The sentiment which would dictate it to me is too abstruse; and besides I think my wife is the proper person to receive the dedication of my life's work. At the same time—it is very odd, it really looks like transmigration of souls—I feel that I must do something for Fergusson; Burns has been before me with "The Gravestone." It occurs to me you might take a walk down the Canongate and see in what condition the stone is. If it be at all uncared for, we might repair it and perhaps add a few words of inscription.

I must tell you, what I just remembered in a flash as I was walking about dictating this letter, there was in the original plan of *The Master of Ballantrae* a sort of introduction describing my arrival in Edinburgh on a visit to yourself and your placing in my hands the papers of the story. I actually wrote it and then condemned the idea as being a little too like Scott, I suppose. Now I must really find the MS and try to finish it for the E.E. It will give you, what I should so much like you to have, another corner of your own in that lofty monument.

Suppose we do what I have proposed about Fergusson's monument, I wonder if an inscription like this would look arrogant:

> This stone, originally erected by Robert Burns, has been repaired at the charges of Robert Louis Stevenson and is by him re-dedicated to the Memory of Robert Fergusson as the gift of one Edinburgh lad to another.

In spacing this inscription I would detach the names of Fergusson and Burns but leave mine in the text; or [10] would that look like sham modesty and is it better to bring out the three Roberts?

I shall send—no, come to think of it, I send now with some blanks which I may perhaps fill up ere the mail goes—a dedication to my wife. It was not intended for the E.E. but for *The Justice Clerk* when it should be finished, which accounts for the blanks.

To my wife
I dedicate
This Edinburgh Edition of my works.[1]

10. Sentence completed by RLS.
1. "I . . . works" in RLS's hand, as are portions of the verses that follow.

I see rain falling and the rainbow drawn
On Lammermuir; hearkening, I hear again
In my precipitous city beaten bells.
Winnow the keen sea wind; and looking back
Upon so much already endured and done
From then to now—reverent, I bow the head!

Take thou the writing; thine it is. For who
Burnished the sword, blew on the drowsy coal,
Held still the target higher, chary of praise
And prodigal of counsel (censure?)—who but thou?
So now, in the end, if this the least be good,
If any deed be done, if any fire
Burn in the imperfect page, the praise be thine! [2]

See, for business remarks, my letter to Melville. I am really concerned about the American affair. Do you suppose I could have six [3] copies of the E.E. for myself? I mean that I should like to give one to my wife, one to Lloyd, and one to the Amanuensis. With a small edition like that I think they will turn out to be—I was about to say portable property but the phrase is hardly descriptive of a twenty vol. edition—real estate will perhaps better express my idea. I should like to, and I suppose it could easily be done, to have six sets marked in every copy, say, on the false title: "To my wife" on one; "To Lloyd Osbourne. *Quorum pars magna fuit*" [5] on the second; "To Isobel Strong, my Amanuensis. *Filiae amicae grataeque*" [6] on the third; "To Sidney Colvin. *Te, Palinure!*" [7] or should it be *"Tibi, Palinure?"* [8] on the fourth; "To Robert Alan Mowbray Stevenson. *Olim Arcades ambo."* [9] on the fifth; and for the sixth, which I mean to be yeur ain, sir, I would put "To Charles Baxter. *Amicus amico."* [1] These six sets may I suppose be thrown off in addition to the thousand copies; and they will form some-

2. "Well, I shall see about this before the mail goes. It don't seem the right thing for the purpose somehow" deleted. The verses were omitted from the dedication.

3. Changed from "three" by RLS.

5. "Of which he had a large share": Virgil, *Aeneid* 2.6.

6. "To a fond and beloved daughter."

7. "To thee, Palinurus": *Aeneid* 6.341. (Palinurus was Aeneas' pilot.)

8. Marginal query in RLS's hand.

9. "Once we were Arcadians together": Virgil, *Eclogues* 7.4. (In view of what RLS had said of estrangement from RAMS, the added "olim" is significant.)

1. "A friend to a friend."

thing of real value for the six of you to keep. And if I'm ever to spend money, this is the occasion.

Please send the books for Henderson to "Care of John Williams, Esq., 2 Macquarie Place, Sydney, N.S.W."

I.[2] Dear Charles, please let me know, after so long an interval, how my investments stand? I am anxious to know. The Edition should as far as possible be mortified to the same purpose. I may get knocked off, or my right hand may lose its cunning. By the way, my wife is of opinion that, on my death, they will have to buy back the house and furniture from the other heirs; this is not so, is it? But she holds to it, so I ask you for your opinion to satisfy her.

II. Please let Johnstone send me:

> *Under the Red Robe,* Stanley J. Weyman,[3] publisher unknown
>
> *The Man in Black,* by ditto, Cassell
>
> *Memoirs of the Mutiny,* Maude and Sherer,[4] Remington
>
> The second Sherlock Holmes book [5] by Conan Doyle.

Also for Johnstone:

> Lady Inglis about Lucknow,[6] name of the book unknown.

St. Ives still plods along: not at an alarming rate, but still so as probably to be in hand erelong. I had miscounted a little and we have no more than 70,000 words. Perhaps you had better consider an application to Scribner's about the American rights? To continue: 70,000 is only about half what a three volumineer should run to; and whether it will run out or not in the sequel is an anxious thought to me. I had miscalculated by counting Belle's page 250 words, and I find it only 200; strange that so little a difference should make up so much in the total! I have been delayed in *St. Ives* by native bothers, and a certain preliminary clearing of decks involved in the E.E.; but it will go on.

Amanuensis: £2,6 this month.

---

2. The letter is finished by RLS.

3. Stanley John Weyman (1855–1928), English historical novelist. Both of the novels named were published this year, *Under the Red Robe* by Methuen.

4. *Memories of the Mutiny,* by Francis Cornwallis Maude, *With Which Is Incorporated the Personal Narrative of John Walter Sherer* (1894).

5. *Memoirs of Sherlock Holmes* (1894).

6. Julia Selina (Thesiger), Lady Inglis (1833–1904), *The Siege of Lucknow. A Diary* (1892). She was the wife of Sir John Eardley Wilmot Inglis (1814–62), who succeeded Sir Henry Lawrence in command during the siege of Lucknow, 1857.

III. What has become of the notes by Macleod [7] that you said would
      follow this month?
IV.   What about McClure and my wife's articles?

R. L. STEVENSON

[Enclosure] [8]

Vailima, 18 May 1894

Andrew P. Melville Esq.

Dear Sir,

I have the pleasure to acknowledge your memorandum and
copies of correspondence in the matter of the Edinburgh Edition.
I certainly feel extremely gratified at the generous treatment I have
received at the hands of my many publishers; and I hope I may
trust you to convey to them the expression of my sentiments.

One point strikes me as doubtful. I mean the sale to McClure. I
suppose he may be trusted to understand for himself the terms of
the late treaty; but according to my opinion, the edition is entirely
excluded from America. But that is nothing. The question is,
whether you have approached my copyright publishers, Messrs
Chas. Scribner's Sons? And what these gentlemen have replied?
I have been treated by them in a manner which leaves me very
sore. I should not like to repay them in kind. Please call Mr. Baxter's attention to these points.

I have been running over the text of several of my books with a
view to the E.E. The corrections are not many, but some of them
decidedly important. For this reason, while I do not think it worth
while to send the corrections home beforehand, I should like to
make sure of seeing in good time the proofs of the E.E.

Yours faithfully,

ROBERT LOUIS STEVENSON

MS, Yale. Dictated to Belle Strong.

Vailima, 18 June [1894]

My dear Charles,

Your long and interesting letter of May 14th [9] duly come to

7. Rev. Walter McLeod (*b.* 1864), St. Andrews M.A., 1887, B.D. 1890.
8. Dictated to Belle Strong; signed by RLS.
9. Not recovered.

hand, but alas not the dummy.[1] It may turn up next month, but upon that subject we can say no more this mail. The title page and specimen are all I could wish; and I wish to explain generally to both you and Colvin that I give you a free hand. I even take back the restrictions announced in my last. It is to be your edition. Please yourselves. And this is not only from humility, which I sincerely feel, but from a sense of what is possible and what is not at so great an interval of posts.

1st. I think you must dismiss Mr. John Lane.[2] I do not feel I have either time or energy to take up the edition or even the introduction, handsome as the terms are.

2nd. *St. Yves.* Practically no progress to be reported this month owing to a miserable cold. At the same time the book is well on the way, and could really be sent off at pretty short notice. I think you couldn't do better than the *Pall Mall Magazine.*[3] About this hitch with Longman and Cassells, I think with you that we are very much committed to the latter. Indeed I scarce see any way of retreat left open to us.

3rd. *Colvin's Name.*[4] His letter to me makes me doubt his real motive. It may only be modesty, it may be the fear of ridicule. I shall put it to him that I would like it so when I write, and then, if he still refuses, what else can we do but leave it out?

4th. I highly approve of the reproduction of *Moral Emblems*[5] myself. I think them far the greatest of my works. But all this I leave to you and Colvin.

5th. Now as to this revising question. How am I to change anything in *Moral Emblems,* for instance? What excuse can there be for reprinting *Pentland Rising* at all, if we change a word of it? I am not now discussing whether it is wise or not to reprint it: that is now yours and Colvin's matter. But what I do say is, you print the piece as an absurdity written by a school-boy, and you can not ask an experienced man of letters of forty-four years of age to re-

---

1. Cf. *Letters, 4,* 347.
2. John Lane published the *Yellow Book,* as well as the works of many of the "new" poets of the '90s. This offer was probably for an edition of Walt Whitman. Cf. below, p. 364.
3. *St. Ives* was serialized in the *Pall Mall Magazine,* November 1896–November 1897.
4. As editor of the Edinburgh Edition.
5. Finally published, with an introduction by Lloyd Osbourne, in 1921.

vise the thing to save a copyright. All these pieces, if they are to go in at all, must go as God made them.

6th. Please take note. If you reprint the "Philosophy of Umbrellas," [6] you must replace Ferrier's name. The piece was written in collaboration with him, although [7] I must confess his collaboration was mainly confined to laughter, and my best real collaborator was my father, who is introduced as the scientific friend.

7th. In the dedication to *Treasure Island,* for *S.L.O.* read *Lloyd Osbourne.*

8th. I suppose it is only next month I can expect an answer to my difficulty about the American copyright and Charles Scribner. I can conceive the whole scheme collapsing over this. Pray be full on the subject—or let Mr. Melville be, and see that he is correct.

9th. This is a list for your faithful bookseller:

> Wolseley's *Marlborough,* Vols. I and II.
> The Duchess of Buckingham's travels, whatever their name be.[8]
> *Chevalier's Songs,*[9] complete with the music.
> Westermarck's *Human Marriage.*
> *Tom Sawyer Abroad.*
> Kipling's Elephant stories [10] and *Many Inventions.*
> *Familiar Letters* of Sir Walter Scott.
> { *Les Opinions de l'Abbe Coignard*
> { *Le Crime de Sylvestre Bonnard,* both by Anatole France.
> *The South Sea Islanders* by William T. Wawn.
> *Scottish Place Names* [11] by Sir Herbert Maxwell.
> Send in my name as subscriber for the *Autobiography of a Cornish Smuggler* [1] to Joseph Pollard, 5 St. Nicholas St., Truro.
> *Social Evolution* by Benjamin Kidd.[2]

6. Published in the *Edinburgh University Magazine,* February 1871.
7. MS, "and though."
8. *Glimpses of Four Continents* (1894).
9. *Mr. Albert Chevalier's Humorous Songs,* etc. (1894).
10. *The Jungle Book* (1894).
11. *Scottish Land Names* (1894).
1. *Autobiography of a Cornish Smuggler, Captain Harry Carter of Prussia Cove* (1900).
2. Added in RLS's hand.

10th. I have to advise you of a bill to the D.H. and P.G. for 400 pounds (£400).

11th. Please credit the Amanuensis with the magnificent figure of £8,11, most of it being household savings. I fear I have put my figures too high. Had Lloyd been at home this month, and claiming *his* savings, I should put my hat down. (I don't deserve that—I only demanded *half* my savings—the whole sum was too large even for my grasping disposition! *Am.*)

Generally, understand that whatever I have not replied to I thoroughly approve.

Yours ever,
R. L. S. [3]

MS, Yale.

[Samoa, received 17 August 1894]

My dear Baxter,

I have received the balloon books from your bookseller, and I must say he is a daisy. I could not have chosen better myself. I desire you to communicate to him this certificate of merit. I would write it to him but cannot for my soul recollect his name.[4]

Your great success over the Edition leaves me gaping. Hip, hip, hurray!

Allow [5] me to congratulate you on the return to duty of the Amanuensis. 'Tis a damned good thing for you and me. I do not quite understand what you mean by the Astor bargain.[6] Does it mean £22,10 for a thousand words? If it does, it means a big deal.

I have still to expect explanations about my American publisher, but I hope to hear next mail and to be satisfied. The eight sets will do me admirably—you must have already received my disposition of (I think) six of them. The exact number I do not remember. But if I am right, the seventh must go to my mother with the dedication: To My Mother.

3. Close and signature in RLS's hand.
4. Johnstone.
5. Letter continued in Belle Strong's hand.
6. "Tomorrow I hope to get from Astor £22,11 per M for *St. Ives*" (CB to RLS, 15 June 1894). William Waldorf Astor (1848–1919), Viscount Astor, 1917, founded the *Pall Mall Magazine,* 1893.

Well, I don't know what I want in the way of this dedication.
Colvin might help. I want something to express (in Latin) that I
am her only son and that these are her grandchildren. I know it can
be well said in Latin, but not by me, who have not so much as a
Latin grammar to aid my stumbling steps.

I have had a letter from Henley, which I thought in very good
taste and rather touching. My wife, with that appalling instinct of
the injured female to see mischief, thought it was a letter prepara-
tory to the asking of money; and truly, when I read it again, it will
bear this construction. This leads us direct to the consideration of
what is to be done if H. does ask for money. I may say at once that I
give it with a great deal of distaste. He has had bad luck of course;
but he has had good luck too and has never known how to behave
under it. On the other hand I feel as if I were near the end of my
production. If it were nothing else, the growing effort and time
that it takes me to produce anything forms a very broad hint. Now
I want all the money that I can make for my family and, alas, for
my possible old age, which is on the cards and will never be a
lively affair for me, money or no money, but which would be a
hideous humiliation to me if I had squandered all this money in
the meanwhile and had to come forward as a beggar at last. All
which premised, I hereby authorise you to pay (when necessary)
five pounds a month to Henley. He can't starve at that; it's enough
—more than he had when I first knew him; and if I gave him more,
it would only lead to his starting a gig and a Pomeranian dog.[7] I
hope you won't think me hard about this. If you think the sum
insufficient, you can communicate with me by return on the subject. And by the bye, don't forget to let me know exactly how I
stand. It is possible that I forge myself fears that need not exist.
The sheet of questions was not returned in my last letter, owing to
some hurry on the day of making up the mail. I believe, however,
all the questions were answered in the body of my letter, but send
it on anyway.

The dummy has never come to hand. Was it registered? It is no
use sending anything connected with business unless you register it.
Now I must end my letter with the same subject that it began with,
your excellent if nameless bookseller. He is to choose at his own
peril the very nicest illustrated edition of *Robinson Crusoe* in ex-

7. The phrase which probably sinewed Henley's posthumous attack on RLS. See
Furnas, pp. 294 ff.

istence and despatch it to Master Louis Sanchez,[8] Monterey, Monterey Co., California. Understand, I mean the nicest edition from the point of view of a young schoolboy of ten, not at all from the point of view of the bibliophile. Your admirable man will certainly be able to fill the bill. There is another thing in his way. We want an old school-book, in use I imagine twenty years ago if not now, called *The Child's Guide to Knowledge*. The child in question is guided by a sort of catechism inculcating as far as I can find out every species of wisdom, from How to Take Care of a Cold, the Remedies of Different Poisons, down to How to Grease your Boots. If Mr. Johnson—there's his name—finds this book not very expensive, he might even send two copies or even three. This is for the deserving native.

I have been and am in communication with Mr. Edmund Baxter, Jr. I trust I am giving satisfaction as his agent in these distant parts. Should he have to complain of any neglect, I'm of opinion that the civility with which the correspondence has been throughout conducted gives me a decided claim to receive a statement and to be allowed to answer it with an explanation.

Ever affectionately yours,
R. L. STEVENSON [9]   P.T.O.[9]

P.S. The account of Mrs. Isobel Strong, Amanuensis and Housekeeper, is to be increased by the sum of £3,8. She begs to ask you for a statement of the amount already to her credit. The amount that the Amanuensis has gained this month is 12/–. The Housekeeper by certain arts known to Housekeepers over the world has earned or claims the balance. Besides which she has been bursting into Authorship in *Harper's Weekly* (June 2nd) [10] and has supplied me with a cheque for $108.35, which please translate into human money and credit to her.

R. L. S. [1]

I have drawn upon you this month for £150 on George Dunnet, Jr. of Auckland and for John Lloyd, San Francisco, the sum of £20.

R. L. S. [1]

8. Fanny's nephew, son of her sister, Nellie Vandegrift Sanchez. Cf. the Envoy "To My Name-Child" in *A Child's Garden*.

9. In RLS's hand.

10. "Within the Reef," by Teuila (Belle's Samoan name, meaning "beautifier of the ugly").

1. In RLS's hand.

To be returned by first mail [2]

Answers to questions raised in C. Baxter's letter of 14–18 May 1894
requiring immediate answer.

Par. in Letter	*Question*	*Answer*
12	Do you approve Colvin being named as Editor on title page of Colld Edition?	Yes by God.
22	Have you any suggestions as to general appearance, size, shape of volume as shewn by "Dummy"?	Not to hand.
24	What do you say to editing an edition of Whitman?	I wunna.
28	What do you wish done about book rights to *St. Ives?*	Leave it to you, sir!
29	What about *Moral Emblems* etc.?	Rather like the idea of *Moral Emblems*.
30	What is H. Henderson's address?	c/o John Williams, 2 Macquarie Place, Sydney, N.S.W.

MS, Yale. Dictated to Belle Strong.

[Samoa] 12 August 1894

My dear Charles,

All previous points approved.

1st. The length of *St. Ives* is as yet by no means decided. The

2. The "sheet of questions" referred to in the foregoing. Heading and questions
in CB's hand; answers in RLS's.

trouble is that I am hopelessly off work. What time did you agree on for its appearance? I must caution you, if it has not been named expressly, that every day gained will be a boon to me and possibly to *St. Ives*. I believe I named the end of the year for it, and of course it's quite possible it may be ready before then, but just now I am incapable of adding one word to the MS and of course take a gloomy view in consequence.

2nd. McClure has sent the MS here, or what was left of it, accompanied by an hysterical letter about the death, suicide, madness, and starvation of all his employees. As if that mattered! 'Tis a whimsical creature.

3rd. I am of opinion that the dedications in my copies would be better printed. Have it set up in a monumental style, like the dedication to my wife, and insert in *every volume* of the series. This will make the whole thing worth more money. A hard-up beneficiary can thus sell his Edinburgh Edition volume by volume [3] for more money. Do not trouble to send me the sheets, as I will not write in them.

4th. The account as far as yet understood is approved. But I wish, my dear fellow, you could hit upon some method of sending me another and simplified statement of my income and expenses. I pass hours of—I think—unnecessary misery in trying to expiscate this result from your account as rendered, and at the end I am never very sure of the result. If you would add a simple statement of income, expenditure, deficit, or balance, I could then easily check it from the account and it would spare me both labour and dubiety.

5th. I shall have the will executed and enclosed.

6th. McLeod's note duly received. Also fresh batch by this mail.

7th. Believe me, I am not in the least sentimental about Chas. Scribner's Sons; for all which I am truly thankful to see them take up the agency, or we should have had a pretty peck of troubles. They could have fought us on the Copyright Act. I have no doubt Stone and Kimball [4] are just as good but no better.

8th. The Mandate also will not be forgotten.

9th. I note the transference to Heinemann.

3. A proposal calculated to make collectors shudder.
4. A highly intelligent and courageous publishing house, recently founded in Chicago. Like all Chicago literary enterprises, it was short-lived.

10th. Note that I have given E. C. Stedman [5] authority to make selections from all my verse for his *Victorian Anthology*. This was unavoidable from divers reasons. But I enclose, for you to deal with at your pleasure, an application from one with the victorious name of Laura Valentine,[6] only observing that this kind of business, while it produces a dull book in itself, tends to form the best advertisement.

11th. Please get and send to us at once the July *Cornhill*.[7]

12th. The Amanuensis has the small sum of fifteen shillings to go to her account. A private letter is enclosed, which the deeds will be tomorrow. I can only trust I have attended to everything.[8]

MS, Yale. Letters, 4, 351.

[Samoa, received 15 September 1894]

My dear Charles,

I have thought well of the matter, and I judge thus: with your father and your sister gone, and the former loss, you would be horribly alone in Edinr. The character of the Godkin or Godlet [9] can scarce be accounted an alleviation. You have always wished to leave the place. Leave it in God's name!

At the same time, remember a change of this sort is, to a man of forty-five, a searching trial; and keep yourself well in hand whilst you make it—and after.

I will confess—going merely by instinctive physiognomical inferences—I am glad to be done with the Godlet. I wonder how your father, worthy man! ever looked twice at him. But he did not know *men;* three of his friends I condemned out of hand: Mitchell, Weir [1] the wine merchant, and Macdonald of Morar.[2] The

5. Edmund Clarence Stedman (1833–1908), the "Wall Street poet" and critic. His *Victorian Anthology 1837–1895* was published in 1895, and included eleven of RLS's poems.

6. Prolific author and compiler of books for children, many of them under the pen-name, "Aunt Louisa."

7. Containing "With R. L. Stevenson in Samoa"; unsigned, but by Marie Fraser. The following year the essay was reprinted in her book, *In Stevenson's Samoa*.

8. Bottom of sheet torn off.

9. William Mitchell, CB's senior partner.

1. Not identified.

2. See *Transactions of the Gaelic Society of Inverness, 15* (1888–89), 63–75.

last justified me, I believe; the other two may not have, but they were insincere and dangerous men.

Well, there is no more Edmund Baxter now, and I think I may say I know how you feel. He was one of the best, the kindest, and the most genial men I ever knew; I shall always remember his brisk, cordial ways and the essential goodness which he showed me whenever we met with gratitude. And the always is such a little while now! He is another of the landmarks gone; when it comes to my own turn to lay my weapons down, I shall do so with thankfulness and fatigue, and whatever be my destiny afterward, I shall be glad to lie down with my fathers in honour. It is human at least, if not divine. And these deaths make me think of it with an ever greater readiness. Strange that you should be beginning a new life when I, who am a little your junior, am thinking of the end of mine. But I have had hard lines; I have been so long waiting for death, I have unwrapped my thoughts from about life so long, that I have not a filament left to hold by; I have done my fiddling so long under Vesuvius that I have almost forgotten to play, and can only wait for the eruption and think it long of coming. Literally no man has more wholly outlived life than I. And still it's good fun.

R. L. S.

MS, Yale.

[Samoa] 9 September 1894

Dear Charles,

1st. Thanks for books received.

2nd. I have sent a most unappetising epitome of *St. Ives* to McClure according to order. The price seems to me exorbitant. But who am I to complain? But give unto the flying hart! Conceive what a misfortune it would be, and how we should bear the ridicule, if we *broke* a publisher these hard times.

3rd. My dear fellow, I need not say I—we—are delighted at this good news. I fear we can't expect you here till February, the height of our bad season—and we have a hurricane due; if my house is blown away, may you be there to see! And anyway I like our bad season best and think it healthiest. Mind and don't drink anything on the voyage: that way lies nervous crash. But I forget, you have been quite the voyager since we met, and this *Pons asinorum* is not unknown to you.

4. *Colvin.* He has been complaining that you do not write to him. So there! Grzz—you pair of mongrels, keep the peace!

10 September [3]

5. I am seedy this morning, but I am thankful to say there seems nothing to be attended to and, for a change, no bills to advise you of. This is a good job, with the precarious balance you declare. However, we shall hope *Ebb Tide* will fill the exchequer again. There will have to be a bill for the German firm next month—I fear a round one. The Amanuensis to be credited with £17.

ROBERT LOUIS STEVENSON

MS, Yale.

[Samoa, 10 October 1894]

Dear Charles,

I am sorry; you have chosen the worst season in the year for Samoa: in February and March it is highly doubtful whether we can even go on a *malaga;* [4] it is possible you may have an even downpour of rain, diversified by a hurricane. I think you may be sure you will be none too soon for the Samoa steamer, and must come on overland, *at least* from Melbourne. I shall tell that excellent fellow Harry Henderson to be on the lookout for you in Sydney. You might send him a despatch from Adelaide telling of your arrival, c/o Henderson and Macfarlane, Sydney. He is a square, jolly fellow, whom we learned to respect thoroughly during a four months' cruise. Be sure you are right in staying aboard: perhaps you should come through overland from Adelaide; but I'll tell Harry to have you posted in that port as to the sailing of the Samoa steamer.

Kindly credit the Amanuensis with two pounds. More cannot

3. Letter finished in Belle Strong's hand; signed by RLS.
4. Excursion.

be said this month as she has been ill, and her housekeeping accounts are not yet *tiré au clair*. I suppose I shall send her money in future months to the firm? We are all much exhilarated at the prospect of your arrival.

Just heard that another steamer has been put on for Samoa from Sydney, which will redouble your chance.

All well as well enough, except *St. Ives,* who ails damnably.

Yours ever,

R. L. S.

MS, Yale. Dictated to Belle Strong.
Note by CB: "Recd. Brindisi, 17
Dec. '94. My last letter from R. L. S."

Vailima, Samoa, 4 November 1894

My dear Charles,

This will be my last letter to you until I shall have the pleasure of greeting you at Apia. I have put it in the charge of Harry Henderson to communicate with you by wire as soon as you shall touch Australia, so that you may be sure of catching the earliest opportunity for Samoa. Note well the man Henderson; he is a prime favorite of mine.

And now to thank you for your letter of Oct. 3rd.[5] It is quite clear and very satisfactory. I should prefer in future that you should give me accounts in this form; not that I had really failed to grasp the meaning of the other, but that to my inveterately un-business-like mind there seems always something illusory and uncertain in results so obtained.

It is quite plain, as you say, that the income I have lately received must be regarded as something quite illusory. At the same time, in consideration of the E.E. and the exceptionally large payments you have secured for *St. Ives,* I venture to hope that we may so arrange it as that my income from capital and royalties shall amount after a few years to not less than a thousand pounds. Now that the house is built, the road partly made, and water just about to be brought in, cacao planted out and doing well, Lloyd

5. Not recovered.

and I have been figuring up that it should be possible to live on 1200 a year. This would practically bring us to a bearing: a circumstance extremely desirable in my present condition of health and mind. Not that I am ill, only that my digestion has quite taken leave of me in the meantime, and that for work I am literally and totally unfit.

At the same time I am making a great effort to finish *St. Ives* anyhow, and I propose to send you by this mail twenty-two chapters of completed copy. If the publishers decide to begin publication, I take my courage in both hands and say they may; but I should infinitely prefer, I need scarcely say, that they should await the coming of the end. It is a tragic thing, when you have done so very well for me, that I should do so very ill for myself.

All that you say of your troubles with Colvin I understand and sympathise with. As to the proposed slip, I put my foot down absolutely. It shall not appear. I have nothing to do with the Edition: no proofs have ever reached me, so far as I can hear no attempts are being made that any should reach me. Colvin writes me by this mail that he has been cutting and carving on my immortal text; [6] I do not say that he is wrong: I do say that "all excisions, alterations and additions" have not been made by me. They have been made by him and he must stand the responsibility. About *Moral Emblems,* what can I say? I have no power, and I am very glad of it. You and he are so kind as to undertake the Edition for me; I have agreed to accept your decisions, and there is an end of the matter as far as I am concerned. At the same time I express an opinion strongly that they ought to go in. I shall express it again direct to Colvin. *Et puis apres, je m'en lave les mains.*

I really think this is all the business I have to transact. Oh! I have forgotten that I wish another cask of wine from the timorous Dieppe. Please tell him the last gave great satisfaction. It is sound and wholesome; perhaps I might prefer a lighter wine, and perhaps some other time he might make the experiment, but for just now we shall just have a repetition of the order.

6. "What he writes about my 'cuttings and carvings' is due to a misunderstanding. They were done in accordance with a *marked copy of his own* sent me for the purpose" (Colvin's note).

Your cablegram received, and I suppose I shall just keep back *St. Ives,* but I will continue to try and get on with it. The first duty is to try to feed my family; it is only the second to publish chefs d'oeuvres. And the chef d'oeuvre is now impossible; as much as I can hope for is to be readable, and not too inexact. This is rather a bitter pill that I have to swallow, but—there!—it is down.

I say, should I not subscribe for the Scottish History Society? I am greatly taken with one I see referred to as being in the press: *The Forfeited Estates Papers, 1745–6.* How are these books sold? If I have to join in order to get them, why I'll join.

I trust this letter will catch you before you go, and I hope your arrival will find me in better case. It is my stomach and liver that have knuckled under. And all I can say is, give me consumption! It doesn't extinguish the rational spark in man. It is possible to go on coughing and be an artist. But no' wi' the stamach! Na!

You [8] may be pretty certain that nothing will arise for you to do, other than the Christmas goose for Mary Ann Watts and the Xmas box for the Boodles. The telegram had the necessary fault of all telegrams: it told me too little. I do not know whether you mean that all these beautiful bargains are off. At the same time I shall go on as though nothing had happened and try to finish the blamed thing as soon as possible. After all, I have still two months of the year, and I shall be surprised if I can't get it done by then. You have never told me who James Dalrymple Duncan is.[9] I hope at least he is a decent fellow. But I own I am just a little puzzled about it. Is it all right with Colvin? I thought I had been to send to him, and just at the present moment when I am feeling just a trifle sore about the editorship, and unfortunately have had to express some of it, I am very unwilling to run the risk of any fresh difference or disappointment to him. In the meanwhile, as I am just to keep *St. Ives* by me until it is done, this does not matter; but in case you get this letter (as you ought to do) before your departure per *Octavia,* I wish you would send me a few lines by

7. Letter continued in RLS's hand.
8. Letter continued in Belle Strong's hand.
9. Not identified.

America to put my mind at rest. These will reach me in time for the January up mail, which you yourself can't possibly do.

33 shillings please for the Amanuensis.

All [1] waiting for you with impatience.

> Yours ever,
>
> R. L. STEVENSON.[2]

1. Letter finished in RLS's hand.

2. "He wrote hard all that morning of the last day; his half-finished book, *Hermiston,* he judged the best he had ever written, and the sense of successful effort made him buoyant and happy . . . He was . . . gaily talking, when suddenly he put both hands to his head, and cried out, 'What's that?' . . . Even as he did so he fell on his knees . . . He died at ten minutes past eight on Monday evening the 3rd of December in the forty-fifth year of his age" (letter of Lloyd Osbourne to RLS's friends).

INDEX

Stevenson, Robert Louis (*continued*)
ings, 184, 296 f., 313, 315, 320 f., 334,
338, 340–2, 351; his mother's financial
affairs, 187 f.; elected to Athenaeum,
189; quarrel with Henley, 189–233, *see
also* Henley; departure for South Seas,
233; almost shipwrecked, 237; at Tautira, 237–9; buys, and plays, flageolets,
238, 249, 258, 264, 270, 278, 283 f.; at
Honolulu, 240–51; drinks with Kalakaua, 240, 243; unusually good health,
241; collaboration with Lloyd, 242,
246; volume of work, 242, 281; plans
for island excursion, 244; happiness in
South Seas, 248, 259; reluctance to have
letters published, 249; makes will, 250;
plans magic lantern entertainment,
250; gathers material for writing,
252 f.; in Samoa, 252–63; description of
Apia, 255 f.; difficulties with Joe Strong,
257 f., 262, 302; buys Vailima, 258;
life there, 258–372; opinions of his
writings, 258, 282; expectation of libel
suit, 265; his anger with Henley over
latter's failure to call on his mother,
274 f.; work in progress, 279–81, 288,
292, 313, 324, 350, 352, 357; schedule of
work, 281; plays written with Henley,
281–2, 291, *see also* Henley; organizes
"band," 283 f.; instructions to change
wife's will, 298; furor over Lady Simpson, 299 f.; judgment of Henley's
poetry, 301; of Kipling's, 301; expenses
of addition to Vailima house, 303–5,
317; libel suit with missionary, 305–8,
310 f.; orders wine, 312, 339, and liqueurs, 341; preparations to publish
letters, 322 f., 325–7, 342–7, 354–6, 358–
62, 364 f.; codicil to his will, 322; new
interest in his family tree, 330; plans
for CB's visit to Samoa, 332, 367–72;
new will, 337; monument for Fergusson, 355; death, 372. For a calendar of
RLS's travels see above, page xxiii

CHARACTER AND ATTITUDES. Attitudes
(toward: art, 102; death, 7, 21; drinking, 18; England, 18; fools, 18; God, 11,
23–5; happiness, 5; himself, *see* LIFE,
illness, poor health; his writing, 51, 67;
illness, 12, 17 f., 108; old age and the
passing of time, 13–15; pain, 13; Poly-

nesians, 248; publishing letters, 249;
success, 270; a weakling, 19–21); concern for others, 19 f.; distaste for senti-
mentality, 63; early atheism, 23–5;
"gospel of cheerfulness," 31, 62, 68; idleness, 45; irreverence, 11, 29; joy in nature, 5; liking for good fellowship, *see*
nostalgia for Edinburgh; moods of
gloom or despair, 12, 17, 22 f., 27–9, 62,
76; nostalgia for Edinburgh and the
Lothian Road days, 15 f., 32, 77 f., 84,
95–8, 116–17, 177, 236, 256 f.; optimism,
5–6, 17 f.; practical jokes, viii–xiv; satirical bent, 2–4, 7–10, 112 f., 121–6,
142–7, 159–62, 179

WORKS. *Across the Plains,* 329, 342 f.,
346; *Admiral Guinea* (with Henley),
157, 282; "Aes Triplex," 55; *Ajax* (projected with Henley), 281, 286; *Amateur
Emigrant,* 67 f., 346; *Ballads,* 271–2;
Beach of Falesá, 285–8, 293–5, 302 f.,
314, 352; *Beau Austin* (with Henley),
157, 281, 285; *Black Arrow,* 343 f.;
"Blame Me Not That This Epistle,"
13–15; *Bottle Imp,* 302; "Brashiana,"
88, 96, 98–9, 105, 107, 109 f., 142, 166;
Catriona, see *David Balfour;* "Character of Dogs," 81; *Child's Garden of
Verses,* 158, 197, 329, 363; "College
Magazine," 44; "Counterblast," 190;
Curate of Anstruther's Bottle, 39;
Darien, see *Heathercat; David Balfour*
(*Catriona*), 295 ff., 300 f., 303 ff., 308,
310 f., 313, 316, 318, 328 f., 331, 335,
337, 343 f., 346 f.; *Deacon Brodie* (with
Henley), 61, 119, 128, 179, 182, 191,
214–5, 282, 286; *Devil on Crammond
Sands,* 39; *Dr. Jekyll and Mr. Hyde,*
177, 179, 183, 324, 343; *Dynamiter*
(with Fanny Stevenson), 157, 343;
Ebb-Tide (with Lloyd Osbourne), 246,
273, 288, 324–5, 335, 343, 345, 348,
368; "El Dorado," 51; " 'Encl' Breathed
the Rustic Maid," 122–3; *Familiar
Studies of Men and Books,* 100, 343,
346; *Father Damien,* 264–5, 271, 343 f.;
"Feast of Famine," 242; *Footnote to
History,* 253, 288, 295 ff., 305 f., 338,
343 f., 346; *Go-Between,* 292, 327; "God
Gave to Me a Child in Part," 150;
"Gospel according to Walt Whitman,"

A

LIFE IN SONG

BY

GEORGE LANSING RAYMOND

FOURTH EDITION, REVISED

G. P. PUTNAM'S SONS
NEW YORK AND LONDON
The Knickerbocker Press

CONTENTS

iii

The course of one born humble . . .
Who yet attained the end of highest aims
As grand as any land or age e'er sought,
Because his plans when struggling toward the light
Emerged where freemen leave to God and heaven
The right to rule the spirit though on earth.

FINALE : A LIFE IN SONG.

A LIFE IN SONG.

PRELUDE.

> "Seven notes make full the gamut.
> Some have said
> Seven ages make our human life
> complete ;

And seven has my life known ; and now the dusk
Folds like a pall above my earthly day.
I would not hold too dear this day that goes ;
Yet who, when he has pass'd through ways wherein
His feet have wander'd and been wellnigh lost,
Would leave no words of guidance for his kind ?
And who, when leaving these where heedless ears
Are disenchanted oft of all distaste
By words men chant in verse whose music seems
To pulse and pant like living blood and breath,
Or leave the nervy lines like breezes blown
From silence into song-land, as they cross
Æolian chords ;—who in a world like this

Would not wish all the current of his thought
To flow to speech amid these waves of rhythm ?
More swiftly and more surely thus, perchance,
The truth that wells from him may clear the space
Between his own and other souls, and swell
The stream of truth which flows from each for all."

So spake, with eyes that fondly sought his works
As mothers' eyes will seek their children's forms,
The man whose care had wrought these tales in
        song.
Then, turning, sage-like, toward a waiting friend,
He slowly said : " Beneath men's outward lives
There flows a force whose current, sweeping on,
Impels to outward good.   But if they start
To gain this good, they oft are driven back ;
And oft then start anew.   Through all their lives
They thus may struggle forward, then draw back,
And move now here, now there, and half believe,
Like half the world, that all their deeds are vain ;
Yet must it be that far above this earth,
Where grander progress courses grander paths
Than mortals ever dream of, aims that urge
Men's hope so vainly to and fro below,
Are seen to swing the pendulums that turn
The hands on heaven's high dials to better times.
A life like this, it is, whose changing paths
The feet that tread the measure of my verse

Essay to follow.   Would the poet's themes
Themselves were worthier !   Then they less **might**
    need
The lyre of fancy to give charm to fact :
Enough of sweetness might attend reports
Of footfalls really heard, and deeds perceived,
Impelled by sweet desire.''

                With words like **these**,
The dying poet turn'd him on his couch,
Sank back, and fell to rest.
                And when, at **morn,**
Friends came to bear to him his early meal,
They found him still and pale, and by him **there**
His poems lay, half held in opening hands.
Alone with these embodied thoughts of his,
Prized so because the forms to which so **oft**
The spirit breathed by him had given its **life,**
That spirit now had all been breathed away.

Of those who mourned him then, none knew his
    past,
They scarcely knew his name.   Some days before,
With locks and beard as white as was the snow
Blown round him when he came, his trembling
    frame
Had drifted hither, like a bark to shore ;
And here, disabled by the strain and stress

Of many a former tempest, he had stay'd ;
And here, erelong, had found the final port
Of all his earthly voyage.

      Nor then had those
Whose friendly doors had open'd for his needs
Been void of their reward.   For such a man,
With so much to draw forth from men their best,
Yet so much to impart beyond their best,
These unversed villagers had never seen.
They could but love him ; yet with all their love,
The more they knew him, something made of him
Still more a stranger.   All about his life
There hung an atmosphere of mystery.
He seem'd through it to see what they saw not;
And as their hush would heed the rare reports
That reach'd them through the music of his voice,
His thought oft seem'd a spirit's ; none could tell
From whence it came ; nor trace it where it went.

So, when he died, the room in which he died,
And writings left there, seem'd like sacred things
To those whose kindly care had tended him.
Nor would they touch them.   "Who can tell," they
  said,
" If friends of his may come in search of him ?
And when they come, if they be like himself,

They may not like it, if our alien hands
Have made aught seem less his."

              And soon it chanced
A friend had come.   One morning, with the sun,
A soldier bright with glittering stars and bars
And buttons on his uniform of blue,
Whose martial mien commanded every eye,
And hush'd the children's play, came down the
    street,
And paused before the house, and enter'd it.
And when he gazed upon the vacant couch
And untouch'd writings of the poet, then
The gem-like tears, pursed in his wrinkling cheeks,
Fell like some rich exchange of value due
Proved wealth of worth within the soul now gone.
" He was my army comrade," said the man.
" Had we but known this," one replied, "his form
Would like a soldier's have been borne to rest."
" He was a true reformer, years ago
The spokesman of the slave," said then the first.
" Had we known this," was answer'd now, " his form
Would like a statesman's have been borne to rest."
" He was a poet," said the first, once more.
" Ah," sigh'd the other, " there his poems lie.
We knew the poet."

             " So you bore him forth,
With no parade of honor," said his friend ;

" And that was well.   He would have wish'd no
        more.
The soldier and the statesman are the state's,
And all the pageantry that can augment
The dignity of office and of power
Befits them, as the king his robe and crown.
Not so the poet.   He is all mankind's,
Akin to both the humble and the high,
The weak and strong.   Who most would honor him
Must find in him a brother.   He but strives
To make the truth that he would speak supreme,—
Truth strongest when the simplest, needing not
The intervention of pretentious pomp,
Plumed with vain symbols of authority
To make men keep their distance."

                          Musing thus,
The man drew near the writings ; and, erelong,
Who watch'd them saw them sorted, one by one—
For all were number'd—into seven groups.
And, at the sight, one bending over them
Recall'd a time in which the man they mourn'd
Had talked of mystic numbers ; and had said
That, " Like the days that part the weeks in sevens,
And tones that run the scales of sounds and hues,
And spheres that seers have seen in heavens and
        hells,
Like these did nature seem all things to group,—
To count the deep formations in the rocks,

And forms in life, till seven made each complete.
Ay, man on earth but seven times ten years lived,
And all mankind through seven like phases yet
Might reach humanity's grand Sabbath-time."
And one, they said, who heard these words, had
    ask'd,
And had discuss'd the question with his mates,
" Could mind and matter then in any sense
Reveal essential oneness ? "   Answering which,
" Why not?" had ask'd the poet.   "Many a sage,—
Augustine, Plato, and Pythagoras,—
Had talk'd of souls as numbers, ay, or spheres.
Yet none," he soon had said, " could really solve
All riddles hidden in the forms outlined
By nature's curves and angles, or amid
The play of her fair features, made more fair,
Like human faces, by the thoughts beneath,
Read all that so has thrill'd in every age
The spirits of the wisest and the best."

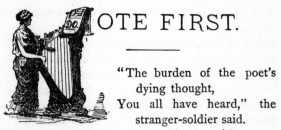

OTE FIRST.

"The burden of the poet's
dying thought,
You all have heard," the
stranger-soldier said.
"'T is fitting then you all should solve with me
His meaning—in these poems"; and he read
The title "Dreaming." "Truly here," said he,
"This man would tell us of his own sweet life;
For he began life dreaming, he himself.
I knew him when a boy, a poet then,
With brain on fire to learn, aye glowing like
A gilder's cauldron, so the crudest thought
That reach'd it from a neighbor's lip or book
Came from it glittering like a precious thing.
An orphan, bound and work'd beyond enduring
By those whose hard, cold natures could not yield
That genial warmth of sympathetic care
For which the spring-time of his nature craved,
Anon, there seem'd for him but one delight:
It came from realms of dreams, while, on his bed,

Too tired for sounder slumber, he would toss;
And, like a galley-slave, forced out to sea,
Yearn for some harbor somewhere in the world
Where waiting love would welcome love that came.
Oft in rare moments that he stole from work,
Would he confide to me his wrongs and hopes.
I seem to see him yet, the straight brown hair
Toss'd wildly backward from the broad white brow,
The sunburnt cheeks, the deep and wondering eyes,
As blue when grand emotion swept within,
As autumn skies are in the northwest wind,
With just as much of heaven back of them—
Dear boy !—and he has told us here perchance
Of what he dream'd."—So spoke the soldier-friend;
And paused a time.   Then, vaguely, with a look
Turn'd inward toward the soul, as if to find
Dear stores in memory, he began to read ;
And one by one the people who had stood
To greet the stranger, softly took their seats ;
And not alone the poem held them there.
The aged soldier's well kept, youthful voice,
The ringing echo of a singing heart,
Charm'd all, like chimings of the old church bells,
Which, sweet in summer, yet still sweeter seem,
When peal'd amid the winter's wind-whirl'd snow.

REAMING.

I.

Life is poised on slender moments; all eternity on time;
And the "still small voice" reveals
the presence of a power sublime.

Footfalls, light as dreams', may wake the slumbering
soul's activity,

Rouse the source whence thought and feeling issue
toward their destiny,—

Toward the good, if lured by movements where a
pathway leads to weal;

Toward the ill, if turning only where the wiles of
craft appeal.

Whether come a sound, a fragrance, or a light that
stirs the mind;

Something wakes a wish within one; something
gleams we glance to find;

And we start; and then press toward it, on beyond
the joys of youth;

On, till old age falls in death, to spring apart the
    gates of truth.

II.

Every thing in art or nature, robed in rich or rude
    attire,
Gains in beauty while it gains in power to lure a
    pure desire.
Surface claims may charm the senses, but the spirit
    from its throne
Waives away all other suitors for what charms itself
    alone.
Thus we find that, while they long to see the scenes
    of which they sing,
Blind or banish'd poets conjure forms more fair than
    sight could bring.
Thus we find, where evening shadows lie reclined
    at close of day,
All the world grows more attractive, veil'd in twi-
    light's guise of gray ;
For, in dim relief, its outlines woo our wonder and
    surmise.
While the stars like sparks that linger where the fire
    of sunset dies
Kindle oft our aspirations, which, as grandly they
    evolve,
Light the brow of meek conjecture with the flush of
    bold resolve.

III.

Is it strange, that such an evening, when my days
    were filled with strife,
Such an evening, far and hazy, seems the sweetest
    of my life?
Is it strange that memory, gazing back through
    many a year's expanse,
Now recalls the scenes I saw then, clad in grave
    significance?

IV.

On that eve, for once, my soul, set free from toil,
    had just been brought,
Through a fairy realm of fiction, near the life for
    which I sought.
Then I turn'd and watch'd the sunset, with emo-
    tions vague and wild,
Till I seem'd a thing scarce human, strange as
    mystery's very child.
Not of earth nor heaven appear'd I. I was one
    with that mild light,
Which had veil'd in awe the hills before the hush'd
    approach of night;
And through all the clouds that floated rose the
    forms of angels fair,
And I seem'd to heed their whispers in the move-
    ments of the air.

Far adown the west I track'd them, till there met
    my wondering gaze
Mountains in the sky that fring'd a sky-set sea
    begirt with haze,—
Haze from shore-sand bright as gold-dust blown to
    clouds by winds of noon ;
But across the sea's blue depth appear'd to sail the
    crescent moon.
Scarce I saw this, when beyond it I descried with
    pleasure great
Outlines of a heavenly port illumed as for a heav-
    enly fête.

v.

Ah, how wondrous was that city, rear'd amid the
    cloud-land bright,
Where that sunset capt the climax of the day's
    completed light.
How the wall that coil'd around it glow'd along its
    winding way !
And how flash'd the floods of flame that in the
    moat before it lay !
What though underneath their splendor stretch'd a
    storm-cloud black and long?
'T was a bass-note held beneath that sweeter o'er it
    made the song.
For, above, as if aspiring toward the heaven's en-
    kindled fires,

Toward the sky in countless numbers, press'd the
    domes and pierc'd the spires ;
Domes, high arch'd, with tints to rival rainbows in
    their every hue,
Join'd with spires from darkness pushing, till their
    peaks effulgent grew ;
Spires like prayers that start from anguish, aim'd
    for where all blessings are,
Spires like hope that falters never while above it
    shines a star.
Then—and how my gaze profan'd them !—what
    retreats for bliss appear'd
In those fair illumined mansions that along the
    streets were rear'd !—
Streets like shafts of light far shooting, fading like
    the sun from view,
Back of trees with leaves like autumn's, when life's
    fires have burned them through.
In my soul I half believed I then should leave this
    earthly star,
Gazing like the seer on Pisgah, toward that prom-
    ised land afar.

VI.

After this, my thoughts, returning back to earth,
    grew mutinous ;
And rebellious meditation to their tocsin murmur'd
    thus :

"Five years—it is long to languish with no teacher
    but desire
In these hours of stolen study, snatch'd from toil in
    sweat and mire.
Wherefore was I left an orphan, and the ward, with-
    out a joy,
Of a man who into manhood thinks to keep me still
    a boy,
Keep me back from needed knowledge, like a weak-
    ling soon to die,
Who, if train'd in-doors, might fail to make my
    friendship with the sky!
Why should he so crush and curse me, dashing
    water on my fire—
Quenching with a hiss each spark that gleams to
    show my soul's desire?

VII.

"Ah! how oft, released from labor, when day's
    heat and dust were stay'd,
By the calm, cool fires of starlight, I have dream'd
    and hoped, and pray'd;
And of things divine had visions, all so complex
    and so vast,
That my mind could comprehend but parts of them,
    the while they pass'd;
Parts that yet so charm'd and thrill'd me, that, with
    all its might and main,

Thought would soar on high to match them, but
    would soar and soar in vain,
Till, to my bewilder'd yearning, in the distance all
    would fade,
Where their long-drawn trains of splendor slowly
    left the world in shade.
Why should mortals be becalm'd amid the earthly
    darkness here,
While the lights from countless havens throng the
    heavens far and near !
Surely sails, wide spread to woo them, heaven's fair
    winds cannot forsake :
That which moves to right moves onward, tho' but
    slowly grows its wake.
Surely, souls, if but persistent in the search of
    truth long sought,
Spy new worlds arise where clouds had coursed but
    watery wastes of thought."

VIII.

Thus with varying moods I sat there, till each radi-
    ant sunset cloud,
Like some living form, seem'd buried in a gently
    gather'd shroud.
Yet my thought still rested on it : naught, oh,
    naught of good so dies :
It but disappears, anon, to don a resurrection
    guise.

Blessings grieve us, when they leave us ; but they
    leave no sunless gloom.

Everywhere new life may spring up, everywhere
    new beauty bloom.

So for me, as died that sunset, all at once there
    came a change ;—

For I slept, and dreamt the sky there flew apart
    with flashing strange,

O'er which clouds abruptly gather'd, as if thus to
    screen from me

Thrice ten thousand flames that lit a path more
    deep than space could be.

Wonder then my brain bewilder'd : reasoning all to
    rapture flew.

"Surely," thought I, "joy celestial crowns the light
    with halo new.

It may be an angel-greeting to some saint !" then
    futile quite,

This attempt of reason left me, for behold ! a
    stranger sight :

Swift from flash to flash augmenting, as a torrent
    seeks the sea,

All those flames that rose and fell appear'd to start
    and flow toward me.

Then my soul within me fluttered.   Here was what
    I long had sought.

"Farewell now to earthly fetters !   Yes, they burst,
    they burst !" I thought.

Ere they did so, all my spirit grew more calm ; for, far away,

Rose a song with words revealing what the light could not convey.

Sweet it was as if the heavens would all their sweet store shower below :

And by one flood quench forever all the thirst of mortal woe ;

And my moods were swept before it in a spell resistless bound,

As a sailor, sinking softly, where the deep sea laps him round.

But can I recall the song now ?—Better bid yon meadow nook

Hold the whole great rain that blest it on its journey down the brook.

IX.

Ay, when men who would direct you onward toward the realms of truth,

Where exhaustless wells of wisdom quench desires of endless youth,

In their efforts falter, blunder, and with phrases vague and blind,

Void of close and clear expression, leave their meaning hard to find,

Blame them not : their case is human : themes and aims as grand as these

Overflow the burden'd words that bear our lesser
thoughts with ease.

Many guiding views beyond us loom but dimly understood :

Many schemes are hatch'd that famish where our
imperfections brood.

O how oft when stirr'd to rescue those we love
from threaten'd woe,

Or to point them toward the pathways, where in
safety men may go,

Our own lack of tact or temper has equipt advice
amiss,

Veil'd like truth with features hid behind a warp of
prejudice.

Ay, how often, when the light that guided us has
gleam'd within,

We have wish'd that our reflections might enlighten
then our kin,

But though brighter minds might aid them, ours, at
least, were dull as night,

Striving ever, failing ever, half our views to mirror
right.

Foremost of our best possessions, faith fails not
that can but feel ;

Yet how blest are they who know and can their
grounds of faith reveal.

They alone, amid the shades, where men who move
toward mystery

Long to know what joy or woe is yet to be their
    destiny,
They alone, with heaven-lit torches, flashing light
    the darkness through,
Can disclose beyond the gloom the looming out-
    lines of the true.

X.

Power like their's, and more were needed, to recall
    what thrill'd me there
In that music flowing round me, as if fountain'd in
    the air.
All the tones appear'd spontaneous ; yet, beyond
    all discord sweet,
By divine and inner impulse made to blend in
    chords complete.
Somehow thus the phrases ran, and roll'd, and
    echoed through the night ;
And the changes that they rang were all to praise
    the Source of Light :—

XI.

Hail, hail, hail,
Eternal Glory hail !
Ye powers of light, high o'er the night
Where only gloom had lain,
Began your sway, ere dawn'd a day,
And evermore shall reign.

Before one star had flash'd afar
      Light fill'd creation's throne,
And, ere the birth of air or earth,
      In growing splendor shone.
      Gleam, gleam, gleam,
      And ever brighter beam,
And far away through endless day
      Forever onward stream.

      Hail, hail, hail,
      Infinite Goodness, hail !
From heavenly height through day, through night,
      And down to deepest hell,
From central throne to circling zone,
      Where'er a world can dwell,
The hosts of right their shafts of light
      Hurl onward through the sky ;
And rear their bow o'er rain below,
      And routed clouds that fly.
      Shine, shine, shine,
      The universe is thine ;
In blackest hell, burst full and fell,
      Like lightning, flame divine !

      Hail, hail, hail,
      Almighty Truth prevail !
At thy command, in every land,
      O'er haunts of lust and lies
The stars, a band of guardsmen, stand ;
      And dawn with ardor hies.
The lightning bounds and thunder sounds,
      And fire and air enroll,

And all that live allegiance give
          To their supreme control.
          Wail, wail, wail ;
          Ye powers of darkness, quail ;
And flee until the wrong be still,
          And right may drop its mail.

          Hail, hail, hail,
          Unchanging Promise, hail !
O'er all that jars the world, the stars
          Burn on the long night through.
Aurora lights her giddy hights.
          The comet cleaves the blue.
The sun and breeze from beds of ease
          The scatter'd fogs pursue.
From land and sky the shadows fly.
          Awaking, winks the dew ;
          Speed, speed, speed,
          With light sow every mead ;
And haste the time when every clime
          Shall glow as grows the seed.

XII.

Ere the echoes that rehears'd it learn'd the tones of
     half the lay
Those who hymn'd it hove in view from out a
     cloud of golden spray.
Such a sight has oft allured me, rous'd by morn's
     first herald-gleam,

Floating up the edge of slumber in a just awaking
    dream.
Angel forms, no man could number, circled in a
    band of light
Round a chariot framed of splendor, drawn by
    steeds of dazzling white.
Softly sped they o'er the vapors ; and, with wings
    of texture rare,
Woke low throbs of murmuring music, as they
    lightly struck the air.
And the chariot bore a Being with a smile so
    sweetly bright,
One could better paint, than it, the fragrance of
    that summer night.

XIII.

" How could mortal dare to face her ? " thought I ;
    "nay, it should not be."
And like veils my eyelids fell to screen my soul she
    should not see.
Then at once my dream had shifted.   Down below
    me met my sight,
As of old, the farm and cattle.   Turn'd away from
    all that light,
Once again my form seem'd staggering through a
    task too hard and mean,
While my very soul was trembling lest my lack of
    strength were seen.

"Cruel fate!" cried I, despairing; "none on earth
 so curst as I!"—

Then my eyes, above me glancing, saw that fair
 one still draw nigh.

On she came, until she reached me, bade those
 angel-bands depart,

And, with accents fill'd with love that thrill'd my
 very spirit's heart,

"Come," she said, "and sit beside me"; and I
 rose, I wist not how,

And within her car I found me; nor had known of
 bliss till now.

Up from earth and through the sky, and over land
 and lake it springs,

Lightly drawn and gently guided by the white
 steeds' beating wings.

Then along the long horizon sudden forms would
 flash in view,

And like suns our skies illumine, as we by them
 swiftly flew.

XIV.

Soon my spirit yearn'd to ask her what these wondrous things could be.

But, while still I dared not do it, she, who knew
 what stirr'd in me,

Said, as if she heard me question: "Mortal homes
 are fix'd in stars.

We have left the bounds of matter ; here are burst
    the prison bars,
Out from which, with powers contracted and a
    weary sense of strife,
Souls, like convicts through their grating, steal a
    luring glimpse of life.
Here are regions where the spirit, freed from fet-
    tering time and space,
Wings her flight through scenes eternal, reading
    thought as face reads face.
Here the good reveal their goodness, and the wise
    their wisdom show ;
And from open minds about them souls learn all
    that souls can know."

xv.

"All they learn," I thought; "learn all things?"—
    and my dream had changed again ;
And my master stood before me, and I dared to tell
    him then,
Till his dark face loom'd like smoke round eyes in
    which fierce anger burn'd ;—
Tell him that the heavens had shown me 't was my
    right for which I yearn'd.
At my words he sprang to strike me—struck—and
    lo ! it seem'd the world
Stagger'd like some drunken giant, while I to the
    ground was hurl'd.

"All is ended now," I thought—when, like a
    mother's voice in youth,
Rose my guide's : " God's children," said she, " have
    a right to know God's truth.
In the world brains mould to bodies, but across its
    border-line
Royal minds must share their purple, slaves with
    kings become divine.

XVI.

"O if but a spirit's vision once could reach a
    mortal's eyes,
In it he might more discover than he else could e'en
    surmise.
Hold, my steeds—while men are slumbering, we
    may note their dreams to-night.
Note, my child, while passing through them, scenes
    that greet angelic sight.
These augment by all the fancies forged in all these
    burning spheres,
From the Pole-star past the Lion, far as where the
    Cross appears ;
Conjure them like minds that muse them, varied as
    their interests ;
Add completed recollection, and all thought that
    each suggests ;
Then conceive a soul's emotions, while such visions
    loom in sight—

You have only dream'd a dream of one short night
of heaven's delight."

XVII.

While she spoke, from out the distance, rose in
view what seem'd a grove ;
But beneath its boughs a dreamland, like a laby-
rinth, unwove.
There were paths like those of Eden. There were
mountains high and grand,
Hung to wild, fantastic fortunes o'er a dizzy dearth
of land.
There were lakes all diamond-dappled ; there were
streams that rushed at meres
Arch'd by bridges, rainbow-girdled, where the high
spray leapt their piers.
There were flowers that flush'd through vistas,
where alternate floods of sheen,
Rich as tides of amber, flow'd through shaded
banks of evergreen.
There were trees whose broad, high branches cradled
all the stars o'erhead.
There were lawns whose tender grasses could not
stand a fairy's tread.
Orchards, gardens, halls, and temples fill'd the
fields ; and in them seem'd

Every creature, of which fancy, past or present, e'er
    had dream'd,—
Birds and beasts of all conditions, dancing, dozing,
    forward, shy,
Strown, as if on isles that throng'd an endless
    ocean in the sky.

XVIII.

"Can it be that heaven," I ask'd, "is fill'd with
    thoughts of things like these?"
"In the heaven's blue vault about us, where earth
    floats in cloud and breeze,
All are held," she said, "that earth holds ; nor
    would past their borders pour
Were the opening voids about them fill'd with in-
    finitely more."
"Can it be that heaven," I cried, "can care for
    beasts that work the field?—
Then for him who works beside them ! "—and with
    this my dream reveal'd
At my feet the well-turn'd furrows where I trudg'd
    behind my plow—
Only now it flew before me, speeded on I knew not
    how,
Only now it drew me upward,—then was not a
    plow at all,
But the chariot where my guide sat. "Heaven,"
    she said, "deems nothing small."

XIX.

Then, anon, she bade me note rare nixes' forms,
    whose golden hair
Flow'd about their sunny faces, fair as clouds in
    sunset air.
Then those clowns that mask and romp she pointed
    out,—Shedeem and Jinn ;
Then, at flower-beds, peris giddy with their fra-
    grance long drunk in.
Near them flitted timid wights, and, where high
    cliffs half hid the light,
Dodg'd the goldsmith-duergar, dragging all their
    gleaming stores from sight.
In a stream were necks and kelpies, pressing down
    a plump strömkarl ;
Near them, gulf'd in water-lilies, dracs who made a
    mermaid snarl ;
Farther off, the leprechaun with bantering brogue
    he hammered well,
Where his quick blows fell more soft than rain-
    drops on the fairy-bell
Then we met with monster-deeves, a korred with
    her shaggy head,
Trolls and trows in gay green jackets, topt by
    fiery caps of red,
And a crowd of sly hobgoblins lugging off some
    cellar's ware ;

And an old-time nis and lutin.   All of Bedlam now
    seem'd there :
Brownies proud of plaids and thistles, kobolds
    flushed with too much beer,
Boggart-snobs astride a lion, roaring so the deaf
    could hear,
And frail elves, like smoke in whirlwinds, dancing,
    while the högfolk sung ;
Or, detected, swiftly skulking toward the leaves
    they hid among.

XX.

Then I saw a stranger marvel :—smaller than each
    mate so small,
Floated near the weëst wonder one could ever see
    at all.
First it seem'd a passing snow-flake ; then repaid
    my steadfast gaze
With the outlines of a skiff there, fill'd with cheery,
    film-like fays ;
And up through the shifting atoms of the air that
    parted us
Oozed in tiny tones a ditty, ; and the lines were
    worded thus :

XXI.

To-night, to-night, my fairies white,
    The fair sweet air we sail.

But first a tune to tease the moon
  That tempts us toward the vale :—
Who cares to go where roses glow
  In sheen the moonlight sheds,
And globes of dew are sparkling through
  The tent the spider spreads ?
Your moonstruck fay may dance away
And crush the rose-leaves all to hay—
  Who cares ?—I don't !—Do you ?

But note you there that maiden fair—
  Ha, ha, a dainty bit !
She dreams a dream of love I deem.—
  Queen Mab 's a wicked wit !
Come, come, a jump; and down we 'll thump;
  And dance about her heart.
'T will beat and beat—aha, how sweet
  The thrills we there shall start !
We 'll tickle her neck, and tickle her toes,
And tickle her little lips under her nose—
  Who cares ?—I don't !—Do you ?

And then we 'll huff that mourner gruff,
  Till he unknits his brow.
We 'll whiz and whiz about his phiz,
  And pinch his lips, I vow ;
Then hide and seek in hair so sleek,
  And down each wrinkle spare ;
And ply his eye, if dry, too dry ;
  And slide the lashes there ;
And when big drops begin to flow,
Oh, how we 'll dodge the flood, oh ho !—
  Who cares ?—I don't !—Do you ?

The moon may keep the earth asleep—
  We 'll twist things ere we go.
The beau shall toss a baby cross,
  The belle shall beat her beau ;
The men be boys ; and boys the toys
  Of girls that at them scream ;
And when they wake, oh, how they 'll shake
  To find it all a dream !
They 'll think of wind and fly and flea ;
But not of you, and not of me.—
  Who cares ?—I don't !—Do you ?

XXII.

Charmed at this, I bent me nearer ; but dismay !
    off dodged the toy,
Shaken like a note of laughter from the bounding
    breath of joy.
"Cruel thing," I cried, provoked then ; "weazen'd
    witchery of delight,
Far too fine for eyes to find you, why should you
    have crossed their sight ! "

XXIII.

Then I thought this whole odd vision might be an
    imagined one ;
Some had deem'd that half life's fabrics were from
    mere thin fancy spun.

" Is it so," at last I question'd ; " are not things
    the things they seem ?

Do souls oft but serve delusions, heeding steps of
    which they dream ?"

" Those who think so," said she softly, " overlook,
    when thinking so,

Truths within man's nature deeper than proof's
    plummets ever go.

Souls reflect all life like mirrors, and their dreams
    by day, by night,

Though distorting oft, oft image facts too fine for
    finite sight.

Borne through life, all move in orbits, whose far
    cycles curve about

Circling spirit-light within them, circled by the
    world's without.

What they call their consciousness is but the focus
    where are brought

Rays, borne in from all about them, burning to a
    blaze in thought.

Few can see, beyond their thought, the source
    whence all that lights them flows ;

Few, except the best whose heaven seems bright
    though earth be dark with foes ;

Or the worst who learn that, when uprightness
    bends to evil's might,

Conscience brings the consciousness that souls have
    lost their spirit-light.

XXIV.

" Thus the good are fill'd with trust, and thus the
    evil oft with fear ;
For they dream of powers about them, swaying all
    in every sphere ;
Powers of good and powers of evil.   Ay, men feel,
    that, bow'd in prayer,
Not with flesh and blood they wrestle, but with
    those that rule the air ;
Nor will vanish thence till vanquish'd by that Spirit,
    whose control
Rolls the star, and waves the sea, and works the
    most self-govern'd soul ;
And can send, for rare communion, cloth'd in rai-
    ment all too white
For the ken of common vision, those who force the
    wrong to flight."

XXV.

We had left that place of fancy, and had reach'd a
    star-lit sea ;
And across its dark, deep waters, clouds, like smoke
    where burned the lee,
Clung about a crystal temple, rising from the surf
    below
Like a dawn of endless promise o'er a night of
    ended woe.

Everywhere behind the cloud-mist, could we see
    the temple rise,
Everywhere, each side and o'er us, till we lost
    it in the skies.
Then, anon, at pearly steps, before an entrance
    dim and vast,
In some way, but how I knew not, we had left our
    car at last ;
And through gold-mail'd hosts were moving, who
    would part, and pass us on,
Swept, like gods, amid a glory blazed from all we
    gazed upon,
Toward a towering portico, a cliff of shafts that
    upward went,
Till the very stars appear'd to trail beneath their
    pediment.

XXVI.

At their base, a sire with thin locks gray from many
    a distant year,
Gazing calmly out upon us, question'd as we ven-
    tur'd near :
"Who is this you bring, my sister, who is this ? ah
    yes, I trace
Restless eyes and flushing cheeks here ; yes, ah
    yes, an earthly face."
"One whose aspiration," said she, "as I rode full
    high at eve,

Craved for light, and aided hither, would not now
  this portal leave."
"Aspiration," quoth he mildly ; "many a bitter,
  bitter woe
Is begot by aspiration. There are easier paths
  below.
He 's the happy man who holds his head not higher
  than his home.
'T is right hard to stoop forever. But I keep you
  from the dome."

XXVII.

For this dome then two to fit me, robed me quickly
  like a knight :
And they whisper'd, when they left me,—" Faith
  alone can find the light."
Then at once wide doors before us open'd like a
  dawning day,
And disclos'd a hall resplendent, sweeping through
  long leagues away.
All about it clouds of incense floated, fringed with
  golden haze,
And within them lamps, half-hidden, shone like
  sparks amid a blaze ;
While huge caryatic figures, carved on columns tall
  and white,
Filed far off like phantom sentries guarding thus a
  phantom rite.

Through the clouds that parted often, loomed
    mysterious choirs anon,
And a slow, low hymn they chanted, surged afar
    and urged us on.

XXVIII.

Come to the love that is coming now,
    Come from the world away ;
Come to the source of joy, and bow,
    Bow to the sweetest sway.
Find but love for the heart that grieves,
Love for the work one never leaves,
Love for the worth that work achieves,
    Love ; and woe will away.

Come to the truth that is coming now,
    Come from the world away ;
Come to the source of right, and bow,
    Bow to the wisest sway.
Find in the way where all is light,
Truth to impel the soul aright,
Truth to make all that awaits it bright,
    Truth ; and doubt will away.

Come to love, and wherever you wend,
    All true life is begun.
Ever in bliss toward which you tend,
    Joy and the right are one.
Love—and the heart shall warmer glow ;
Love—and the mind shall brighter grow ;
Love with truth—and the soul shall go
    On to the lasting sun.

Come to the truth, and come as you may,
    All of love is begun.
Whether you feel or think your way,
    Love and the truth are one.
Love is the warmth, and truth the ray ;
Truth is the light, and love the day ;
Come to either, you wend your way
    Under the lasting sun.

XXIX.

As the anthem ceas'd—ah, music of such import
    knows no death :
Evermore its tones refresh us, like a draft of angel
    breath,—
As it ceas'd, I sigh'd aloud, " O would that I their
    light could share ! "
When, behold, high, high uplifted, I was borne
    along the air,
On and on, with slippery speed, far sliding still to
    swifter flight,
Where strode by us tall, white columns, like gigan-
    tic ghosts of night ;
Where high arches fell and rose up like an ocean
    in the sky,
And bright lamps like lines of lightning on the
    clouded wall flew by.
Then more steadfast came a splendor, and, amid
    the burning air,

Checks that gently stay'd our progress, in a domed
    rotunda there.

XXX.

Broad this was and high, heaved heedless of that
    lavish'd wealth of space,
As all else had been,—a marvel even in that
    marvellous place.
Such a sight creation's dawning might have seen,
    when first arose
Morning mists to end the night of an eternity's re-
    pose.
All the pavement gleam'd as bright as could that
    first chaotic sea,
When it floated all the germs of all the beauty yet
    to be.
And the shafts that held the dome, and might have
    held in half the skies,
Rose with lines of earthly grace, but wondrous in
    their hues and size.
Far above, their hazy flutings burst in blazing
    capitals,
Where amid encircling glory hovered hosts of
    terminals.
Did they live or not, I knew not, but to my con-
    fused suspense
Their high distance made them holy ; and I bow'd
    in reverence.

XXXI.

Underneath the dome's great centre loom'd a
    mighty throne, it seem'd ;
But with outlines indistinct, for back of glowing
    clouds they gleam'd.
And the clouds were smoke that hover'd over fires
    that brightly shone
On a vast white altar, built before and round about
    the throne.
From the pavement rose the altar, as from waves
    a coral reef ;
But through lifting smoke its front show'd figures
    carved in deep relief.
One by one the smoke would leave these, and
    appear'd revealing so,
Through successive scenes, a tale of which my soul
    had need to know.
On the scenes my gaze I fix'd then.—In the first,
    there met my eye
Figures of a youth, and angel pointing out the
    headlands high
Of a land of peerless grandeur past an ocean wide
    and lone.
In the next, near harbors lured the youth to shores
    where wrecks were strown.
Next, he sail'd o'er rough seas bravely ; next, did
    drift becalm'd awhile ;

Next, flew on where fairest breezes blew toward
    many a flowery isle.

Next, great clouds were sweeping toward him, and
    his frame was bent with fear ;

But the last scene show'd a port with heaven-high
    mounts that he drew near.

XXXII.

Whose could be that life there outlined ?—so I
    question'd, till the fire,

Blazing on the altar, led me to appease a fresh de-
    sire.

On all sides, I saw about me, stretching outward
    far and wide,

Long, deep halls that radiated from the dome on
    every side.

All the halls were lined with statues, white robed,
    such as art redeems

From the fate of fellow-fancies, when, too soon,
    they die in dreams.

All the halls had pictured walls, of brightest hues
    which, far away,

Stream'd like oriflammes of dawn before a march
    of coming day,

XXXIII.

Soon I heard that "In the halls and on the walls I
    gazed at then,

Art in finest forms had outlined all the ways and
     works of men.
Each event in life was traced there, till all sank
     beneath the tomb;
Then, beyond it and above it, rested past the reach
     of gloom.
All the halls were open to me.   If I wish'd I might
     select
One I chose, and might explore it; and, when
     in it could detect
What befell the man whose course was limner'd
     there, when earth was left,
And the spirit journey'd onward, of its worldly
     powers bereft."—
Hearing this, I gazed about me, and resolved that
     hall to test,
Where was pictured most of promise for pursuits
     that seem'd the best.

XXXIV.

Thus resolved, I found one soon, in which were
     frescoed on the walls,
Wharves and ships that fill'd a harbor, busy streets,
     and market-halls,
Fruit-red trees, and yellow corn-fields, open mines
     that gemm'd a land,
And a gay-dress'd throng that drove through wind-
     ing ways to mansions grand.

"Truth's position aids its mission," thought I;
 "men will serve his voice
Who commands what most they treasure. Let
 me make this hall my choice.
Now to find what wealth will bring me!"—and I
 turn'd without delay,
Where, at first, the brilliance dazed me, as I
 met it down the way.
But the hall soon fill'd with smoke, and then the
 walls, in graver hues,
Loom'd to picture but the ills of those who would
 their wealth misuse.
Then, as yet I push'd on farther, by and by, all
 light was gone;
And a sound of floods drew near me; no one could
 have ventur'd on.
So I turn'd and sought the altar; but, alas, I sought
 it long
Ere I spied its light, then wonder'd why it was I
 went so wrong;—
What could mean the gloom and terror?—asking
 which, anon, I thought
How a night would come, at last, when light with
 wealth could not be bought.

XXXV.

Then I found another hall, and watch'd it with a
 beating heart!

For, portray'd upon its walls, were artists famed
    in every art.
And about them had been pictured works of chisel,
    brush, and pen,
Fit to body forth the thoughts breathed into them
    by Godlike men.
Here, too, far and near, were statues ; and o'er
    each a gem-set crown
Flash'd with light, and thousands like it shone the
    hall's whole distance down.
"This," thought I, " is what was wanting ; why was
    I so dull before ?
Here the way is all illumin'd," and I enter'd, awed
    no more.
Lighted onward by the crowns, my spell-bound soul
    had lost its fears,
While the thought of scenes I saw there bore me
    past my mortal years.
My works, too, seem'd not forgotten ; past my
    death they linger'd still,
Thron'd a living recollection, sceptr'd o'er a living
    will.
Ah, do not deny the soul its hopes of immortality ;
Where did ever noblest living seek a lesser destiny?—
But, while thus enrapt in revery, scenes about me
    lost their light,
Introducing dusk to darkness, dodging doubt to
    crawling night

And again cold mists were round me, while the
    unseen water's roar
Fiercely rose again to drive me toward the dome I
    sought once more.
" Ah," sighed I " those jewell'd crowns are void of
    all that made them bright,
As the moon would be, if sunlight could not reach
    that orb of night.
All the radiance that has left them from the far
    bright altar came ;
When 't is hid, no art can ever make them kindle
    into flame."

XXXVI.

Now, when I had reach'd the altar, I remained a
    while in doubt,
Sworn to try no other hall that I had not thought
    long about.
But, in one, some bright-robed artists linger'd
    painting deftly still,
And it seem'd less lonely here, where their fair
    forms the hall did fill.
So I paus'd where one was picturing waters to re-
    flect like dreams
White-draped clouds, on hill-sides, tending slender
    wants of suckling streams.
Flowers were bending by the waters, grown in
    fields of varied green

Stretching off toward heaven-hued mountains,
    which some shroud-like mists would screen ;
Then, where summer fields appear'd to melt to
    yield their golden grain,
Boys came bounding from a school-house, out
    toward men who reap'd a plain.
Toward the reapers roll'd a carriage. They were
    but in laboring guise
Yet the lordliest came to greet them ; and respect
    was in his eyes.
" Here where nature rules and gives its due to all
    humanity,
Here must be the land," I thought, " of all the
    dearest prophecy.
His way surely ends in brightness, who is ruled in
    every plan
By a love like God's, not slighting one whom God
    has made a man."
So I tried this hall ; but shortly I had all its work-
    ers pass'd ;
And I found myself with shadows, which by slow
    degrees were cast
Over all the walls, now picturing not pure love but
    low-aim'd zeal,
Making men, who strove for right amid a storm of
    lead and steel,
Lose their rights in flame and smoke ; and when, at
    last, this fill'd the wall,

Naught was left me, once again, but back through
　　pall-like gloom to crawl.

Ah, the depth of my despair now !　Could one hall
　　be wholly bright ?—

"Nay, not so," I thought, "if even love can lure
　　the soul from light."

XXXVII.

Yet, at last, my heart, still anxious, bade me one
　　more effort make.

But, ere that, I sought the altar ; and, when cour-
　　age dared, I spake,

Faintly asking one who walked there, "Is not some
　　hall wholly bright?"

"Yes," he said, "and they who find it, nevermore
　　can lose the light."

Then I thought, if there be only, anywhere, a single
　　choice,

Fit to bless me, could the blessing come from one
　　with sweeter voice?

And I whisper'd : "O, good spirit, tho' my endless
　　home this be,

Only breathe one word to aid me, I will ever serve
　　but thee."

XXXVIII.

He replied then ; "Are you kneeling ?—well for
　　those who kneel in youth.

Self-reliance tends to failure, even where it starts
    with truth.
Yet hope not for gleams of wisdom lighting all
    life holds in store.
Finite souls must journey onward, learning ever
    more and more.
Only signals can be given ; look to these ; and, by
    and by,
Through the pure white air beyond you grander
    views will greet the eye."

XXXIX.

As he spoke, one near the altar, at a hint of his
    desire,
Brought a ring, wherein, like gems, were sparks
    that held the altar's fire.
On my finger then he placed it, saying : " All things
    are your own.
Choose the hall that seems the brightest ; choose,
    as all men must—alone."
Near me then the hall of wealth was, which I
    enter'd ; and behold,
Found it, to its utmost limit, shining bright as
    brightest gold.
And the pictures far within it, that before had
    seem'd so sad,
In the darkness had deceived me : they were now
    in beauty clad.

And the floods that I had fear'd so, flow'd around
    the temple-side,
Weird and grand ; and grand, across them, rose a
    land beyond their tide.
And the other halls ?—their story was the same.—
    Ah me ! how strange !—
How the lights we carry with us make the scenes
    about us change !

XL.

After this, when turning backward toward the cen-
    tral dome once more,
Forms of glory gather'd round me, thousands there
    not seen before.
Bright they were to indistinctness, and bright robes
    they brought for me,
Where within the folds were jewels it might blind a
    man to see.
And my whole soul felt the nearness of the love
    these friends confess'd,
Where no end of welcome check'd the full com-
    munion of the blest.
And, anon, I found me joining in their joy that
    watch'd the sight
Seen in stars where souls in bondage sought for
    freedom, love, and light.
Then, as one star rose, there rose this chant as rare
    in harmony

As if all the souls that sang, had melted into
   melody.

XLI.

See the world that whirls forever,
Round and round and weary never,
Leaving sinning, glory winning
   Through its ever brightening way.
Oh, in worth the deeds of duty
Rival all the claims of beauty.
Onward world, with steadfast spinning,
   Learn to turn a perfect day.
   Work cannot go wrong for aye.
   Woes but roll to roll away.

World of faith, the years are dying
In which clouds about thee lying
Robe a wondrous waste of sighing,
   Empty throes of vain unrest.
Life, if right, whatever bearing,
Still for true success preparing,
Must outwit the wrong's ensnaring.
   Faith will find that faith is blest ;
   Wrestle through its prayer for rest ;
   Dwell with good a constant guest.

World of hope, the stars are o'er thee.
Dawn is waiting just before thee.
Heaven's own light, thy life invoking,
   Every promise bright reveals.
Fast shall rays that days are sending
Heaven and earth in one be blending ;

Showing what the storm's dark cloaking,
　Tho' with rainbow belt, conceals.
　Night, too, blesses him who feels
　'T is a star in which he kneels.

World of love, the heavens above thee
Hold the clouds, and can but love thee.
Though in spring the storm sweep o'er thee,
　April's rain is autumn's gain.
Rock'd by wind and nursed by shower
Life will grow to leaf and flower ;
Every harvesting before thee,
　Shows the vintage is but rain
　Turn'd to wine the grapes obtain
　From the floods that fill the plain.

Onward world, desponding never,
Round and round, yet onward ever,
On where sense and sorrow sever,
　Onward move thy mission through.
Wisest deeds thy safety highten.
Wisest words thy thoughts enlighten.
Wisest views thy visions brighten.
　Holy wings thy way pursue.
　Heavenly outlines loom in view.
　Bliss is dawning down the blue.

XLII.

Round and round me rose the chorus, like a flood
　to cleanse all space.
Far on high its waves would lift me; down as far
　would fall apace.

Then, as all at once above me, bright and clear,
      appear'd the sky,
Wide awake, my eyes, in opening, found those dear
      delusions fly.
Gone they were with sleep and dreaming, and the
      star-gemmed canopy
Night had borne beyond the west ; and sworn to
      ceaseless constancy,
Day had come, his fair suite with him, all their
      armor burnish'd bright,
Searching, as they search forever, for the flying
      forms of night.
"Dawn has routed all my dreaming !" sigh'd I, as
      in dew and rill,
All the van of sunbeams early shot reflections from
      the hill.
"Yes I only dream'd." I sigh'd; and then I roused
      myself to find
Where had fled the phantom feet that left such
      sunny tracks behind.

XLIII.

All had vanish'd ; but, long after, left like footprints
      where they pass'd,
Lo, I found within my spirit this impression, there
      to last ;—
That for him who hears anon by day or night the
      spirit's call,

Naught is fitting save to be and do and speak the
    truth to all.

Let the world refuse to heed it,—he at least is not
    to blame ;

For the truth still rules his action, and the heavens
    direct his aim.

Let the world with force oppose him,—he may lead
    a worthy life ;

And his words may prove prophetic, tho' his works
    insure him strife.

Let him make mistakes in methods,—who can learn
    these till he tries ?

And the world that brings him failure, makes him
    fail to make him wise.

He alone can hope to prosper, who has learned to
    use the light,

Ray by ray, that shows the spirit, step by step, the
    way of right ;—

Only he, who, when his dreaming lures him toward
    ideals rare,

Wakes to gird and venture on, to be, to do, at least
    to dare.

OTE SECOND.

———

The reader paused and said :
    " The daylight fades,
And many times must fade,
    before I close
My work here for the poet whom we mourn.
Enough for one day that our souls have felt
The flood of fresh suggestions coursing down
From this first poem as their fountain-head.—
But come to-morrow near the sunset-hour."

So on the morrow near the sunset-hour
The people gather'd ; and the soldier read
The title " Daring."   " Here again," he said,
" The poet's fancy is a veil for facts,
Through which, not dimly, those who knew him best
May trace an early, rash attempt of his
To match his dreams of doing good by deeds.
What gave these deeds direction, was the aim,
Which, just as he emerged from boyhood, stirr'd
Kind men through all the region where he dwelt

To face the persecution sure to come,
And band together that their words and deeds
Might free the friendless, kidnapp'd Afric slaves,
To whom our nation, ruled by selfish greed,
Denied all rights of body or of soul.
In those dark times of fierce dispute, our youth—
Scarce better than a slave himself—infused
With admiration for these workers, vow'd
To aid, or fit himself to aid their work.
And, while to deeds his nature's currents rush'd,
As rills to streams, all, soon, that strove to check
But swell'd their tide. His pent-up powers burst
        forth,
And swept all patience out of him : less wild
Had been a war-steed, stirr'd by blasts that bid
To onset.   Do you ask with what result ?
Hear then this poem.   Too impetuous
And stormy was the temper of the youth ;
And blustering weather blew about their ears
Who cross'd his pathway, like November winds
That shake the mad red leaves, turn pale the
        flowers,
But leave the vales as barren as a waste.
His deeds wrought little.   He intended well ;
But good intentions, if they be not mail'd
In prudence and well train'd in self-control,
Are no more fitted to contend with wrong
Than half-stripp'd serfs with steel-clad veterans."

ARING.

I.

Above vague moon-lit forms of
mount and vale
There lies the haze-wrought
mantle of the night.
The winds are hush'd ; the clouds are still and
pale ;
The stars like drowsy eyes just wink their light.
Earth sleeps, except where on the seashore white
The tumbled waves are waked by distant gales,
Or where the calls of owls and nighthawks fright
The startled slumberer of the silent dales
With sounds they never make till night their plun-
dering veils.

II.

But hark ! amid the stillness now a tread
Disturbs the dews that tremble in the grass.
What form impell'd by what pursuing dread,
So speeds across this dark and drear morass ?—
A youth it is, whose eager mien, alas,

Bespeaks an aim that seems beyond his years.
 Anon, where o'er a hill his path will pass,
He gazes backward ; then, tho' naught appears,
Anon renews his haste, and with it, too, his fears.

III.

He flies from home ; nor first nor last is he
 To leave his friends for midnight's chill embrace ;
Nor first nor last is he, whom dawn shall see
 A wanderer cheer'd by no familiar face.
 Ah, homes forsaken thus, can aught displace,
In after years, the sadness that ye wear
 For mourners who the childhood-love retrace
Of those thus lost whose youth appear'd so fair,
Ere storms had swept away hope's buds that blos-
  som'd there ?

IV.

The rose that with the fondest care we tend,
 May grace a bush whose briers but cause distress,
And those on whom we most of love expend
 Give sorrow in return for our caress ;
 Yet need we not despair of their success ;
For oft, where others would move on no more,
 Those who in youth these headstrong wills pos-
  sess,

Their way so push that every check, in store
To stop the weak, becomes for them an opening
　　　door.

V.

But think not headstrong aims alone impell'd
　　The course of him now borne along this plain.
Against harsh treatment had his will rebell'd ;
　　And so he thought that he but strove to gain
　　His rights, long sought through other means in
　　　vain.
And yet what were these rights, he hardly knew.
　　He merely felt an impulse to attain
A life where each could freely seek the true,
And in the world do all the good a man should
　　do.

VI.

Times were, when, arguing his projected schemes,
　　He might have told you, souls had need of light;
He might have told you of desires and dreams,
　　All vague enough to make you deem them right,
　　Who strove to hold in check his ardor's might.
But heaven of late had sent what roused his thought
　　And routed vagueness as the day the night,
And oft would show, with endless blessings fraught,
A brightest goal and paths through which it might
　　be sought.

VII.

That dawn which brings the light of coming years
　　Had blest his native land with liberty ;
And through its Northern borders all were peers ;
　　But, southward, one race held supremacy,
　　And one, as yet, was held in slavery.
A wrong was this that many more wrongs brought;
　　For man is man, whate'er his ancestry ;
And in a land where speech is free as thought
Whoe'er do wrong, erelong, will find their ruin
　　　wrought.

VIII.

So in this land, a call to free the slave
　　Had sprung to some few lips, and fill'd the air.
And when our youth had heard the call, it gave
　　Direction to his hopes enlisted there.
　　And now his life seem'd pressing on to share
The fate of those—as yet despised and curst—
　　Brave souls who in dark times had turn'd them
　　　where
The light of coming good on earth should burst ;
Nor knew 't would gild themselves with all its
　　　glory first.

IX.

The youth, scarce heeding where he was or went,
　　Moved wildly on as thoughts that moved his will;
As if, within the present strength he spent,

Unfolding wings his earth-wrapt soul did thrill.
　At last, he paused upon a higher hill ;
And, looking downward through a moon-lit dell,
　Like one entranced, he stood a moment still ;
And then his welling feelings broke their spell,
And utter'd forth this fond and passionate farewell:

X.

"You hills, and vales, and streams, and woods, and
　　lawns,
　You never, never, never seem'd so dear.
What beauty shall be yours when morning dawns !
　But I who love you so shall not be here.
　Yet still the hopes, if I be far or near,
Which you alone were told, shall stay with me.
　Would man had lent to them a willing ear !
Ah, then, how fill'd with joy my life might be,
For I had had no need of flying to be free."—

XI.

You ask me now, why I, who write here, seek
　My mirror for my face that gazes down ?—
This face was his, who, spurr'd by fancy's freak,
　O'erleapt the limits of his native town.
　But his eyes then were fields for fancy's clown,
Not homes like these wherein sad memories rest ;
　Nor smiles were his, all check'd by Fortune's
　　frown ;

Nor did white locks about his brow attest
How rays of ghost-land's light had touch'd its com-
    ing guest.

XII.

A few short years, how soon their sun and storm
    And shifting seasons change one's face and frame;
And what one vaguely deems himself, transform
    To that which friend and foe alike disclaim:
      How calm the heart, which once those calls to
      fame
Thrill'd through like beatings of a signal drum!
    Those throbs, by turns, of hope and fear, how
      tame!—
Familiar ticks of life's old pendulum,
Wound up to vibrate on till hope and fear are dumb.

XIII.

A few short leagues, and, calm and sluggish grown,
    The fickle brook has left the mountain steep;
And now, no more in boisterous torrents thrown,
    Through fertile fields, flows noiseless, broad, and
      deep,
    Alive with sails and lined with those who reap.
So may our lives, altho' no more allied
    To narrow rock-bound brooks that wildly leap,
Send forth an influence no less grand and wide,
Because a gentler motion moves its growing tide.

XIV.

The boy—to speak of him and term him " I,"
  Would break the spells of strangeness, as I write,
Which make these life-scenes that behind me lie
   So sacred that their shadows all seem slight,
   Or only render dark forms near them bright,—
The boy pass'd on; and, just as dawn began
   Erasing all the stars with lines of light,
Along the road before him he could scan
A house, and barn, and fence, on which there lean'd
    a man.

XV.

Brought near the man, he finds his frame is bent,
  As if by long devotion to his lands ;
His arms are brown with heat by sunlight sent
   To turn red-ripe the fruit served by his hands.
   His chest is broad, and gratefully expands
To feel the generous air his health renew,—
   A master of his house and farm he stands,
Who, fearing no man, dares to all be true,
With open eyes and lips that let the soul speak
      through.

XVI.

He saw the youth ; and said, the while there flew
  From off his questioning lips a whistled lay :
" You had an early start, to bring you through

A marsh like that by this time in the day.
And those who tramp for hours across it, say
They find no dwelling, let them try their best.
And you were coming east,—eh?—toward the
bay?
So could not wait till sunrise reach'd the west!—
And now—ay, sit you here—or in the house, and
rest.

XVII.

" 'Good farm,' you say?—why yes, we think it is.
No richer land in all the State, than here!—
Grows grain so fast, one wellnigh hears it whiz!—
The crops are somewhat changed about, this year;
But on the hill-side lot, beyond that steer,
Where now those buckwheat buds puff out like
leaven,
Last fall the corn—I swear I am sincere—
Grew stalks full ten feet high, instead of seven,
As if to beat the tree-tops in their race for heaven.

XVIII.

" 'T is just our breakfast-hour; but spare your
dimes:
To what we have—not much—we 'll welcome
you."
With this, both sought the house; and there, betimes,

The boy had given his genial host a view,
  With words that wellnigh let more secrets through,
Of all those aims that made his nature brave,—
  His wish for schooling, and intention, too,
To help to loose the fetters from the slave.
But thus his host would all the plans, he spoke of,
      waive :

XIX.

" Uncommon sense is nonsense, boy. Your schools
  Are good for some ; but are you sure their drill
Trains men for work ? Fact is, these thinking tools,
  Are hard to handle—have too much self-will.
    They need more meat, than mind.   Here, let me
      fill
Your plate up?—No?—Be dainty, I may vow
  You came from snobs, and may present my
      bill.
These ribs came off as fat and sleek a sow
As ever warm'd a litter—There, try that one now.

XX.

"' All men should learn ? '—not as you state it,
      boy ;
  All men should learn enough to make them work.
Too little schooling may a man annoy ;
  Too much may make him lazy as a Turk.—
    And ' all men should be free ? '—Ay, but no jerk

Can root out all the wrong in just a trice.
　　Wherever grain can ripen, tares must lurk
And grow till harvest come. 'T was Christ's ad-
　　　　vice :
Impatience cannot force the fruits of Paradise.

XXI.

" ' I have,' you think, ' no public spirit ? '—No ;
　　But private spirit, boy, which does less harm.
Last year, some city folk came here to show
　　How wise 't would be—and well their words
　　　　could charm—
　　To rip a rattling railway through my farm ;
Then cut it up in town-lots ; just as tho'
　　Against a pet lamb one should lift his arm,
And kill and quarter it, and take it so
To market, for the few dead coin it brought, you
　　　　know.

XXII.

" And so I told the strangers they must face
　　Men who would fight their plan for many a year;
Nor wish'd the farm and farmyard to give place
　　To park and palace they would bring us here.
　　Besides—old-fashion'd folk they knew were
　　　　queer—

We scarcely cared to pay for tripled rents
  With even doubled gains ; and had some fear
Our girls, whose gowns now half cocoon'd their
    sense,
Might burst to city-butterflies at our expense.

XXIII.

" Ay, far from pining after city-life,
  Where things moved not so slowly, as they said,
Our folk had found enough of stir and strife
  In this more quiet life that here we led.
  We might but watch the seasons as they sped ;
Yet some new task or sport gave each its leven ;
  And, whether suns or storms were overhead,
Compared with city-air, all stench and steven,
Although outside their world, our own seem'd
    nearer heaven.

XXIV.

" To this they said, as you yourself would say,
  ' I lack'd in public spirit.'   May be so ;
And yet our country folk all thought my way.
  'T was public, in that sense.   In their sense ?—no :
  My own wish did not publicly o'erflow
My neighbors' wishes.   Yet a spring may be
  A good spring that makes things around it grow;
Tho' not a grand spring ; no ; until, bank-free,
It makes a public swamp the whole way to the sea!

XXV.

" What, must you go so soon ?   Nay, nay, but rest.
　Brows always knit grow wrinkled in their prime.
You 'must go'?—then good-by, and stride your
　　　best.—
　But pardon one word more, my boy :—one time,
　When young, I, too, saw heights I thought sub-
　　　lime ;
And tried to drive toward them some older folk ;
　But, boy, 't is only young blood cares to climb.
Try it : you cannot drive, and may provoke
Old heads, too long ago grown steady to life's
　　　yoke."

XXVI.

At this, the youth pass'd out along the road,
　His eyes bent downward, gazing on the ground ;
Nor did he once look back, as on he strode ;
　Till, far away, a shaded place he found,
　And paused to rest upon a wayside mound.
Then bursting tears rain'd downward o'er his
　　　cheeks
　From clouds of grief in which his brain was
　　　bound.
"Ah, who could think," he cried, "that one, who
　　　seeks
No kindly aims, could smile so kindly when he
　　　speaks ?"

XXVII.

But where was youth, that in the scales had cast
　His hope and fear, and watch'd them balancing,
Who found not hope outweigh his fear, at last?
　And thus, erelong, from grief recovering,
　The boy grew sure that time would changes bring,
And other souls that would with his agree,
　This farmer even—'t would be no strange thing—
Might wish perhaps the self-same good as he;
But did not understand him; no, it could not be.

XXVIII.

More calmly then he walk'd; and when, at noon,
　The trees drew in their shade, as birds their wings,
He found beneath broad oaks a grateful boon,—
　Three fair-faced women dining near some springs.
　They bade him rest there from his wanderings,
And share their meal; then, baiting for his thought,
　Threw out so many flattering, gracious things,
That every secret to his lips it brought.
" Ah, here were souls," he felt, " who yearn'd for all
　　he sought."

XXIX.

" You left your home?"—they cried, " How grand a
　　flight!"
　" And for a fancy too?"—" Aha, you blush!"—
" Who might she be?　Had black eyes, eh?—or
　　light?—

Like this maid here ?"—"Not strange a lad
  should flush !—
Where could he elsewhere find fair fruit so
  lush ?"—
"And he shall rest with us, he shall !" one said ;—
  When, touch'd as by a snake, he sprang to brush
Her fingers from his neck, and free his head ;
Then, pelted well with laughter, from the three he
  fled.

XXX.

Escaped from them, his feet approach'd a town
  From which a railway stretch'd invitingly ;
And in its train he soon had sat him down.
  It moved, and filled his mind with ecstasy.
  The hum recall'd his favorite melody.
The trees wheel'd by like dancers in their flight ;
  And, as they whirl'd with mad rapidity,
Spell-bound, he slept and dream'd all wrought for
  right,
And made the world they wrought in, beautiful
  and bright.

XXXI.

Anon, awaking, he could hear the sound
  Of vying voices from a seat behind,
And saw two men there, as he turn'd him round.
  One seem'd all eyes of that swift glancing kind
  Which hint the culprit, whose too cautious mind

The secrets of his inner self would shield.
　　Low views of others and himself combined,
Had given this man distrust, not all conceal'd
　　In manners taught to stay what should not be
　　　　reveal'd.

XXXII.

Beside him sat another, all whose face
　　Bore marks of patience, train'd by years of care.
His glasses, lifted oft with easy grace,
　　Great coat, large pockets, and abundant hair
　　Marked him—"physician," one whose calm, wise
　　　　air
Can bid the raging fever sink to rest ;
　　And turn to smiles his patients' weary stare,
While children wonder at his bottle-chest,
And how a still pulse tells him just what pill is
　　　　best.

XXXIII.

By chance, the two men, as they sat, spoke now
　　Of one well known and honor'd through the
　　　　land,
To whom the lad had learn'd, long since, to bow
　　As his ideal of all things true and grand.
　　"Can you conceive how one like him should
　　　　band

With those," the first said, " who would free the
    slave ?
  No public man can ever hold in hand
His party's reins, till wise enough to waive
His own ideals for ends which all his party crave."

XXXIV.

The other said—to skip words harsh for rhyme:—
  " 'T was all quite true ; a ventricle should not
Congest an auricle : there was a time,
    Place, ad captandum vulgus: this was what,
    Hygien'd all influence: ne'er had he forgot
His diagnosis, Medicinæ D.,
    Not D. D.: some of these would tell a sot,
Half dead, the truth, and wholly kill him; he
Would lie to save a life—if thus his doctor's fee."

XXXV.

He paused; for while he spoke, the boy's wide eyes
  Confronted his there, like an opening soul;
Whereat the man increased their deep surprise
  By asking if his talk seem'd strange or droll.
  The lad first blush'd; then, gaining self-control,
Confess'd the wonder that his face had shown.
  He said: " He might not rightly judge the whole
That he had heard; but, if so, had to own
That he had deem'd it sad, more this than strange
    alone."

XXXVI.

The two men smiled, and, drawn to trust in them,
　　The boy was led with ardor to proclaim
His reverence for the man they would condemn,
　　In terms the two seem'd pleased to hear him
　　　　frame,
　　But, as he spoke full long, at last they came
To view his tribute like some long-drawn jest,
　　Not pointed till cut off.   He mark'd their aim,
And, flushing red, pour'd forth what well express'd
How madly hot the zeal was which he thus con-
　　　　fess'd.

XXXVII.

"Had not I seen," he cried, "enough to know
　　Your slight regard for me, without this test ?—
No need to laugh your mask off so, to show
　　What could, without the showing, have been
　　　　guess'd !
　　Yes, yes, I was a dupe, I own, to rest
Content to trust in you who dared to spurn
　　The views divine, with which such souls are
　　　　bless'd,
As, always looking up, forget to earn
Earth's praise, because of joy in heaven's to which
　　　　they turn."

XXXVIII.

His quivering lips could hold no further word ;
    Nor was there need : the two soon left the
        train.
Some further jest of theirs was all he heard ;
    And then was left alone to nurse his pain.
      These men knew not how their light thrusts
        would drain
The tears like life-blood from a soul so faint ;
    Nor thought how much of good is often slain
By small, sharp shafts of wit, without restraint
Shot forth in sport, and lodged where one hears no
        complaint.

XXXIX.

Our poor boy in his anguish thought of home—
    Friends, love, truth, slaves, and all things,—who
        can know
Round what the most our surging fancies foam
    When depths of feeling rise, and overflow,
    And swamp the reason in their floods of woe ?
Alas, one can but feel (while all sweep on,
    And, flitting through their mist-hung midnight,
        show
Grim ghosts of buried good with features wan)
Sensations too acute for thoughts to poise upon.

XL.

" I wonder if it be that yonder star
  Shines now on those I love," so mused he here:—
" Those dear old faces there !—how dim they are !
  And shall they nevermore my spirit cheer ?—
  Alas, how could I let, without a tear,
Mere empty-handed hope outweigh each claim
  Of friends though few, who made my whole life
      dear ?
And are they sad, those friends, that here I came ?
Or do they miss me not ? or, if so, but to blame ?

XLI.

" On every side, I see some stranger smile,
  And hear anon his ringing laughter bound.
I heed it, as within some chapel aisle
  One in his coffin seal'd might hear the sound
  Of his own burial hymn, when it had drown'd
His last faint cry of 'murder !'   He were blest
  To have those friends his final woe surround.
But who would mourn for me ? my soul's unrest
The very grave might shrink from, as a worrying
      guest.

XLII.

" I read a tale, once, of a spar that bore
  A ship-wreck'd sailor o'er a storm-swept sea,
Away from beacon-fires upon the shore

That rose and fell with waves that sought the lee.
　So here, some power, that will not let me be,
But bears away from earth my reeling brain,
　Seems drifting, far from love and life, with me ;
Yet ever fails to bring the final pain,
To snap each straining nerve, and burst each
　　swelling vein.

XLIII.

" But, far cold World, could not I show to those
　Who, pitying my desire, would venture near,
That they to friends yield most, whose whole love
　　flows
　But for the few ?—Yet, ah, could aught appear
　Attractive in my woe to draw them here ? "
Thus mused our boy, too young as yet to know
　How youth alone to human love is dear,
Before warm tides of life in veins that glow
Have lost the heat and hue of heaven from which
　　they flow.

XLIV.

The train had stopt ; and from the crowd there
　　came
　A youth who, after many a bow and smile
To friends who waved their hands, and call'd his
　　name,

With swaying gait had trod the car's long aisle,
  And sat in silence by our boy awhile.
Then, when the train dash'd through a tunnel near,
  "A blasted bore !" he cried. "A man could file
His ear-bone off and less confusion hear.—
But you—what ails you, man ?—There 's nothing
      here to fear.—

XLV.

"Ah, you are blue, you say ?—The skies are so—
  Not gloomy tho', till clouds their blueness hide !—
Then, why hide yours ?—Ay, doff the hide ! You
      know
  To flay a folly slays it.   If you sigh'd
  Your sigh out once, it to the winds would glide.
Naught like an airing would you oust a moan ! "
  And rattling on thus like a wag defied,
This new friend's talk had such an old friend's tone
That soon our boy, who heard it, felt no more alone.

XLVI.

Besides he had no secrets now to hide.
  So soon had shared them with his new-found
      friend ;
On whom his woes all seem'd, anon, to glide ;
  Would God our older cares found such an end !
  "With only that much in your purse to spend,

You started out," he heard, "to free the slave?—
    Your zeal, at least, was rich, and to commend ;
And freedom to yourself, at least, it gave :—
When free from him, who made a slave of you, the
        knave !

XLVII.

" Now hear you this : I serve a guardian too—
    A good one tho' :—he always pays my bills.
He runs a school—a school were well for you—
    And edits a gazette too, which he fills
    By talking at a scribe, whose whole frame thrills—
Not always tho', electrified with joy—
    At such discharges emptied through his quills.
This guardian, could he find one, would employ
A scribe in place of me he talks at now, my boy.

XLVIII.

" So go you south with me to Baltimore,
    And all you wish is there, and close at hand ;
Though, as for freeing slaves, you 'll think that o'er.
    In our right merry State of Maryland,
    No Yankees with their endless reprimand
Make men run mad with isms fit to wear
    Strait-jackets ! we their notions will not stand ;
Nor them, till sure they do not come to bear
Our own pet slave-girls off for their free love up
        there."

XLIX.

Our youth here frown'd; yet felt as one when streams
  Upon his waking eyes the morning light
That swings the golden goal-gates of his dreams.
  Where slaves were, could he live? and learn to
      write?—
  It distanced hope he had not dared excite.
And, as it thrills him, ah, how wrapt he bends
  To catch the stories told, too swift of flight,
About this coming home, and coming friends,
While round about each form his joy a halo sends!

L.

He hears about the school : " the queerest set
  Earth e'er had jarr'd together ; down from Pool—
The pest of tutors, but the students' pet,
  Who gain'd more discipline than all the school
  Through working hard to break through every
      rule—
Way down to Sims, whose jingling pocket-toys
  Outweigh'd his brain, a fop and fawning fool,
Too mean to join in other's jokes or joys,
The gull of all the girls, the butt of all the boys."

LI.

He heard too of its matron—" sharp and slim—
  Whose eyes were flintlocks, and whose hair of hue
To fit them when they flash'd ; and every limb

Stiff as a gunstock.   At each boy she flew,
　As if they all were cats that she would shoo
From her choice milk.—Ah, 't would be soured to
　　dwell
　With her hot temper!—Not a chum she knew,
For all her hints of news that she might tell,
Who found out all folks did, and not one doing
　　well."

LII.

The master too was pictur'd—whom our boy,
　When soon he join'd the school, soon dared to
　　show
His very heart of hearts.   E'en now his joy
　Went forth to meet a soul he yearn'd for so :—
　" A man who loved a 'yes,' but dared say 'no' ;
Strict, yet with smiles ; and gay yet earnest too.
　They said his life had weather'd many a blow ;
Still was it staunch : when gales of laughter blew,
To hold one's own with him was more than most
　　could do."

LIII.

Some men there are, whose moods, on fire for truth,
　Burn like that bush that Moses, one time, saw,
And never lose the fresh, fair charms of youth.
　Their souls from heaven itself their ardor draw,
　Nor burn according to an earthly law.

Their zeal, when kindled, kindles joy in those
  Whom worldly heat would but repel or awe ;
Nor ever warps the soul that near them goes,
But by its warmth allures to love that through it
     glows.

LIV.

A man like this it was, with judgment sound
  And kindly heart, to whom our boy was brought :
And whom, the while he toil'd for truth, he found
  Prepared to aid the groundwork of his thought.
    Hard strove the youth, aye feeling, while he
     wrought,
That but from deep foundations, grand in size,
  Life-structures rose like that for which he
     sought ;
And, tho' he oft would think this ne'er could rise,
Anon in visions fair he saw it fill the skies.

LV.

And now he lived for weeks in that bright land
  Where youth appears in endless dawn to dwell ;
Where skies of pearl o'er golden clouds expand ;
  And every breeze o'erflows with sweets that well
    From warbling birds, and burst each blossom's
     bell ;
Where every thorn that yet shall pave one's way
  Is hung with dews that coming joys foretell ;

And all the glitter of the opening day
Still blinds the eye to all that else might cause dis-
    may.

LVI.

He lived, with restless eyes and merry voice
    And yielding ways, whose yielding gave them
        grace,
One fond of friends, who yet sought oft by choice
    In soulless forms to find a spirit's face,
    In wordless tones a subtle thought to trace.
For this the youth would search through dust and
        noise
    Queer buildings, or the bustling populace ;
Or wend, where on the green some crowd enjoys
A firemen's fight to quench the ardor of the boys.

LVII.

Or, tired of sounds and scenes that thus one meets,
    His feet would turn, and wander down the hill
Along the shady sides of grand old streets :
    And reach the wharves, and watch the water still,
    Or ships about it sail'd with subtle skill,
Long charm'd he knew not why ; and there would
        stay
    Till sunset's fire his glowing heart would thrill,
Whose throbs within seem'd felt as far away
As bells' whose echoes broke like breakers round
        the bay.

LVIII.

Again, desires that spurr'd his eager mind
    Would dash it through the lines of some chance
        book,
Much thought to seize, and much to leave behind.
    Alas, how many truths did he o'erlook !
    How many rich-robed lies for guides he took !
How dazed grew hope, that follow'd in the track
    Of forms that vanished !   Conscience, how it
        shook,
Charged by each innuendo's base attack,
Smooth-tongued as knaves are when they stab be-
        hind one's back !

LIX.

But books brought good with bad.   At last, he
    learn'd
    How faith reacts on doubt ; if truth be sought,
How most for those who most have ask'd and
    yearn'd
    Ring echoes from the boundary walls of thought.
    But deem not moods nor books were all that
        taught
His growing nature.   There were friends to read,
    With whom he banter'd, argued, pleaded, fought;
But soon forgot the passion he had freed,
Half doubting if the strife had been in dream or
    deed.

LX.

But, more than all, the woes of slavery
　　Impell'd him on, as often wrong as right,
To plan and work for all men's liberty;
　　And while he longed to champion this fight,
　　His life appear'd a tourney, he a knight.
A young Don Quixote, most on guard to dare,
　　He harm'd more good, through zeal in need of
　　　　light,
Than any wrong his efforts could impair;
And fill'd with dust the way just where all needed
　　　　air.

LXI.

For, then and there, what was it save a crime,
　　To aim one blow at what, as all men knew,
Upheld the social structures of the time?—
　　A crime against both wealth and custom too?
　　And where all Northerners waked suspicions,
　　　　who
But gazed upon the slave with pitying eyes;
　　As if men thought these eyes were heavens of
　　　　blue
To lure the slave to cloudless, clear, free skies,
How could this youth escape, who had not yet grown
　　　　wise?

LXII.

He could not.　And, on one sweet eve, when all
　　His earth-germ'd thought had bloom'd in dreams
　　　　most bright,
He woke to watch strange shadows cross the wall;
　　And, glancing up, beheld the welcome sight
　　Of two who oft had praised him for the might
With which his ardor had assail'd the wrong.
　　But now, alas, he heard them both make light
Of all they once had praised; and lay there long,
Until his love grew faint, which he had thought so
　　　　strong.

LXIII.

For who that loves can think a human heart
　　Can ever lightly lay its love aside?—
The spirit's life, whose gentle thrills impart
　　Each separate ripple of the power supplied
　　For every act, can aught its presence hide?—
Ah, sooner might the heaving sea attest
　　Its life, without the movement of the tide;
And sooner might the sunlight sink to rest,
Nor trail the sunset hues adown the glowing west.

LXIV.

The words he heard, erelong, were, "Did you know
　　The boy was off again to see the slaves?"—
"Aha, found Venus a brunette, I trow!"—

"Nay, worse than that!—A lip, like his, that braves
 Our cuffs by cursing slavery, also raves
Of it to them. I'll track him; and do you;
 And if we find it so, then nothing saves
This bird, that fouls our nest for which he flew,
But flying home again, with tar and feathers too."

     LXV.

"'My friend,' you thought him?—Ah, some friends we use
 Like opiates, when our spirits are alone,
And would be lonely, could not these amuse"—
 "And make us dream," chimed in the other's tone,
 "Of things that elsewise hardly would be known!—
A dream like Joseph's, of the stars to fall
 With all created things about the throne
Of one, whose dream has proved the spirit's call,
And who, some day, shall rule in Egypt o'er us all."

     LXVI.

Our youth knew love was no love, that loved not
 What made his life worth living. So he cried:
"Rare friends, behind one's back! had you forgot
 Your Joseph lived his dreams before he died?

And I may mine.   A blockhead may take pride
In never dreaming.   Blocks are n't made for it,—
   Live not in clouds.   Yet clouds not often glide
O'er barren soil ; nor rich dreams often flit
O'er minds too poor to yield the deed such dreams
         will fit."

LXVII.

Alas, the youth—how vain an egotist
   He seem'd indeed, to trump his own claim so !
And yet, when sworn to enter honor's list,
   Of which his fellows could or would not know,
   His frank soul merely thought the truth to show,
But he had stopt at words ; and earth, that yells
   To cheer the gold-laced swaggerers, who but go
Unwhipt before their trump to onset swells,
Will stand no words in protest—better cap-and-
         bells !

LXVIII.

The youth talk'd raving on, till, glancing up,
   His favorite teacher's coming he espied.
Then soon the froth that foam'd o'er reason's cup,
   Dissolv'd in timid tears, flow'd down the side.
   " Alas, and could I help myself ? " he cried ;
" They came and roused me rudely from my
         dreams ;
   And proved pretended friends, who could deride

And drive me hence for having—not low schemes,
But aims all just and right, no matter how it
    seems."

LXIX.

"My boy," the teacher said, "our nearest friends,
    In judging us, our works, not wishes, take,—
Works oft as far from what the soul intends
    As dreamland from the life to which we wake.
    Full oft our traits that temper it may make
Impure the coloring of our purest aim.
    So need we caution, and for truth's own sake ;
Lest those who watch love's fire within us flame
Shall doubt if it from love or something baser
    came.

LXX.

"Remember Him, that once men sacrificed,
    But now rules over souls in every land.
The world had long His gentle spirit prized,
    Ere it had come to heed His each command.
    Remember Moses :—with his mission grand,
His meekness was the trait his race knew best ;
    Nor can our restless world ere understand
How one can lead it toward a promised rest
Whose own soul has not yet this promis'd boon
    possess'd.

LXXI.

" A seer should know that truth, like morn, comes on
   By slow degrees, enlightening every sight ;
And, tho' he wake the world it dawns upon,
   His faith should wait till souls can see the light.
   'T is he that waves his own torch in the night
Who feels that he must force on men its glare ;
   And, though, ere dawn, it seem the one thing
       bright,
If taken for the sun, it leads men where
Their leader's oil burns out, and they themselves
      despair.

LXXII.

" So, friend," he went on, " you and I and all,
   If passion suddenly o'erflood our will,
Should just as quickly our quick words recall.
   Thus love may seem our life's controller still.
   Bear this in mind, too :—ere above earth's ill
Heaven's light of freedom dawns on all mankind,
   You scarce can lift the sun by human skill ;
Nor toward one mount it gilds draw heart or mind
By lips or lives through which no love can be
     divined."

LXXIII.

Some more he said ; then left our boy alone.
   'T was well : no voice could now recall the dart

That, tho' without intention, had been thrown,
  To wound the youth within his inmost heart.
Why should he mask his aims, he ask'd, in art?
  "Nay, nay; God knew that he would rather die
  Than live a life from all life's worth apart."
He sought once more his bed, awake to lie,
Or sadly swoon to sleep, as fearful dreams went by.

LXXIV.

And then he woke, half-crazed. There may be souls
  Can lose, and not lose all things else beside,
What seem to be life's only worthy goals.
  But he knew not enough yet to confide
  In good unseen. He thought how he had tried
To seek the right, and caused his friends but pain,
  And done what now he saw he could not hide,
And what must force him from them. Ah! 't was
      plain,
He could no longer there beneath their roof re-
      main.

LXXV.

And so he rose and left it, tho' the night
  Already shook beneath the threatening tread
That brought, anon, a storm. Oh, fearful sight,—
  That black car of the thunderer overhead!
  Those fierce bolts flashing down their track of
      red,

And crashing on amid the shatter'd sleet !
　　And one broad elm, like Cæsar, stabb'd and
　　　　dead,
Flung up its robes and tumbled at his feet,
While hoarse winds howl'd about, and made his woe
　　　　complete.

LXXVI.

But not once turn'd he back, until the bay,
　　The while a deafening peal of thunder came,
Flash'd forth before him, his quick feet to stay.
　　But, ere it check'd them, lo, the lightning's flame
　　Lit up, out o'er the deep, a human frame,
Whose outstretch'd arm sank down beneath a
　　　　wave.
　　At this, forgetful of each other aim,
The youth plung'd through the deep—drew forth a
　　　　slave—
Who curst him for the favor—had he sought a
　　　　grave ?

LXXVII.

Nay, freedom !　Dragg'd on shore, a shot, well
　　　　aim'd,
　　Brought down the slave, whose piercing shrieks
　　　　cut through
The fitful surgings of the storm, and maim'd
　　The sever'd thunder.　Lamps then gleam'd in
　　　　view,

And swift police, who spied but to pursue
Our youth, whose flight, they felt, proved guilt and
      fear.
   Then oh, how fast through lawn and lane he
      flew,
Till all were still again, when, drench'd and drear,
He hid beneath a shed to wait till dawn drew near!

LXXVIII.

At last, it came. Above his crimson couch,
   The sun drew back the curtains of the east;
While pale-grown shades began in vales to crouch,
   Or, hurrying westward, leave the world releast
   From spells that long had silenced man and beast.
Then winds, arising, shook the rustling trees,
   As if they said, "'T is time your rest had ceast";
And birds that sang soar'd high, as if to seize
The last of flickering stars, blown out by morning's
      breeze.

LXXIX.

Soon o'er the hills ascends the sun's bright crown;
   And, richly robed, as welcoming thus their king,
The dew-deck'd groves and bushes bend low down
   Bright limbs o'erladen with rare gems they
      bring,—
   Rare gifts, borne all too soon, on sunny wing,
Toward clouds that in the blue dome o'er them
      blaze.

Then sounds of labor join with bells that ring ;
And one more dawn has heard the prayer and praise
Of those who past it see the day of all the days.

LXXX.

They see a day, where heaven's bright grain of life
    Sprouts in the last black death-urn of the night,
And buds of peace burst through the thorns of
    strife,
    And souls awake to praise enduring light.
    Ah, even now, they see, with earthly sight,
That men may track the rain-storm by the rose,
    And make the wake of war the way of right,
And learn, as each fresh breath of morning blows,
How sweet and fair a life beneath the darkness
    grows.

LXXXI.

So might our youth have hail'd this morn ; but he,
    For whom the soft winds whisper'd in their round,
For whom the brisk birds chirpt their calls of glee,
    For whom the bright sun up the heavens wound,
    And all the world of work awoke to sound,
While men moved gladly and the children leapt,—
    He, dead to hope and happiness profound,
His dreams begun, while all his heavens had wept,—
Upon the chill, damp ground, through all the dawn
    had slept.

NOTE THIRD.

The people waited till another
    day,
Then met their genial soldier-
    friend again.
"We found our poet all alert for deeds,"
He said, ere reading, " and he fail'd in these.
We now shall find him, like a storm-check'd bark,
Put back to port and waiting.

            " Many weeks,
As his own lips have told me, from the night,
When he forsook that Southern teacher's home,
He drifted like a waif from town to town,
Now toiling in the fields ; now seeking work
From door to door of shop or factory.
Anon, as news-boy, then as printer's boy,
Almost a slave by day, a thief by night,
He taught himself to print, and gain'd a time
Of leisure, when he read, and thought, and wrote.
But still for years he lived in misery,

Half starving both in body and in soul.
And doubt rose round his growing powers of
      thought,
Like vapors reeking from the refuse heap'd
On undevelop'd germs in early June.
Perchance his manhood's fruit was ripening then,
For always would he say, and always, too,
While saying, have that tremor in his voice
Which seems to make the soul's pulse audible,
That even in those times of woe to him,—
E'en through his daring, since he meant it well,—
The soul succeeded though his projects failed.
He lost his outward end, indeed, but gain'd
An inward end that, for his youthful years,
Had far more value.   But I weary you.
Who hears his words may judge them for himself."

OUBTING.

I.

Fate gave me feelings all my
own,
And dreams that others had not
known,
And forced me thus to dwell alone ;
And sad, where no one else cared aught
For what I was or wish'd, I wrought
These rhymes to bear and share my thought.

II.

All day, as printer's drudge, I earn
My bed and board, the while I turn
To moulds of type the thoughts that burn
In other minds ; but in my own
What thoughts may burn can turn alone
To ashes that away are thrown.
At night, when like the printed sheet,
I bear them up and down the street,

None there my records care to greet.
So, past where street-lamps light the walls,
At last, through dark and mouldering halls
My form a tumbling stairway crawls ;
It crawls, until I reach on high
My attic-home, in which I try,
Till no more sounds go passing by,
And others' lamps no longer burn,
To gain the skill for which I yearn,
With so much still to do and learn.
I strive to force my sweating brain
To grow me truth, but till in vain
A soil that heaven sends only rain.
What grows, I long to sow again ;
But who can tell me how or when
One gives his best to grateful men ?

III.

I like to think this frame of mine
Contains a spark of life divine,
Enkindled there with some design.
I oft have thought, there ought to be
Some light to glow and flow from me,
And show what all men long to see.
And oft I deem, the while I find
Some men are slaves whom others bind,
That my light now might bless my kind,

Would men but look where I can see
How all could thrive, if all were free.
But much I fear that few can lead
The world to wiser wish or deed,
Because the world so few will heed.
The men who scan us, as a class,
Turn always toward themselves, alas,
Their magnifier's largest glass ;
And small and far seem all they pass.
There may be some ordaining grace
That priest and prince of every race
Have sought through mystic lines to trace ;
A something back of sword and gown,
Power apostolic, handed down :
There are no wise men to the clown :
The royal mind in tent or town
To loyal genius owes its crown.

IV.

Why is it, all men hate and hound
And hunt me down, if by a sound
I hint the truth my soul has found ?
I changed my city : 't was no use ;
E'en here, this devil's cur, abuse,
Is ever barking at my heel,
Provoking sighs I should conceal,
And making all my reason reel.

To-day, why could I not have stood
The test of inward hardihood,
Content to know my aims were good ?
Why did I meet the man I hate ?
Why did he stand there with his mate,
Smirk at me, and commiserate,
And anger me ?—Were anger wise,
The face that would its force disguise
Would not so blush to feel it rise.

v.

More sweet than heavenly harps are hearts,
When love her low throb in them starts ;
More sweet than sweetest songs, when sung,
Are harmonies of deed and tongue
Where two together think as one.
Alas, and what have my moods done
To part me so from all my brothers ?—
Yet how can I accord with others,
When all the strings I play, though nerves
That every feeblest feeling serves
To fill with thrills, oft bear a strain
Of stretching fibres wrench'd with pain
That wellnigh snaps them all in twain,
Ere fitly strung to sound aright
Some highest pitch of scorn or spite ?
No wonder, gentle souls will say,

The while they softly shrink away,
And learn to shun me, day by day,
"Far better than a friend so wild,
His rival, wrong, perchance, but mild."

VI.

Had I, who know that slavery
Fits not God's heirs of liberty,—
Had I but more self-confidence,
The men who give me such offence
Might yield my thought more reverence.
When foes are sworn to cow their zeal,
Those who would do good work should feel
That none can rightly make right kneel.
Some men have manners dignified
By nature ; others learn to stride ;
But others yet, with no less pride,
Can never show what will not screen
And keep their inner worth unseen.
The brute that shakes at these his mane,
Lets fly his hoof, nor minds their pain,
If only whipp'd from his disdain
And broken once, might mind the rein.

VII.

O could some Godlike soul look through
My outward life, like God, and view

And judge my soul, with judgment true,
By what I am, not what I do ;
By what I am, not where I stand,
Which souls of low, short sight demand
Before they dare give bow or hand !
Mean, cowardly souls, whose natures feel
That they were born to cringe and kneel,
And heed like dogs a master's heel,—
They show a due respect alone
For those who fill, if not a throne,
At least a station o'er their own.
So must one's worth that these despise
Press on and up, until it rise
And reach a place that all will prize.
Awake, my soul, and strain each power
That hints of effort.   Let the hour
Of sleep, that was, watch armor-clad ;
Calm seem a pest ; contentment mad ;
And slander'd patience onward press
Till steadfast force achieve success.
Come wounds ! come jeers ! where were they miss'd
By one who sought the noblest list ?
Zeal ne'er did sigh, but some drone hiss'd,
" Be dunce with me, or egotist."
Wise world, that you our due begrudge us
You yet, years hence, may understand.
If we work out the good, so judge us ;
If ill. time then to use your brand !

VIII.

How sad, when thoughts, proud once to roam,
Abused and bruised, came mourning home
With their young ardor overthrown,
How sad is life that lives alone !
There was a time, when, brave and bare,
The little hands, all soft and spare,
Claspt all, and hoped that love was there ;
Not gloved in fear, claspt every thing,
With every rose to grasp a sting ;
Then dropt it, sad and suffering.
And what are now those thoughts about ?
Oh, they have turn'd from deed to doubt :
They work within, if not without.
Oh, they have turn'd from all the pain
That came from earth they served in vain,
To that still world within the brain,
Where fancy forms its mead and main.
There many a fairest vision, sought
In clearer light than sunlight brought,
Is mirror'd in the wells of thought.
But oh, how oft must one surmise,
While o'er the soul's wild sea of sighs
Imagination's glories rise,
That, as at sunset, every form
Derives its best from cloud and storm !
Oft fancy works but to appease
A restlessness that shows disease,

A fever that the brain would ease.
Oft crimson floods of thought impart
Their brilliant hues to speech and art,
When thus a pierced and bleeding heart
Is drain'd in drawing forth a dart.

IX.

They call me morbid—if they mean
I hate the wrong, wherever seen;
And make supreme my own ideal;
And grieve to find it not made real;
I hail the term.   No titles go
From earth to bias heaven, I trow.
Men's normal moods may sink and swell
At one with tides that drift to hell.
E'en what the world calls holiness,
Which ardent youth can ne'er possess,
Is oft—so white and colorless—
The ashes where heaven's fires are spent,
Calm, cold, accurs'd, and yet content.

X.

This home of mine is in a place
Where dwell alone the poor and base,
And I partake of their disgrace.
But, even here, some good I find
Awaits a watchful patient mind.

For, where our wants are numerous,
And fashion's robes are stripp'd from us,
We learn of human nature thus.
On earth, 't is but "the few" can find
The gold that gilds the sordid mind
And common dross of all mankind.
And here "the many" live, and so,
Unable to afford the show,
In nature's naked truth must go.
At first, I shrank from life so mean ;
And oft would blush when I had seen
How man could boast, yet be unclean ;
But, oh, I feel, as weeks wear on,
Vice, oft unveil'd, appears not wan,
And stings of sin wear blunt anon :
One learns to know with little fear
How seldom love and life appear
Full wedded in this lower sphere.

XI.

At times, my door shakes to and fro,
And voices call, until I go
To ask within some drunken foe—
A foe, though in his hand he bears
A draft that, if I quaff, he swears
Shall drown beneath it all my cares.
At times, there comes a softer voice

That vows to make my veins rejoice :—
Ah, they know not his better choice,
Who with ideals for his friends
Finds, in the light toward which he wends,
What all the lure of wrong transcends.

XII.

At times, when wrapt in sleep profound,
Loud cries and crashing sound around.
Bewilder'd then from bed I bound,
Too wise to speak, yet wild to call,
I wander out, explore the hall,
Dodge all I meet, yet dare them all.
A bird, whose wings had glanc'd a dart,
Felt not more flutterings at the heart.
I linger, till in fear I start,
Lest, if my cup of fear I fill,
Insanity, the glee of ill,
Shall rave upon the throne of will.
Then, when I turn from all before,
Swift flies from under me the floor,
And swift with bolts I bar my door,
As if some fiend behind me ran
To scathe the spirit and the man.

XIII.

Calm sleep to weary limbs were sweet :
Who cannot sleep, may scan the street,

And search for watchmen in their beat —
Slow, dusky forms with echoing feet.
I stretch far out : I gaze far round :
'T is weird to hear no human sound,
And be so high above the ground.
I fancy I am thrown adown,
Think how the news will stir the town :—
" A youth was found stone dead, they say " ;
" Ah, yes, I heard ; good-day, good-day."
Ho, ho ! what now ?—why did I start
And slam, with such a beating heart,
The sash, yet leave the blinds apart ?
This mirror mocks my wild grimace !—
Men differ slightly in the face :
And how might mine a madman grace ?

XIV.

How near proud reason's realm may be
That fierce Charybdis-craving sea,
That drags toward madness you and me !
We wander toward its misty strand :
There swells the wave ; here stops the land.
How bright the sea ! how dull the sand!
" Oh Guardian Sense," we cry " away ! "
We wade the surf ; we feel the spray ;
We leap !—and God prolongs our day.
Ah, Holy Wisdom, if Thou be
The Logos from the Sacred Three,

Who all men's good and ill decree ;
And if the wise above us dwell,
The unwise then—but who can tell ?—
May madness be the mood of hell,
Where God, who ruleth, ruleth well ?
If it be true that death translates
To other spheres the self-same traits
Our souls acquire in earthly states ;
If it be true that after death
The heat of some accursèd breath
Can into fever'd action fan
All lusts that once inflamed the man,
Till life grow one intense desire,
A burning in a quenchless fire,
A worm that gnaws and cannot die,
Since worldly things no more supply
What worldly wishes gratify,
And flesh and blood no more remain
To make a fleshly craving sane ;—
If then the passions, anger'd sore
Because indulged, as once, no more,
Rise up, and rave, till reason swerve,
And lose command of every nerve,—
What state can anarchy preserve ?
What state ?—O Christ, I see them now—
Those teeth that gnash !—and see why thou,
To save our souls from future strife,
Didst cast out devils in this life.

XV.

Far off, I hear the midnight bell,
And watchman's cry, and, like a knell,
My conscience calls : " For heaven or hell,
One day toward death, and is all well ?"
Like wrecks that up and down are toss'd,
Till plunged beneath the waves and lost,
How aimlessly, through blame and praise,
Through depths of nights and heights of days,
We men are swept along our ways !
But have our lives no nobler state
Than drifting on with tides of fate ?—
No power to stem them, while they feel
The filling sail, the whirling wheel,
The steadfast helm that guides the keel ?
Tho' oft our course be turn'd about
By wind and wave of hope and doubt,
Come all our motives from without ?
Does not some impulse oft begin
With mind's propelling power within ?
Is not the soul, whose low depths thrill,
An offspring of perfection still ;
And Godlike by creative will ?
And yields not heaven some gleam to thought,
Or hope by spirit-whispers brought,
To guide toward all our souls have sought ?
Ay, ay ; do not clear skies reveal,

At times, to cheer our wavering zeal,
Bright realms that mists no more conceal ?

XVI.

I know how deep and dark the vale
Where some, fair fortune's heights to scale,
Equipp'd with sword and shield and mail,
Have found the power to wound the wrong,
And dash aside its lances long,
And press between its yielding throng ;
Till all else wonder'd at the fight
Whose brunts had made their mail so bright
That older glory shunn'd its light.
Anon, triumphant o'er the wrong,
And thron'd above earth's cheering throng,
As chosen chiefs of all the strong,
Behold, they stand where honor dwells,
And earth with pride their story tells,
Nor envy evermore dispels
Their joy that swells at victory's bells.

XVII.

Yes, all made men are self-made men :
We ask too much of friendship then :
The soul's best impulse, in the end,
Is evermore the soul's best friend.
And when truth's whispers all pertain

To our souls only, why complain,
Tho' none but us their import gain ?
Let one, who honor craves, be strong
In worth, to make dishonor wrong :
Or, if he crave a sceptre, find
A task that fits a sovereign mind.
Their high ambition, do not doubt,
Is heaven-directed and devout,
Who strive, to plan, and then work out
What God has given them souls to will ;
With thankful hearts remembering still
That shallow depths the soonest fill,
And endless blessings wait in store
For those alone who long for more.

XVIII.

Where so much good is yet untried,
Our souls must all, if satisfied
With what they have or are, abide
Untaught, unhonor'd, and unblest ;
For but to-day what is is best.
The morrow's gain is all possess'd
By those who journey ere they rest.
Yet ne'er at daybreak had begun
One ray a shining course to run
But snakes crawl'd out to hiss the sun ;
And e'er, if truth then dawn'd in view,

Would tongues, whose fangs in fury flew,
Cry : " Who have seen the like ? Have you ? "
Ah me ! and what, forsooth, is new
And strange to men's experience,
'T would libel all their own past sense
For them to treat with reverence !
Oft in earth's bigot-brotherhood
The fools alone are understood,
And stupid souls alone seem good.
But, while the rest are dozing late,
The genius, quick to sight his fate,
Will wake and wish, and work, and wait,
And fix his aim on looming schemes,
Apart from those that earth esteems,
Else would he mind but common themes.
We are not always curst, when born
By throes of nature's freak or scorn
With moods abnormal and forlorn ;
We are not curst ere we consent
To dam our own development
By choking down our discontent.
If truth be something sought and learn'd,
He most may gain, who most has yearn'd
To fill a need he most discern'd.
Ay, let the earth, too stern but just,
Crush all our pride of thought to dust :
If still for growth in truth we trust,
While faith can dare, it cannot die.

With facts against it, 't will espy
Far distant lights that guide its eye,
Snatch hope from talons of despair,
And welcome flight with fancies fair.
In the vague light of ages old
The poets were the first who told
The truths to make late logic bold.

XIX.

If only once the souls that climb
So slowly up this mount of time,
Could, with prophetic vision clear,
See views that from its peaks appear ;
Then gaze below, where foul mists creep
Along black waters of the deep,
Note slippery stones that trip the feet,
Or slide beneath the indiscreet,
How closely would they watch and tread
The narrow, narrow paths ahead !
And then, should one a safe way trace
O'er some supremely dangerous place,
What could he do there save to try,
Tho' plains were wide, and hills were high,
To make those heed his warning cry,
Who in the paths behind him moved ?
Though means he chose to some but proved
His madness and his meanness both

Which they must hound with many an oath ;
Though he were kill'd where loom'd the danger,
His corpse might save some coming stranger,
Who in the stare of death could trace
The aims that flush'd his living face.

XX.

Woe me, I boast, but cannot be !
A poet is a babe, whose plea
Is whined in words.   Alas for me,
Can screaming scare away one's pain ?
The rattlings of a restless brain,
What good did ever rhymes obtain ?
What is there good on earth but gold ?
Life's bright paths hold a sordid fold,—
Hold men like cattle bought and sold,
Who treat each sky-born child of truth
As valiantly as bulls, forsooth,
That goar, and tramp, and leave to moan
Sweet children caught in pastures lone.
Nay, none who pass his protest by
Will stop to heed the poet's cry,
Or care if he survive or die.
None aid, or deem his aim sublime,
For only those who try to climb
And reach the far-off heights of rhyme,
Can know their distance.   Fast flies time :

Too hard I toil, to gain but bread ;
And I would rather far be dead
Than leave my life's report unsaid.

XXI.

How many men, compared to me,
Tho' counted slaves, may still be free?
Those yet possess heaven's liberty,
Whose minds are not in slavery.
But ah, what hell-forged fetters rest
Where one's own conscience must attest
He would, but dare not, do his best,
Because his lust or hunger waives
The truth that but the spirit saves!

XXII.

The truth for which I boast I care,—
Who knows what it may be, or where?
Where is the man that owns the truth?
Do I ? or I alone forsooth,
Who scarcely have outgrown my youth ?
The minds that think I err, had done
Much work ere mine had been begun :
And they are many ; I am one.
If they and I thus disagree,
And I doubt whether truth can be

In what seems true to only **me**,
Humility may be my plea.

XXIII.

What right have I to blame the earth
When I have woe and it has mirth?
Its throngs around me feast and dance,
And all their joys in life enhance
With friends, who prize their every glance;
While I, like some physician, trying
His poisons on himself, am lying
A martyr where none need my dying;
But scout my sick, insane idea,
Too well to test my panacea.
Why should they not? A man of sense
Trusts first his own experience;
Nor waives the truth he draws from thence
For all mankind's experiments.
But I, who seek the good of earth,
Do I concede that it has worth?
Or does the world in me perceive
That which can make it long to leave
Its gains behind, and mine achieve?
Nay, let me seek some better way.
When into doubtful paths they stray,
The wise turn back, tho' fools may stay,
Consistent—but that title lacks

One word to make it fit the quacks,
Where wisdom grows and change attacks,
Consistent—monomaniacs.

XXIV.

Grand it is new life to borrow ;
Like a spirit dead to sorrow,
Dead to all earth's dread to-morrow,
And to wake in realms of laughter,
Free from grief before or after.
Hail the eye, so brightly glancing.
Hail the music, and the dancing.
Hail the feast, and, echoing o'er us,
Hail the wine-brought cheer and chorus.
When such joyous deeds employ us,
Why should graver thoughts annoy us ?

On the dance !—but ah, what feeling
O'er the soul is vaguely stealing
Through the blaze and buzz and wheeling ?
When the best ideals lure one,
Only then can aught assure one
That his motive is a pure one.
Who would let a soul, nor fear it,
Be embraced with no love near it,
Both to cherish and revere it ?

Back to music ! Ah, to use it,
Seems all holy when we muse it.

Surely wrong could not abuse it !
All our lives, we start and wonder,
In this under world, what blunder
Woke in heaven the voice of thunder.
Yet it peals ; and oh, how sadly,
Like the storms that gather madly
Over days that dawn so gladly,
Burst on heavenliest harmonies
Notes from where no music is!

Back to feasting !   Ha, they cheer it.
Here 's to health !—they do not hear it ?
Here 's to health !—what, dare they jeer it ?
Lo, they tremble—Do they fear it ?
Look—my soul !—a man has tumbled ;
Shown himself a beast, and humbled
Man and God, at whom he grumbled.—
Moans a wife now never sleeping,
Babes that her thin hands are keeping :—
Waits a grave where none are weeping.

Back from earth !   No, fruit is in it
Fit for peeling.   Who begin it,
Find the fruit has worms within it.—
What, my soul, does good decay so ?
Let me lie before I say so !
Heaven would let the devil never
Rile clear springs that gush and ever
Thus refresh our faint endeavor.

Our own spirit, when too near it,
Taints the good that comes to cheer it :
We debase until we fear it,
Joy that was not meant to curse us,
But to nerve us and to nurse us.
Oh, for right to re-imburse us !
And the day, to dawn above all,
Where, at last, we all can love all!

XXV.

When sad from self-satiety,
Why should one shun society ?—
It rouses him from introspection,
And routs his dreams of drear dejection.
I think, as pools, whose overflow
Not freely off through earth can go,
Will breed foul mists, that reek and rise
And dim the earth and cloud the skies,
Our thoughts, if not allow'd to flow
Toward others freely—who can know ?—
With vapory whims may blear the mood,
And thus deform the objects view'd,
And half the light of life exclude.
An eye, made dim, may facts gainsay
And see, in fairest forms at bay,
But lions fierce that fill the way.
When dull to sounds, a man may fear

And take the rumbling he may hear
Within his own disorder'd ear
For footsteps of advancing strife.
Whate'er we seek or shun in life,
Too often we ourselves conjure
The direst foes its veils obscure.
Come then, my soul, and open wide
Those doors that keep the world outside ;
And welcome, as thine own, the worth
Of sunlight, beauty, friendship, mirth,
Design'd for him whose home is earth.

XXVI.

Amid the traits of multitudes
The Maker speaks through many moods
Of truths that are not understood
By those who by themselves do brood.
And better be, in lone despair,
Some king's court fool, astride a chair,
Who dreams he rules a kingdom there,
With stock-still statues his hussars,
And scarfs of Knighthood, but the scars
Deep-whipt across his bleeding back,
Than be a man whose life must lack
The love that waits on friendship's throne.
For all our worth is crown'd alone,
When friends have made our cause their own.

XXVII.

What power on earth compares with love?
It rules alone in heaven above.
But love in heaven is always just;
And so I think I would not trust,
But fear a friend, by day or night,
Whose love contain'd no love of right.
The world is wide, and wisdom strange;
To find it one must freely range;
And, when from this to that we change,
We lose our friend, unless his mood
Will justly weigh our former good
With what is now misunderstood,
And though he cannot see our goals,
Have faith enough to trust our souls,—
Faith man as well as God demands
From every soul that near him stands.
Oft, when so far and hid, how could
We point our goals out, if we would;
Yet then we like to be thought good!
And oft there comes a need of rest,
No strength have we to do our best;
And then, if friends yet seek a test,
Our home is like a sick bird's nest,
Whose fellows' beaks all pierce his breast.
Strange cure!—yet 't is an old complaint,
That much of love, when only faint,
They peck to death to make a saint.

XXVIII.

Within our souls is much of yearning
That patient thoughts are slowly turning
To deepest and to broadest learning
That cannot answer back a " why?"
Like sailors, when they watch a sky
Where fogs, offscourings of the sea,
Becloud their sight, so often we
Must guess our reckonings, it may be.
Then ye who with us onward sail,
And watch our ways, with faces pale,
And, hissing fiercely as the gale,
Our right of reticence deny,
Ye force us, if we must reply,
To make your fears increase, or lie.

XXIX.

Ah, in our good society,
(Where things that gain acceptancy
Are fashion's phrases, and an air
Which, caught with neither thought nor care,
Make wits and fools both equal there),
Lies oft seem wiser than the truth.
Like bodies why should souls, forsooth,
Not be well padded, stay'd, and laced
To suit the world's prevailing taste,
Till through the form no truth is traced?

And so to play with lies may be
The surest way to sound the key
That makes all social tones agree ;—
Ay, it the one sure note may strike
That moves all men to act alike.
And yet if love must love the soul,
What power more lovely can control
The men we meet, than words and ways
Unveiling life so all can gaze
On thought behind the outward phase,
While every eye serene and bright,
Transparent with the inward light,
Reveals what thrills angelic sight !
If one in friends like these confide,
He need not fear what veils may hide
In moods that back of them abide.—
I watch'd a man and maid, to-day :
Each dimm'd the other's eyes with spray.
He dash'd from his life's dregs unseen
What pleased the lady's wistful mien,—
A maid not vicious, yet I ween
Not loath to be, with open eyes,
His mate whom honor could not prize.
Ah, lust is lush in flatteries wise !
Full well she liked her dash of danger
With such a spicy, saucy stranger—
But let them pass.   For conquest girt,
The man a rake, the maid a flirt,

Will get, when caught, their own desert ;
Be prey ; and prey are always hurt.

XXX.

Who craves the fruit of friendship knows
How worthless now is much that grows.
Our friends, at times, are parasites,
Who drain our strength, to crawl to heights
On which they thrive on other's rights.
At times, not made for light, they spring,
As fits an upstart underling,
Beneath the shade our branches fling.
In either case, it scarce would suit
Their aims, to bear the best of fruit.
The usual yield that fills the stalk
Is promissory buds of talk,
Or gossip-tales—which spring around,
If low-lived friends gain slightest ground,
Like toadstools where decay is found.
These gossips all are scavengers
Of nobler people's characters.
And how can one of taste or sense
Be made, and yet take no offence,
The cess-pools of their confidence ?

XXXI.

They scarcely let one rest in bed ;
They whisper so, till all have said

Their worst about some heart or head.
Mean slanderers of characters,
These friends that stick to us like burrs,
Throng every home, and boast an ear
Well hugg'd against one's heart, to hear
Each secret throb of hope or fear.
Why tell they what they ne'er have known?
And force one, since he cannot own,
To leave their untrue love alone?
A time there was I thought mankind
Had all an inborn right to find
How truth appeal'd to every mind.
How noble is the task, I thought,
When one has wisdom gain'd in aught,
To show what he has thus been taught!
And this to do, my every nerve
I strain'd and pain'd, so all might serve
For men to harp on. But the strings
I held to them, were scarce the things
For them to harp on with content.
Men guess not oft the whole truth meant
By words that voice another's thought.
The truth would seem too cheap, if brought
To souls that ne'er for it had sought.

XXXII.

A man who cannot bear abuse
Would better live a mere recluse,

Than turn his own soul inside out
Because, forsooth, men stand in doubt
Of what he thinks the most about.
Alas, where foes our souls assail,
Not all can conquer, stript of mail,
What spurs the firm may wound the frail.
Ere more I stoop to be earth's fool,
I swear to figure as its ghoul,
And chum with nightmares, to affright
A world that keeps my soul in night;
Or play the owl, and rouse a toot
So mean that all shall at me hoot.
Hail open hatred ! but earth's fangs
And secret hissings bring one pangs
No nerve can measure.   These I fear
And from them seek my attic here
That shields me like a soul in clouds,
When one has left the grave's white shrouds
And crawling worms that gnaw'd his heart,
Ere he and things of earth did part.

XXXIII.

It is not wholly misery,
To be bereft of sympathy.
Perchance, a wise Omnipotence
Makes plain mere surface-difference
To join men in a deeper sense.
Beneath the whur of worldly strife,

All undisturb'd, there dwells a life
That feels the tender infant-plea
Of something grander yet to be.
There winds do whisper, waves have speech,
And shapes and shades have features each
That friendly to the soul appear,
And bring a Spirit subtly near,
And make the truth of heaven seem clear.
Perchance, when driven to gaze away
From earth, to find life's perfect day,
A soul so yearns for what should be
That God, who always will decree
His presence where men bend the knee,
Trails, through the strange unearthly light,
His robes that, while they blind the sight,
Yet lure men onward toward the right.

XXXIV.

Of late, when I am all alone,
I try to make the tests my own
That wise Philosophy has known.
My questioning thought to satisfy,
With eager soul but patient eye,
I search in every moving thing,
To find, at last, its hidden spring.
I fancy it is fire or air
Or mind itself so conjuring there.
I press against the window pane,

Ask—feels my nerve ? or feels my brain ?
What is it joins my sense and soul ?
Is it the Absolute's control ?
Or is it faith ? or is it aught
Beyond the ebb and flow of thought ?
Am I, who muse thus, made to be—
Responsible in no degree—
The vagrant wave of some vast sea ?
Or am I more than most men deem,—
Are forms that round about me gleam,
Things not substantial as they seem,
But only phantoms of a dream ?
If so, if not, can men, forsooth,
With all their searching, find the truth ?
Or do their eyes, approaching near
The grandeur sought, with vision blear
See all things falsely looming here ?—
Then flashes right, as lightnings glance ?
Or dawns it o'er some dozing trance ?
Shall one know more when earth is done ?
Reach misery ? or oblivion ?
Or through some mystic, spiral way
A Babel mount, and there survey
An earth become a heaven for aye ?

XXXV.

But hold ! thus thinking, I but hie
Some new-robed heresy to try